Chris Argyris

Reasoning, Learning, and Action

Individual and Organizational

 Jossey-Bass Publishers

San Francisco • London • 1989

REASONING, LEARNING, AND ACTION
Individual and Organizational
        by Chris Argyris

Library of Congress Cataloging in Publication Data

Argyris, Chris
        Reasoning, learning, and action.

        Includes index.
        1. Problem solving. 2. Learning, Psychology of.
3. Organizational effectiveness. I. Title.
BF441.A64   658.4'03   81-48662
ISBN 0-87589-524-7   AACR2

Manufactured in the United States of America

JACKET DESIGN BY WILLI BAUM

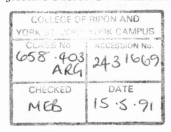
JACKET DESIGN BY WILLI BAUM

FIRST EDITION
        First printing: May 1982
        Second printing: October 1982
        Third printing: December 1983
        Fourth printing: April 1989

Code 8214

A joint publication in
The Jossey-Bass
Social and Behavioral Science Series
and
The Jossey-Bass Management Series

Contents

vii

.

To Donald Schön

with whom I have spent many wonderful hours
double-loop learning

Preface

The purpose of *Reasoning, Learning, and Action* is to describe the results of ten years' research on how to increase the capacity of individuals and organizations to solve difficult and underlying problems. The focus is on those problems that cannot be solved without changing basic values, policies, and practices. All the research has been conducted in actual organizations (private and public, voluntary and nonvoluntary, large and small), as well as in educational environments especially designed for increasing leadership effectiveness. The book is constructed around my own work; I did not intend to—nor do I—include a review of the literature.

This book is for the practitioner and the action researcher. I seek, on the one hand, to reach consultants, educators, and executives in all kinds of organizations. On the other hand, I seek to reach those who conduct basic research intended to produce usable knowledge.

Individuals or organizations who achieve their intentions or correct an error without reexamining their underlying values may be said to be single-loop learning. They are acting like a thermostat that corrects error (the room is too hot or cold) without questioning its program (why am I set at 68 degrees?). If the thermostat did question its setting or why it should be measuring heat at all, that would require reexamining the underlying program. This is called double-loop learning.

We strive to organize our individual and organizational lives by decomposing them into single-loop problems because these are easier to solve and to monitor. Unfortunately, we get increasingly better at the routine and increasingly more frightened about questioning the program that makes the routine possible. So we may be good at accomplishing the routine, but only with increasing costs, one of which is an unquestioning acceptance of the routine that appears to get the job done. As a result, we may produce something for today but lose control of tomorrow.

We do value double-loop learning, and we all believe we are good at it. Indeed, most executives, professionals, and educators consider double-loop learning to be more important and of higher status than other learning. The problem, I suggest, is that the reasoning and skills we use and the conditions we create in order to attempt to double-loop learn are actually counterproductive for that purpose. A discrepancy is created between our intentions and our ability to achieve them. Moreover, most of us are unaware of this discrepancy, and we create organizational and societal conditions to reinforce and legitimize our unawareness.

To understand why this is happening, we must separate what individuals and organizations espouse and value from how they act. "Do as I say, not as I do" is a very old truism. But we must find propositions that are valid descriptions of real life and can form the basis for changing it.

Generating such propositions is not easy. We will have to explore the very essence of human nature and of organizations and social systems. I hope to show that some of our most fundamental concepts about effectiveness in everyday life are themselves barriers to effectiveness. I have suggested that the problem is epidemic because of concepts and skills that most of us possess. The primary source of the problem is what we are taught early in life. The discrepancies arise because we are successfully socialized with ideas and skills that are counterproductive to double-loop learning.

How is it possible for such socialization to occur, as I will show, in so many different people across countries and cultures? One possibility is that, worldwide, the human mind may work to create similar constraints and opportunities for itself. For example, it is now well established that the environment is far too complex for the human brain to deal with as a totality. So problems must be decomposed, and rich, complex data must be organized into more abstract concepts. The processes of decomposition and abstraction enable us to maintain control but, if used incorrectly, can create problems that cause us to lose control. This book is replete with examples in which decomposition and abstraction were used ineffectively even though people were following accepted rules and norms for their effective use.

Another reason for this socialization may be the way we think about, design, and manage our organizations. For example, organizations are seen as mechanisms by which to coordinate the actions of many individuals. But the way we coordinate is through a theory of control that inhibits organizational double-loop learning. Indeed, it appears that the very act of using information to manage an organization, given the new information technology and given that it is used well, will lead to internal conflicts and injustice.[1] Yet I know of no other way to administer an organization except through the use of information.

Thus, at the individual and organizational levels, we have some very fundamental inner contradictions. Inner contradictions exist whenever an action that is necessary for success necessarily also leads to failure. For example, the mind works to keep us in control but may inhibit the double-loop learning required to remain in control. The way we use information to control organizations may inhibit the double-loop learning required to control our organizations.

How can we deal with these inner contradictions? First, we probably must forget about getting rid of them. That is not possible. But we should examine exactly what we do and what organizations do to cause them. As we know, organizations do not reflect and reason; it is individuals acting as their agents who do so. But if some of the inner contradictions exist because individuals have no choice but

[1] Chris Argyris, *Inner Contradictions of Rigorous Research* (New York: Academic Press, 1980).

to reason and act as they do (it is the way the mind works or the way we are socialized), and if the same people become anxious when facing these double-loop problems, then whatever is causing them to behave as they do and whatever leads them to feel anxious will necessarily influence the way they think and act as agents of their organizations. It is important that we strive to correct the factors at the individual level so that when we turn to redesigning organizations, the activity is not tacitly dominated by culturally induced constraints and by tacit fears related to organizations' going out of control.

It makes sense, therefore, to begin with individuals and to examine the way they reason about action. One of the central findings of our research is that people reason differently when they think about a problem simply to understand it than when they intend to take action. For example, if the objective is to discover and understand (as is true for scholars), then there is plenty of time—and many rewards—for elegant and comprehensive understanding. But such rich and complex analyses are rarely of help in acting under real-life conditions. One reason may be that the rich and complex maps would require much more time to use than is usually available. A second reason is that most maps assume that whatever they describe will not change. If there is a river or mountain on the map, the assumption is that this will not change. But such an assumption may be dangerous when the map is one of human action. People have the nasty habit of changing without notice. As someone has said, "Under carefully controlled conditions, people behave as they damn well please."

If people can choose to be unpredictable, then how will we ever develop a science of human action with which we can predict and generalize? What makes this dilemma solvable is that people cannot normally be unpredictable to themselves. They must design and execute the actions that others will experience as unpredictable. Unpredictable action must be predictable at least to the actor. This means that actions are designed. Behind every major action is a process of reasoning, no matter how automatic and spontaneous the action appears to be. For example, when we ask people to reflect on outbursts, they are able to give the reasoning behind them. To do so means that they can retrieve programs in their heads. It is these programs which inform our actions that we must understand and change if errors are to be corrected in ways that make it unlikely they will recur. Our task, therefore, is to discover the reasoning processes that people use to make themselves predictable.

Such knowledge will not guarantee perfect prediction, because people may still choose to act unpredictably. But the gap may not be as wide as we had originally thought. In order to behave unpredictably, people must design their actions. In order to design their actions, they must have some theory in their heads about what and how to design. I hope to show that they do have such theories in their heads—that if we understood the theory, we would be able to predict when they will be unpredictable and the limits of what they will design to be unpredictable. For example, I will illustrate from seminars and real-life situations in organizations where we tell people how they will behave; there they deny that they will behave that way; where they go ahead and act and then assert that their actions confirmed the predictions; and where, with a little help from their fellow participants in reflecting on their actions, they rather quickly admit that they were wrong.

People may have the freedom to design their unique actions, but they must limit that freedom by holding a theory about unique action in order to actualize it in a given situation. If we understand that theory, we can go far in predicting the unpredictable.

I focus heavily on usable knowledge, but not simply because I am interested in application of research. Application is a much more basic process. It is largely the name of the game in real life. Hence, basic research about human beings requires a focus on how they go about acting in order to get things done. Basic research about human beings and organizations is research that focuses, *at the outset,* on how human beings and organizations use knowledge in order to act. I emphasize *at the outset* because many of us were taught, and continue to teach, that sound basic research which seeks to understand is cumulative, and someday it will all add up to a comprehensive guide for action. Elsewhere[2] and in this book I assert that for double-loop problems this assumption is not valid and is, in fact, a myth. It is a myth probably developed by social scientists so that we can remain distant from the limits of our action and disconnected from the reasoning processes that we use to create the distancing.

Distancing and disconnectedness, I hope to show, are necessary consequences of the theories of action in our heads and of skills learned for the purpose of *not* distancing ourselves and being disconnected from our reasoning—another inner contradiction!

[2] Argyris, 1980.

On the Nature of Data and Evidence

The majority of the data presented in this book are observations and transcripts from tape recordings of actual encounters in different types of settings. Such case material is usually categorized by social scientists as "anecdotal" and is usually evaluated as "soft" rather than "tough"—as rich descriptions of individual, unique events that do not by themselves lead to generalizations that apply beyond the individual case. This evaluation is valid in the sense that it is congruent with methodology that is in good currency in normal science.

For some researchers, this position leads to a dilemma. On the one hand, they value the basic standards of science (such as disconfirmable causal theories and explanations that combine comprehensiveness with minimal necessary complexity) because they help to reduce error. On the other hand, ruling out the data that are so rich in meaning appears to create wide gaps between the knowledge that researchers produce and the likelihood that such knowledge is usable.

Interesting progress is being made in finding rigorous ways to generalize from the single case. For example, scholars are developing statistical procedures to be used with the qualitative anecdotal data embedded in cases.

Another thrust has been made more likely by the advent of the cognitive and informational processes perspectives. These perspectives view the production of qualitative data, such as conversations, as the result of identifiable and describable rules, schemata, or theories of action. The meanings in the anecdotal data are therefore predictable, and hence they can be used as the basis for testing theories. That means, for example, that the transcript of a one-hour meeting, which may contain 40 to 80 double-spaced typewritten pages of conversation, may contain meanings that are both predictable and generalizable to other meetings. For this to be possible, we must have a theory from which to generate these predictions ahead of time, and the predictions must be stated in ways that are disconfirmable.

Human beings in their everyday life produce much conversation, and they probably listen to even more. Hence, they, too, have the problem of making sense out of anecdotal data and individual cases. Indeed, such data are the fabric of their lives. It is my position that they solve the problem by developing their own theories of action. They use these theories of action to understand and to act in the world in which they are embedded. The theories of action are like master programs in their heads. It is also my position that these master programs have a formal structure that is stable, identifiable, and organizable into rules and propositions. The more we can come to know about these theories, the greater is the likelihood that we can use qualitative case material, such as conversations, as the basis for unambiguous tests and valid generalizations.

A key feature of this approach is the identification of two types of meanings embedded in everyday conversation. The first type may be called the culturally acceptable meanings. The second type is the effectiveness of such meanings given what the actors are trying to accomplish.

Consider a superior, Y, talking to a subordinate, X. Y says to X, "Your performance is not up to our standards." Such words carry a meaning that most people understand without having to learn our (or someone else's) theory. They have learned, probably through socialization, that the meaning embedded in such words is something like "X, your performance so far is unacceptable." Let us call this meaning the culturally understood meaning.

If we stopped at this point, then case materials and conversations would not be the basis for a test of a theory of effectiveness. They could be used as a test of a theory about how well people have learned culturally sanctioned meanings. The focus of our work, however, is on individual and organizational learning and effectiveness. This focus, we maintain, is also held by human beings and organizations in everyday life. When they act, they, too, must seek to learn about their effectiveness.

For example, the sentence spoken by Y contains the culturally understood meaning that X's performance is unacceptable. How effective is such a meaning in helping X? Most respondents, as we shall see, evaluate such statements as being blunt. These imposed meanings are on rung 3 of the ladder of inference. Rung 4 on the ladder represents our evaluation of the probable effectiveness of the rung 3 meaning. When Y said what he did, he made a unilateral evaluation that was unillustrated—that is, he provided no concrete examples of X's behavior to back it up. Using our theory of effectiveness, we can predict that the more the conversation is composed of such meanings, the greater is the likelihood that the recipient (X) will feel misunderstood and unilaterally judged and hence will become defensive.

We focus, therefore, on at least four levels of inference in every conversation. First is the relatively directly observable data—that is, the words and nonverbal cues. Second is the culturally understood meaning. Third is the meaning that the actors impose on the first two levels regarding their effectiveness for double-loop learning. Fourth is the meaning the researcher imposes. So we have the first four rungs of a "ladder of inference":

Levels of Inference

4. Meanings imposed by the researcher about effectiveness
3. Meanings imposed by the actors about effectiveness
2. Culturally taught meanings
1. Relatively directly observable data

The meanings imposed on effectiveness in the example of X and Y are related to interpersonal interaction. As we shall see, this is just the beginning of the hierarchy. There are levels of concepts that deal with group, intergroup, and organizational realities. The advantage of such a theory is that the user can go up and down the ladder of inference and connect organizational issues to group and individual ones or vice versa.

All the cases I will present contain conversations and actions that will be evaluated using our theory. For this purpose, any case will do as long as it contains double-loop issues. Therefore, we do not have a serious sampling problem. But this very advantage also means that our theories are subject to a tough test. If we have little problem of sampling, so do those who may seek to disconfirm the theory. All they have to do is find a case that contains double-loop issues and use it as a test of our perspective. If such attempts are made and our perspective holds up, then not only is it a more generalizable theory, but it is one that can be made usable by human beings in everyday life. For example, the insights, generalizations, and rules that can be inferred from the Davis College case (in Chapter One) will be valid, we predict, for the way all future executive classes will handle the case, even if they have read this book. We would also predict that executives in private industry, government, trade unions, and churches will behave in similar situations by doing what the educational administrators in the Davis College case did. For example, they, too, will make issues undiscussable; they, too, will act as if they were not making the issues undiscussable; and they, too, will expect that all this will remain undiscussable. We would also predict, from another case presented in Chapter One, that the problems Califano had with his policy team, with the president, and with Marshall, the secretary of labor, will be repeated by other secretaries who are placed in the same competitive situation and given a deadline by which to produce a new policy about a very complex and controversial issue.

All our predictions are at the third and fourth levels of imposed meanings, not at the first two levels. In effect, we are asserting that no matter what people say at levels 1 and 2 of the ladder of inference, we can understand and predict their impact on effectiveness by using our theory. This means readers should find that our theories hold in any case which involves double-loop issues and whose participants hold the theories about effectiveness that we will specify. If they do not, they have data that disconfirm our theory (and I would very much appreciate hearing from them).

Some readers may wonder whether we have not slipped a hooker into the argument by requiring that participants hold the kinds of theories we specify. This, indeed, might be true except that, as you will read, we assert that most people and most organizations conform to our theory. Hence, the generalizations should apply to a wide range of instances. Again, such an assertion is easily disconfirmed because all that is required is an example or two from a very wide universe.

The Craft of Intervention and Knowledge Generation

For nearly the past three decades, I have been interested in intervention. In the late 1950s and throughout the 1960s, I published several books describing my interventions in various kinds of organizations in order to be of help to them. *Intervention Theory and Method*[3] was my first attempt to reflect on my practice and to make explicit my views on intervention.

Intervention has always meant to me the activity of helping individuals, groups, and organizations solve problems, especially those that require double-loop learning. I have focused on double-loop issues because I believe that social science should question the status quo and offer people alternatives that have been rare or not avail-

[3]Chris Argyris, *Intervention Theory and Method* (Reading, Mass.: Addison-Wesley, 1970).

able but that are highly valued (for example, systems with high trust, risk taking, and high internal commitment among the participants).

I also believe that intervention activities should be subject to the most demanding tests because those practicing them may be affecting human lives in nontrivial ways. We must be especially careful to make sure that we do not knowingly or unknowingly kid ourselves and others. The best way to achieve this, it seems to me, is to state our views in ways that allow them to be publicly tested and falsified. To do so, we must make our reasoning explicit and organize it in such a way that it is testable. In this sense, I have always seen interventions, be they for ten minutes or two years, as experiments. Our interventions could be derived from a theory and then tested in practice, whether in a ten-minute episode or a ten-year program decomposed into episodes. The craft of intervention, therefore, means a coexisting activity of helping and producing generalizable knowledge.

But what does it mean to test? Although I have always been committed to the underlying features of science (such as disconfirmability of propositions), I have had doubts about the use of many of the currently accepted methods for rigorous research in intervention. I do not believe that interventionists can or should have the amount of unilateral control that a researcher requires to design rigorously controlled experiments, because that very unilateral control can lead to implicit and tacit distortions on the part of the subjects, as well as on the part of interventionists, that can unknowingly and significantly limit the validity of the data. Also, unilateral control significantly influences the kinds of propositions that can be tested. For example, elsewhere I have tried to show that normal scientific methodology tends to lead to propositions that are consistent with the status quo. Finally, propositions that are tested under conditions of rigorous unilateral control also require that these conditions be met whenever someone, such as a client, uses them. Thus, clients will have to replicate the conditions embedded in rigorous research methods if they are to use the knowledge produced from such activities. But to do this is to create an authoritarian world that, whatever one's values, forces a particular way of life on its users and does not provide people with chance.[4]

I am not proposing that we abandon testing. As I have indi-

---

[4] Argyris, 1980.

cated above, I believe that by constructing certain kinds of theory and refocusing on what it is that we are testing (Levels 3 and 4 in the ladder of inference described above), it is possible to test publicly intervention activities and, at the same time, to design these tests to disconfirm (as well as to confirm, if you are not a Popperian) features of theory and produce generalizations.

This book, therefore, focuses heavily on the craft activities of intervention that are simultaneously related to the production of basic knowledge and generalizations.

The Importance of Reasoning

Although there are numerous approaches to intervention activities, there has been an underlying agreement on the focus of understanding and changing behavior.[5] This has led to numerous studies of interpersonal behavior, group behavior, intergroup behavior, and organizational behavior. Each of these foci was assumed to be distinct and to have its own causal theories. Consequently, different propositions were generated about each.

In this book, I begin to question this practice (even though I have defended it in previous publications). The point is not, however, that the individual, group, intergroup are not distinct levels of inquiry or that they should not be represented by different propositions. The thrust will be to show that individual reasoning underlies many of the activities in all these units. Moreover, in more cases than I, at least, believed was possible, the reasoning is the same whatever the unit. If this is true, then we have found a way to simplify greatly the theories that are needed, the advice that must be given, and the new ideas and skills that must be learned by the client.

We have also greatly increased the toughness of the empirical tests that can be used. It is now easier to disconfirm the theory because discrepancies at any level become the basis for questioning the validity of the theory. To compound the toughness of the test, recall that I am asserting that the interventionist should not have the degree of unilateral control that is normally expected in the design and execution of experiments. Yet I am also asserting, and expect to

[5]Wendell L. French and Cecil H. Bell, Jr., *Organizational Development* (Englewood Cliffs, N.J.: Prentice-Hall, 1973).

illustrate, that a priori hypotheses can be stated and tested under these conditions. Moreover, many of the tests are simultaneously episodes for client learning. Hence, learning and testing go hand in hand. If we can succeed in coupling the two, then we should also be able to help clients become testers and learners in everyday life; hence, we can create the foundation for a learning society.

Organization of the Book

I begin in Chapter One by describing examples of double-loop learning problems in three contexts. Next I examine the reasoning processes that people use to deal with these types of problems (Chapters Two, Three, and Four). The reasoning processes turn out to be remarkably similar. This may be indicative of a powerful socialization process. In Chapter Five, I describe models of the theories that people use, as well as models of the context or behavioral environments that they will necessarily create when they use these theories. The approach may be described as one that combines socialization and context. People are seen as the carriers of the rules embedded in these sociological and contextual phenomena.

The theories that we use to make sense out of everyday life turn out to be counterproductive for double-loop learning. A consequence is escalating error, which leads people to distance themselves from the resulting mess. When people distance themselves, they tend to get poor or inadequate feedback about this effectiveness because accurate feedback might dig even deeper holes for the participants. Soon they not only become distanced from others, but they become distanced from their own tacit reasoning because they lack the data to become aware of the gaps in their effectiveness (Chapters Six and Seven).

In Part Two, I focus on how to begin to learn a theory that can be helpful for double-loop learning (Chapter Eight). These ideas are illustrated at the individual level (Chapter Nine), at the group and individual level (Chapter Ten), and at a group level (Chapter Eleven). Part Two closes with an analysis of the puzzles and paradoxes in the educational processes that we have been designing (Chapter Twelve).

In Part Three, attention is turned to illustrating some of the payoffs and difficulties in attempts to use the new theory to deal with double-loop problems in an organizational setting. The data come from the study of a consulting firm (Chapters Thirteen through Eighteen).

In Chapter Nineteen, attention is on some of the implications of the research on the practice of individual/organizational development. The book closes with some thoughts on the development of action science, which purports to produce usable knowledge about double-loop learning (Chapter Twenty).

I would like to thank my colleagues for their very helpful advice and time: Larry Lynn, Andrew Pettigrew, and Donald Schön; my teaching fellows Nancy Brodsky, Robert Putnam, and Diana Smith for their reading and comments; and my secretary Joan Ames for her typing and editing assistance.

Cambridge, Massachusetts   Chris Argyris
March 1982

The Author

Chris Argyris is James Bryant Conant Professor of Education and Organizational Behavior at Harvard University. He was awarded the A.B. degree in psychology from Clark University (1947); the M.A. degree in economics and psychology from Kansas University (1949); and the Ph.D. degree in organizational behavior from Cornell University (1951). From 1951 to 1971, he was a faculty member at Yale University, serving as Beach Professor of Administrative Sciences and as chairperson of the Administrative Sciences department during the latter part of this period.

Argyris's early research focused on the unintended consequences for individuals of formal organizational structures, executive leadership, control systems, and management information systems—and on how individuals adapted to change those consequences (*Personality and Organization,* 1957; *Integrating the Individual and the Organization,* 1964). He then turned his attention to ways of changing organizations, especially the behavior of executives at the upper levels of organization (*Interpersonal Competence and Organizational Effectiveness,* 1962; *Organization and Innovation,* 1965).

This line of inquiry led him to focus on the role of the social scientist as a researcher and interventionist (*Intervention Theory and Method,* 1970; *Inner Contradictions of Rigorous Research,* 1980). During the past decade he has also been developing, with Donald Schön, a theory of individual and organizational learning in which human reasoning—not just behavior—becomes the basis for diagnosis and action (*Theory in Practice,* 1974; *Increasing Leadership Effectiveness,* 1976; *Organizational Learning,* 1978).

Argyris is currently working on a project that will relate the perspective presented in this book to the ideas of other researchers and practitioners.

Reasoning, Learning, and Action

Individual and Organizational

Part One

Sources of Ineffectiveness

1

Introduction
to the Problem:
Academic, Business,
and Government Cases

Case A

A group of 79 senior-level university administrators in a senior-level executive program read a case called "Davis College."[1] The president of Davis College had appointed a committee composed mainly of senior faculty members and a few senior administrators to prepare concrete recommendations for the future of the college.

The substance of the recommendations is not relevant to this analysis. The relevant fact is that the participants evaluated the recommendations during the class discussion as follows:

"Vague—typical of committees with no specific goals."

[1]"Davis College," Parts 1 and 2, mimeographed (Institute for Management of Lifelong Learning, Harvard University, 1980).

"They said nothing and said everything. That's what happens when individuals are not given specific instructions."

"Bunch of abstractions covered up with bull."

"The committee acted irresponsibly by producing these cliché-ridden recommendations."

After the evaluation pattern was placed on the blackboard, the interventionist[2] asked whether the views of any persons in the room were not represented by that pattern. The interventionist repeated his request, saying he wanted to make certain that everyone's views were represented on the board. The participants confirmed that they were.

These participants' reactions are not unusual. Indeed, similar reactions have occurred in many executive programs in which the Davis College case has been used. What is behind these reactions?

Several assumptions about organization and management are embedded in this diagnosis. The first assumption is that if people are given specific goals and directions, the recommendations they produce will be more relevant and specific. And this assumption includes another—namely, that clarity of goals and directions will motivate people to produce specific recommendations, or if they are not so motivated, it will at least be easier to confront them on the quality of their performance. This assumption, in turn, includes another that is frequently stated as "People respect what you inspect," meaning that effective control over performance requires objective performance criteria and ongoing inspection. So the diagnosis is based on a microtheory of management. A key proposition in that theory is that if you specify the job and reward fairly, employees will produce what you expect; if they do not, you have a right to question their actions or even punish them.

These propositions are so much a part of life that they are taken for granted. We rarely question the underlying fear embedded in them, which is that people may choose not to follow the rules and perform their tasks. Management theory is partly designed to minimize the possibility that employees will choose not to obey. Those in

---

[2]Throughout the book, the term *interventionist* designates the author except when used in an obviously general sense.

management understandably see rules and expectations as the basis for order.

Implicit in this view is that the rules and propositions of the managerial theory cannot themselves ever cause consequences that would make the rules and the propositions counterproductive to that order. But that is what may have occurred at Davis College. The faculty committee was given a task to perform and (we assume) compensated for it. On the basis of the theory of order just described, the president rightly expected the committee to produce what it was asked to produce. Our class participants also had the same expectations and therefore also believed that the faculty acted ineffectively and incompetently.

Note that the participants were not surprised. This, they proclaimed, is typical of faculty committees when they have a tough task. They produce vague commitments, abstractions, and bull. Thus, we have a result that is counter to effective management, but it is seen as so typical that it, too, is taken for granted.

Origin of Paradoxes

How is it possible to have opposite outcomes both taken for granted when executives believe that order, loyalty, and performance are key to organizational effectiveness? Why are these counterproductive consequences permitted to live side by side?

To answer that question, let us return to the case. The faculty committee could have concluded during its deliberations that concrete recommendations to the president of places to cut or expand the financial commitments could pull the organization apart. The committee members may also have concluded that neither they nor the president would be able to deal with the reactions effectively. Hence, they developed as vague a set of recommendations as they could without being vulnerable to the charge of negligence. To ensure their safety, they may have spent hours writing "specific" recommendations in such language that they could weasel out of them with impunity.

Why would a loyal group of faculty members who are committed to Davis College conclude that they should not make tough recommendations? One obvious answer is that they did not want to be responsible for individuals losing their jobs or for the realignment of departments. Important as this explanation is, it is not adequate, for several reasons. First, there is the responsibility to the college and to its students; someone will have to take this responsibility. Second, faculties are known to have acted similarly even when money was available to ensure job and department continuity.

There is another reason—namely, that faculty members have learned to distance themselves from such responsibility. By "distance themselves," I mean that they do not see their personal responsibility for having produced the problems, nor do they see it as their responsibility to try to solve them.

The faculty members at Davis College would probably have liked nothing better than to have their task force dismissed. They would then feel free to speak ill of the project with their colleagues so as to reinforce their own distancing and infect their colleagues with the same attitude. This points to another feature of distancing. If the "carrier" of distancing infects another, the carrier's own attitude is reinforced. Thus, he or she both entrenches and expands the distancing going on in the organization.

The president may soon feel discouraged, if not betrayed. "They produced these recommendations, and now they are not backing them up." If his attitude gets communicated to the faculty members, they may react by feeling maligned and by asserting that such attitudes are more evidence that the administration does not understand the faculty. Such reactions would tend to sanction and reinforce distancing from the president and the administrative activities of the college. This distancing decreases the probability that either the faculty or the administration will blow up and consequently be accused of negative behavior.

All these consequences reinforce a fundamental problem of many educational institutions—that faculty and administrators do not work together on the issues critical for survival. The end result may be self-fulfilling prophecies ("You can't get the faculty to be concerned about administration" and "Administrators do not understand the faculty"). These self-fulfilling prophecies can become self-sealing processes. Because each side privately blames the other for the problem, there is no testing of the validity of the attributions that each side makes about the other. The self-fulfilling prophecies are now sealed.

As our classroom discussion developed, a number of administrators suggested that there may be an advantage to keeping the instructions and goals vague. Given the climate of mistrust between faculty and administration, they reasoned, the faculty might interpret specific instructions as too restrictive or as not allowing the freedom required to think creatively about the issue.

Note that most of the administrators believed that specifying goals and instructions was the best strategy, but only if in a climate of trust. As the issue of low trust developed, however, some administrators were willing to subvert rationality in order to protect relationships. In doing so, they were still acting rationally through subverting the rules of rational management and taking the risk of poor performance. Many of these administrators were quick to point out that the risk was not great. If the faculty recommendations were vague, then the president should accept them because their very vagueness would enable him to keep his options open. For example:

> "I think the president should accept the recommendations as is; it makes good political sense."
> "Maybe the president should let the tension build up [then he can step in to deal with the crisis]."
> "Maybe the president has no idea what to do. Hell, if he had a clear idea, he might have never been hired. If he doesn't, he should focus on the fact that the solution should be arrived at jointly."

A well-known phenomenon may be occurring here. The faculty developed vague recommendations to keep its options open. The president may have accepted the vague recommendations—acting as if they were not vague—in order to keep *his* options open. In this process, the genuine doubts that the players have about each other are only reinforced. Again, we have self-fulfilling prophecies that are self-sealing.

This leads to a fourth feature of distancing in organizations. The managers begin to use managerial strategies that tacitly accept the distancing and to act as if the distancing did not exist. Now we have management colluding in the game and thus legitimizing it. How can managers condemn distancing when they themselves use it?

Let us return to the class discussion. The 79 participants were placed in six groups. They were given several hours to write a letter to the president concerning what his response to the faculty recommendation ought to be. In all six groups, the participants recommended that the president (1) withhold his sense of disappointment, (2) accept the recommendations with a note of gratitude, and (3) appoint a new committee, which would be given a more specific charge and would include people the president knew would take action (the exact composition of the committee varied in the different letters).

When the interventionist noted that the recommendations appeared to be a form of face saving, the administrators responded, "Of course; what else can one do in such a situation?"

The point is that all the class groups recommended the face-saving games combined with the appointment of a new committee that would be under very specific and binding directions. Even more interesting is that the class explicitly stated that none of the face-saving devices was to be made explicit. This is understandable because making a face-saving device explicit undercuts its face-saving function. So we have the university executives distancing themselves from the problem even in the classroom, where they do not have to act.

If the president writes the glowing letter of thanks to the faculty, and if the faculty sees the conclusions and interprets them as the class did, and if later the president appoints a new committee "with teeth," the faculty will infer that a game was being played. We would also predict that the faculty would not make the game discussable, because (1) it would violate the norms, (2) disclosure could threaten the faculty's own game, and (3) the faculty can use the president's game to reinforce and validate its acts of distancing.

The underlying rules of the game being played can be described as follows:

I (the president) know that I am playing games; you (the faculty) know that I am playing games.

You (the faculty) are playing games; I (the president) know that you are playing games.

All of us know that we should keep the rules and the gameplaying undiscussable.

We also know that in order for these rules to work, and the game to succeed, we must keep them undiscussable. One important rule for keeping the undiscussable undiscussable is to act as if the undiscussable were not undiscussable.

The entire class concluded by recommending that the president play a game of deception in order to save face for himself and the faculty and in order to keep his options open. They suggested that he say one thing ("Many thanks for your fine recommendations") but have a different evaluation and action in mind ("The recommendations are useless; I will appoint a new committee").

If the president takes this advice, it is likely that the deception and games will become evident the moment another committee is appointed or when it takes a different action. If the faculty does not confront the deception and games—a very likely outcome of self-distancing—then it, too, is playing a game of deception and face saving.

These games must be played consistently to be effective, and the fact that they exist must be undiscussable. Moreover, the undiscussability of the undiscussable must also be undiscussable.

These conditions may reduce motivation for performance, make the participants feel mistrusted, and lead to expectations of disloyal behavior. Superiors and subordinates are now moving toward unilateral control coupled with face-saving games. The undiscussability of these consequences will help to assure the continued existence of self-fulfilling prophecies and self-sealing processes.

We now see a fifth feature of distancing. It necessitates making the actions associated with it undiscussable and making the undiscussability of the distancing also undiscussable. The faculty and administration of Davis College, and the participants in the class, distance themselves from their responsibility to deal with the issues. They then make this distancing undiscussable and act as if it were not. Can people actively strive to deal with life by such acts of distancing and undiscussability? Aren't such acts passive? How can people take responsibility for being irresponsible?

Summary and Conclusions

The administrators' original diagnosis can be summarized as follows.

When groups produce recommendations that say everything and say nothing, the consequence is a set of vague and unusable recommendations.

To correct this situation, the president should define a new set of highly specific goals and directions while developing ways to monitor and control the performance of the committee. A strong leader is one who is willing to implement this strategy.

If this strategy is implemented, the faculty may feel mistrusted and unfairly controlled. Emotional reactions could result that would inhibit faculty performance. If the strategy is not implemented, the president runs the risk of inaction or ineffective action. The situation is paradoxical in that both options lead to success *and* failure, with the failure feeding back to undermine the success. So we see that, in the interests of rationality, people act to produce consequences that paradoxically inhibit rationality.

It is important to point out that group after group of executives recognized the problem in the Davis College case. Many reported their own examples of the same phenomenon. What makes the case real is that they can identify with the problem. Moreover, their reactions to the case are, I believe, common. Most of us have had experiences of giving or receiving advice similar to what the president received.

We will see that the distancing, undiscussability, and counterproductive advice are predictable responses to such problems. It is as if people were programmed (much as a computer is) to automatically react the way the university faculty and the class administrators acted, and they were programmed to be unaware that they are acting paradoxically. By that I mean that the blindness or unawareness is skilled, perhaps caused by earliest-age instruction.

There is a second feature about this automatic response and paradoxical unawareness: Many people can recognize the paradox, and their unawareness of it, almost immediately if it is pointed out. However, as we shall see, they appear doomed to repeat their automatic response.

Finally, a third feature is that people choose to deal with these difficulties by using games whose primary features are that they are known by all players, they are undiscussable, and their undiscussability is undiscussable.

All these features tend to inhibit the production of valid information for problem solving and decision making. Yet they are present precisely when valid information is most needed—that is, when people are dealing with difficult and threatening problems.

It is important to keep in mind that people produced these

paradoxes and counterproductive consequences even when they analyzed the case away from the classroom. Such consequences are not the result of a particular setting; they are caused by the very way human beings reason. Hence, people should produce these consequences in any setting, not only in a class.

Case B

The organization from which Case B was obtained was in the business of selling highly sophisticated knowledge that utilized complex technical skills. The key to the firm's success was the professionals who created the knowledge and used it to make individual diagnoses and solutions for clients. In an organization such as this, attracting and keeping first-rate professionals is a central issue, and not surprisingly, the officers hold strong opinions on it.

Some officers believed that career development programs were needed to attract outstanding young professionals. Another group had serious doubts about career development programs, believing that if the firm hired the "right type" of professional (that is, one with high analytical and conceptual skills), such professionals would be so engrossed in their work that it would be easy to attract and keep them. This second group was not against career programs per se; rather, its greatest fear was that the programs might be used to retain the duller professionals. This group also feared that, in the long run, these less competent professionals would depend on these programs for their commitment rather than on the actual job tasks. Hence, career development activities might attract and retain professionals who really should leave the firm. The former group of officers were known as "liberals" and the latter group as "conservatives."

The debate about the career program had been going on for several years. Every time a young professional quit (not often), the liberals used his or her departure as evidence for the validity of their position. The conservatives expressed doubt of this. They maintained that if professionals with the right attitude and proper skills were hired, they would not leave.

Both sides saw the problem as a central one requiring some action. A committee including liberals and conservatives was formed and was asked to recommend future policy. I want to focus now on some of the problem-solving dynamics of the meeting in which the committee made its presentation to the executive group. The data presented here were collected from tape-recorded interviews and from observation of several preliminary group meetings.

How the Liberals and Conservatives Framed the Problem

We learned in interviews held before the final meeting that the liberals framed the problem as follows:

1. The firm is being unfair, foolish, and bloody irrational about education, evaluation of professionals, and career development programs.
2. The conservatives are, mostly, well-meaning people who are blind to the unfairness and irrationality of the present policies.
3. The conservatives see us (the liberals) as overprotective alarmists: "If the liberals were let loose, they would produce policies that require much more attention and money to implement, and this might spoil the younger professionals."

The conservatives believed:

1. There is a morale problem among the younger professionals. The problem can be solved through proper recruiting.
2. The liberals are overreacting to the cues of dissatisfaction. If we are not careful, we may undermine the firm's emphasis on high standards, analytical excellence, and autonomous professionalism.
3. The liberals see us (the conservatives) as well-intentioned but out of date with the current social changes about careers.

These frames illustrate that there is a basic agreement that the firm should hire and keep first-rate personnel. There is also honest disagreement on what action to take. These agreements and disagreements are discussable. The liberals can talk about career programs in general, and the conservatives can talk about "proper recruitment procedures" in general.

The difficulty arises when the whole group tries to design the specific actions the firm should take. Before an agreement can be reached, each side must explore the doubts it has about the other.

The difficulty is that each side questions the other's reasoning processes. To compound the problem, each side privately explains the ineffective reasoning of the other side by making attributions that the other side is unfair, irrational, foolish, blind, overprotective, and overreacting or that it is responding to political pressures from its coalition group.

Although each side doubts the other's reasoning processes, it explains the ineffective reasoning by using motivational "political" concepts—as if the explanation lay in the motivations and defenses, or in the political action, of individuals. It is as if each person assumed that when others act, they intend the consequences that follow. But this assumes that they are accurately aware of the consequences of their action and that if they are acting ineffectively, their ineffectiveness is related to motivational or political factors. The possibility that their reasoning processes are wrong and that they may not be aware of this is not considered. We have already glimpsed that people may be unaware of the consequences of their own actions yet aware of the consequences of other people's actions. Moreover, their reasoning processes may be automatic but flawed, and accompanying each automatic response is yet another that keeps people unaware of their ineffective reasoning and the consequences of their actions. The motivations and political factors may be the *cues* that trigger off the automatic responses. Hence, they are necessary but are not a sufficient focus for detecting and correcting errors.

It follows that both groups will have to suppress much of their diagnostic frames about the other side when they meet to discuss the issues. It is not surprising, therefore, that both the liberals and conservatives affirmed prior to the meeting that their meeting strategies should be guided by "good common sense." The definition of good common sense varied somewhat. For example, the liberals framed their action as follows:

1. Do not do or say anything that makes the conservatives publicly defensive. Such action would be viewed by all as unfair and uncivilized and could lose us support for our position. Therefore, do not mention the conservatives' blindness and irrationality.
2. Focus on the negative consequences of the present policy by citing data that clearly support our views.
3. Do not polarize or overstate the case, because the conservatives

will interpret such statements as confirming our alarmist tendencies and will confront us on those issues. That would lead to personal attacks, which would get us away from the issues.

The conservatives framed their action as follows:

1. Do not say or do anything that makes the liberals publicly defensive. Such action would be viewed as unfair and uncivilized. This could lose us support for our position. Do not discuss our view that the liberals are blind, are alarmists, and tend to overprotect the young professionals.
2. Let the liberals talk so they cannot accuse us of being obstructionists. Respond with data that clearly illustrate our views.
3. Do not polarize, because that will only confirm the liberals' fear of our rigidity and stodginess.

The two groups appeared to hold the same views about factors that would inhibit effective problem solving. Both ruled out discussing their view of the other side's poor reasoning. In doing so, they ignored the opportunity to test the validity of their views; yet they continued to act as if these views were valid.

After the meeting, representatives of the liberal and conservative positions were interviewed and asked whether it would have been helpful if they had tested the validity of their attributions. All the automatic responses included the following reasoning:

> "Of course; that's obvious."
> "That is not possible, though, because it would only upset others."
> "If people are upset, you get neither a valid test nor a civilized discussion."
> "After all, all of us are striving to be rational."

Is a paradox embedded in this reasoning? At the heart of rationality is the rule that inferences should be subject to test. It is fundamentally irrational to assert that a premise is true when it has never been tested. The paradox, therefore, is that, in the name of rationality, the participants are acting irrationally.

However, at another level this irrationality is rational. It is rational in the sense that if people act on the basis of attributions they know others will not confirm, then to state these openly will indeed upset others, and this may block that particular action.

When the participants said they were acting rationally, they meant that they wanted to minimize the expression of negative feelings and defensiveness, and this is rational. But it makes little sense to expect that such expression will be minimized if each side believes that the other is reasoning incorrectly and if each is making unjust attributions about why that is so.

Because both sides planned not to discuss these matters, a powerful norm was generated that all would hesitate to violate. The norm assured that negative feelings and defenses would not be expressed, but it did not influence the way people secretly felt.

What Happened During the Meeting

The meeting was opened by the liberals. They recommended establishing a high-level career development committee to define and monitor policies. They frequently repeated the following points, making suggestions for new career development initiatives.

Career development:

Is not a panacea to solve all problems.
Will do better what we are already doing. We are building modestly
    on existing practice.
Will not alter the firm's norms on first-rate technical competence.
Will be experimental.
Will be informal. It is not designed to threaten anyone.
Should be managed by officers with a wide range of perspectives.

The liberals also noted that a study of the younger professionals suggested that one of the most important complaints had to do with the executives' behavior when evaluating subordinates. They recommended that this topic undergo further study—a recommendation that might be described as an "easing-in," cautious approach.

The conservatives interpreted the approach in precisely these terms. They began their counterreaction with such statements as "I'm glad to hear that we are moving carefully and experimentally, that we are trying to make better what we are presently committed to." Interviews after the meeting confirmed the inference that those who spoke this way saw it as a means of publicly holding the liberals down.

At the same time, the conservatives agreed that there was room to improve the quality of the feedback to younger professionals; emphasized the importance of recruiting fine professionals with "the attitudes of the builders of the firm"; and agreed that they may not have fulfilled their share of career development responsibilities but mentioned that they were an already overloaded professional group.

Not all liberals and conservatives followed the guideposts. At times, a liberal's impassioned plea cited such dangers as impairment of the firm's growth and excellence if the firm could not get the best professionals. The response was that there was little evidence that the firm was not getting its share of the best professionals. Or a liberal said that younger professionals were overcommitting themselves to ensure promotion, to which a conservative responded that this might be a plus for the firm if kept within appropriate limits.

The meeting concluded with a vote to create a career development committee and program. The career committee was explicitly told not to generate initiatives costly in terms of attention and money without reporting these to the total partnership. The conservatives asked that the committee's representation include an appropriate range of views. The managing partner assured them that this would be done and, indeed, asked for volunteers. The meeting ended with public comments about the spirit of cooperation, the common sense used, and the progress made.

Case C

In Case C the subject is an episode that occurred in a governmental setting over a much longer period than those in cases A and B. The substantive issues were related to welfare reform.

The case authors[3] describe in careful detail the problem-solving activities related to welfare reform that occurred at the high-

---

[3] Laurence E. Lynn, Jr., and David de F. Whitman, "The President as Policymaker: Jimmy Carter and Welfare Reform," mimeographed (John F. Kennedy School of Government, Harvard University, 1981).

est level of the Department of Health, Education and Welfare (HEW) and the Department of Labor, as well as with President Carter and his advisers. The authors go beyond description and analyze the entire episode to provide their explanation of the problems and their recommendations.

Lynn and de F. Whitman conclude that (1) at no time did the president's advisers seem to be doing what Carter wanted them to do, (2) a proposal that Carter liked never became a major part of his policy, and (3) HEW and Labor representatives created intergroup relations that made it impossible for them to resolve their differences. Moreover, very little real political discussion occurred about a problem that was "foremost a political problem." "The process as a whole seemed feckless and fumbling, wasteful of the time and energies of the officials involved. The president appears to have lost control of it altogether" (pp. 325-326). The authors concluded that part of the cause was the type of presidential leadership—or lack of it—that Carter showed. They also concluded that the problem-solving processes used at the level of the secretaries of HEW and Labor were faulty. It is these processes that I wish to examine, especially their descriptions of (1) the relationship of Joseph Califano, Secretary of Health, Education and Welfare and his group and (2) the relationship between the HEW and Labor groups, relating these to the relationship with the president.

Internal Dynamics of the Califano Group

The authors report that Secretary Califano's team had difficulty figuring out his ideas about welfare reform. They appeared to be hesitant to ask him to clarify his views, for at least three reasons. First, he had asked *them* to make the studies to generate relevant views. Second, they were aware that he did not know at the outset what he should recommend to the president. Third, there was the danger that any answers they got might foreclose their initiative to show what a good and creative policy team they were. Neither these attributions about Califano nor their own motives were discussed openly with the secretary.

Partly because these stances were not discussed candidly, and partly because Califano was an extremely busy man, the team had to gather its intelligence about its boss in meetings with him. These opportunities were not only rare, they usually were connected with making presentations on the very projects about which the team members wished to query him. They were in the predicament that the best opportunity to learn was at meetings whose effectiveness depended on their already having learned.

Not surprisingly, there was a good deal of apprehension about these meetings as well as a good deal of reaction afterward about their effectiveness. For example, the first team meeting with Califano was described by one member as a "disaster." Califano was "completely, totally, absolutely bored. He was not interested in anything that he was briefed on. Our presentation . . . fell flat, the material fell flat" (p. 76).

The team never publicly tested these attributions with Califano. If Califano had validated them, the team members could have sought to take corrective action. They might have asked for insights into the kind of information and reasoning that he preferred, as well as any thoughts he had about the possible nature of the welfare program. They might also have asked for his reactions regarding their mode of presentation. But to discuss these attributions openly was difficult because they were undiscussable. Hence, it was important for the team to act as if it was not hiding something that was undiscussable.

This did not prevent individuals or groups of members from making further attributions privately. John Todd (senior member of the HEW team), for example, described Califano as not schooled "to sit there and believe that all this [information he was receiving] was essential and important information. . . . Califano is motivated only when he can . . . seize upon an issue of public policy where [he] see[s] a genuinely difficult choice to be made which requires [his] attention" (p. 77).

Note that the first set of untested attributions about Califano is now explained by another set, which is also untested. If Todd is correct, then the team members did not present any issues that caught Califano's attention. If so, and if they were interested in doing so, then why not test out their attributions? Again, the answer appears to be "Because such attributions were undiscussable."

Nevertheless, the participants continued to make attributions. The subordinates were beginning to hold Califano responsible for the limitations of the analyses because he never gave them the necessary criteria and because the time constraints made it difficult to get the information that the team thought he required. Henry Aaron, one of the most senior and distinguished analysts, realized that "Califano wanted something [other than what we were giving him], but we did not know what to give him" (p. 93). Later Aaron commented that he knew what Califano needed but there was not adequate time to obtain the data because of the time required for a particular model to become operational (p. 93).

Califano was seen as a poor reader who disliked linear presentations, who was capable of absorbing quickly what he believed was important, who remained aloof from other information and close-mouthed. The close-mouthed feature was partly a personality characteristic and partly a situational constraint due to Califano's lack of clarity about what the president wanted. (Califano may have had problems with the president similar to those his team had with him. He, too, may have been making private attributions and not testing them.)

One consequence, according to Aaron, was that the team did not operate effectively. "We could have used clearer [instructions and cues].... We never [got them], so we had to feel our way along the wall of a dark closet, so to speak" (p. 94). And as another senior member put it, "We were guessing at what he wanted, as well as trying to make ourselves look good, communicate our analytic capabilities" (p. 95). Again, we see a team which knew it was not pleasing its superior, which knew what information it wished it could get in order to be more effective, which could not discuss this knowledge, and whose members acted overtly as if none of this were going on.

The actions that they took with Califano were consistent with their psychology but were destined to be ineffective because they did not get at the underlying issues. For example, in one meeting Califano told the team that "memos should use lots of bullets and underlining, along with white space, to accentuate important points.... So we were at this staff meeting where Barth ... said things like ['Not enough white space, Califano won't read this page full of print']" (p. 95).

Incidentally, Aaron himself was subject to covert attributions from his fellow team members, who never tested them publicly. Thus, one staff member commented that Aaron was playing the in-house Brookings analyst: "A fine analyst, the best in the tribe, but

largely functioning as a one-man analyst [instead of] as a staff director" (p. 135).

Intergroup Issues

There were many intergroup issues between the HEW team
and a competing one created by the president in the Department of
Labor. These teams created win/lose dynamics that polarized the issues so much that Carter asked one of his senior White House aides
to intervene between HEW and Labor. Even with the intervention, as
Lynn and de F. Whitman point out, the issues were never reconciled
and integrated into a report that the secretaries of Labor and HEW
could approve.

Examples of the intergroup dynamics between HEW and Labor included the following.

Two teams were composed of members who knew each other
and their positions on welfare reform. One informant believed that
many of them did not read the papers written by the other team but
came to the meetings to advocate their views. Moreover, "instead [of
talking] about criteria that might have illuminated [their] differences, they wanted to talk about those differences in the context of
concrete proposals" (p. 83).

A welfare rights advocate group set up to defuse charges of not
including representatives outside government believed that the HEW
and Labor groups were wasting time and producing poor papers.
Little did they know that these groups were holding secret meetings
that, according to several of their members, "generally turned into a
random airing of people's views about the specific reform approach
that happened to be on the table for discussions that week" (p. 87).

As time grew short, the intergroup attributions between HEW
and Labor teams intensified. HEW saw Labor as inconsistent and difficult to control. Labor and HEW wrote notes to themselves about
what the other group was doing that was counterproductive; yet
these notes were never discussed. The mistrust between the groups
increased. One day the Labor representative accused Califano of holding secret meetings (something that Labor, too, had probably done).

Labor felt that HEW was sending "junk" to the president.
Junk apparently meant memos trying to criticize Labor's views by
misrepresenting them. "We were just livid" (pp. 141-142). Another

Labor representative accused HEW of acting unethically and unpro-fessionally (p. 165).

Not surprisingly, when the time arrived for the two teams to integrate their views in one approach, there was little agreement. The team members agreed to a compromise approach for the president that few believed was adequate. For example, the HEW parts of the memorandum were seen as deliberately withholding information from the president, giving him ambiguous data and muddled logic. The result was that the president did not get the quality of analyses that he should have received. As one member of the HEW staff group described it, "My impression of the agreement is that very significant issues have been papered over" (p. 238). One observer clearly related this to the win/lose dynamics that were frequently present and oper-ative, yet never discussed: "A lot of the [participants] have rough edges on their personalities. Their reaction [as a group] is not to roll with the punch . . . it is to bristle and try to put the other guy down" (p. 238). Another observer stated, "Packer and Aaron were like kids arguing back and forth. A lot of it was silly nonsense. . . . There was a lot of one-upsmanship in those meetings" (p. 238). And, finally, another observer recalled, "There was a crazy dynamic . . . [it was] troublesome [to see a] group of people getting together, and it had to do more with their 'out-machoing' each other" (p. 238).

Common Features of the Cases[4]

1. The actors, whether representing themselves or their sub-group, appeared to advocate their position in such a way that they would win and not lose. Statements were made with a degree of cer-tainty or with persuasion that inhibited inquiry into their views. For example, the administrators in Case A were "sure" that the faculty committee had performed poorly. The liberals in Case B designed their meeting strategy to overcome the conservatives' resistance in order to obtain new career development policies for the organization.

2. In order to win, the actors coupled their advocacy with ac-tions that would inhibit the expression of negative feelings. Although the administrators in the role of observers in Case A were also upset

---

[4]This analysis will focus heavily on Cases A and B. Case C is discussed in detail in Chapter Four.

with the faculty committee's performance, they recommended that the president not communicate such feelings. Moreover, they recommended that the president tell "white lies" to minimize upsetting the faculty and simultaneously get on with the appointment of a new committee.

In Case B the liberals designed their presentation to assure the conservatives that there was nothing new or radical in their recommendations. The conservatives, for their part, were cautious, and they carefully examined the liberals' sales approach for hidden messages and implications.

3. The actors appeared to design their behavior to be rational. By "rational" they meant suppressing issues that might upset others and simultaneously focusing on the task. The administrators in the class and the executives in the meeting focused on necessary and attainable goals and on defining realistic ways to reach these goals, the assumption being that rational human beings would be influenced by the requirement of defining objectives and ways to achieve them.

4. People strove to control the meeting so they could maximize winning, minimize losing, minimize the expression of negative feelings, and keep the actors rational.

Under these conditions, it is quite likely that problem solving would be less effective, the internal commitment to any decisions would be low, and suppressed negative feelings might build up to cause distortion of views in future meetings.

Several consequences may flow from the preceding. We have all attended long meetings where little new business is approved because everyone is using an easing-in process. This process assures people that no major changes will be made and teaches the players to be inherently conservative. It also teaches them to play games in which undiscussable issues are overlaid with discussable ones. Further, it teaches people not discuss these games and simultaneously to act as if no game were being played.

It is precisely such games that lead people to take a stance of what one executive called "adaptive paranoia." Whenever someone is assuring everyone that the changes being recommended are small and/or an extension of present practice, first, do not believe it, and second, hold the speaker publicly to that commitment.

A second consequence is the impact on the norms of, and expectations people have about, organizations. For example, organizations become known for escalating error when dealing with double-loop problems; for developing a polluted culture of mistrust and conformity; for games that cover up errors, the pollution, and the cover-ups. This, in turn, reinforces the probability of inconsistent, counterproductive actions. This circularity is not evidence of poor reasoning but evidence of the self-reinforcing quality of certain organizational factors.

It is not surprising that under these conditions difficult substantive issues do not get discussed candidly. For example, in Case B, a deeper and more profound issue is the design of the next generation of services the firm should offer. Some believe that the firm may no longer be able to invent and produce the next generation of services. Most partners are aware of these issues, and as they reported in interviews with the interventionist, are aware that they are "hot issues."

A "hot issue" is usually an emotionally laden, politically sensitive issue. Once substantive issues are framed as hot issues, people tend to deal with them in the same way they dealt with them in the cases. The hot issue will be cooled off by translating it into something discussable. The result may be what Donald Schön has described as "dynamic conservatism." Basic changes are unlikely under such conditions unless someone can violate these norms and rules with impunity. This is usually accomplished by bringing in a new executive team or, at lower levels, by some form of revolution, such as a strike. Once the problems are corrected, the irony is that the new team will generate the same norms and rules around its position, and hence those who survive have understandably concluded that the more things change, the more they remain the same.

The consistency of data such as these leads us to believe that they are not random. They are intended and designed, although the design may have unintended consequences. It is difficult to believe that actors are not aware of these consequences. Yet they continue to behave in accordance with the design to control unilaterally, to maximize winning and minimize losing, to minimize the expression of negative feelings, and to remain as rational as possible.

Why do people create and use designs that have such counterproductive features? One possibility is that they are coerced to do so by the organization. Another is that the designs produce both productive *and* counterproductive consequences. A third possibility is that individuals are acculturated to these designs long before they enter an organization, and they find the organization congenial to their designs. This should not be surprising, since organizations are created by individuals, and understandably the organizations that they manage and control will sanction such designs.

A fourth possibility is that all three possibilities are likely. If so, we are dealing with a highly powerful set of individual, group, organizational, and cultural forces that are intimately connected and self-reinforcing. It also follows that this set of forces contains the foundation for inner contradictions. The forces lead to success *and* failure; the very act of achieving the success leads to failure.

One reason these inner contradictions are difficult to attend to is that success does occur, but it is related to routine performance. People are not required to pay attention to the deeper issues until the counterproductive forces are so powerful that they inhibit even routine performance. Once this occurs, organizations are seen as being in crisis. Drastic action is now possible, such as replacing administrators, firing employees, and creating new policies.

Yet, as I hope to show, all these changes ignore the fact that the system was programmed to make errors, to be unaware when it was making errors, and to reach the point at which it could self-destruct. However, the new regime will be headed and managed by people programmed with the same old design. The prediction is that soon a new set of counterproductive features will develop, the buried legacies of the old regime may arise to reinforce the new, and soon the organization will again be locked into generating a new crisis and inviting a new revolution, a revolution that again changes many of the single-loop features but none of the double-loop issues. Hence, there is change in order to remain constant.

Under these conditions, it is not surprising that an increasing number of people believe organizations are not the place for double-loop learning. To hold this belief, individuals must also believe that they themselves are not responsible for this. The organization is the culprit. But is this the whole truth? Why, for example, do executives in advanced seminars consistently advise the president of Davis College to expect incompetence from the faculty committee, to act nevertheless as if the committee were competent, to "accept" the report, to take new action that belies the authenticity of his acceptance? Doesn't such action reduce the probability that organizations will double-loop learn? Then why place all the blame on organizations? There is no formal organizational policy that says executives should play these games, but the executive would respond that there exist unwritten, informal rules to do so. Indeed, the ability to play these games is a key criterion of success. The executives would conclude that they advised action complying with these games because they were asked to deal with the problem as if it were a real-life situation. And "real life" means organizations are not the place for double-loop learning.

But even if all that is true, and organizations are not meant for double-loop learning, it does not necessarily follow that individuals *are* meant for double-loop learning and that it is only the organization that keeps them from using double-loop skills. As we shall see, individuals espouse and value double-loop learning, but the skills they have to produce it are counterproductive to such learning, and they tend to be unaware of this fact.

If this is true, individuals are, in effect, focusing on only one feature of the problem—namely, the system—and ignoring their own personal responsibility for creating these problems. I call this *distancing*. Distancing occurs whenever human beings act in ways that reduce their personal, causal responsibility for the problems they are trying to solve. Distancing is, I suggest, a very common and powerful force in organizational life as far as double-loop learning is concerned.

But why should young and old, wealthy and poor, male and female, majority and minority, exhibit distancing, especially when dealing with double-loop problems? After all, they are not similar in personality, nor economic or social background, nor personal history.

Our data suggest that one explanation is that when it comes to reasoning for *action,* not simply for understanding, individuals show a striking similarity. Moreover, the reasons for this similarity may be few. If this idea raises eyebrows, let me add two more that may seem even more surprising. Individuals are not aware of the reasoning processes that they use to design and implement actions related to double-loop issues. Moreover, they have programs in their heads that keep them disconnected from their reasoning processes.

Distancing and disconnectedness combine to make it unlikely that individuals will be good at double-loop learning. They also combine to allow individuals to ignore their personal responsibility for creating organizations where double-loop learning cannot take place.

Pessimistic as this diagnosis may sound, it has a very optimistic prognosis. We find that people *want* to be more effective at double-loop learning, and it is possible to turn distancing and disconnectedness around. If the turnaround is effective, it marks the beginning of new capacities in individuals to continue to double-loop learn, even in the face of adversity. We find almost no forgetting curve, even years after the initial learning, because individuals are constantly sharpening their competence on the endless supply of double-loop issues that characterizes life.

What is most optimistic about all this is that the ultimate choice of facing these problems is up to the individual. We, as social beings, can choose to reduce our distancing and disconnectedness and to create organizations and institutions where double-loop learning is a norm.

2

Self-Reinforcing
Patterns of Learning
and Problem Solving

What causes the self-reinforcing patterns that make it hard for individuals and organizations to double-loop learn? From the late 1940s through the early 1970s, the major causes were assumed to be the hierarchal structure, unilateral power, differential status, the dependence and conformity of subordinates, and the lack of time for effective problem solving.

The result was a spate of research to redesign organizational power structures and to get employee involvement. Power equalization, employee participation, and mutual decision making were key concepts of these experiments. A criticism of those experiments is that they did facilitate some single-loop learning but did little to alter the difficulties organizations had in double-loop learning. For example, alternative schools designed to achieve double-loop learning by creating conditions of power equalization and participation have largely failed, even when the teachers and students were all volunteers, when the schools had adequate funds, and when they were protected from hostile environmental forces.[1] Moreover, where organizations have allotted more time and opportunity for problem solving, as in matrix organizations, there is no evidence that double-loop learning occurred.

This failure does not necessarily mean that the factors just mentioned are unimportant. It may be that there is another set of factors, equally or more powerful, that operate jointly with those factors to create the problems I am discussing.

This possibility led us to design an experiment in which as many of the factors as possible were favorable for double-loop learning. We created a situation in which the participants were asked to help an individual become more effective in dealing with the double-loop problem of evaluating and counseling a subordinate whose performance was no longer adequate—a problem frequently encountered in most organizations. Ostensibly the evaluator had asked for such help. We wanted to see whether individuals would create the counterproductive factors identified in Chapter One if they were placed in a nonhierarchal environment designed for learning, if there was no time limit on their task, if they had the initial involvement of the person whom they were to help, and if status and history were not operative.

The experiment was designed to be used in graduate programs in schools of education, business, public administration, and law; in executive programs; and as part of organizational development programs in many settings. The exact conditions and personnel of the case material can be tailored to fit the particular study group. For university administrators, for example, the subordinate, X, was a university staff member. A superior, Y, was assigned to talk with X in order to help him alter his performance. The top administrators told Y to communicate to X that they wanted to keep him on the job but this was his final warning. If there was no improvement, unpleasant but appropriate action would have to be taken.

The study group was given the following transcript of some of Y's statements to X and was told to assume that these statements represented the entire range of meanings that Y communicated to X.

---

[1]Chris Argyris, "Alternative Schools: A Behavioral Analysis," *Teachers College Record*, 75(4) (May 1974): 429-452.

X, your performance is not up to standard, [and moreover] you seem to be carrying a chip on your shoulder.

It appears to me that this has affected your performance in a number of ways. I have heard words like *lethargy, uncommitted,* and *disinterested* used by others in describing your recent performance. Our supervisors cannot have those characteristics.

Let's discuss your feelings about your performance.

X, I know you want to talk about the injustices that you believe have been perpetrated on you in the past. The problem is that I am not familiar with the specifics of those problems. I do not want to spend a lot of time discussing something that happened several years ago. Nothing constructive will come from it. It's behind us.

I want to talk about you today, and about your future in our system.

The participants were asked to write, on one sheet, (1) a short analysis and critique of the way Y dealt with X and (2) any recommendations or advice they would give Y to make his performance with X more effective. They were then asked to assume that Y came to them and said, "How well did you think I dealt with X?" In answering the question, they were to assume that Y wanted to learn.

They were then asked to divide several sheets of paper into two columns. On the right-hand side, they were asked to write exactly what they would say, how they would expect Y to respond, and how they would respond to Y's reply. In short, they were asked to write up an actual conversation with Y. In the left-hand column, they were to write any concurrent thoughts or feelings they would have that, for whatever reason, they would not communicate to Y.

The participants completed the cases before the executive study program and, for the most part, mailed them directly to me, the interventionist in the program.

Participants' Evaluations

Seventy participants completed the first part of the case. A simple content analysis was made of their diagnoses of how Y dealt with X. All but 6 of the 70 evaluated Y's actions toward X as negative. Those who made some positive statements connected them with negative evaluations. For example, they described Y as being "bold," "straightforward," or "honest" toward X and followed these evaluations with "but you came on too strong," "but you should have been a bit more careful," or "but a softer approach would have been more effective."

The evaluations by the 70 respondents contained 96 items, which may be categorized as follows: 48 were attributions of Y's motives, 30 were evaluations of Y's actions, and 18 were attributions of the impact of Y on X.

Attributions of Y's Motives

Y wanted to attack and be blunt	18
Y's mind was made up before the session	8
Y was uncaring	8
Y was controlling	8
Y was threatening	4
Y was unwilling to face the issues	2
	48

Evaluations of Y's Action

Y did not listen to X	6
Y passed the buck	6
Y's actions were negative	5
Y never permitted a dialogue	4
Y had the wrong approach	4
Y made destructive comments	3
Y made unfair evaluations	2
	30

Attributions About Y's Impact

Y made X defensive	13
Y set up X	1
Y produced anger in X	1
Y put down X	1
Y aroused X's anxieties	1
Y created an unreceptive atmosphere for X	1
	18

Here are three diagnoses verbatim:

Example A

Blunt and insensitive to feelings of X. Contradicts self in that dismisses "past history" from X's point of view but uses past as basis of own value judgments . . . .

Very structured and intimidating in approach and style. Requests feedback from X but does not establish a receptive environment.

Wants to talk about "feelings" but gives impression of really not caring unless they are the right (acceptable) "feelings." Today and tomorrow will not exist in a vacuum. They are a factor of yesterday. Dismissal of past and curtailment of that opportunity by X to discuss (vent) will certainly impact negatively on quality/quantity/willingness of X to discuss today and tomorrow.

The model teacher (supervisor) may be a construct of Y but never shared with X (or others). Without knowing expectations, X is performing at a disadvantage. Subject to arbitrary analysis and evaluation.

Example B

Y, in a dictatorial tone, took over the platform and never permitted X to dialogue with him/her. Communication was, at best, one-sided. Y used terminology [such] as *lethargy, uncommitted,* and *disinterested* to further place X in a defenseless position. Performance was questioned based on the *un*documented charges of others.

To speak of the past as having perpetrated injustices on X, and then refusing to address these injustices, Y demonstrated insensitivities of a magnitude to destroy any relationship.

The professional style of Y was *un*professional.

Example C

Jumps in without explaining a) we've a standard, b) which is . . . . This is what, at the outset, appears to be "denigration without explanation"—a "theme" in this scenario.

A cheap shot—an observation which is couched in

a loaded term. A poor use of language at best, an unsub-
stantial nonbehavioral-explained indictment at worst.
Character assassination. An attempt to anger?

Again, loaded language from unknown sources.
How does this set of words manifest itself as behavior?
Who is observing this "lethargy," etc.? Others? *Why*
mention others? Is this a way to ease the pressure of this
uncomfortable situation?

There is an interesting inconsistency about these diagnostic
frames: They contain attributions about Y that are blunt, judgmental, attributive of bad motives, and so on. That is, the group
framed their diagnoses using the same features that they identified as
being counterproductive when Y used them with X. Why would the
group members frame their diagnoses with features that they identify
as counterproductive for helping people to learn?

One answer is that, with possibly two exceptions, the group
members were unaware they were producing these inconsistencies.
As in the cases in Chapter One, the inconsistency was seen and accepted by the participants once it was pointed out. But we can still
ask what makes people unaware that they are producing frames that
violate their own concepts of providing effective help. And why is
the unawareness so widespread and profound, yet so easily seen and
accepted once pointed out?

We will have to present much more data and many more inconsistencies before the answers to these questions can be given. Let
us turn to additional illustrations that permit a closer look at the reasoning processes used. The following responses come from the two-
column conversation with Y that the group members wrote.

Response 1

"Y, your statement ('You seem to be carrying a
chip on your shoulder') is projective and interpretive."
"Y, your statement ('Our teachers cannot have
those characteristics') is a putdown for X."

The contradiction is that the first statement is interpretive and the
second may be experienced by Y as a putdown of him. Hence, this
writer is behaving in ways that he asserts are not helpful although his
intention is to be helpful.

Response 2

"Y should know that generally people feel their performance is up to standard. So to begin the evaluation [as Y did] sets the stage for a denial and an argument as well as a rejection of whatever else may follow."

If the writer believes that people generally feel their performance is up to standard, then why wouldn't this hold for Y? Wouldn't telling Y that he "sets the stage for a denial and an argument" increase the likelihood of argument and denial on the part of Y? Again, in an attempt to help Y, this respondent is using actions that he is asking Y not to use.

Response 3

"It is illogical and poor human relations to have expected anything except hostility on the part of X."

Isn't it illogical for this writer to believe that comments such as this will not produce hostility from Y?

Response 4

One respondent began to recognize that she was being as evaluative and punitive toward Y as she had accused him of being toward X. Then she wrote a scenario of how to correct this problem: "[I should say to Y] I know my remarks may seem harsh, but I can help you only if I am candid."

The contradiction embedded in this statement is that this may be precisely what Y felt about X—namely, that he could help X only if he was candid and harsh. The respondent is telling Y that she will help him by behaving in a way that Y should not use when he is trying to help X.

Roleplaying

Finally, let us explore some roleplaying vignettes. It is important to keep in mind that the roleplaying occurred after several hours of class discussion and after all the participants had agreed that they

had produced diagnostic frames containing the inconsistencies described above. In this first example, a university executive roleplayed
the following scenario:

Roleplay 1

"Y, this is too sharply worded. It is guaranteed to
rouse immediate resentment and hostility. . . . I would
suggest a 'let's get together and see if we can help each
other' approach."

The first inconsistency is that telling Y his conversations are too
sharply worded and are guaranteed to raise resentment and hostility
may be experienced by Y as "too sharply worded" and, hence, may
arouse his resentment and hostility. The second inconsistency is that
such an approach is not likely to have a "let's get together" impact
on Y.

Again, in order to help Y, the actor is using practices similar to
those he criticizes Y for using.

Roleplay 2

The next class member invented a strategy that he
described as "softer," saying that he wanted to be cooperative and participative. The invention was congruent
with one he had written several days before.

"I agree that he [X] is going to resent anything
you say. But you must be patient and communicate to
him your hope and willingness to work with him to
change the problem. By telling him he has a chip on his
shoulder, you're creating more resentment than you
need. I think you'll have to take it a little softer so he'll
work with you."

This actor stated in the first sentence that he expected X to resent
anything Y said. In the next sentence, he recommended that Y express his hope and willingness to work with X. The actor made it
clear during the discussion that he did not recommend making explicit the hypothesis that X will resent anything Y says, because that
might upset X. Hence, the logic is to give Y abstract advice, such as
"communicate hope and willingness to work together," when Y
judges that the client has little hope or willingness to work together.

Next, he advises Y not to discuss the attribution of "chip on your shoulder" but "to take it a little softer so he'll work with you." The logic is: If you minimize statements that might upset X, and if you are softer, X will cooperate.

Y can minimize statements that might upset X ("X will probably resent anything you say") by not saying them. Presumably this leads to a softer approach. But it also makes undiscussable some very important issues that may be at the heart of X's problem. If this analysis is correct, then X will be predisposed to mishear and mistrust Y. To advise Y to be softer, which in this case means not to test out the attributions that Y made about X, is to rule out of the discussion the very factors that eventually must be discussed.

Moreover, Y may pay special attention to X on these factors because Y is on the lookout for any signs of mishearing and intransigence. But again, these attributions will not be tested, because that would violate the "soft" strategy. Holding untested attributions about X may predispose Y to overreact to X's responses and to see more resistance or hostility than is there or to see the resistance and hostility accurately but to interpret it as evidence (untested) that X is stubborn.

The softer approach appears, in this case, to drive underground the issues that require discussion. It also enhances the conditions for X and Y to mishear and misperceive each other, thereby increasing the probability of error. Because these issues are not discussable, the strategy can lead to escalating error. Y could interpret X's errors as "proof" of X's chip on the shoulder. X could interpret Y's errors as evidence of the unfairness and unilateralness of Y (and the organization). These interpretations can become the basis for self-fulfilling prophecies. Because they are undiscussable, they also become self-sealing.

Roleplay 3

Actor said to Y: "Y, I think you have already made X paranoid by suggesting to him that everyone on the campus is gossiping about him. You, as Y, should take responsibility for having noticed the changes. But don't say that other people have been telling you those things."

Actor said to X: "X, as of recent months I have noticed a change in your attitude. You seem to be

lethargic, on the defensive. Possibly there are problems
I'm not aware of. Would you like to discuss them with
me?

"... Perhaps things change for an institution
more rapidly than for an individual. Maybe you're not
aware of what's going on here because you have been so
busy doing your own thing."

We note that the actor attributes to Y that he has made X more paranoid. He then advises Y to deal with the changes in X's performance
by saying that Y himself has noticed them.

The actor asserts in roleplaying that he has observed X being
lethargic, defensive, and so on. Then (1) he asks X to tell him the
cause of these attitudes, which means (2) he assumes his diagnosis is
correct; (3) he then attempts to explain his untested attributions by
making additional ones: The organization is changing faster than X
can cope with, and X is unaware because he is doing his own thing.

X may again feel prejudged and unfairly so. If he were to say
this, he would risk offending Y. If he did not say it, he could feel upset and frustrated—again, conditions that are not discussable. We are
back to the increased probability of escalating error, self-fulfilling
prophecies, and self-sealing processes.

Roleplay 4

Actor said to Y: "The point is, if you really want
to help him, you've got to decide how much of yourself
you want to put into it. You have to try to establish
some common ground with him. You really have to invest in it."

Actor said to X: "These are the things that need
to be improved, and these are steps that you need to
take."

The advice to decide "how much of yourself you want to put into
this" is abstract and, more important, is designed to be unilateral. Indeed, this seems to be, in X's judgment, the same problem he has
with company policy. To X, it appears that the organization is unilaterally deciding how much to invest in him. But in his eyes, even to
make a unilateral decision requires that his superiors observe and
interpret his actions. As we have seen, X has little confidence that

they are observing and interpreting correctly. Moreover, because Y is not testing his interpretation (in any of the roleplays), X may understandably infer that the attributions are undiscussable, and if he acts consistently with that inference, then we again have the conditions for escalating error, self-fulfilling prophecies, and self-sealing processes.

So far we have seen that, when asked to write a diagnosis privately, all the participants develop diagnoses that contain action implications similar to the ones they advise Y not to use, and they seem unaware of the counterproductive features. When the participants write scenarios or actually roleplay them, most of them try to be softer and more diplomatic. However, as we have seen, this strategy leads to consequences that are also counterproductive. The written diagnoses, inventions, and productions all generate actions that lead to escalating error, self-fulfilling prophecies, and self-sealing processes.

The class members were then asked to invent some strategies to deal with X and to come prepared to produce them through roleplaying the next day. All continued to invent and produce solutions that contained the same counterproductive features.

Group Discussion of Strategies and Roleplaying

An analysis of the tape recording of class members' interactions indicated that in all cases the participants were able to identify the counterproductive aspects in others' roleplaying before the interventionist presented his views. Hence, the participants were effective at diagnosing the errors of their colleagues. Second, the participants counseled each other using the same counterproductive actions they used in their diagnoses and in the roleplaying. For example:

> "I think the essence of the message (the way you made it) gets downgraded."
> "First of all, the message has to be gotten through that he's fired."
> "He's giving me [as Y] advice which ignores the problem that I may have to fire X."
> "The examples you just gave [in your roleplay] are irrelevant."
> "Are you *really* trying to save him, or are you set-

ting him up for one last time and he's going to go down
the drain?"

"There is a difference between getting rid of him
and accusing him—of trying to destroy him personally.
Be positive, communicate that you don't want to destroy him."

All the comments made by the participants could be categorized as unillustrated attributions and evaluations or as advocating
a position in order to win and not lose. Indeed, the interventionist
had to interrupt the dialogues because they would only result in escalating error, self-fulfilling prophecies, and self-sealing processes. In
other words, the class discussions created the same counterproductive conditions that the members created in their written diagnoses
and in their roleplaying. All this occurred over a period of seven
days, including four two-hour discussions about the counterproductive features of their actions.

As you might predict, bewilderment and confusion among
the participants increased. It is important to note that the confusion
and bewilderment did not result from the interventionist's diagnoses
of the class, for even though he judged the class members' interventions to be counterproductive, that judgment was illustrated and confirmed by the class members. The bewilderment came from each
member's apparent inability to invent and produce the interventions
that he or she wanted to. Frustration increased when members realized they had been unaware of their inability to do this. Finally, all
these feelings were compounded as it became clear to the class that
they could diagnose correctly the errors of others but they themselves were unable to produce effective intervention.

Summary

Learning may be described as a process in which people discover a problem, invent a solution to the problem, produce the solution, and evaluate the outcome, leading to the discovery of new
problems.

In our experiment, people were asked to act as consultants to
Y in the matter of how he dealt with X. They were asked to diagnose, or to discover, Y's actions, to invent new ways that Y could
have dealt with X, to produce these inventions in the form of role-

playing, and to evaluate their effectiveness, thereby leading to new discoveries.

The participants diagnosed Y's actions as ineffective. They invented solutions that they were unable to produce. Hence, they began to discover that they were not as effective as they thought. If we can assume that Y also was not as effective as he thought, then we have a case of the blind helping the blind, the helpers being unaware of their blindness.

When we examined the reasoning processes of the participants, we found that they diagnosed the problem of Y by framing it with attributions and evaluations that were as counterproductive as those that the participants inferred Y had made about X. When we asked them to produce the solutions that they had invented, we found that they were unable to do so. When we examined the consequences for learning that they created, we found the same counterproductive features that the participants accused Y of using with X. When members tried to help each other in class, they repeated all these features. Hence, they were creating with each other the same counterproductive features that they were advising Y not to produce.

As in the cases in Chapter One, people tended to be unaware of their own inconsistencies but aware of those produced by others. Moreover, whenever they tried to communicate those to each other in order to be of help, they created conditions that led to escalating error, self-fulfilling prophecies, and self-sealing processes.

Finally, by acting in ways that created the very conditions they were condemning, they also created conditions in which those being helped felt that their consultants were not acting competently and justly.

As you will see in the next chapter, we have obtained these results in 27 other experiments. Thus, the findings are not unique. It is the consistency of such findings that leads to the hypothesis that people may be disconnected from their reasoning processes that lead to action. How else can we account for their advising Y not to evaluate X, yet evaluating Y; not to put down X, yet putting down Y; to be supportive of X while being forthright, yet being destructive of Y while being forthright? How can people diagnose accurately the negative impact of Y's action on X and be blind to the fact that they are producing the same negative impact?

Indirect evidence for the hypothesis that people may be disconnected from their reasoning processes when dealing with double-loop issues is that they are able to identify the counterproductive actions in others or at least can readily confirm their inconsistencies once they have been pointed out. It is as if they first became connected to the reasoning processes because they observed the behavior, and then they became able to infer the underlying reasoning.

We may also begin to see one of the root causes for distancing. If people are disconnected from their own reasoning processes, if they act in ways that escalate error, if they create self-fulfilling prophecies, self-sealing processes, and escalating error, and if they create and are embedded in systems that reinforce these factors, it is understandable that they distance themselves from their personal causal responsibility. On the one hand, they may literally not see it; on the other hand, the culture and the system in which they are embedded reward and reinforce the blindness.

3

Reasoning
Processes
and Action

People rarely produce actions that do not make
sense to themselves; they have intentions about what it is they are
trying to accomplish. The degree to which they are aware of their intentions varies, but so far we have found that their actions are intentionally rational. Their actions are explicitly or tacitly designed to
achieve some intended consequences.

This chapter will focus in more detail on the reasoning processes that people appear to use when they diagnose situations and
act in them. By "reasoning processes" I refer to the premises that
people create, the inferences they make from the premises, and the
conclusions they reach.

A premise is a fact or proposition that is proved or assumed to
be proved. A premise is grounds for an inference and conclusion. An
inference is the process by which a person deduces a conclusion from
the premise. Inference processes vary in degree of looseness and
tightness. Conclusions vary in degree to which they follow compellingly from the premises.

Everyday actions involve many premises, inferences, and conclusions. Most of them are performed at very high speed; indeed, many appear to be automatic responses. If they are automatic, it is probably because they are learned, highly skilled responses. If they are skilled responses, and if many people use them, then there is a strong probability that they have been learned through socialization. And if this is so, the responses are probably tacit; that is, they are performed without much conscious attention.

It is difficult to study these automatic responses because they occur at such rapid speed, and people may not be fully aware of the reasoning processes that underlie them. We had to find a way to slow down the process, to get people to repeat their actions, and simultaneously to avoid creating conditions whereby the slowdown and conscious attention to responses altered them.

There is a natural way to create these conditions. People will slow down, pay attention to, and continually repeat their responses if they find that the responses they expect to be skillful turn out not to be (that is, they do not produce the intended consequences). For example, tennis players are willing to slow down their tennis game and concentrate on their backhand if their backhand no longer produces the results they had intended.

The case of X and Y presents such an opportunity. To date, our participants diagnose Y as behaving largely ineffectively. They all provide advice on how he could become more effective, writing scenarios or roleplaying to produce that advice. And to date, their recommendations lead to conditions that contradict their advice. Under these conditions, people begin to feel frustrated and ineffective. Consequently, many of them are willing to repeat their automatic responses and to reexamine them in order to better understand the cause of the inconsistency.

In this chapter, we deal with a class taking advanced degrees in counseling and consulting psychology, a contrast to the executives of the previous chapter. These professionals make a living at facilitating client double-loop learning. Yet, as we shall see, they use the same reasoning processes and produce the same inconsistencies as line executives do.

Why is this so? It is not because they are at Harvard; I have obtained similar results in other universities that have similar programs.

It is not because they are in the helping professions; the same results occur with consultants in microeconomics and strategic planning as well as with consultants designing actions for clients based on highly complicated statistical models. It cannot be age, sex, or race; the results are the same when age ranges from 12 to 70 and when males, females, and minorities (see Table 1) take the course (designed as a 4-

Table 1. Groups in Which the X and Y Case Was Used

Type of Participant	Number	Percentage Female	Percentage Minority
1. Master's and doctoral students	100	35	25
2. Master's and doctoral students	40	55	20
3. Master's and doctoral students	80	55	20
4. Master's and doctoral students	85	41	11
5. University administrators	75	35	25
6. Senior government officials	39	26	25
7. Senior government officials	53	26	26
8. Senior private executives	16	0	0
9. Senior private executives	95	0	5
10. Senior private executives (Europe)	22	0	0
11. Senior private executives	4	0	0
12. Senior private executives	6	66	0
13. Senior executives and spouses	8	50	0
14. Senior executives and spouses	20	50	0
15. Senior organizational development (OD) consultants	20	40	30
16. Senior OD consultants	4	0	0
17. Senior OD consultants	12	50	8
18. Senior OD consultants (Europe)	20	40	0
19. Senior OD consultants (Canada)	35	71	30
20. Senior OD consultants (England)	25	20	0
21. Senior consultants other than OD	25	2	0
22. Junior consultants	10	0	0
23. Junior consultants	25	5	0
24. Junior consultants	20	10	10
25. Junior consultants	20	5	0
26. Government executives	100	46	16
27. Scandinavian executives	90	11	0

to 24-hour seminar). Moreover, similar results have been obtained in a sample four times as large as the total represented in Table 1. That sample included professionals from South America, Israel, India, and Western Europe. The major difference was that the cases the participants wrote described important problems that they faced in their everyday professional and managerial lives.[1]

There is one underlying similarity in all our data. Whatever the substance of the case, it required double-loop learning. Participants had to break the frames that they normally used to understand and act in their world. Helping people to "framebreak" is the common activity depicted in these cases, whether the participants are line executives, teachers, consultants, or parents.

Framebreaking is what this book is all about. We have found that individuals or organizations are able to detect and correct errors as long as such learning does not require framebreaking. Such learning is important, but it is not powerful. For example, during the past decade, through the use of information sciences, a myriad of managerial information devices have been produced to help administrators manage and control their organizations more effectively. Yet during this very period, confidence in organizations and in most of the professions decreased.[2] One reason is that most of the technology is effective only within the existing individual and organizational frames. The problem of confidence, however, is related to framebreaking and the development of new individual and organizational frames.

Diagnostic Frames Developed by the Participants

The 40 participants, students in a special master's and doctoral program in counseling and consulting psychology, had two or more years of experience as counselors and consultants. There were slightly more women than men (55 to 45 percent). Twenty percent of the students represented minorities. These consultants, like those in Chapter Two, evaluated Y's actions as being largely ineffective. In doing so, they used unillustrated evaluations and attributions.

---

[1]Chris Argyris, *Increasing Leadership Effectiveness* (New York: Wiley-Interscience, 1976); Chris Argyris, "Theories of Action That Inhibit Individual Learning," *American Psychologist, 31*(9) (September 1976): 638-654; Chris Argyris and Donald Schön, *Theory in Practice: Increasing Professional Effectiveness* (San Francisco: Jossey-Bass, 1974); Chris Argyris and Donald Schön, *Organizational Learning* (Reading, Mass.: Addison-Wesley, 1978).

[2]Chris Argyris, *Inner Contradictions of Rigorous Research* (New York: Academic Press, 1980).

The majority of the experienced consultants were eclectic in their use of interpersonal and group perspectives. Most had participated in such learning experiences as T-groups, client-centered therapy, Gestalt therapy, cognitive behavior modification, and analytically oriented psychotherapy. Six might be termed "sociologically oriented" in that their preferred point of entry for change was the social system.

Consultants' Diagnosis of Y's Action

Let us first examine the consultants' discoveries, or diagnoses, of Y's actions and of Y's impact on X, as well as the inventions they made to help Y.

Diagnosis: All 40 class members saw Y as behaving toward X in this pattern:

Judgmental, evaluating, threatening, degrading, imposing, accusatory, recriminating, giving mixed messages (asks for feelings and yet ignores them).

Giving negative feedback without any positive feedback, cutting X off, putting X down without any specifics, using second-hand information.

The impact of the foregoing actions on X would be to make X feel:

Unheard, bullied, pressured, rejected, dismissed, unsupported, panicky, defensive.

The impact of Y's actions on his effectiveness was described as:

Counterproductive, unjust, closed system.

Invention:

To help Y become aware of his counterproductive attitudes and actions in such a way that we minimize creating feelings in him that he is being judged, thereby making him defensive.

To help Y become more aware of his own defensiveness and how it causes him to be autocratic, insensitive, and a poor listener.

To help Y examine the extent to which he (and his organization)
    really wants to understand X's problems.
To help Y articulate what he felt was wrong with X.
To help Y express his feelings of frustration and anger with X.
To help Y soften his technique; to help Y learn how to give X an
    opportunity to express his anger and pain.

We see, then, that all the class members evaluated Y's actions
negatively.

The way they expressed their evaluations differed somewhat.
The majority evaluated Y in such terms as "threatening," "judgmental," "degrading," and "accusatory." A smaller number agreed but
included illustrations of Y's actions to back up their diagnosis. This
difference is not important for the moment, because the point being
made is that the class, like the administrators in the previous chapter,
diagnosed Y as being ineffective.

There was also a high degree of agreement in their inventions.
About 75 percent of the inventions are covered in the first two
items. The difference among all the alternatives is not great.

Another way to illustrate the data is to present two actual
diagnoses. Example A contains more evaluations and attributions
that are not illustrated than Example B. Example A had 24, or 60
percent, and Example B, 16, or 40 percent.

Example A

Y's approach to X can be characterized as accusatory and recriminatory. He is clearly establishing that X
is indeed a subordinate and that it is time to "shape up
or ship out."

Y begins his confrontation with X by delineating
X's negative attitude and performance. Thus, his approach is an offensive one which further underscores the
inequity of power in the relationship between the two.
Statements such as "Our teachers cannot have those
characteristics" are belittling and aggressive. Y leaves little room for dialogue or open confrontation as he has
set up a one-way situation where he maintains control.

This setting of limits to the discussion also characterizes the interaction. Y states, "I do not want to spend
a lot of time discussing something that happened several

years ago. Nothing constructive will come from it." This statement cuts off areas of discussion which are most probably of great importance to the issue of a deteriorating performance over a period of six years. This statement also conveys an attitude which is, at best, unsympathetic and unwilling to change.

A third characteristic of the interaction is that it is closed. Y confronts X with a variety of accusations, and leaves no room for response to his statements.

Example B

Y evaluates X—"Your performance is not up to standard." This will put X on the defensive.

Y attributes unattractive motives to X—"You seem to be carrying a chip on your shoulder." This will reinforce defensiveness.

Y suggests causality—"It appears that this has affected your performance. . . ."

Y is impersonal. Y uses the comments of others to convey his own concerns about X's performance—"I have heard words like *lethargy, uncommitted,* and *disinterested* used by others in describing your recent performance." This conveys an unwillingness to become personally involved.

Y is judgmental. Words like *"lethargy, uncommitted,* and *disinterested"* convey this. These words also categorize Y, making X feel threatened and reducing the probability of X being open.

Y is dominant and controlling in stating, "I do not want to spend a lot of time discussing something that happened several years ago." This statement also indicates an unwillingness on the part of Y to consider (or to discuss) problems in the organization and closes off the possibility of a discussion of any problems X may have in his relationship with Y.

In focusing on the problems and ignoring mention of the earlier fine record of X, Y appears as unsupportive.

Y appears to be task-oriented rather than people-oriented.

Y's empathy toward X is limited to "X, I know you want to talk about the injustices that . . . have been perpetrated on you in the past."

Collage of the Consultants' Responses

The consultants unanimously felt that Y's way of dealing with X would have the following effects:

X will feel threatened and defensive.
X will feel that he is not accepted.
X will not believe that Y is genuinely concerned.
X will not believe that Y really wants to hear what his problems are.
X will not feel free to discuss any perceived (by either party) short-
    comings or inadequacies.
Without openness, it is unlikely that real problems will be brought to
    the surface, where they can begin to be dealt with.

Notable Features of the Responses

The first feature of the collage, as well as of Examples A and B, is that the sentences can be organized into propositions of a kind that exist in theories of action. For example:

If people (in this case, Y) behave in ways such as being judgmental,
    evaluative, and so on,
then they will tend to make others (in this case, X) feel unheard, bul-
    lied, misunderstood, and so on.

These first-order consequences combine to produce second-order consequences. For example, these relationships will feed back to reinforce Y's defense-producing action, which in turn will reinforce the defensiveness, thereby reinforcing and escalating error. These consequences will combine to inhibit double-loop learning.

All these propositions have embedded in them assertions about causality. Y's behavior causes X's defensiveness, and X's reaction may reinforce Y's ineffective actions. Embedded in these causal relationships is a theory of defense. That is, all these consultants (as well as the executives in the previous chapter) must hold a theory that unilateral and untested attributions and evaluations lead to defensiveness. The consultant in Example B makes this implicit theory explicit. We will examine this theory in more detail later.

Second, in the diagnoses, all participants imputed their own meaning to Y's sentences. This is a necessary first step in taking action. One must decide the meaning of the events that one is trying to understand and, in this case, alter. But the act of creating a meaning is an act of making an inference from data. The diagnoses show that people saw different meanings in the sentences; hence, the meanings that they created are impositions or enactments. The meanings are never out there statically waiting. The variance in meanings, however, was not large. Patterns of meaning could be identified.

Third, although there was some variance in meanings, there was no variance in the causality inferred from the meanings. Everyone saw Y's actions as counterproductive to learning. Some meanings (for example, "Y is recriminatory and power-oriented") require a number of inferences because they are not directly illustrated by Y's actions as depicted in the X-Y scenario. Other meanings may be described as close to the relatively observable data (in this case, the transcript from a tape recording). For example, one could turn to the transcript and show that Y did refuse to talk about history or that Y quoted others to attribute lethargy to X. One important feature of these latter meanings is that they can be more easily falsified.

At the other end of the continuum were inferences that were much less easy to connect to the relatively directly observable data. For example, statements such as "Y was recriminatory and power-oriented" may be true, but the ladder of inference that would be required to test these assertions is much more complex. The longer the ladder of inference—the further the inference is from the relatively directly observable data—the greater the difficulty of testing the validity of the meanings, and hence the greater the likelihood of misunderstandings.

How are people's reasoning processes ordered on a ladder of inference? The first level is whatever the person considers to be the relatively directly observable data. For example, in the X and Y case, the sentences taken from the transcript are relatively directly observable data; they are the first rung of the ladder. The second rung represents the culturally understood and acceptable meaning. For example, Y's statement "X, your performance is not up to our standard" has a meaning of "X, your performance is unacceptable." Figure 5 (p. 181) is a diagram of the ladder of inference.

Inferences made beyond the first two rungs express the meaning the second rung has for whoever is reading the sentences. Examples of consultants' third-rung inferences about Y are "Y was blunt," "Y was insensitive," "Y was punishing." These third-rung meanings became the premises for the consultants' diagnoses of Y's effectiveness: *If* Y is blunt, *then* X will feel angry, prejudged, and so on. Such statements of causality could not be made without an implicit theory of human defensiveness. This implicit theory of what makes people defensive also influences the consultants to see bluntness or insensitivity in Y's statements.

Finally, participants' third-rung inferences vary in their degree of abstraction, but no matter how abstract, the participants see them as concrete. Whatever meanings people produce on the third rung of the ladder, they see as obvious. Perhaps the inference processes required to produce the first three rungs are so highly skilled, automatic, and tacit that the creators see their inferences as close to the data. If the inferences are obvious and close to the data for the creators, then they will see little need to test them. However, the recipient—in this case, Y—who may not agree with the inferences may wish that the inferences made about him were tested. Until he is convinced through his own reasoning processes that others are correct, he will probably respond by attributing bluntness, insensitivity, and misunderstanding to those others. The creators, also holding a theory of defense, will see Y's actions as evidence that he is defensive and perhaps closed to learning. Hence a self-fulfilling and self-sealing prophecy is created.

Consultants' Inventions to Help Y

So far we have focused mainly on how the consultants framed their diagnoses. The next step is to see how they would actually behave, as illustrated by the scenarios they wrote. What meanings did they create when they began to talk with Y? How consistent were the meanings with their diagnoses? How effective was their help?

As in the previous chapter, all the scenarios could be described as ranging from nondirective, inquiry-oriented to directive and telling Y what to do. There were more inquiry-oriented scenarios among the professional consultants than among line and staff persons. The consultants' easing-in strategy tended to last longer than the line and staff strategies. As in the previous chapter, a few consultants became more directive as their scenarios went on and finally told Y that he had to alter his behavior. However, there were more consultants who remained inquiry-oriented and never dealt with the problem they had identified. For example, in their scenarios many appeared to ask for further study and enlarged consulting activity before they could help Y. The consultant who wrote Example B produced the following easing-in scenario.

Example C
Easing-In Inquiry-Oriented Approach

Thoughts and Feelings	*Conversation*
Listening to the tape allows me and Y to have a common starting point. Also, I can watch Y's reactions.	*Consultant:* Y, let's listen to a little bit of your taped conversation with X. [They listen to tape]
Solicit Y's reaction. Obviously, a reply didn't help his recognition of the problem.	*Cons.:* What are your feelings about what we have heard?
	Y: Well, it's a fair representation of the problem and what was said.
Still trying to lead Y to a recognition of the other guy's perspective. He's obsessed with the future. Sounds like he prejudges everything.	*Cons.:* Did X indicate what may have been the cause for his sudden substandard performance?
	Y: Nothing more than he's said before. Besides, if he's going to do the job for us in the future, we've got to forget the past and get on with it.
More of same. He still doesn't see the problem.	*Cons.:* Wouldn't it be helpful to have his perspective on why his performance has changed so drastically?
	Y: Oh, it would be just the same old stuff.
	Cons.: What stuff do you mean?
	Y: Oh, I've forgotten, and X has

Thoughts and Feelings   *Conversation*

been around long enough that he isn't going to change.

The discussion has now turned into an evaluation of Y's performance. But he still doesn't know it. He has given up on X.

Cons.: There had to be some reason for X's change in behavior. Don't you think it would be helpful for us to listen to him carefully again and try to determine what it is that is bothering him?

Y: It probably would be a waste of time.

Cons.: It seems to me that one of the characteristics of a good manager is to know enough about his people that he can assess the cause of the problem. How can we do this if we don't listen carefully to what he has to say?

Y: He'll just tell us about all the things we do wrong.

Cons.: That's important to me. As managers we should be willing to listen to fair suggestions and criticisms from our people, especially from men with the demonstrated talent that X has shown.

Obviously, the conversation could go several ways here. A more direct approach to Y is possible *and likely.* But I have to try to live within the organization as much as possible—and who knows, Y's evaluation of X may be correct. It's how he arrived at it that is bothersome.

Y: I'll try again if you say so, but I'm sure it will do no good.

Cons.: Perhaps I should talk to him and listen to what he has to say.

Y: That's not necessary. I'll do it.

Cons.: Are you sure you can?

Y: Can what?

Cons.: Listen? . . . carefully?

How can we explain the predominance of the easing-in inquiry-oriented approach? One explanation is related to the causal theory embedded in the diagnoses. For example, let us reexamine the diagnosis of the consultant who produced the foregoing scenario. Column 1 of Table 2 shows the meanings that the consultant produced

Table 2. Implications of Consultant's Diagnosis of Y

Consultant's Meaning of What Y Did	Consultant's Prediction of Consequences	Implications for Consultant's Action
Y evaluates X.	Negative evaluation leads X to become defensive.	Do not make negative evaluations.
Y attributes unattractive motives to X.	Reinforces defensiveness.	Do not make unattractive attributions.
Y suggests causality.	Causality could be wrong.	Do not imply causality.
Y is impersonal.	Will make X feel that Y does not want to become personally involved.	Do not be impersonal.
Y is judgmental.	X will feel categorized, threatened, and less open.	Do not judge.
Y is dominant and controlling.	Reinforces defensiveness.	Do not dominate.
Y is task-oriented rather than people-oriented.	Reinforces impersonality.	Be people-oriented as well as task-oriented.

when she was diagnosing Y's actions. Column 2 states the predictions she made of the consequences of Y's actions. Column 3 identifies the actions the consultant must *not* produce if she is to remain consistent with her own theory of defense. That is, we assume that the consultant will not knowingly try to produce the same conditions with Y that she believes are counterproductive to effective help or learning. For example, she must not make negative evaluations or unattractive attributions and must neither judge nor dominate. These constraints make it highly unlikely that the consultant will be candid, direct, and forthright, because her diagnosis contains negative evaluations, unattractive attributions, and negative judgments. Hence, if she must try to be personal (the opposite of her "Do not be impersonal"), and if she must not dominate, then asking questions becomes the rational approach. The problem is that such action does not help Y learn.

Perhaps if the scenario had been longer, she would have solved the problem. We have tried this by asking people to write an additional scenario and/or by roleplaying. The results are consistent: People may become more candid and direct, but they do so in ways that reproduce the conditions that they are telling Y he should not have produced.

Why do people fluctuate between easing in and being directive? One answer is that they appear to have master programs in their heads that lead them to produce either the directive or the easing-in scenario. But where did these master programs come from? What do they look like? How did so many people learn similar master programs? To answer these questions, more data will be presented, and a possible explanation provided, in Chapter Four.

Most Frequent Diagnostic Pattern

The consultant whose diagnosis was reproduced as Example A uses a frequent form of diagnosis and action (especially among the consultants studied to date). Column 1, Table 3, contains some of

Table 3. Consultant's Inferences About Y and Some Alternative Interpretations

Inferences Made by Consultant	Possible Alternative Inferences from Y's Point of View
1. "Y begins his confrontation with X by delineating X's negative attitude and performance." *Inference process:* The episode in which Y delineates X's negative attitudes and performance can be used as an illustration of *confrontation,* and *confrontation is negative.*	Delineating negative attitudes and performance is descriptive of an ineffective employee.
2. "Thus, his approach is an offensive one which further underscores the inequity of power in the relationship between the two." *Inference:* Since this is confrontation, it is *offensive,* and it *reinforces inequitable power relationships.*	X has had the upper hand for years. He is the one who is offensive to all the other hard-working employees.
3. "Statements such as 'Our teachers cannot have those characteristics' are belittling and aggressive." *Inference:* Telling X that his performance characteristics are not acceptable is *belittling* and *aggressive.*	Acting as a responsible manager requires that I tell him that his performance characteristics are unacceptable.

Table 3 (Continued)

Inferences Made by Consultant	Possible Alternative Inferences from Y's Point of View
4. "Y leaves little room for dialogue or open confrontation as he has set up a one-way situation where he maintains control." *Inference:* Since Y is confronting, offensive, reinforcing inequitable relationships, belittling, and aggressive, then he *maintains unilateral control* and *leaves little room for dialogue or open confrontation.*	If I were all these things, then I would agree with your conclusion. But I do not agree with the premises.

the sentences that appear in the consultant's diagnosis and the inference processes that we presume the consultant used in order to produce the sentences. For example, the consultant read the first sentence in Y's transcript and inferred that Y was confronting X and that such confrontation was negative. Once she established that Y was behaving offensively, then it followed that Y was reinforcing inequitable power relationships.

Column 2 includes other possible meanings that could be inferred from Y's scenario. For example, Y could maintain that he was not confronting X; he was describing X's ineffective performance. Y could also maintain that X had the upper hand because he was being given another chance even though his performance had been poor for years.

In Table 4 we present the consultant's reasoning, or logic, plus

Table 4. Consultant's Logic and Comments on It

Consultant's Logic	Comments
1. Delineating means confrontation.	Not necessarily so—but the logic is not made explicit.
Confrontation is bad.	Not necessarily so—but the logic is not made explicit.
2. Given that confrontation is bad, then Y is offensive; and given that, then Y reinforces inequitable power relationships.	Logic is compelling if one accepts that Y is confronting and is offensive, but these are premises of doubtful validity.

(continued on next page)

Table 4 (Continued)

Consultant's Logic	Comments
3. If you tell another that his performance characteristics are negative, you are belittling and being aggressive.	Not necessarily so—but the logic is not made explicit.
4. Since Y is confronting, offensive, reinforcing of inequitable relationships, belittling, and aggressive, then it follows that he maintains unilateral control and leaves little room for dialogue or open confrontation.	Logic is compelling if one accepts that Y is all these things—but that he is has never been tested and never been accepted by Y.

our analysis of that reasoning. We indicate that other perspectives (such as Y's) may exist. Hence, the consultant's assertions are seen for what they are—namely, inferences that require testing. But note the consultant's logic in items 1 and 2. She begins with two assertions that are assumed to be true; then she develops a conclusion that is validly based on those assertions. The problem is that the premises from which the conclusion was drawn were not tested. The same occurs in items 3 and 4.

This type of reasoning occurs in all the scenarios analyzed. People state premises that they assume are true, from which they therefore may deduce consequences that are valid. They appear unaware of the problematic nature of their premises. The behavioral strategies implicit in this logic might be stated as follows:

1. State premises that are not tested, but act as if they were true.
2. Derive conclusions from these premises from which one can derive further conclusions.
3. Behave this way toward the client, and advise him not to behave this way toward others.

To begin to infer this consultant's theory-in-use, let us examine the conversation she produced:

Thoughts and Feelings	Conversation
	Consultant: I'd like to know about how you're doing with X.

Thoughts and Feelings	*Conversation*
	Y: Our conversation didn't seem to do any good. He had nothing to say for himself and doesn't seem to want to improve his performance.
I am trying to focus on the issues underlying the performance.	*Cons.:* What are your feelings about the reasons behind his negative performance?
Y is labeling X and has his mind made up.	*Y:* He just doesn't seem interested in his work. He is resentful and lazy.
I ask this to point out the direct and bluntly negative approach Y has taken with X.	*Cons.:* Did you tell him that?
	Y: Well, not in so many words, but yes, I let him know I was not pleased with him.
	Cons.: What was his reaction?
	Y: He didn't say much—just scowled.
I am trying to suggest a different approach to X and to point out the futility of an accusatory one.	*Cons.:* You seem to be getting nowhere with that. He sees that you are unhappy with his performance but does not want to cooperate with you?
	Y: It certainly seems that way.
	Cons.: Did you give him a chance to cooperate with you?
	Y: Of course. I told him I wanted to talk about his future in the system.
	Cons.: And he saw no future for himself in the system?
	Y: I don't know. We really didn't get that far.
	Cons.: Not much good came of the talk.

Thoughts and Feelings	*Conversation*
	Y: I guess not. The guy has a chip on his shoulder.
Pointing out the one-way interaction.	*Cons.:* You see him as having a negative attitude. Do you think he might pick up on that?
	Y: It's possible. What else can I do?
I want Y to reflect on the consequences of the previous interaction and to think about a more open approach.	*Cons.:* How do you think you might change your approach?
	Y: I didn't find anything out. . . .
	Cons.: Why did that happen?
	Y: Maybe I came down on him too hard.
Confirming this.	*Cons.:* Perhaps you did.
	Y: I have no idea of why he's having problems at work.
	Cons.: Is there a way to find out?
	Y: I guess I need to ask him. And to give him room to answer.
Reiterating a new approach.	*Cons.:* That may be. Is that your goal for the next time you talk with him?
	Y: Yes. I'll try to hear his side.

The consultant begins by inquiring into Y's views about his relationship with X. After Y responds that X is still a poor performer, the consultant asks for Y's view of what causes X's poor performance. She writes: "In asking, 'What are your feelings about the reasons behind his negative performance?,' I am focusing on the underlying issues."

When Y responds, "He just doesn't seem interested in his work. He is resentful and lazy," the consultant infers that this is evidence that Y is labeling X and has already made up his mind about him. I infer that the consultant makes this inference confirming her view of Y because Y's view of the "underlying issues" is different from the consultant's. But all Y is doing is remaining consistent with his diagnostic frame about X. The consultant is also remaining consistent with *her* diagnostic frame. When Y does this, it is a sign of being closed; when the consultant does this, it is a sign of trying to help Y see his closedness.

The consultant then asks, "Did you tell him that?," because she believes it will lead Y to see that his approach is bluntly negative. The inference is tenable if Y admits that he did not feel free to speak openly with X. Y admits that he did not speak openly. The consultant does not inquire what prevented him from doing so. Perhaps one reason is that the consultant is using a theory-in-use similar to Y's— namely, withholding the attributions that she has made about Y.

The consultant then tells Y, "You seem to be getting nowhere with that [approach]." She asks whether X "does not want to cooperate with you" even though he "sees that you are unhappy with his performance." The intention is to help Y see the futility of his approach.

The meanings produced by the consultant may lead to the intended consequences if Y sees himself (or the organization) as responsible for X's poor performance. There is no evidence that Y feels this way. There *is* evidence that the consultant has diagnosed it this way.

When Y asks, "What else can I do?," the consultant asks, "How do you think you might change your approach?" Her intention is "to get Y to reflect on the consequences of the previous interaction and to think about a more open approach." This intention might come about if Y were ready to see himself and the organization as causally responsible for X's poor performance, a view that is part of the consultant's diagnostic frame.

To summarize, the consultant states conclusions that do not follow from the X-Y conversation. They do follow for her, however, because she imposes meanings on Y's conversation that are consistent with her diagnostic frame. She accepts the conclusions as valid. She then expands these conclusions into premises that are presumed true in order to make further inferences about Y. None of these inferences is made explicit, and none is tested publicly with Y.

This consultant's approach has some unintended consequences. First, the consultant appears to focus on communicating and maintaining her frame about what is going on between X and Y. In doing so, she appears to ignore Y's questions; to ignore, or not to create, opportunities to help Y explore his untested attributions about X; and to be unaware of the unintended attributions that she makes about Y. Second, Y may feel misunderstood and may feel that the consultant does not understand the problems of superiors and organizations. Finally, the consultant creates in her relationship with Y the same conditions that she advises Y not to create with X.

Consultant States:	*Consultant Acts:*
1. Y is accusatory.	1. To accuse Y.
2. Y establishes power relationship.	2. To establish power relationship.
3. Y appears to care only for system.	3. To focus on maintaining her system (of logic).
4. Y leaves little room for dialogue or open confrontation.	4. To restrict dialogue to her view and to prevent open confrontation of her view.

Summary

In closing, let us summarize how the consultants dealt with Y and the implications of this for double-loop learning and effective consulting.

The Diagnostic Frame

Both the consultants and the line executives diagnosed Y as being judgmental, recriminatory, and so on. This frame of the problem became a premise, which they considered to be valid. They could then deduce that acting on the attitudes they had attributed to Y would make X defensive. This conclusion became a premise for the next step in their reasoning. Given X's defensiveness and Y's predisposition to create defensiveness, they were able to deduce that the situation would probably be filled with escalating errors and defensiveness.

Validity of the Diagnostic Frame

If the criterion for validity was consensus, then the validity of the frame would have to be judged high, because almost all members of the class arrived at that frame independently. But the issue of validity was not so easily settled. Our frame about Y contained un-illustrated judgments, evaluations, and condemnations, which, if communicated to Y, would make him defensive. The class members generated a frame in order to understand Y that contained the same counterproductive features they had identified in Y's frame for dealing with X.

Why should the class of consultants use a frame that contained the same features that they had judged counterproductive in the frame used by Y?

Nature of the Conversations with Y

To answer this question, we must examine the scenarios that the class members produced. In these scenarios the overwhelming majority of the consultants invented what may be called an "easing-in" strategy. The basic features of this strategy were the following: (1) Hide from Y their diagnostic frame, and hide the fact that they are hiding it. (2) Ask loaded questions that, if Y answers them, will bring him to see what they are hiding. (3) If Y does not generate that insight by answering these questions, then begin to "unwrap" the diagnoses by asking leading questions or, in a few cases, by telling him directly.

Validity of the Productions

The easing-in strategies were not very effective. They could have led Y to feel indirectly misjudged, unfairly judged, or mis-understood and to be attacked indirectly.

In other words, the counterproductive consequences that the consultants had identified in Y's interaction with X were also pres-ent in their frame of Y, and these consequences surfaced in their own productions. The consultants found themselves acting toward Y in ways that they had advised him not to use with X.

Consultants' Awareness of the Puzzles and Dilemmas

The consultants appeared to be unaware of these counterpro-ductive features until they were pointed out. They confirmed the validity of this diagnosis, once it was made explicit, with almost no major disagreement. So something was operating to "cause" them to create the very conditions that they identified as counterproductive *and* to be unaware of this fact.

How Do We Explain These Findings?

We have four elements of an explanation.

1. Counterproductive reasoning. The first step in producing an explanation was to go to the relatively directly observable data. In the case of the diagnostic frame, we used the consultants' own descriptions of their frames. We noted that the consultants made inferences from premises which were either false or incomplete but which were used as if they were complete and true. Conclusions drawn from these premises followed logically, as if the premises were true. These conclusions were used as premises for further diagnoses or actions. Again, the reasoning from the consequences was logically valid; the problem was that the premises were not. So the consultants were somehow blind to the incorrectness and incompleteness of their premises.

2. The consultants' theory of help and consultation encouraged conditions for counterproductive reasoning: Be supportive; be minimally responsible for making the client defensive or for the client's leaving; be egalitarian; be close to the client. There are problems with this theory of help. It does not differentiate between defense that can enhance learning and that which inhibits it, and it does not differentiate between competently produced information or feedback and that incompetently produced.

A client who was highly closed to learning could become defensive even if he was told something that was valid and even if it was done competently. Yet, given this theory of help, the consultants would hold themselves responsible for this outcome. Their theory of help places the consultants under the control of the neurotic, nonlearning aspects of a client's behavior.

If the consultants used their theory of help as the criterion for judging effectiveness, then it is understandable that they concluded that Y was unsupportive, defense-producing, power-differentiating, and distant. The consultants were in the position of being controlled by the nonlearning behavior of Y, whom they saw as predisposed to use such behavior if they questioned it. It is also understandable that they were especially careful not to upset Y. This in turn, reinforced the self-censorship and "easing-in" strategies.

The consultants were in a passive stance vis-à-vis Y. Once they became more active, they began to behave like Y.

3. The consultants did not have an effective theory of organization. This gap in knowledge may have reinforced the weakness embedded in their theory of help because a theory of organization would have helped them define the conditions under which attributions, evaluations, defensiveness, and the like are legitimate and necessary.

4. The apparent blindness to features in the consultants' own theory of help and their lack of an effective theory of organization, which led them to see premises as valid when they were not, to see illogical inferences as logical, and so on was reinforced by their theories of how to act toward Y—basically strategies of unilateral control and censorship in order to be in control and to win and not lose.

Distancing and Disconnectedness

We now have further illustrations of reasoning processes and their relation to distancing and disconnectedness. The consultants distanced themselves from their responsibility in creating the very counterproductive conditions with Y that they advised Y not to use with X. Whether easing in or relatively forthright, they placed the responsibility for Y's resistance to their help on his defensiveness. And the theory of defensiveness that they held and the reasoning processes that they went through made it unlikely that they would ever test for their personal causal responsibility. Moreover, as the scenarios suggested, Y rarely confronted them with his doubts and frustrations. One explanation is that Y may have held the same theory of defensiveness as the consultants. He may have seen the consultants as becoming defensive and withheld his doubts about their effectiveness as they did about his. Thus, distancing may result from the very skills we have in reasoning about situations that require framebreaking.

Disconnectedness is more difficult to explain. The consultants appeared connected to their reasoning processes in the sense that they generated premises, inferred conclusions, and acted on them. However, they appeared unaware that (1) their premises were often wrong, (2) their premises were abstractions that required testing, and (3) they were somehow seeing abstractions as concrete descriptions.

4

Individual
Reasoning
About Others'
Performance

We have shown that people seem to use reasoning processes that produce consequences counterproductive to their own intentions. Moreover, people appear to be unaware of these actions and consequences, as well as distanced from their personal responsibility and disconnected from their reasoning processes.

In this chapter, we answer two frequently asked questions: (1) To what extent do people use the same reasoning processes when they are diagnosing larger units as they use in diagnosing a two-person relationship, such as the X and Y case? (2) Do the same results occur when a subordinate is evaluating the effectiveness of a superior?

According to our position so far, the answer to both these questions is that the same counterproductive actions and consequences should occur. In this chapter, I illustrate this answer for each situation.

Analysis of the Califano Case

Case C in Chapter One represents a problem that involves group, intergroup, agency, and interagency relations. People diagnosing this case clearly would have to deal with more than a two-person relationship. If we asked a group to diagnose this case, what kind of reasoning would they use, and what kind of action would they take?

An opportunity arose to answer this question with a class of 100 graduate students in a school of public administration. Briefly, most of the class participants had five to ten years' experience as administrators in government agencies. About 10 percent were senior-level administrators; fewer than 5 percent had less than two years of experience in the world of practice. The class was about 40 percent female.

The class had no previous exposure to the concepts in this book. The two discussions (two hours each) were led by a faculty member whose theory of instruction was based on a different stream of thought. He began the discussion by asking the class how effective they believed the players in this case were in accomplishing their objective of defining a new welfare policy, and why. The analysis that follows is based on tape recordings of the session, as well as the notes that I took as an observer.

In keeping with the format of the previous chapters, let us first look at a collage of the responses. The words, phrases, and sentences are direct or nearly direct quotations.

During the first session, the problem was related to the following causes:

1. Working groups—
    With entrenched positions.
    Unwilling to change.
    Lots of disagreement.
    Miscommunicating.
    Not accustomed to working with each other.
    No one confronting the real issues.
    Delegates from Moscow.
    Each group pushed its agenda any time it could do so.
2. Califano was "Washington-hip"—
    Let things boil.
    Keep options open.

      Smart enough to know that if he accepted responsibility, he
          also would get all the trouble.

      He appeared to have a secret agenda.

      Vintage Califano:

          He learned to humiliate his staff from Lyndon Johnson.

          He acted like a trial lawyer.

          He acted bored in order to collect his thoughts.

3. The problem was the deadline—place people under pressure.

4. The problem was that no one was willing to make firm decisions.
      Each player thought, "It is not my decision to make."

5. The problem was that this is the dynamic of the first six months
of any administration. The players are finding their way around,
jockeying for position. Turf is being defined.

6. The problem was that Califano did not know his staff.
      They were afraid to level with him.
      They told him what they thought he wanted to hear.

7. The problem was that the groups had the typical Washington
mentality:

    a. Throw money at problems.

    b. Take care of constituents.

8. The problem was that everyone was acting rationally.
      Each group felt it had the answer and acted as if it did.
      It is rational to resist (carefully and adroitly) being required
          to give up one's position.
      Hence, Carter may be able to push a button and launch a
          missile, but he pushes Califano and nothing gets done.

9. The problem was an underlying tension between the Georgia
hicks and the Washington sophisticates.

During the second session, the class members repeated the
same features just described and some that were different. Examples
of the latter are these:

1. *The task itself.* The task itself contained conflicting features: On
the one hand, redesign welfare; on the other hand, add no more
cost in order to keep inflation down.

2. *Classic power struggle.* Why do we expect anything but what
happened? Why are we surprised? The players are heads of agencies and are born winners, ambitious men who want to win. If
they lost, they would lose the respect of their staffs.

3. *Selfish, self-centered players.* Everyone is looking out for number one, obsessed with maintaining "my truth." People's self-esteem is wrapped up in game-playing, and they are fearful to say they do not know what to do.

4. *No one with a vision.* None of the players had a great vision, an important organizing idea about welfare. No one really seemed to care about welfare reform.

   We lack mature leaders; no one with wisdom. We have dropped the "philosopher" from "philosopher-prince."

5. *Self-centered institutions.* Each institution had its own learning experiences and perspective; none wished to cooperate.

6. *Too big a task.* The task was too large to do all at once. It might have worked out if done incrementally.

The class participants judged the actors to be largely ineffective, just as the previous groups had judged Y to be ineffective. Thus, both cases drew negative evaluations.

What reasoning processes did the participants use to make these evaluations? To answer that question, we reorganize their responses into categories related to the causes of the problem. Causes were identified at the individual, group, intergroup, and cultural levels of analysis.

1. *Individual.* For example:
   Califano acted like a trial lawyer.
   Califano humiliated his staff.
   Carter did not take initiative.

2. *Group and intergroup.* For example:
   They never listened to each other.
   No one was confronting the real issues.
   Everyone had an entrenched position.
   People were unwilling to change.

3. *Cultural.* For example:
   Washington sophisticates know that it is best not to take charge under these conditions because you'll likely wind up losing.
   It is best to keep your options open; play it cool for as long as possible.
   They acted with the Washington mentality—that is, throw money at problems and take care of constituents.

It is easy for the president to push a button and set off a missile; it is much harder to push a secretary's button and get something done.

The problem was tension between Georgia hicks and Washington sophisticates.

Two features of these responses are relevant to our inquiry. First, they represent the same kind of reasoning that participants used in discussing the X and Y case. The statements made were primarily (1) Unillustrated, untested attributions or evaluations; (2) advocacy of participants' views with little encouragement of inquiry into them by others; and (3) attributions that placed the responsibility "in" individuals or in forces in the culture. The second feature is that the diagnoses contained an implicit causal theory of effectiveness that may be characterized as follows: *If* individuals, groups, or intergroups behave in accordance with these features, *then* there will be hardening of positions, intergroup rivalries, mistrust, and distancing from taking responsibility to confront process issues. These outcomes, in turn, will lead to escalating error, undiscussability of the counterproductive features in settings where they are occurring (but discussability among friends or cliques), and acting as if there were nothing undiscussable (one cannot discuss the undiscussability of the undiscussable).

Finally, if the actors in the Califano case had asked the class to evaluate their effectiveness (as Y theoretically asked the class to do), and if the class stated these causal microtheories directly, they would be using the same counterproductive reasoning that they had used in the X and Y case. In other words, if the Califano players listened to the class dialogue, they would probably become defensive, as Y did.

During the class discussion, a number of opportunities arose to illustrate the hypothesis. Frequently, the faculty member would ask the class how they would communicate to the actors in the case what the students were saying about them in class. Almost always, the student would try to ease in. In the few instances when students were forthright, many of the class members laughed. When asked why, they answered that it was unrealistic to think that one could be forthright with the president, Califano, Marshall, and all the other major actors.

Interestingly, the type of advice given in the Califano case differs significantly from that given in the X and Y case:

1. Carter should have appointed one person to be in charge, given him a definite set of orders, and told him how to proceed.
2. Califano should have taken charge and told Carter it couldn't be done or told Carter to give him the parameters within which to work.
3. Carter's staff should have defined the process, thereby reducing the mixed orders; they should have forced Carter's thinking so that he could say what he wanted.
4. Someone outside (such as John Dunlop) should have brought them together and said, "No one leaves until we arrive at a decision."
5. Someone was needed who could knock some heads together after they had all had their say.
6. What was needed was mature leaders with wisdom—the "philosopher-princes."

In the X and Y case, much of the advice was humanistic, person-centered. Y was advised to be more sensitive, to encourage X to give his views, to listen to X's failings—in short, to deal with X more as an equal who needed help. The advice the class gave in the Califano case was to bring in a strong "take charge" leader who had vision and could "knock heads together if necessary." Why the difference?

I believe that each set of responses can be related to tacit theories that people hold about what actions are effective in a particular situation. When the issue is counseling or helping a colleague in trouble, the theory of defense I have already described is assumed operative. People try to minimize the defensiveness of others so that learning can take place. When the issue is how to deal with a conglomerate of factors that lead the actors to behave in a way that is counterproductive to their own desires and even to their agency's objectives, then a microtheory of organizational learning, based on experiences that people have in organizations, will become operative. In Chapter Five, I identify such a microtheory of learning and show that the advice the class members gave is consistent with it.

The X-Y Case in Reverse

Often students and clients who complete the X-Y case (see Chapter Two) ask what the results would be if subordinates were evaluating the ineffective performance of superiors. According to our theory, nothing should change. The persons giving the feedback should produce either easing-in or forthright strategies. These should lead to misunderstandings and inconsistencies that, in turn, should lead to escalating error.

An opportunity arose to illustrate this hypothesis. The junior members in a professional organization reported low morale among their ranks, due mainly to the leadership style of the managers and the officers. The officer in charge of the firm asked them to conduct their own study to diagnose the problem and report the results to the officers and managers. I was invited to the feedback session, which lasted about three and a half hours. Three hours were tape-recorded. The four consultants used overhead transparencies to illustrate their major points.

Two sets of data were available about the meeting—the transparencies and the transcript. Excerpts from both will be included here to illustrate that both parties behaved largely as predicted. The consultants' diagnosis contained many unillustrated attributions and evaluations that they never attempted to test publicly with the officers/managers (O/Ms). When the O/Ms began to defend themselves, the consultants responded with the abstract advice that they "should not become defensive." As one O/M put it, the suggestion "represented motherhood." His particular problem was that he did not know how to be an effective and sensitive listener to the satisfaction of the consultants. The consultants used phrases such as "*Really* listen" or "Try hard" or "Tell it to them straight."

Many O/Ms believed that the consultants were bringing up important points. However, both parties had an increasing sense of underlying hostility, which obstructed their listening. The consultants accused the O/Ms who expressed such views of trying to undermine their presentation. In short, inconsistency, misunderstanding, and escalating error were generated.

Analysis of the Transparencies

First, let us examine some of the transparencies to illustrate the meanings communicated to the O/Ms and to infer the dilemmas and inconsistencies embedded in these transparencies. The first, quoted in full here, was a scenario of a problem frequently experienced by consultants.

Transparency 1

Case team meeting.
Discussion.
Consultant proposes another way of looking at problem.
(O/M privately considers it not too helpful.)
Silence.
O/M nods and goes back to previous point.

The import of the consultants' message appears to be that if the O/Ms believe that a consultant's performance is not adequate, then they should say so. If they do not say so, the consultant is likely to react by making three attributions: (1) O/M does not want the new ideas. (2) Maybe I am wrong and O/M should say so. (3) O/M is threatened by other people's having ideas. The consultants followed up the analysis with notice that they wanted "better communication [by O/Ms] of negative information feedback." Yet they also warned the O/Ms that consultants saw them as powerful and therefore tended to overinterpret and overreact to O/Ms' comments.

Perhaps the O/Ms did not give negative feedback because they realized the consultants saw them as all-powerful and hence expected that the consultants would overinterpret and overreact to any such feedback. Being forthright about negative evaluation would be asking for trouble. How should the O/Ms deal with consultants who overreact? If they followed the consultants' advice, they would be honest. But to tell a consultant who has overreacted that he or she overreacted may be a "cure" that makes the illness worse. Considering the normal pressures on the case team during a typical meeting, silence may be one way for the O/M to protect the consultant and the team.

Transparency 2

O/M asks Consultant 1 to do lead work.
Consultant is busy but is interested in case and does three days of
    work.
Following week O/M meets consultant in hall:
    Thanks consultant for his work.
    Says may not turn into case.
    O/Ms are doing a seminar on case possibility.
    Will let consultant know if a case develops.

Consultant 1 talks to Consultant 2 and finds out Consultant 2 has
been asked to work on developing the seminar. Reaction:
   Anger at not being told the whole story.
   "Why didn't the O/M tell me directly?"
   "Maybe he/she didn't like my work."

In this scenario, the consultant believed that he was not properly informed and that the manager had purposely not informed him.
Again, the O/M may not have known how to inform the consultant,
given his predicted overreaction. Or, as we have suggested, if managers are not skilled in leadership, and if they are dealing with consultants equally unskilled, and if they are embedded in organizations
where such tactics are considered proper responses, they are likely to
respond this way because that is the skilled response they have at
their command.

Later, in another transparency, the O/Ms were told, "When
people are unhappy or thinking about leaving the firm, it is more
often than not a function, in part, of 'insensitive management.' "
Now the O/Ms' dilemma deepens. They could now be held accountable for a consultant's leaving because they behaved in ways that
they felt protected the consultants.

Finally, the consultants told the O/Ms that "if people are comfortable, feel they are performing well, and are not spending energy
at being annoyed, they will do better work more efficiently." As several O/Ms stated, this is the equivalent of "being for motherhood."
They wish they could create such conditions not only for the consultants but for all employees, including themselves. Now they are
being warned, in effect, that if they are unable to create the conditions over which they believe they have little control, they may be
evaluated as insensitive and hence may be a cause of some consultant's leaving. To compound the dilemma, the O/Ms are advised to
make consultants feel comfortable and to minimize their annoyance;
yet they are also told to give negative feedback forthrightly so there
will be no surprises.

The consultants' view of a major cause of their problems is
that the managers were never trained to be effective managers and
that they "lack incentives to train and develop consultants."

We can agree that the O/Ms would benefit by education in
managing people. Indeed, the O/Ms themselves agreed to this when

they asked the consultants to make the presentation. But the consultants add further attributions by telling the O/Ms that they do not grasp how important it is to be sensitive and concerned. Moreover, they infer that the sensitivity should come from the managers. Do the consultants believe the O/Ms already have many pressures on them? The O/Ms may wonder whether they do, because in all the diagnoses, responsibility for both the problem and the solution was placed solely on the O/M group. Thus:

If a consultant is afraid of "putting his foot in his mouth"	The O/M should be aware of these feelings and act to correct them.
If the consultant is ready for new responsibilities but believes the manager cannot shift him	The manager should be aware of these feelings and act, whenever possible, to correct the problem.

Note that the O/M is being asked to second-guess the feelings of the consultants. The consultants are not expected to take the initiative, to express their views, because they may fear the manager. The burden is on the manager to be sensitive and to take the initiative.

Similarly:

If the consultant feels he can be a more effective team performer by knowing what the other consultants are doing	The O/M should call a meeting so that such information can be shared.

Moreover, O/Ms are admonished to hold "more frequent informal interactions" with consultants, "to set a meeting style conducive to brainstorming at appropriate times," "to maintain constant liaison with officers," and "to minimize 'huddling' of officers and managers" so that consultants do not feel left out. Finally, the O/Ms are instructed, on the one hand, "Never underestimate consultants' reactions to your actions," and, on the other hand, "Don't avoid or put off the difficult actions."

The presentation contained many recommendations similar to those observed in the X and Y case. They are so abstract that they do not differentiate between effective and ineffective actions. More frequent interactions may be counterproductive if the O/Ms behave ineffectively and if the consultants believe that they can legitimately place the major responsibility for interpersonal problems on the O/M group.

Advising the O/Ms to set the stage for brainstorming is a fine invention, but it is doubtful that they can produce such conditions if they act in accordance with their present theories of action. Moreover, it is doubtful that the consultants could support such a session, if we may judge from the conditions they created in the feedback session. It is not unfair to suggest that the consultants' diagnoses and action recommendations contained the seeds for O/M bewilderment and possible rejection.

Analysis of the Transcript

Let us now analyze a segment of the transcript of the session. I begin with a scoring of the comments made by the consultants during the first few minutes.

Transcript	Analysis
Consultant 1: There is a real sharp break between initial skills of analysis and skills required for manager. We feel there is not adequate training for managers [in leadership].	*Explicit unillustrated attribution:* The managers are not adequately trained in leadership. *Implicit attribution:* The managers are not effective leaders.
O/M: Is that a consensus?	
Cons. 1: No, it is an observation in general. There are structural inherent conflicts—for example, the consultant would rather not fall flat on his face [in order to learn] and you obviously would prefer not to teach.	*Unillustrated attributions* about consultants and O/Ms.
[A manager has the] tension . . . of both pleasing an officer and not creating problems for the case team [when the officer wants to be updated on the case].	*Unillustrated attribution:* Managers wish they did not have to bring officers up to date but do so to please them.

Transcript	*Analysis*
When there is a trade-off between better management and better analysis, the manager prefers better analysis.	*Unillustrated attribution:* Managers prefer better analysis to better management of people.
[Managers generically prefer to develop analytical skills over any of the softer skills of managing.]	*Unillustrated attribution:* Managers prefer to develop analytical skills over human skills of managing.
O/M: I see these as conflicts but I do not believe that they are inherent.	
[Another O/M agrees with consultants.]	
[More discussion]	
Cons. 1: It is even worse. If I were a manager in our firm, and I knew that I would work with the same consultant over a period of time, I would then invest in developing individuals.	*Unillustrated attribution:* Managers do not want to help consultants develop because they do not work with them over a long period.

The messages embedded in the next few pages of transcript were summarized by Consultant 1:

You guys are powerful.
You guys decide our fate.
We tend to react very strongly in all sorts of subtle ways.
And more often than not, people who have left the firm have done so on one of the soft issues.
You people are not good at soft skills.
You prefer not to learn soft skills.

When the O/Ms raised questions about whether they are to be blamed when people report they are not happy, the reply was this:

Cons. 1: We're not blaming you that you aren't good managers. We want to suggest better ways.

The implicit logic in this response is as follows:

You O/Ms are beginning to act defensively.
Although we attribute to you poor managerial skills and a low inter-
       est in bettering them, we are not blaming you.
Just listen to our recommendations.

The consultants' next complaint was that the managers "do
not wish to spend time with us" and that this indicated what the
managers thought of the consultants and their development. The
managers denied the validity of the unillustrated attributions and
suggested that they did not have the margin to "spend time." This
was the reply:

Cons. 2: I personally wouldn't mind if you lied a little [so that such
a discussion would not take too long] as long as you don't place all
of the responsibility on the consultant. . . .

The consultants repeatedly emphasized that consultants are
sensitive people: "Would you want an O/M to say that to the consultants?" an O/M asked. The immediate response by the consultant
was an example of unilateral face saving coupled with advocacy and
unilateral control—coupled, in turn, with a "however, but" argument.

Cons. 4: No, I'm not sure any comment of that kind is appropriate.
If it were, then the way I would couch it would be "Let's not overreact to this. As far as I can tell, you are doing excellent work. However, there are a few points. . . .

O/M: That's what we're doing now.

[Much laughter]

The discussion continued with the consultants making more
unillustrated attributions about the motives and competence of the
O/Ms while maintaining that the reason the consultants do not communicate more openly with the O/Ms is that they are afraid. Then
the following conversation ensued:

O/M 1: Implied in the last three transparencies is that somehow we
are not doing it. Do you have any suggestion as to how we can do it
better?

O/M 2: Part of my reaction to that transparency [of suggestions] is that is nice, like apple pie and motherhood. What I'd like to discuss is how do we handle the issue.

Cons. 1: Well, more often than not you can look ahead for a couple of weeks [and not wait until the last minute].

O/M 3: This implies that the officers may be doing some of these bad things and not for good reasons.

Cons. 2: No, we think it can be done a lot better.

O/M 4: What I am saying is that changing commitments does happen all the time. But most of us do not do it because we think it is not a good idea.

Cons. 2: [Maybe you can do it better.]

[Later]

Interventionist: You are communicating that consultants feel that managers may not give a darn because they make these unilateral last-minute changes. Then O/Ms are saying, "That is not our view." Then they ask, "What is it we can do to correct the situation?" The response they have been getting is "Well, that's what the consultants feel!"

Cons. 3: Well, our role is being a funnel, communicating what the consultants tell us.

The conversation continued with unillustrated and untested attributions and evaluations from the consultants. Some of the O/Ms denied the validity of these by using their own unillustrated attributions and evaluations. However, a substantial number sought advice from the consultants. The responses were abstract, as was the advice in the X and Y case—for example, "Be more patient," "Listen to them," and "Spend more time" with consultants.

Next, an officer raised the puzzling fact that when the young consultants were hired, it was because they were strong and independent, whereas in this presentation they were depicting themselves as weak and dependent.

O/M: I have a curious feeling. I believe that I know the first-year class [of hires] through the recruiting process. They came across as extraordinarily strong-willed, they would test you out all the time and wanted to be independent, et cetera. Now I hear that they are afraid to go to a guy about a problem. The implied contract they made with us is that "we are strong and independent individuals."

They are willing and capable of putting their asses on the line. Now I'm hearing: "Hey, please take care of me!" "Give me feedback every time I want to make a move."

Cons. 4: They're now in a position of working with the firm.

O/M: But we hired them because they sold themselves as being creative and independent people.

O/M: I am hearing a message [from the consultants] that "we do not want to be anxious: we do not want any uncertainty." Uncertainty and anxiety are part of the job.

Cons. 1: [Emotionally] I think you're really taking the rug out from under this whole presentation by saying that. What you are saying is that you don't have to listen to any of these things because the consultants don't want to be anxious. We're not saying that. We're trying to make some *really* specific—make clear—some really specific suggestions. We haven't thought too much of ways to do it. Maybe [one way] to do it is for you guys to figure out how better to tell us these negative things and for us guys to better figure out how we can tell you or ask for negative feedback.

O/M: There are two sets of messages that are coming. One is the specific things that you are talking about. The other is a general underlying tone of real hostility towards us. [You appear to be saying to us] "Here are the problems, and we do not believe that you are going to listen to us, but we're going to tell you, whether you like it or not."

O/M: Yes . . . yes.

Cons. 2: I think the hostility is widespread.

Cons. 1: We thought you guys would listen. Somehow we are conveying the wrong messages.

Cons. 4: I'm astonished that you said that—that we are coming across as aggressive and hostile. Let me back up. We are trying to be a little more assertive because [although] I think there is a lot of genuine satisfaction, . . . we do think there are some definite concerns. This is one of a few situations in life where you [superiors] have asked us to help you evaluate your performance. And now when you're hearing these evaluations, you are reading too much hostility—which means that you may overreact the way we do.

Note that when an O/M attributed to the consultants that they do not want any uncertainty and anxiety in a job that is loaded with it, the consultant's response was not to discuss and test the attribution, but rather to attribute nasty motives to the O/M ("You're really taking the rug out from under this whole presentation").

Then an O/M expressed concern that the consultants were conveying an underlying tone of "real hostility towards us." The response was (1) the hostility is widespread, (2) we have to hit you in order for you to listen, (3) we are not aggressive and hostile, and (4) you O/Ms overreact just as we do.

In sum, the transparencies and discussion contained diagnostic frames and action frames that led to dynamics similar to those reported in the X and Y case. Subordinates can create for superiors and themselves the same distancing and disconnectedness that superiors can create for subordinates. This has important implications. Subordinates, especially in professional organizations, usually seek to equalize power relationships with their superiors. Hence the popular notion that power equalization should help reduce the unintended consequences of pyramidal structures. Our data suggest that even if individuals were somehow made more equal, this would not make much difference in terms of framebreaking, because they are programmed to generate escalating error, self-fulfilling prophecies, and self-sealing processes. Equalizing power without altering reasoning processes and behavioral strategies will lead to failure and hence to greater frustration. The genuine participation that is effective for solving difficult problems requires reasoning processes and skills that people do not seem to have.

Disconnectedness

We can now identify several features of how people disconnect from their reasoning processes while designing and implementing actions to deal with double-loop issues.

1. People are unaware when their premises or their inference processes are faulty.
2. People see their diagnoses as concrete and obvious when they may actually contain abstract ideas and inferences that are nested in other inferences.
3. They rarely see the necessity for, nor do they act with the intent of, testing their reasoning processes publicly. They believe their reasoning is based on the concrete and the obvious.

The data from which we make our inferences were produced under a pattern of conditions. First, the data were produced by our clients almost instantaneously. It frequently appeared that what they were doing was second nature to them. Second, they were rarely able to state what they were doing before they acted. However, they could, with some help, re-create the reason for their actions after they acted. Third, even though they were able to identify the counterproductive features of their actions and reasoning processes, and even when they wished to change both, they were unable to. It was as if they were programmed to continue that action.

One possible explanation is that the actions people produce are highly skilled and are therefore effective in achieving the intended goal. They are produced automatically, with little effort, and little attention is paid to them while they are being produced. But if they are highly skilled, how did people learn them? Why do so many different individuals appear to have learned the same skills?

Another explanation is that people do believe that they are testing their ideas but that they are doing it covertly. The test is covert because they do not wish to influence the results and because publicly stating the attributions and evaluations they have about others might upset or hurt those others. As we have seen, however, covert tests generate automatic responses from the tester himself. For example, people who eased into a situation interpreted an unexpected response as evidence of the other person's defensiveness.

Distancing

Distancing occurs when people act to reduce their awareness of, and their actual personal causal responsibility for, creating the very conditions that they criticize. One source of distancing is the state of being disconnected from the reasoning processes. Another may be that people are programmed to produce the self-fulfilling prophecies, self-sealing processes, and escalating errors that I have described. A third cause is that if the first two are valid, then it follows that human beings create cultures and systems that reinforce and protect the first two causes. Once systems and cultures reinforce and sanction distancing, the loop is closed and a self-reinforcing condition exists. Individuals will be socialized in accordance with the systemic and cultural features.

If disconnectedness and distancing occur among the well educated as well as the poorly educated, among the powerful and the powerless, the young and old, male and female, it is not surprising to observe these features in organizations populated by a well-educated, relatively wealthy elite who are highly involved in satisfying work. This is precisely from where most of our examples have been, and will continue to be, drawn. We focus on professionals in consulting organizations who are very well paid (beginning salaries about $45,000 a year) and who, by their own declaration, find their work very involving and satisfying. Thus, some features of alienation may be found even among this privileged population.

Our reasoning is based on the assumption that people are programmed to be disconnected and to produce distancing. This assumption is implicit in the notion that these responses are highly skilled. If such programming exists, what is the nature of this skilled program? How does it work? How does it lead people to become disconnected and to distance themselves? How does it lead to systems that reinforce the program? And finally, can we teach new programs that can overcome these problems?

To answer these questions, we have to generate a theory. The theory should explain the results we have obtained. It should be able to specify the mechanisms by which these results occur and hence should also be the basis for making valid predictions over time and under different conditions.

Finally, we also need a theory of how to help individuals and organizations double-loop learn. This theory will help us test the first one. As Lewin said, "If you wish to understand something, try changing it." The theory should also help us design learning environments and produce theories of instruction on how to get from here to there.

5

Theories-in-Use:
Model I and Model II

We have covered three important themes so far. First, individuals could, on reflection, tell us what was effective and ineffective about Y's, their own, and others' actions. All their answers contained propositions of causal relationship. For example, when Y is unilaterally judgmental of X, X will feel misunderstood and eventually defensive. Most statements that participants made were in characteristic theory form—that is, "Under these conditions, if someone behaves in a stipulated manner, certain consequences will follow."

Second, individuals appeared to be unaware that they were frequently producing consequences which they did not intend, which seemed to contradict their stated values, which led to actions that they would, upon reflection, judge ineffective, and which led to conditions they would consider unjust.

Third, we identified several possible causes of this unawareness: (1) The actors tended to act in ways that could easily lead others to infer that they were unaware of possible inconsistencies. Recall how often individuals spoke in unillustrated evaluations and attributions, all containing high levels of inference, and yet they acted as if the evaluations and attributions were concrete and obvious. (2) The actors appeared to develop incorrect premises from which they drew incorrect conclusions but to be unaware of doing so. The incorrect premises were not due to a lack of skill in defining premises or in making inferences and drawing conclusions. Most of the reasoning processes were carried out automatically and effortlessly, indicating that they were highly skilled. (3) The norms and mores about helping others were consistent with not expressing negative feelings, remaining in unilateral control, striving to win and not to lose, and withholding valid feedback lest the other person become emotionally upset and events go beyond control.

During the past decade, my colleague Donald Schön and I have been evolving a theoretical perspective to explain these results. This perspective is discussed in detail in other publications[1] and will therefore only be outlined here.

We begin with the proposition that people hold theories of action about how to produce consequences they intend. Such theories are theories about human effectiveness. By *effectiveness* we mean the degree to which people produce their intended consequences in ways that make it likely that they will continue to produce intended consequences. Theories of action, therefore, are theories about effectiveness, and because they contain propositions that are falsifiable, they are also theories about truth. *Truth* in this case means truth about how to behave effectively.

These views, in turn, assume that a key activity of life, if not *the* key, is acting to bring about the consequences one intends. Because we appear to conceptualize our actions and intentions with propositions about how to get things done, and because these propositions contain views of causality, then we must be designing creatures; we design the actions that we intend to produce.

The designs that we are able to infer from the cases and interviews are much too rich and complex to have been produced *de novo*. It follows that actors must carry these designs with them to

---

[1] Chris Argyris and Donald Schön, *Theory in Practice: Increasing Professional Effectiveness* (San Francisco: Jossey-Bass, 1974); Chris Argyris and Donald Schön, *Organizational Learning* (Reading, Mass.: Addison-Wesley, 1978); Chris Argyris, *Increasing Leadership Effectiveness* (New York: Wiley-Interscience, 1976); Chris Argyris, "Theories of Action That Inhibit Individual Learning," *American Psychologist*, *31*(9) (September 1976): 638-654.

use in appropriate settings. But no design discovered so far has been adequate and complete for any given situation. There are information gaps that individuals have to fill in. The actors can rarely slow down real life enough to fully design their actions, because these gaps have to be filled in within real-life constraints.

The designs that people bring to a situation are not situation-specific; rather, they are general designs about how to effect action in a generic situation. These theories of action, therefore, are more like master or executive computer programs, which can be used to design and execute action in a given situation. These master programs, or theories, appear to have been learned early in life through socialization.

We have found that a crucial skill is the ability to limit the information gaps, so that even though people do not go into a situation with a full-fledged design, they have enough of a design that they do not feel insecure in the situation. People who tend to apply their executive designs as if sufficient for a specific situation create an impression of rigidity. Those who appear to have incomplete executive designs create the impression of being confused and vague. In other words, one key human skill—one not sufficiently recognized—is the ability to design one's ignorance. A corollary skill is the ability to produce learning while acting so that the designed gaps can be filled in effectively with the cooperation of others.

As we began to develop our systematic picture of people's theories of action from cases and interviews, we discovered, as amply illustrated in the preceding chapters, that whenever people dealt with difficult and threatening issues, they did not behave congruently with the theories of action that they had recited or that we had inferred from their cases or interviews. The frequency of this inconsistency was so great that the rational reaction would have been for us to scrap the idea of theories of action as executive design programs. But in order to scrap the idea, we also had to scrap the idea that there were identifiable connections between what went on in people's heads and their observed actions.

To salvage the concept, we took what appeared to us a risky, if not arrogant, step. We asked ourselves: What if there *are* identifiable connections between what goes on in people's heads and their actions, *but they are not aware of them?* Could we use the tape recordings or the scenarios written in the cases as approximations of what actually happened? If we could, would it be possible to infer the theory of action that must be in a person's head so that the actions in the tape recordings or the scenarios made sense—that is, followed a theory of action?

We reviewed the cases and tape recordings and found that a theory of action could be inferred. We also found that it could be used to predict how people would act in future situations. In fact, we found that this theory of action predicted their actions more accurately than they themselves could. For example, in the 27 learning experiments listed in Table 1 (Chapter Three), we predicted that the participants would not be able to produce certain meanings, even though they intended to do so. We were able to design learning environments to help people produce meanings that they had been unable to produce before.[2]

We called the theories of action that people actually used their *theories-in-use*. The theories of action that they wrote or talked about, we called their *espoused theories*. Whenever they were dealing with nonprogrammed, difficult, and threatening situations, they did not act congruently with their espoused theories.

If our research had stopped here, our perspective would not be contributing anything particularly new. A great deal of literature shows that people do not always behave congruently with their beliefs, values, and attitudes (all part of espoused theories). Our perspective made an additional assertion: Although people do not behave congruently with their espoused theories (in the situations just described), they do behave congruently with their theories-in-use, *and* they are unaware of this fact.

Given our axiom that people design all their actions, since unawareness is an action, then unawareness, too, must be designed and highly skilled. If it is highly skilled, it must be related to components in the actors' theories-in-use as well as to components that make them unaware of being unaware.

We come, then, to a puzzling conclusion. People have theories-in-use, which they use to design and maintain control over their actions; yet somehow they have developed components within these

---

[2] Argyris and Schön, 1974; Argyris, 1976; Argyris, 1976.

theories-in-use that make it unlikely that they will be in control when dealing with double-loop issues.

To understand this puzzle, we must first understand the nature of theories-in-use.

Model I Theory-in-Use

Picture human beings who have programmed themselves to behave in ways that are consistent with four governing values, or variables (Table 5). These variables are (1) achieve the purpose as the actor defines it, (2) win, do not lose, (3) suppress negative feelings, and (4) emphasize rationality. Human behavior, in any situation, represents the most satisfactory solution people can find, consistent with their governing variables.

We found through our research that people create certain behavioral strategies that are congruent with their governing values, or variables. The primary behavioral strategies are to control unilaterally the relevant environment and tasks and to protect oneself and others unilaterally. The underlying behavioral strategy is control over others. As we shall see, people vary tremendously in the way they control others, but few people behave in ways that do not control others and the environment.

One of the most effective ways to control others is to control the meaning of valid information. The basic act of creating a concept whose meaning is given by us to others and whose validity is defined by us for others is a powerful control. It is probably the most powerful control we have over our children. We give them the meanings that we believe their lives should have.

These behavioral strategies have *consequences for the actor, for others, and for the environment.* Briefly, these strategies tend to make people defensive and closed because unilateral control does not usually produce valid feedback. Moreover, others may see unilateral control as a sign of defensiveness. Groups of individuals programmed according to Model I also tend to create defensive group dynamics, to reduce the production of valid information, and to reduce free choice.

We also hypothesized that the consequences just mentioned

Table 5. Model I Theory-in-Use

1 Governing Variable for Action	2 Action Strategy for Actor and Toward Environment	3 Consequences for Behavioral World	4 Consequences for Learning	5 Effectiveness
Achieve the purposes as actor perceives them	Design and manage environment so that actor is in control over factors relevant to him	Actor seen as defensive	Self-sealing processes	Decreased effectiveness
Maximize winning and minimize losing	Own and control task	Defensive interpersonal and group relationships	Single-loop learning	
Minimize eliciting negative feelings	Unilaterally protect self	Defensive norms	Little public testing of theories	
Be rational and minimize emotionality	Unilaterally protect others from being hurt	Low freedom of choice, internal commitment, and risk taking		

will tend to *generate a particular kind and quality of learning* that will go on within the actor and between the actor and the environment. There will be relatively little public testing of ideas (especially those that may be important and threatening). Consequently, the actors will not seek feedback that genuinely confronts their actions, and those controlled will tend to play it safe (they are not going to violate their governing values and upset others—especially if the others have power). As a result, many of the hypotheses or hunches that people generate will become self-sealing or self-fulfilling. Moreover, whatever learning people develop will tend to be within the confines of what is acceptable. This is called single-loop learning because the actor learns only within the confines of his or her theory-in-use. Few people will confront the validity of the goal or the values implicit in the situation (such confrontation would lead to double-loop learning).

Under these conditions, attempts to solve technical or interpersonal issues will be ineffective. Effective problem solving occurs to the extent that people (1) are aware of the major variables relevant to the problem, (2) solve the problem in such a way that it remains solved (at least until the external variables are changed), and (3) accomplish the first two goals without reducing the present level of problem-solving effectiveness.[3]

People programmed with Model I theories of action produce Model I group and organizational dynamics that include quasi resolution of conflict, uncertainty, avoidance, mistrust, conformity, face saving, intergroup rivalry, invalid information for important problems and valid information for unimportant ones, misperception, miscommunication, and parochial interests. These, in turn, produce ineffective problem solving and decision making. Under such conditions, top administrators become frustrated and react by striving to increase control, by increasing secrecy about their own tactics and strategies, and by demanding a degree of loyalty that borders on complete acquiescence.[4]

[3]Chris Argyris, *Intervention Theory and Methods* (Reading, Mass.: Addison-Wesley, 1970).

[4]Chris Argyris, *Integrating the Individual and the Organization* (New York: Wiley, 1964); Chris Argyris, *Intervention Theory and Methods*, 1970; Chris Argyris, "On Organizations of the Future," *The Sage Professional Papers in Administration and Policy Studies*, No. 03-006 (Beverly Hills, Calif.: Sage Publications, 1973).

In addition to these defensive interpersonal group and inter-group dynamics, pyramidal structures and management information systems (including budgets) will compound the consequences just described,[5] eventually creating an ultrastable state.[6]

Model I theory-in-use has embedded in it causal theory that states that if people behave according to Model I action strategies (column 2 in Table 5) in order to satisfy any combination of the four governing values (column 1), then the consequences stipulated in columns 3, 4, and 5 should occur *and* the opposites should not occur, by design. For example, we should observe single-loop learning, self-sealing processes, defensive norms such as low trust and low risk taking, and undiscussability of issues so that they are not publicly tested. The prediction also states that high trust and risk taking, publicly disconfirmable actions, and double-loop learning should *not* be observed to occur, by design. There should be no exceptions to these predictions. If, for example, people who are judged to hold a Model I theory-in-use were observed to intentionally produce double-loop learning or to write cases whose scenarios were intended to illustrate double-loop learning, then our theory would be importantly falsified. The reader is asked to recollect that in all the examples given so far, not one instance of double-loop learning was noted in the cases or discussions during the early phases of the classes.

Model O-I Learning Systems

If the consequences are as inevitable as we suggest, and if most people studied so far use Model I theory-in-use, then we can predict that they will create systems with identifiable features that form a self-maintaining pattern.

Figure 1 displays a Model O-I learning system (*O* is for *organization*). Reverse arrows along the bottom indicate feedback loops that close the system. The order of columns, from left to right, and the numbered arrows in the reverse direction show the interaction effects that seem to us to be most important. Complex as it is, the

[5] Chris Argyris, "Alternative Schools: A Behavioral Analysis," *Teachers College Record*, 75(4) (May 1974): 429-452; Chris Argyris, *Organization and Innovation* (Homewood, Ill.: Irwin-Dorsey, 1965).
[6] Donald Schön, *Beyond the Stable State* (New York: Random House, 1971).

Figure 1. Model O-I: Limited-Learning Systems

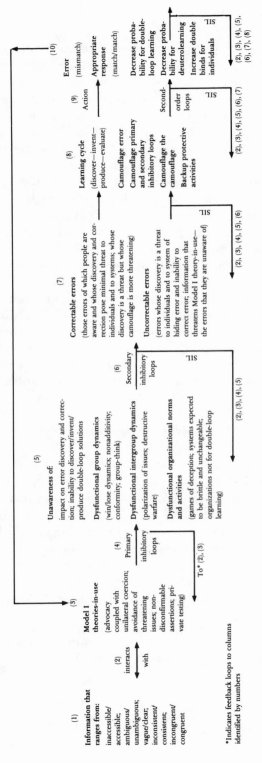

*Indicates feedback loops to columns identified by numbers

model is still oversimplified in a number of ways. For example, arrows along the top might also have been numbered; secondary loops, to take one instance, lead not only to correctable and uncorrectable errors (column 7) but also to camouflage of error (column 8). Each column has its effect not only on the one immediately following but on others further down the line. However, we have tried to arrange the columns so that left-to-right order is a reasonably good representation of direct effects.

The model does not describe the etiology of limited-learning systems. Its meaning is *not,* for example, that primary inhibitory loops came first in the evolution of organizations and that they later led to dysfunctional group and intergroup dynamics, and so on. We think it more likely that a limited-learning organization, at any period of its evolution, displays, at least embryonically, the full configuration of the system.

What the model does reveal is the set of direct and indirect effects and feedback loops that interconnect with the principal element of a limited-learning system. Given any column (such as column 8, Camouflage), one can look to the left to find its immediate and less immediate antecedent conditions and to the right to find its immediate and less immediate consequences.

We begin with primary inhibitory loops because they seem to us the best starting point in order to explain a limited-learning system and the best starting point for intervention. They are "primary" not in the sense of temporal order but in the sense of their importance among the processes making up the system. The model, then, has the principal function of being a guide to mapping and diagnosis of limited-learning systems.

Column 4: Primary Inhibitory Loops

Elements of an organization's instrumental theory of action are inaccessible, unclear, or inadequate. One or more of the features of the organizational theory of action gives rise to error (column 1). In a good dialectic, such conditions of error would be confronted and reduced through organizational inquiry. In a Model I behavioral world, however, such conditions trigger Model I interactions (column 3), which reinforce those conditions for error or create new ones. Within such loops, conditions for error become uncorrectable and trigger the very responses that make them so.

Column 5: Unawareness; Dysfunctional Dynamics

Primary inhibitory loops reinforce unawareness of their effect on organizational learning.

Primary inhibitory loops yield intragroup and intergroup dynamics (secondary loops) that mirror and amplify the properties of primary loops. These secondary loops feed back, in turn, to sustain primary loops. Sustained primary loops lead to the expectation that organizations are brittle and unchangeable. When members learn to despair of double-loop learning, the stage is set for games of deception.

Games of deception, of gaining credit and avoiding blame, tend to occupy the foreground of organizational attention. They loom large in each person's universe of concerns, blunting awareness of the uncorrectable error and the related processes that underlie it.

Column 7: Correctable and Uncorrectable Errors

The processes described so far do not prevent members of an organization from detecting and correcting errors in first-order performance so long as that detection and correction does not confront Model I governing variables. Given the primary and secondary loops characteristic of these living systems, however, such errors become uncorrectable. Given the frame of conditions for error and Model I theories-in-use, efforts at error correction tend, in fact, to amplify error.

The constraints imposed on organizational learning by limited-learning systems depend on the scope of uncorrectable error. We have argued that errors tend to be uncorrectable whenever their correction entails double-loop learning—that is, when norms central to organizational theory-in-use would have to be questioned and changed. We have also argued that errors tend to be uncorrectable when their correction would threaten Model I governing variables—that is, when it would require double-loop learning at the level of the behavioral world. Within the range defined by these criteria, however, there is room for great variation. And organizations vary greatly along these lines, as we will see in the chapters that follow.

Column 8: Camouflage

In a Model I behavioral world, discovery of uncorrectable errors is a source of personal and organizational vulnerability. The response to vulnerability is unilateral self-protection, which can take several forms. Uncorrectable errors and the processes that lead to them can be hidden, disguised, or denied (all of which we call *camouflage*), and individuals and groups can protect themselves further by sealing themselves off from blame should camouflage fail.

Camouflage may resort to espoused theory ("We are open, trusting, and cooperative with one another") in which everyone makes an open secret of the incongruity. Or the uncorrectable error may be attributed to external factors over which members of the organization have no control. Members of the organization may make a public show of attacking the problem while covertly sharing an understanding of the ritual nature of that attack.

Protection often takes the form of anticipating the consequences of uncorrectable error so as to give the anticipator a margin for acceptable performance.

What is less familiar is the consequences of camouflage and protection. Camouflage is a response to uncorrectable error which draws off energy that might be used to engage such error. The hiding, disguising, and denying of uncorrectable error tend to protect it from further inquiry and thereby to reinforce second-order loops.

Moreover, when camouflage and protection are broadly practiced, they set the conditions for a second layer of camouflage. The hiding, denial, or disguising of uncorrectable error cannot come to light without actualizing this double layer of vulnerability. Hence, these processes must be hidden, denied, or disguised.

Column 9: Second-Order Loops That Inhibit Learning

These are second-order loops that arise when inquiring into an organization's first-order activities. They are generated by the same kinds of factors—conditions for error, the Model I behavioral world—that create primary and secondary loops. And they feed back to reinforce both primary and secondary inhibitory loops.

Column 10: Decreasing Probability for Double-Loop Learning: Increasing Double Binds for the Individual

Double-loop learning depends on awareness of error, which primary and deuterolearning loops prevent. When errors are uncorrectable, they cannot trigger double-loop learning.

Members of limited-learning systems might inquire into the features of their system that make errors uncorrectable, except that deuterolearning loops prevent such inquiry. Hence, in limited-learning systems, double-loop and deuterolearning are unlikely.

From the viewpoint of an individual living in such a system, the organizational world is apt to be peculiarly frustrating and constraining. Such a person is apt to find himself or herself in lose/lose situations that present intractable dilemmas. A government staff member, for example, is likely to experience a world of ambiguity in which he fears punishment for delays he does not see as his responsibility, fears the consensus-seeking process and equally fears avoiding it, feels he does not understand the problem and believes he cannot discuss with others the factors that put him in that situation. A school principal finds herself ineffective in getting a teacher to recognize his poor performance and feels vulnerable as a consequence, but the prospect of a more direct confrontation with the teacher makes her feel equally vulnerable. The resulting dilemma is one that she is also unwilling to surface, since it could be taken as a sign of poor performance, a judgment that would again increase her vulnerability.

These situations meet the conditions Gregory Bateson has laid down for "double binds"[7]—one is caught in a no-win game, and the rules of the game are undiscussable.

Predictably, limited-learning systems generate situations such as these. They require that members assume the double layers of vulnerability inherent in camouflage and games of deception. Discussion of these conditions is taboo, as is discussion of the process by which one has been caught in them.

Implicit Assumptions About Human Nature

The theorizing above contains implicit assumptions about human nature that should be made explicit.

The Underlying Rationality of Life: Human Beings Are Self-Governing and Personally Responsible

We found out that people designed their actions to achieve the consequences that they intended. This means that people design

[7]Gregory Bateson, *Steps to an Ecology of Mind* (New York: Ballantine, 1972).

their actions in a given situation with a causal microtheory in mind. For example, they diagnosed Y as judgmental and noncaring and as unilateral, and they predicted that these qualities would lead X to feel defensive. Moreover, many realized that such a diagnosis of Y was itself judgmental and unilateral. Applying their own causal microtheory, most concluded that they could not tell Y what was in their diagnostic frame, while a few concluded that they should be candid but should expect Y to become defensive.

Furthermore, people reported feeling a sense of failure or success, depending on whether they achieved their intended consequences. If they succeeded, they tended to repeat their actions in similar situations. If they failed, they were predisposed to try to understand their errors in order to correct them. People believed they understood their errors when they could identify the flaws in their causal microtheories and design new ones with which to implement new actions.

It is data such as these that lead us to the idea that people are fundamentally rational. To be rational means (1) to intend to bring about certain consequences, (2) to have an explicit or tacit design or theory about how to accomplish one's intentions, (3) to act intentionally consistent with the design, (4) to feel a sense of success or failure, depending on whether one's intentions were achieved, and (5) to correct mismatches so that designs lead to a match between intention and outcome.

This concept of rationality assumes that human beings design their actions (tacitly or explicitly) and hence are personally responsible for their actions. It also assumes that human beings cannot knowingly design error (or mismatch), because to bring about an error knowingly and by design is a match. Finally, this concept of rationality means that people seek to control their own capacity to design and implement their actions; they are predisposed to be origins of their actions rather than pawns.

People become frightened and judge themselves in trouble if they cannot make a connection between what is in their heads (their designed intent) and their actions. They also become frightened when they realize that the actions they design are counterproductive and that they are unaware of this fact. Whenever this occurs, people report that they are concerned or frightened because it means that, as one person stated it, "I am dangerous to myself." This judgment assumes that if the person designed his actions, and if his actions are counterproductive and he is unaware of this fact, then something must be wrong in the way he designs, implements, and monitors his own actions.

According to this view, to be irrational is to be unable to govern and design one's own actions. Human beings are rational in the sense that they strive to bring about their intended and designed consequences. To act rationally also means that people never knowingly harbor designs or intentions that are destructive to this sense of governance. Thus, our meaning of *rationality* is not the narrow meaning of intellective or purely cognitive features. Our meaning is related to the assumption that human beings are designed to be designing systems and to be held accountable for their designs and implementations.

Feelings are, as we have seen, a central component in this form of rationality. In all situations studied so far, people experienced feelings ranging from confusion and bewilderment to shame, frustration, guilt, and anger whenever they realized that they were unable to design and implement what they intended to design and implement and that they were predisposed to be unaware of this fact (although colleagues were easily aware of their unawareness).

Our proposition that people are fundamentally rational should be interpreted to mean that they are self-governing, personally responsible organisms, or, to put it another way, they seek to carry out their designs effectively. All designs for diagnosis and action have components that vary in intellective and emotional degree.

Intimate Relation Between Competence and Justice

Competence may be defined as designing and implementing matches (between intentions and outcomes), including the detection and correction of mismatches. In order to know whether they have implemented a match or corrected a mismatch, people require feedback from the environment. If it is to be helpful, the feedback must have at least two features: it must contain valid information, and it must be communicated in a way that does not make the receiver defensive and hence unlikely to hear the information.

If people knowingly communicate information that is invalid and yet act as if it were valid, they are judged as acting unjustly and unfairly. Such actions are unjust because they are intended to harm or violate our capacity to govern our actions and be self-responsible.

Injustice occurs whenever anyone asserts that a rule applies to everyone under a given set of conditions but acts in ways that violate the rule under the same stipulated conditions. The reason injustice is so closely connected to competence is that one of the best ways to make self-control or governance ineffective is to unilaterally alter the rules that are central to governance. Under such conditions, people never know whether they can design effective action because the applicability of the rules on which their designs are based is no longer predictable.

People can govern themselves if they live in an environment where rules about inconsistency and injustice are stable and predictable. When this is the case, they can design and implement action. If they succeed or fail, they can look to themselves or to the actions of others to correct the situation. If the underlying rules are changed unilaterally, the very basis for detecting and correcting error is gone, and self-governance is threatened.

Self-confidence, Competence, and Justice

Within this framework, self-confidence is central to effective action. Self-confidence means that people believe they are effective, self-governing systems in the world in which they are embedded. This belief is developed through experience in everyday life. Self-confidence is critical because in everyday life people have little time or help to design and implement their actions and cannot expect to be fully informed in any given situation. Therefore, they have designs about how to design action. These master designs are based on actions that their culture and the systems within which they are embedded accept as valid (or label invalid). If people's master designs are incorrect, they are in real trouble, because their situational designs will probably be ineffective.

People who feel self-confident are those who have had success in designing and implementing their actions and in detecting and correcting any errors that they may have produced. Such people enter a situation with a greater degree of certainty that they can behave competently. This sense of certainty makes them less vulnerable and hence more likely to identify and correct error. This outcome reinforces their sense of competence and their sense that the world is basically just.

Implications

Let us now turn to the question of how people create the conditions described in Chapters One through Five when they are dealing with double-loop learning.

1. People hold Model I theories-in-use (although many of them hold espoused theories that approximate Model II, to be discussed later in the chapter).

2. Whenever people are faced with a difficult issue that may threaten them or others, they confront the possibility that they or others will become upset and express negative feelings, inhibiting rationality; therefore, they begin to lose control and thereby increase their chances for losing, not winning. These consequences will be resisted because they violate Model I governing variables and inhibit Model I action strategies.

3. The automatic reaction will be to focus on the causal responsibility of the others involved. By framing the diagnosis in terms of what to do with others, people remain within the Model I governing values and bring into action their highly skilled Model I action strategies.

People will not focus on their own causal responsibility (if any) because, as we have seen, it is unlikely that they will be aware of it or that others will provide the feedback required for awareness.

4. The maps that people have learned to use contain concepts very high on the ladder of inference. This is necessary if only because the human mind cannot deal with the complexity involved without using abstraction.[8] Hence, this feature is not related to theories-in-use; it is related to the finite information capacity of the human mind.

What *is* related to Model I theory-in-use is the predisposition to use high-level inference concepts without relating them to the directly observable data for testing the inferences implicit in them. Recall that we found all respondents made attributions about and evaluations of Y's actions. But no one wrote scenarios or roleplayed actions to test these attributions.

---

[8] G. A. Miller, "The Magical Number Seven, Plus or Minus Two: Some Limits in Our Capacity for Processing Information," *Psychological Review*, 6(3) (1956): 81-96; Herbert A. Simon, *The Science of the Artificial* (Cambridge, Mass.: M.I.T. Press, 1969).

5. One explanation for the almost automatic reaction against testing is that it could lead to data that would place the evaluations and attributions in doubt. Then the person might lose control over the situation.

Although none of our respondents acted to test his or her attributions and evaluations of Y when this explanation was pointed out, many expressed bewilderment over how to test the validity of their inferences with someone who is bound to become defensive and who will thus make valid falsifiability impossible.

This argument is sound, given the Model I strategies used and the O-I learning systems that were created. You may remember that most participants held a view of defensiveness that led them to believe that if they were candid with Y, he would become defensive. Given that view, the automatic reaction was to use face-saving strategies to minimize the probability that they would be accused of making Y defensive. The result was the easing-in strategy, which only produced further counterproductive consequences. However, because Y was also programmed with Model I, at no time did Y provide the feedback the helpers needed to become aware of their errors. The few helpers who did use a forthright approach expected Y to become defensive. They acted in ways that were counter to their theory of defense because they felt that, in the interests of the firm, someone had to be candid with Y. When Y responded defensively, they too used their diagnostic frame and interpreted his reactions as lamentable proof of the validity of that frame. Again, there was no valid test, just a condition for self-fulfilling and self-sealing processes.

6. Even if the Ys had been candid, all the helpers held a diagnostic frame that contained a causal statement that Y was responsible for X's defensiveness and that Y was both incompetent and unaware. Recall that, whether people used the easing-in or the forthright strategy, whenever Y responded in ways that seemed to question the validity of their diagnoses, the helpers' automatic reaction was to interpret Y's action as defensive. Hence, the automatic response was not to test but to create self-fulfilling prophecies and self-sealing processes.

7. All these actions were reinforced by the O-I learning systems that were created in the cases, during the roleplaying in the classroom, and in the meetings observed in organizational settings. In other words, people tended to feel that cultural norms and mores supported their actions.

8. The result is that it was highly unlikely that people would become aware of their errors. When a few persons became even slightly aware of their possible responsibility, they either reacted toward Y ("I'm doing this for your own good") or reacted to their classroom critics ("What else could anyone do?").

The theories-in-use and the O-I learning system create a world where the cues that the actors will see are those that automatically trigger Model I meanings. Once these meanings are generated, we produce incorrect premises. From these incorrect premises, we infer conclusions that are wrong. Given the nature of the behavioral world in which we are embedded, we neither stop to test our inferences nor encourage others to do so. Those are the mechanisms that lead to this proposition: Given people programmed with Model I theories-in-use, and given the O-I learning systems that necessarily follow from that programming, whenever people try to deal with double-loop issues, the ultimate result will be self-fulfilling prophecies and self-sealing processes—and, hence, escalating error.

Summary

An explanation for the results reported in the previous chapters is that most people are programmed with a Model I theory-in-use and are embedded in O-I learning systems. If this is true, then Model I is a powerful example of learning through socialization in the systems in which people live and work, as well as through socialization in early life.

It is this theory-in-use, supported by O-I learning systems, that leads people to reason in counterproductive ways—that is, to create incorrect premises but then use correct inference processes to reach wrong conclusions; to refrain from testing their attributions and evaluations; to be unaware of the high levels of inference embedded in their constructs; to believe that their ideas are highly concrete and, in fact, obvious. In our opinion, it is the reasoning processes that must be altered if the features of Model I that militate against double-loop learning are to be reduced. They are basic in that they are the processes by which people make sense out of their world and by which they design, implement, and monitor their actions. They are also basic because they contain individual, group, organizational, and societal factors, the results of the socialization process.

The reasoning processes are the social genes that contain the information needed to ensure that people will think and act in accordance with what is socially acceptable, no matter what the environment in which they are placed. In other words, we should find that persons who use Model I are able to behave in accordance with Model I (directively) or, if they wish, in accordance with the opposite to Model I (easing in), but they should not be able to behave in accordance with a model designed to overcome the counterproductive features of Model I.

Model II Theory-in-Use

Schön and I have developed a model of a theory-in-use that, if used correctly, should lead to effective double-loop learning. We have called this Model II. As we have illustrated elsewhere[9] and as we will illustrate in this book, the major features of this model have not been disconfirmed. Furthermore, without help, people are unable to produce action congruent with Model II even if they espouse it, value it, wish to learn it, and practice it.

Model II has a causal theory embedded in it, parallel to the theory embedded in Model I. That is, if people behave according to Model II action strategies in order to satisfy Model II governing values, then certain consequences, to be described, will follow.

Table 6 shows the Model II theory-in-use. The governing variables, or values, of Model II—valid information, free and informed choice, and internal commitment—are *not* the opposite of those of Model I, and the behavior required to satisfy these values is not behavior opposite to that of Model I. For example, Model I emphasizes that people be as articulate as they can be about their purposes and goals and simultaneously control others and the environment in order to ensure that their purposes are achieved. Model II does not reject the skill of being articulate and precise about one's purposes. It does reject the unilateral control that usually accompanies advocacy

[9]Chris Argyris and Donald Schön, *Theory in Practice: Increasing Professional Effectiveness* (San Francisco: Jossey-Bass, 1974); Chris Argyris and Donald Schön, *Organizational Learning* (Reading, Mass.: Addison-Wesley, 1978); Chris Argyris, *Increasing Leadership Effectiveness* (New York: Wiley-Interscience, 1976); Chris Argyris, "Theories of Action That Inhibit Individual Learning," *American Psychologist*, *31*(9) (September 1976): 638-654.

Table 6. Model II Theory-in-Use

1 Governing Variable for Action	2 Action Strategy for Actor and Toward Environment	3 Consequences for Behavioral World	4 Consequences for Learning	5 Effectiveness
Valid information	Design situations or encounters in which participants can be origins and experience high personal causation	Actor experienced as minimally defensive	Disconfirmable processes	Increased effectiveness
Free and informed choice	Task is controlled jointly	Minimally defensive interpersonal relations and group dynamics	Double-loop learning	
Internal commitment to the choice and constant monitoring of the implementation	Protection of self is a joint enterprise and oriented toward growth	Learning-oriented norms	Frequent public testing of theories	
	Bilateral protection of others	High freedom of choice, internal commitment, and risk taking		

because the typical purpose of advocacy is to win. Model II couples articulateness and advocacy with an invitation to others to confront one's views, even to alter them, in order to produce action which is based on the most complete, valid information possible and to which people can become internally committed. This means that the actor in Model II is skilled at inviting double-loop learning.

Every significant Model II action is evaluated in terms of the degree to which it helps the people involved generate valid and useful information (including relevant feelings), solve the problem in such a way that it remains solved, and do so without reducing the present level of problem-solving effectiveness.

The behavioral strategies of Model II involve sharing power with anyone who has competence and who is relevant to deciding or implementing the action. Definition of the task and control over the environment are now shared with relevant others. Saving face is resisted because it is a defensive, nonlearning activity. If face-saving actions must be taken, they are planned jointly with the people involved.

Under the conditions just described, individuals will not compete to make decisions for others, to "one-up" others, to outshine others for the purpose of self-gratification. Individuals in a Model II world seek the people most competent to make the decision. They seek to build viable decision-making networks in which the major function of the group is to maximize the contributions of each member; when a synthesis is developed, the widest possible exploration of views has occurred.

Finally, if new concepts are created under Model II conditions, the meaning given to them by the creator and the inference processes used to develop them are open to scrutiny by those who will use them. Evaluations and attributions are minimized. When used, they are coupled with the directly observable data that led to their formation. Moreover, the creator feels a responsibility for presenting evaluations and attributions in ways that encourage open and constructive confrontation.

If the governing values and behavioral strategies just outlined are used, the degree of defensiveness in and between individuals and groups will decrease. Free choice will increase, as will feelings of internal commitment.

The consequences for learning are an emphasis on double-loop learning, in which the basic assumptions behind ideas or policies are confronted, in which hypotheses are tested publicly, and in which the processes are disconfirmable, not self-sealing.

The end result should be increases in the effectiveness of decision making and policy making, in the monitoring of decisions and policies, and in the probability that errors and failures will be communicated openly and that actors will learn from the feedback.

Model O-II Learning Systems

As with Model O-I, we begin the description of Model O-II (Figure 2) with the conditions of error shown in column 1. They now interact with the Model II theories-in-use (column 3), which couple advocacy with inquiry, encourage the surfacing of threatening issues, and sanction disconfirmable statements and the public testing of these statements.

Error is detected and Model II inquiry begins. Model II inquiry (column 5) increases the probability that a corrective response will be made. Mistaken assumptions will tend to be reformulated, incongruities will tend to be specified, ambiguity will tend to be clarified, testability will tend to be substituted for untestability, scattered information will tend to be brought together in concert, information withheld will be surfaced.

The conditions of error that met with dysfunctional responses in Model O-I now will tend to be met with functional responses. Instead of the reaction's maintaining or magnifying the errors, errors will now tend to be corrected. The feedback is negative in the sense that it is corrective.

Two kinds of learning are possible in an O-II learning system. The first kind that would be encouraged is single-loop learning. This is relatively straightforward learning because the errors are usually attributable to defective strategies or actions. Consequently, with Model II inquiry it is not too difficult to invent, produce, and evaluate effective actions to correct errors. As Figure 2 shows, inventions are produced to correct the error in strategy or assumption. Because the behavior required fits within the existing theory-in-use, the task of producing it is relatively straightforward. Evaluation then follows: If the response corrects the error, learning is terminated; if the response is a mismatch, the actor returns to diagnosing the error.

The second type of learning is double-loop learning. Here the

Figure 2. Model O-II Learning Systems: Facilitating Error Detection and Correction

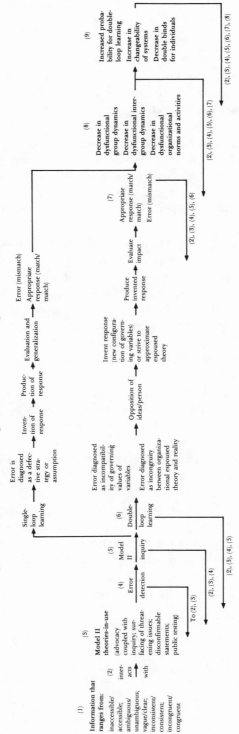

error is diagnosed as incompatibility of governing values or as incongruity between organizational espoused theory and theory-in-use. Correction of such error requires the conditions of the good dialectic, which begins with development of a map that provides a different perspective on the problem (for example, a different set of governing values or norms). The opposition of ideas and persons then makes it possible to invent responses that approximate the organization's espoused theory. Next, the inventions are produced and evaluated. If the error is corrected, and hence the response is appropriate, the learning cycle ends. If the response is a mismatch, there is further inquiry (column 7).

Such a learning process should decrease dysfunctional group dynamics because the competitive win/lose, low-trust, low-risk-taking processes are replaced by cooperative, inquiry-oriented, high-trust, and high-risk-taking dynamics. Finally, dysfunctional norms and games of deception should decrease, as well as the need for camouflage, camouflage of the camouflage, and the defensive activities described in O-I (Figure 1, column 8).

The results should be that participants will experience that double-loop learning is possible for themselves and their organizations, that organizations can change, and that the double binds experienced by individuals can decrease (column 9). Both columns 8 and 9 reinforce the previous columns, and hence we have a learning system that is simultaneously stable and subject to continual change.

A word of warning: It is important not to isolate a full cycle of organizational learning from the larger organizational dialectic. In good dialectic, new conditions for error typically emerge as a result of organizational learning; hence the quality of stability combined with continual change. This means that the good dialectic is not a steady state free from conditions for error but an open-ended process in which cycles of organizational learning create new conditions for error, to which members of the organization respond by transforming them so as to set in motion the next phase of inquiry.

6

Individual Distancing
from Responsibility
for Problem Solving

The data presented so far in this book indicate that whenever people face double-loop issues, they will act in ways that are counterproductive; they will tend to be unaware that they themselves are doing so, yet tend to be aware when others are doing so. They will tend, therefore, to believe that any difficulties are being created primarily by others. Moreover, when they try to help others, they will use easing-in or forthright actions that compound the counterproductive consequences and create conditions of injustice.

All these consequences are caused by Model I theories-in-use that are probably taught through socialization. People come to accept Model I theories-in-use as being quite natural because they use theories-in-use spontaneously and automatically. Moreover, they spend most of their lives in organizations (family, school, work, and so on) that contain O-I learning systems. These systems reinforce Model I theories-in-use as well as such norms as "You can't change human nature," "Neither organizations nor individuals are meant for double-loop learning," "Being concerned and civilized means playing games of deception and unilateral face saving" in order not to make these issues discussable and thereby risk opening a Pandora's box.

It is not surprising, therefore, that double-loop problems are increasing in our society while people simultaneously are striving to solve them by translating them into single-loop problems. Model I theories-in-use and O-I learning systems are more effective in dealing with single-loop problems. One of the most frequent uses of information science is to handle double-loop issues with detailed work specifications and monitoring procedures suitable for single-loop error, thereby hiding crucial double-loop error. As we have noted, the same can be found at the level of government regulation.[1]

How can people live in a world that deals with double-loop problems by, in effect, ignoring them? The answer is straightforward: People ignore such problems, regardless of the fact that they may focus on performing their tasks well, so that no one can accuse them of irresponsibility, disloyalty, or incompetence. To this end, they emphasize being individual contributors. They have, in effect, distanced themselves from others to play down the issue of interdependence.

A sense of alienation, withdrawal, hopelessness—long held to be typical of the poor, disadvantaged, and lower classes—may also be experienced by the highly educated, by professionals, and by those with substantial power. The difference is that distancing by the latter group is related to double-loop problems. This group, presumably charged with solving society's difficult problems, are the very ones who may distance themselves from doing so. The paradox is that this distancing, or escape from responsibility for double-loop problems, is seen as an act of responsibility in getting on with the single-loop issues.

The following three cases illustrate aspects of this disconnectedness. In Case D, we will show that not only do people disconnect themselves from their reasoning processes, but they probably *must* disconnect themselves because their reasoning processes are full of inconsistencies and injustice. People become quite upset if they realize that they act counterproductively in order to be effective. As one of our participants said, "This is crazy thinking!"

[1] Chris Argyris and Donald Schön, *Organizational Learning* (Reading, Mass.: Addison-Wesley, 1978).

It may well be crazy thinking. It may also be that what prevents people from going crazy is that they disconnect themselves from their own thinking. If confronted, they may have many societally sanctioned ways to blame a problem on the system rather than on themselves. Disconnectedness from their reasoning processes may help them maintain sanity, but it can also numb the sense of responsibility for solving double-loop problems.

Cases E and F illustrate these features of distancing. In Case E, we present the reflections of a case team of highly skilled professionals who provided to the client, by their own admission, a less than acceptable product and service because the members acted as individual contributors and ignored the problems of interdependence and of building an effective team.

In Case F (Chapter Seven), we present a case of distancing in progress. We were able to interrupt the action and get the case team to explore how various members were distancing themselves from their responsibilities.

Case D

Case D (written by Gerry Garnett Ward) illustrates the essential difficulties that subordinates encounter when dealing with a superior who is suspected of controlling the situation to his or her own ends. The dilemma facing the subordinates is that they would like to discuss the situation, but they believe that the superior will protect his or her hidden interests at all costs. To speak openly is to risk the wrath of the superior. To withhold one's views violates one's sense of responsibility.

The writer of the case, the subordinate, chose to pursue the familiar path of not discussing his suspicion, focusing instead on the "facts" of the situation. "Inevitably," he writes, "that route leads to my feeling dishonest and being a partner in protecting the superior's hidden interests. However, the approach has some merit in that it may allow [the superior] to feel freedom enough to allow some movement toward my position."

The description of the situation and the scenario of the case are quoted directly from the subordinate's write-up. Only minor editorial changes and name changes have been made.

The situation around which this dialogue centers is drawn from my professional experience as an assistant director of admissions at a large university. The admissions staff there is composed of twelve assistant directors, four associate directors, and one director. All the assistant directors are responsible for carrying out university promotion and student recruitment activities as well as evaluating applications. Each of the associate directors is responsible for researching and planning one of the larger aspects of the admissions program—promotion and recruitment, alumni relations, staff supervision, and institutional research. The director is the chief executor of the entire operation, making the final and major decisions in all areas.

At the time that this dialogue took place, the director was aware that morale among his assistant directors had dropped significantly. He thus encouraged them at their annual retreat to consider means of creating professional growth and satisfaction on the assistant director level. He was fearful that the morale problem would reverse the success for which he and his staff had received credit over the past few years.

Throughout the staff, Mr. T, the director, had established an undisputed reputation as an autocratic administrator. In spite of the likelihood of T's negative reactions, the assistant directors made a proposal for a major change in office responsibility that would involve them in some of the associates' planning and research. T and the associates did not react with encouragement at the time of the initial proposal, yet chose not to dismiss it completely, perhaps being aware that an immediate denial would create further dissatisfaction among the assistant directors. The following dialogue is a reconstruction of one that took place in a subsequent meeting between the director and myself for the purpose of further discussing the proposal.

Thoughts and Feelings	*Conversation*
That's an insincere question. I know from our explanation and his reaction at the retreat that he fully understood the essence of	*T:* Well, Gerry, what is it exactly that you and the other assistant directors had in mind concerning your proposal?

Thoughts and Feelings

Conversation

the proposal. He's asking me to describe details of the plan that we can't possibly have. Therefore, it will appear to be ill-formed. From experience I know that T is much too defensive for me to say that. I'll simply explain the assistant directors' position.

Gerry: We haven't formed any of the specifics of the plan, since it will require a great deal of time and effort by a number of staff members—assistant directors and associates. We don't think that such an investment could be made without your commitment, at least to the theory of the proposed change. The assistant directors feel that since all of us have been on staff for at least a couple of years, expanding our responsibility would allow us to contribute more and would be more satisfying professionally.

I'd better reemphasize the fact that we're in need of a change and underline that it's necessary by alluding to our dissatisfaction. Otherwise he could completely dismiss this.

That praise is gratuitous. He's trying to prove that he appreciates us before he squelches the proposal.

T: I'm aware that most of you have done a good job and probably have something more to offer. But I can't give any commitment to the proposal until I've seen the specifics. I think that this proposal will have to be developed by the assistant directors as a group and then we'll consider it.

He's avoiding the central issue: Will he commit himself to expanding our responsibilities? He's hiding behind the supposed need for specifics. He knows that, given the present schedule, many of the assistant directors aren't available and will be pressed with other work when they return. His strategy is to put us off, since in six weeks planning will be impossible.

Thoughts and Feelings	*Conversation*
I'll skip the judgment of his ultimate strategy and simply present our dilemma.	*G:* The proposal is a major change and would require hours of meetings for the assistant directors and the associates in order to adequately plan. Such an effort couldn't take place without an initial commitment from you. I don't think that anyone, especially the associates, would risk spending hours of time on something so tentative.
He's staying with his demand for specifics, knowing that there's little hope for us. He's also playing on "professional responsibility" and "initiative," one of T's favorite ploys.	*T:* And I can't approve anything that's so tentative! Such a proposal, with its specifics, has to come from the assistant director level. You're the people who are proposing it.
I'll simply reassert my position and partially acknowledge his.	*G:* I realize that we are the ones who are proposing it and therefore are responsible for the specifics. But the specifics are difficult to come by without time, effort, and cooperation.
He's employing his usual tactic of demanding his position and then concluding that we're irresponsible if we don't meet it. It's a great way to put me on the defensive and to protect his position.	*T:* Well, you know that if the assistant directors are really committed to exploring the possibilities for change, then they should certainly be willing to make the effort that's necessary.
I'll counter his implication that we lack commitment.	*G:* It's not a matter of the assistant directors' commitment to the effort; they are willing to work hard on this. But as I've explained, we can't invest so much with no positive indication from you that you'll accept it.
I'm repeating myself and sounding frustrated. He knows that he has successfully prevented our getting this proposal off the ground.	

Thoughts and Feelings	*Conversation*
He's creating the guise of remaining open but is actually closing the lid on the discussion and, in effect, is eliminating the proposal's chances. One more power play for T!	*T:* Gerry, as I said before, I'll consider the proposal when it appears in a fully developed form submitted by the assistant directors.

Gerry did appear to meet his intentions. He never mentioned his mistrust of his superior; he held back his feelings of anger and frustration (left-hand column) and dealt mainly with the substantive issues. Further, he maintained and reinforced his views of T as a person who connives, uses ploys, hides his intentions, and lies to maintain his position.

But let us examine the reasoning processes that Gerry used and the action strategies he took. They could be described as follows:

> I (Gerry) am dealing with an individual (T) to whom I attribute several intentions: (1) to control the situation to his own ends, (2) to act as if he were not doing so, (3) to use his greater organizational power to accomplish 1 and 2, (4) to act as if 3 were not the case, and (5) to consider all these actions undiscussable.

This cluster of attributions becomes the premises that Gerry holds about T. They will guide his reasoning processes and his actions toward T.

In order to create these premises, it is necessary that Gerry know and believe these attributions about T. If Gerry is to know and believe these "facts" about T, they cannot be hidden to him. Hence, the "facts" that he believes T is hiding are not hidden to Gerry. We can infer, therefore, that Gerry's premises (attributions about T) require an additional set of attributions:

1. T is unaware that his intention to hide these "facts" is not working.
2. T is unaware of the negative impact his actions and their undiscussability have on myself and the others.
3. To discuss the undiscussable would upset T and could lead him

to become angry with me, which, in turn, could make me vulnerable to T's greater power.

The scenario that Gerry wrote suggests that (1) he never tested these attributions, (2) he acted in front of T as if they did not exist, (3) he therefore made them undiscussable, and (4) he acted as if they were not undiscussable.

To maintain the premises that Gerry held about T, *he had to reason and to act in precisely the way that he considered T should not act.* These represent the conditions described in Chapter Five as being the basis for injustice and for feeling incompetent. Gerry's approach, then, not only makes it less likely that he will deal effectively with T but creates conditions in which Gerry must hold himself responsible for acting unjustly and incompetently.

If we assume that people will not feel comfortable about being their own worst enemies, then it is rational to predict that they will blame others for the injustice and incompetence and will not test their attributions. Hence, we have Gerry describing T as "closed," "autocratic," manipulative," and "punitive." If Gerry sees his superior as having these characteristics, he may understandably believe that it is necessary for him as well to become "closed," "autocratic," and "manipulative" in order to survive. His negative responses are caused by his interpretation of T's actions.

But how closed T is to Gerry's influence may also be related to how he interprets Gerry's action. What if T senses that Gerry (and the other assistant directors) sees him as closed, autocratic, and manipulative? It is unlikely that he will feel understood and respected by the assistant directors or that he will take risks with them. He will probably create his own set of attributions about Gerry and the other assistant directors, which will be as counterproductive to dialogue as those created by Gerry. T may indeed depend on his organizational power, because that is what will make it likely that he will win in this relationship of minimal trust and understanding.

Returning to the dialogue, we note that T, like Gerry, focused on the substantive issues. He asked for more facts about the proposal. Gerry's reply was to argue that the details were best worked out by the assistant directors. In effect, Gerry's action strategy was this:

When T asks me to work out the details, I will respond that his suggestions are inappropriate.
I will also ask for a commitment to the theory underlying the change
that I am proposing.

Gerry was using an action strategy that violated his own premises about T. Gerry saw T as unilaterally controlling the situation for
his own interests and afraid to share influence. Hence, Gerry had
now created a double bind for himself. If T accepted Gerry's suggestions, then Gerry would have to conclude that his premises, his actions during the meeting, and the reasoning processes that he used to
create both were distortions. If T rejected them, then Gerry could
fear that he had lost or jeopardized his standing with T.

One way for Gerry to prevent himself from experiencing either
feature of the double bind would be to reason and act in ways that
identify T as the culprit. Indeed, Gerry made this strategy highly
probable by the way he framed the problem at the outset. Gerry believed that he was caught between leveling with T and going along
with him in ways that might "allow T to move toward my position"
without T's realizing that Gerry was managing the movement. This is
a heuristic commonly observed in everyday life. It is often touted as
a great skill of leaders—namely, getting others to do what you want
them to do in such a way that they believe they are following their
own choice. Gerry appears to be as manipulative as T.

In this connection, Gerry remarked during the discussion of
his case, "Ironically, I believe that I still am on good terms with T."
Why not, we may ask? He utilizes the same theory-in-use that he attributes to T and is very careful not to discuss the undiscussable. But
much of Gerry's inconsistency could be caused by the possibility
that T was closed to being influenced and was powerful enough to
maintain the closedness. We created an opportunity to test this hypothesis by asking Gerry to roleplay T in the meanest form he could
conceive of while several of us tried to create a scenario that might
influence T. Gerry agreed. A scenario was produced within five minutes that Gerry believed had a decent probability of working, or if it
did not work totally, at least it would minimize the necessity for
Gerry to act in ways he considered dishonest.

The roleplaying began with one participant suggesting the following response after T says (in the transcript), "I'm aware that most of you have done a good job. . . . But I can't give any commitment to the proposal until I've seen the specifics."

Proposed Reply	*Analysis of the Reply*
Participant 1 (roleplaying as Gerry): I can understand that you cannot commit to a plan you haven't seen.	Confirms T's hesitance to commit.
I would like to design planning processes that would enable us to discuss our plans with you as we go along.	Suggests a joint process, with T periodically involved.
I'd like to have your ideas incorporated into the plan so that we don't end up putting lots of time into something that you believe is unrealistic.	T could see this as a potential trap, requiring time that he does not have and involving him in discussions that he wishes to avoid.

Participant 1 then asked Gerry to please respond as T would "if he were being tough." Gerry said he would be glad to roleplay T using "the attributions I make about the guy of *really* wanting to protect his position, the suspicions that I have of him . . . is that what you want?" Yes, was the response.

Roleplay	*Analysis*
Gerry (roleplaying as T): I don't have the time to really sit down with you people. Moreover, it really has to come from you people. You're the ones who are proposing it.	T distances himself from responsibility to work with assistant directors by repeating his lack of time and focusing on the assistant directors' desire to create and propose the new ideas.
P1 (roleplaying as Gerry): OK. I'd like your thoughts on one potential problem. Developing a detailed plan would require lots of hours of work (without your help). The chances are greater that the plan would be unacceptable to you.	The suggestion that the plan might be better if T participates may not be relevant if T's intention is to stonewall the plan.

Roleplay	*Analysis*
At the same time, those who have worked on it would feel highly committed to it.	T might feel that this is a risk that he would take, because if the plan is not acceptable, then he may have put down such action for quite a while.
If we become highly committed to a plan that you find unrealistic, then we've not only wasted staff time but we've created a morale problem.	
Gerry (as T): I understand the choices are difficult, but I am so swamped [enumerates] that I must take that risk. I do not have the time.	T continues by protecting his time, by acknowledging the risk, and by suggesting that the probable morale problem would be less severe if the assistant directors were committed and loyal.
And I really do think that it is your responsibility to come up with this. I know there's a risk involved, but it is a measure of your commitment.	
P1: I can understand you're busy. I think it is unfortunate, but that is your decision.	Respects T's decision but is also clear that he has communicated the potential problems to T.
These are the problems I see, and I wanted to make it clear to you what I see going on.	

Then Gerry (speaking as T) said that he felt the assistant directors would now be "back to square one . . . I think it would settle down to an impasse." P1 agreed and added, "If I were an employee, I would not know what to do next." Another participant said, "It is almost an impossible situation." Gerry added, "Yes, that's the problem in the case."

But there was one important difference between this roleplay and Gerry's scenario. In this roleplay, P1 was able to state some of the views that he believed were important. He did not collude in the same way as Gerry did (by talking about details). Hence, he may have felt that he had been more honest and had generated more valid information about the situation.

Assuming that the roleplay produced more valid information about the dangers of T's not becoming involved, it also led T to maintain his position of distancing himself from any responsibility for the plan.

Participant 2 then asked to continue the roleplay, even though the situation appeared impossible. First he reviewed what P1 had said.

Participant 2: I'm sorry that you do not have the time. I hope that I have communicated to you that I can understand your dilemma.

I also hope that I have communicated my belief that if we do not do something, we will continue to exacerbate the morale problem, and if we do it the way you suggest, we will have a morale problem.

I would not recommend that we go either way, and would say that to the assistant directors.

Reviews his judgment and informs T that he would not recommend either action because both would make the situation worse.

Gerry (as T): Look, I'm not totally shutting down the plan. You can still go ahead. I'll still look at the proposal when it is done.

T does not want to be held responsible for shutting down the plan, and yet his actions do create a "no win" situation for the organization.

P2: You're saying that the assistant directors should trust you; that you're going to remain open but that they have no right to involve you. [It is difficult for them to feel trusted under those conditions.]

T's position requires of Gerry unilateral trust when he and the assistant directors imply that low trust exists at the moment.

G: I agree that this is not ideal. But we have no time for the ideal.

Again, time is critical.

P2: What is your view of the time frame that I am asking for?

G: Meeting periodically with the assistant directors over the next four weeks.

P2: What I am asking for is a

Asks for a short period of time

one- to two-hour meeting at the
outset. We would like to learn
what your concerns are about
such a program. We could use
them as guideposts in designing
our plan or at least be able to tell
you explicitly why we did not
follow some of them.

to establish criteria and guideposts.

Gerry stated that he believed that T would agree to one meeting of the kind that P2 had suggested.

Why was it possible for two others to create a scenario that
was acceptable to T, as roleplayed by Gerry, to be as tough and resistant as Gerry could imagine? A frequent response to this question
is that the seminar members were not as emotionally involved in the
situation as Gerry. This is a valid but inadequate answer. It is inadequate because it implies that if Gerry had been less involved, he
might have acted more constructively. The difficulty is that involvement is inescapable when people are dealing with critical everyday
challenges. Gerry and others require knowledge and skills to help
them become more effective while being involved.

In order for Gerry to test the idea that his emotional involvement was responsible for his inability to produce effective roleplays,
he could examine his reasoning as follows:

> I, Gerry, diagnose T as closed, manipulative, and
> interested in remaining in unilateral control and not los-
> ing.
> I, Gerry, am aware that I am behaving toward T
> in the same way.
> Any time I act in ways that I assert are unjust and
> incompetent, my reasoning is faulty and the conse-
> quences will be counterproductive. Under these condi-
> tions, it is highly likely that I will interpret what T says
> to confirm my diagnosis. Because I keep the diagnosis
> tacit and the testing of it secret, I run the risk of gener-
> ating self-fulfilling and self-sealing processes.

Such reasoning should not allow Gerry to design any scenario
other than the one he did design. Nor can Gerry design a more candid scenario in which he moves the ideas and feelings from his left-

hand column to his right-hand column in order to test the attributions. T has not asked Gerry to be his interpersonal consultant. Indeed, T gives Gerry clues that T does not wish to deal with such issues.

If Gerry should not use untested attributions, and yet he cannot test these attributions with T, then what *can* he do? The foregoing roleplaying suggests that Gerry can focus on the requirements of organizational effectiveness. Thus, he can show that T's strategy will lead to a "no win" situation with escalating problems. He can also show that the assistant directors may hold T responsible for such consequences. In other words, Gerry can help T examine his own reasoning processes and the impact they will have on problem-solving effectiveness. Once it is established that T can be held responsible for worsening the situation, then T may be more willing to give a few hours' time for a meeting. The assistant directors could then develop a list of guideposts so as not to violate T's constraints. However, they can also go ahead and violate the constraints but come prepared to subject their reasoning to public test.

Reflecting on the entire case, we can now see that T (as described in Gerry's case) was distancing himself from dealing with the assistant directors *and* from those features of himself that related to subordinates asking for more autonomy and influence. Although T never said to the assistant directors that he was distancing himself from them, they felt it. Gerry's case was an attempt to help T become more involved with his subordinates.

But to accomplish this, Gerry used a strategy that also distanced him from the problem. He never told T that he (and the other assistant directors) sensed the distancing and the mistrust that it implied. Moreover, Gerry was aware that his own strategy was leading him to collude with T's strategy to keep the mistrust issue hidden. But Gerry became detached from his reasoning processes. He diagnosed the problem as being T's fault. He framed the dilemma as either leveling with T and being rejected or hiding his true feelings and views and acting as if he were not doing so. Gerry eventually placed himself in a situation in which he would have to become aware of his own reasoning in order to test his attributions publicly. To view himself as a rational and just human being, he had to overcome his nonrational and unjust reasoning.

There is a fundamental optimism in the foregoing comments

and in the material presented in Part Two. Distancing and disconnectedness can be overcome by first making the reasoning processes
explicit. Once their counterproductive features are identified, it is
not difficult to invent new designs. But to produce these new designs, the group members must develop a new theory-in-use and a
new learning system. Once there is a commitment to doing so, it is
possible to take to the road of double-loop learning.

The main requirements (beyond the insight and understanding described so far) are practice in reflecting on one's reasoning,
discovering any inconsistencies, inventing new ways of reasoning,
and trying to produce the new inventions. These actions, which combine inquiry with experimentation, begin to create features of an
O-II learning system. New actions are established, such as identifying
and testing attributions and combining advocacy of one's position
with inquiry. These actions begin to reduce the competitive win/lose
games and to repudiate the norm that individuals and organizations
cannot double-loop learn. As we shall see, individuals begin to produce Model II actions under zero to moderate stress. If they strive to
do so and fail, they are open to being confronted and to correcting
their errors.

The trip from I to II is not linear, nor is it easy. It is full of experiments that succeed and fail, of paths that sometimes prove useful
and sometimes do not. But as we shall see, the learning can go on
while other technical tasks get done. Indeed, even when the new behavior is not clearly Model II, the intent is recognized and respected.
Moreover, double-loop learning is not easily forgotten—people remember lessons of several years earlier. People seek an appropriate
situation in which to experiment without harming the organization.
As one participant put it, "After the first few hurdles, you can have
your cake and eat it too." He meant that it was possible not only to
get the work done more effectively but to continue to learn and to
periodically raise the ante for learning.

Case E

The vice-president in charge of a consulting team asked the
five members to meet with him to reflect on their effectiveness as a
team and on the service provided the clients. He was interested in
learning why a team of two very competent consultants and three

managers, all of whom had successfully completed a similar project in another part of the client organization, did not produce the high-quality work expected by the firm and the client. He believed that self-reflection could strengthen the capacity of the firm, through its professionals, to detect and correct its own errors.

The material that follows is an edited version of the meeting transcript.

Vice-President: One reason I called this meeting is because I don't understand [why we did not produce as good a product for the client as we could have].

This is probably as good a case team as can be put together. The people are good, the level of experience is good [for the most part], the client liked and respected us, our client skills are quite good, [and finally, we had done a similar study for the client in another location].

The officer then asked the case team to be candid. He stated:

> I'll talk last because I do not want to bias what others of you say. I'll give my report [and I promise to be candid]. And I would say that we are all strong enough and big enough around here that we should be straightforward in our evaluations. I don't think that we gain anything by not being straightforward about all our roles, including officers as well as managers.

The vice-president then asked that the persons around the table give their views:

Manager 1: I think we had a lot of chiefs and no Indians. Second, we never made explicit our internal [case team] organization. As a result of changing [client] conditions, redefinition of the case, we ended up not being clear, and the changes over time caused a lot of resentment and were counterproductive.

M2: [Adding] Everybody had his individual piece, but people did not know what the others were doing.

M1: And finally, there was some backbiting as well. Also, the vice-president had to change his time commitment [in midstream], and [Manager 3] was to compensate for his time. But I do not believe that was made explicit.

Consultant 1: I agree. We went into the field intensively, and once in the field, it was kind of irretrievable. [Later on, when new issues surfaced, we could not] go back to the field in a cost-effective way. So I think we could have done more thinking before we went into the field.

M2: Also, since the order was to go out to do the market interviews, we had little time to interact as a case team. Nobody was really coordinating the case from a holistic point of view. [Provides detailed example.] The whole thing was basically out of control.

Interventionist: When did you sense that the project was out of control?

M2: Between the start of the project and the first presentation.
[Another thing], we [rarely] met as a case team without the client so that we could integrate our work. It was always more of a "show and tell" presentation. We never had a normal case team meeting without the client and without the "show and tell."

M1: We also needed you [vice-president] during the first presentation to the client. Just the fact that you weren't there in a situation where we were getting nitpicked to death. . . . I don't think any of us, and many of us tried, could stop [the nitpicking]. I think maybe you could have. I don't know why we couldn't stop [it]. I remember sitting there saying, "My God, we just killed ourselves for a week and I'm watching this presentation just get torn to hell for nonsensical reasons."

Int.: What could the vice-president have done that none of you could have done?

Cons. 1: Acted vice-presidential!

M1: "Acted vice-presidential" is probably the perfect answer. It climaxed for me in [Consultant 2's] presentation. It wasn't one of his greatest, and it wasn't particularly bad. . . . The message didn't come through and they were nitpicking us on numbers that were their own creation.

[Later]

I remember sitting in that meeting and saying [to myself], "You have three choices. You can keep your mouth shut, and that wouldn't work. You can try to contribute when [the client is] getting off the point. Or you can try and stand up and say, 'Listen, you turkeys, you're being idiots. Stop the nonsense. Here is our message.' "
    And I did not have the guts to do that.

M2: Yes, that would have helped.

M1: Which you [vice-president] would have done as a matter of course.

Int.: What would you have expected the vice-president to say?

M1: [Roughly, he would say], "Today's session is an interim presentation. We are here to update you as to our progress. We also want to make sure that we're not getting totally off the track. I think the level of detail that you people are trying to explore *is* getting us off the track." Then he would give some examples and literally bring the meeting to a halt until that issue was resolved.

Int.: And you do not think anyone on this team would have done that with credibility?

M1: I think [Manager 3] could try.

Cons. 1: I heard [another officer] once say to the clients in a meeting, "It doesn't matter what the number is. The point is, your performance in that area is lousy. It doesn't matter if it is 80 percent or 70 percent lousy. Once you're below 95 percent, it is awful. All right?" And he just totally shut the client up, and [the client's] boss kept a quiet approval. He can probably get away with it because officers have equal-level relationships with the client. And none of us would dare do it, no matter how senior we are. Or even if we did it, it wouldn't come off the same.

M3: [I tried several times to do something like Consultant 1 describes], but there were so many levels of the client organization present—Smith was sitting there having a field day. It was a zoo.

I would like to put the mantle on you [vice-president]—and you probably could have pulled it off, but it was a difficult situation. It was difficult in a curious way because it wasn't particularly rancorous, it was just nitpicking.

M2: [Returns to the issue that] we never had a chance among ourselves to say what the hell are we trying to accomplish. . . . What are the issues, anyway?

[To another case team member] I remember you said [such-and-such], and I sat there and I didn't even know what that meant. You made it sound important, but I didn't know what that meant.

Cons. 2: [Since there was a lack of coordination], I didn't know how to really pitch in and take the burden off [someone], because I didn't understand what we were doing as a whole, but I never said so.

And everyone was working madly . . . and the harder people work, the more frantic it is . . . the harder it is to tell anyone to do something or to give someone something to do.

M3: I think I agree with most of what has been said. As I hear this, I have learned that probably I should have been a little more forceful [about the lack of coordination and who is the leader].

It was difficult to do so because I did not have the vice-presidential imprint so that I could say, "Now look, I want you guys to do this." And so I was listening to [the case team members] in a sounding-board sense rather than trying to take control. . . . Maybe that was a mistake.

I think the client was not easy [during the first presentation]. To this day, I haven't figured out whether we were talking at one level and hearing something back at a different level, or what the heck was going on.

As a result, [we created our own explanation. We decided] that they were crazy, not us, and you know, don't worry, we'll come around in the final analysis and we'll give them value for the money.

Finally, [because we had done this case before], there was an incredible fixation to come up with something that was different. And I think you [Manager 2] created a segment out of whole cloth, just to try to satisfy yourself that in fact you had added something new and creative. Because I think that we were all disappointed . . . you know, this is a pretty boring business. I mean, there was nothing new under the sun. This was not my favorite assignment.

Oh, yes, and finally, I think in the final analysis we came up against a client to whom we were saying things that the client did not want to hear [illustrates].

VP: OK, let me add a few more points. Our senior client contact, Jones, had just been made head of another outlet. They did not want their operation to report to the U.S. The old story of the U.S. overtaking. Hence, Jones was reluctant to force us down the throats of the client organization. That was why he asked for the most senior case team he could have so there would be lots of interaction with the clients. One reason we went into the market early was that Jones believed that his organization did not know what they were doing in the market.

[Later]

We have learned that it is difficult to have three levels of clients who all think they are clients. On the other hand, I do not think that we coped with it. We knew about this problem, and I do not think any of us, me especially, did a particularly good job.

[Later]

The case team meeting in May left me with the impression that you hadn't learned a damn thing. And not only that, you focused so explicitly on the businesses that they were in and so little on the peripheral sides of the business that [our presentation] would have been a disaster.

That is why I made the changes [that you described]. I said to myself that we can't show something that ignores half of the other guy's business.

And I think one of the major lessons here is that never through the whole case, until the end, did I feel that I could turn to any one of you for a holistic view of what the client's products were. I felt that each of you knew your own little piece and you were all going to do your own little piece as well as you could do it, without getting your ass in gear.

Not only that, but each of you specifically thought the other guy was not doing his job. There were people saying, "[Manager 2] didn't do his job," and [Consultant 1] said, "Did you see [Consultant 2 is] going to get credit for what [Manager 1] did?" [and I could give more examples].

And so I had no one coming to my office and saying, "I think, in fact, we're not facing the real issue." I didn't have a single guy come in and do that. Not once in the whole study did somebody come in and say, "I think we're looking at this wrong." [Manager 3] and I did do that toward the end, which is why we finally wrote the report ourselves.

And look, I was guilty too, because I just left the scene, so I can't claim that I'm a great help.

We each had our own little piece, and we came in here and showed it, and they [the client] came in the next day and said it was terrible. They did it at every single meeting after that. [Manager 3] and I could fend them off, [and so we privately] reorganized the presentation so that it covered more of the whole.

I think that the reason the first meeting went bad was because we had bad stuff. I do not think that it went bad because I was not there. I don't think if I had been there I could have done what many of you said. I'm very glad I wasn't there, because I would have had to stand up and defend you guys, and it was probably bad stuff.

[Later]

I don't think our stuff was as good as it should have been. For example, we produced the wrong forecast, and that is serious. I do think that they picked the hell out of us, but they would have tried that with me there. It would have taken some amount of chutzpah to get us through the meeting, no matter what.

After that, I'm sure we made a mistake in having them there for the briefing. That was a terrible mistake. [However, it is working in another client situation because we are maintaining intimate on-going contacts with them, something we did not do in this case.]

[Later]

If I were to state the generic problem. I think the Indians/chiefs is the real one. That's important because if we are to be successful, we will have to have a lot of Indians. [In the future], we've got to sell more million-dollar-at-a-whack cases, which means more cases like this one down the road. That's the way we've got to go.

We've got to learn to work together, each carrying the weight of our salary in our billing range. And that means we need to identify, keep the whole in place, and then be able to approach each other when the work isn't good enough.

[We also must] approach the person who is leading [the project] and say, "I don't think that we're addressing the big issues here" —instead of each guy looking like "All I have to do is just make sure I don't get my ass in a sling and I'm billable and then I'll be doing good work."

M3: The vice-president gave me a lot of free rein, short of saying explicitly . . . I mean, you know, he said to me, "I'm going to be busy at another case, so I'm going to rely on you." I think that put me in a difficult position because that statement was never made explicit to anybody else. Nor did I make the statement any more emphatically to anybody else than you made it to me.

Maybe an error was that I didn't begin to behave in more of a general/admiral kind of fashion. I found it difficult to have two fellow managers on the case. It got difficult to go to you and say, "Look, damn it, go do that." In my experience around here, two reactions can ensue from that approach. One is "Go screw yourself, [Manager 3]." The other is "That's terrific, [Manager 3]"—and then all of a sudden it starts coming back through the grapevine [that the person] was really upset.

Let me ask, is there anything that I did that dissuaded you from coming in and telling me, "This thing is going wrong?"

Unidentifiable speaker: I didn't see much of you.

M2: I guess there is really no good answer. We should have come to you. I know that I didn't say a peep and I don't think that I heard much of a peep from anybody else other than the kind, you know, on the airplane. The question was asked, "Why are we doing this?," but nobody ever said, "Maybe we should stop right now and do something else." [Several persons say or nod yes.]

Cons. 1: But [to return to your question], I didn't get the feeling that if I said something to you about it, . . . things could change that much.

M3: What do you mean by that?

Cons. 1: If I have a feeling that we are poorly organized but do not have real hard data or facts, how is talking about it going to change what you are doing?

I saw you [and others] busy. You were running around. I figured the last thing you're going to have time to do is to sit down and spend a lot of time trying to figure out if something's wrong when the only reason I'm saying it is because I do not see much interaction going on.

The interventionist reported that Jones had said he was disappointed with the case team's performance and he blamed the vice-president for it. Jones felt that a case team was as good as its VP. This VP, he said, was superb. The problem, as he saw it, was that the VP had become overcommitted. Jones had expected that the VP would pull together a case team report that was technically good, understandable, and communicable and that the VP would have the team working more cooperatively with the client's inner group. The interventionist gave excerpts from Jones' conversation: "Regarding the VP, he is very bright. But more important, he can come alive and make something complex become clear. It makes it possible for us to understand him and also to question him. Without the vice-president, I wouldn't buy this. I don't think that I could have sold this case to the group."

Reflections on the Case Team

Diagnoses: Factors That Inhibited Performance. As we have just seen, the case team members identified the following causal factors as inhibiting their performance:

1. Too many chiefs and not enough Indians. Chiefs like to manage, and there was no one to be managed.
2. Not enough time set aside at the outset of the project to think it through.

3. The consultants did their own work in ignorance of what others were doing and did not take the initiative to find out. They saw themselves as individual contributors rather than as team members.

4. Team meetings should have been held without the clients present.

5. Some backbiting among consultants.

6. Vice-president withdrew from active management, and no one filled the vacuum.

7. The manager who was the logical successor did not take adequate initiative to manage the case team.

8. The team lacked a vice-president who could "act vice-presidential" at the first client presentation and stop client's nitpicking.

9. Managers felt helpless in dealing with nitpicking client and suppressed their frustration. The client reps escalated their counterproductive activities, infuriating the team members. Meeting result: a disaster.

10. Parts of the case were so routine that some members overinvested time and energy just to come up with something different.

Reasoning Processes Embedded in Inferring These Inhibiting Factors. The causal factors just listed are inferences made by the team members about what caused the team's below-par performance. The partial and complete transcripts show that all the participants confirmed the relevance of each factor. Factors 1, 2, 3, 4, and 6 were identified as important, the first one, "Too many chiefs and not enough Indians," being the key factor. The existence of a strong consensus among the members is not adequate evidence that these were the only causal factors. The team members might unknowingly be ignoring important factors. Indeed, I hope to show that they were.

The next step in the analysis is to answer this question: What were the reasoning processes used to arrive at the consensus?

One objective of the meeting was for each member to state what he believed were the causal factors that produced the less-than-desired performance—that is, to make a diagnosis. Each person gave his views, illustrating them whenever possible by sifting through his experiences as well as he could recollect them.

These conclusions become the basis for our analysis. For example:

Participants' Comments	*Inference About What Team Members Experienced*
1. Nobody was really coordinating the case from a holistic point of view.	Individuals recognized coordination problems but did not discuss them or take corrective action.
I remember you said . . . and I sat there and I didn't even know what that meant.	Members were reluctant to discuss issues if it meant stepping on each other's toes.
I didn't know how to really pitch in . . . because I didn't understand what we were doing as a whole, but I never said so.	
2. We went into the field intensively [too early] . . . We could have done more thinking [about the case] before we went into the field.	The team members realized early on that they could produce a better product if there were greater clarity about objectives early in the case.
3. We rarely met . . . without the client so that we could integrate our work. It was always more of a "show and tell" presentation. We never had a normal case team meeting without the client.	Consultants experienced difficulty in case team meetings because client representatives were present.
4. The whole thing was basically out of control.	Once the vice-president withdrew, the manager who was the logical choice for second-in-command did not take charge.
I did not have the vice-presidential imprint so that I could say, "Now look, I want you guys to do this."	

The team members' experiences described in the right-hand column became the premises for the next step in the reasoning process. For example:

Team members reported:	*They therefore concluded:*
1. The managers and consultants recognized the coordination problems as they occurred, but they neither discussed them nor took corrective action. It seemed as if	Too many chiefs, not enough Indians.

Team members reported:	*They therefore concluded:*
the managers and (perhaps less so) the consultants did not wish to step on each other's toes.	
2. It was soon obvious that the experience of a similar case was not an adequate guide. Team members felt they would have produced a better product if objectives had been clearer at the outset.	Team leadership did not take time to examine the assumptions and directions of the case because they did see these matters as important.
3. Consultants experienced difficulty in several case team meetings because client representatives were present.	Some team meetings should have been held without clients, but team leadership did not schedule such meetings.
4. Once the vice-president withdrew, the manager who was the logical choice for second-in-command did not take charge.	Manager did not wish to, or did not feel free to, take charge.
5. Case team members felt helpless to control client's nitpicking during early sessions.	Vice-president could have blunted counterproductive behavior of client.

Responsibility for the Causal Factors. Embedded in these reasoning processes is a second, deeper level of causal factors. The team members place responsibility for the first-level factors on gaps in judgment, inherent limitations of participants, and unforeseen events. For example:

If	*Then*
Not enough time was allocated during the early stages to think the case through	The responsibility was the officer's and we (managers and consultants) had better not question his judgment. He is highly skillful; therefore, (1) he will realize when the case is not progressing and blow the whistle and (2) he knows how to deal with difficult clients.

If	*Then*
There were too many chiefs and not enough Indians	The managers did not act as if they had the capacity to be simultaneously managers and effective case team members.
Each participant acted as an individual contributor	Good team members need only to make their individual contributions. It is the vice-president's responsibility to generate and maintain effective team interdependence.
We had too many meetings with the clients	The vice-president must have known what he was doing by inviting the client to our meetings; we had better acquiesce.
The team lacked a vice-president who could act vice-presidential	The vice-president was responsible for creating a gap that could not be filled by others.

These second-level factors fall into three categories:

1. Gaps in judgment. For example, the vice-president erred in not allocating more time to early case team meetings and in inviting clients to meetings.
2. Self-imposed limitations embedded in members' actions. For example, Manager 3 did not exercise leadership; no one integrated the individual contributions into a whole until the end.
3. Unforeseen actions counterproductive to team's effectiveness. An example is the vice-president's withdrawal.

We now see that we have two levels of factors operating to cause the poor team performance. The first and more manifest factors—that is, those closer to the surface—are the ones the case team identified. The second and more latent factors—those below the surface—are those inferred from the reasoning processes that led to the first factors.

The two levels of factors give significantly different targets for change. Moreover, if the second level causes the first, then correction of the first level is no guarantee that the second will not continue to exist and create difficulties in another situation. To complicate matters, the first-level factors can be used to avoid examining the second-level factors. Therefore, there must be a tacit consensus, or group-think, operating among the team members of which they are unaware. What could cause their tacit consensus, and why the unawareness?

The Primary Recommendation. To answer the question, let us turn to the primary recommendation made by the case team members. Embedded in the recommendation is the change target that the members agree on—and in their agreement is our first clue.

The overwhelming consensus was for a chief who could be tough and forthright and could exhibit take-charge leadership. This consensus continued even after the team members read a draft of the transcript. For example, the vice-president said, "Looking backwards in order to deal with the future, I think that I would get mad at these guys sooner," and "I could have endorsed [Manager 3] more directly, but he is a senior and respected manager [and so] I did not believe that he needed the mantle."

Their target, therefore, is to create a clear chain of command under someone who is able to coordinate and give orders and to whom the team members can communicate their views. Unilateral power in the hands of a case team leader is the recommended solution.

This recommendation, however, has limited effectiveness. Holding meetings to set the objectives of the case and holding meetings without the client present could not be achieved solely by the appointment of a chief. But the major requirement is that the chief sense, and/or the team members tell him, that such action is necessary.

Now, the vice-president might have been willing to take such action if he had been so advised by the case team members, although he expressed doubts about the advisability of excluding clients. One could add further reservations about the team's recommendation: Appointing a chief may not solve the problem if the chief makes errors but is not particularly confrontable. His effectiveness could be seriously compromised in a team where the trust level is low. Appointing a chief, therefore, is no guarantee that problems will be solved in such a way that they remain solved.

A chief does assure, however, that team members do not have to focus on the errors in their own actions and reasoning processes.

For example, the team members could have communicated upward information about the factors that were harming the team's effectiveness; they could have explored the reasoning processes that led them to place the responsibility elsewhere; they could have explored the implications of their lack of initiative. They could have done this and more, but they did not, because in their minds their actions were not errors and their reasoning was not faulty. They sincerely believed that what they did was in the interest of the organization. (The analysis that follows will partially support this belief.) Hence, we have a paradox: Actions that are in support of the organization necessarily also harm it.

But how was this paradox created? Who is responsible for such conditions?

Several individual and organizational factors combine to cause the problem. The professionals have developed a strategy to protect themselves from pressure and from feelings of failure, a strategy *distancing* them from any responsibility for the internal system of the organization. For example:

Team Members' Actions	*Features of Distancing*
1. Identified factors that inhibited the team's effectiveness and chose (a) to act as if they did not see them and (b) to hide the act of hiding. There were a cover-up and a cover-up of the cover-up.	Individuals distanced themselves from their personal causal responsibility for both the cover-up and the cover-up of the cover-up.

2. Chose not to go public with the cover-up when the VP requested that they do so in the interests of individual and organizational learning.
 	
     They also chose not to go public about the cover-up of their cover-up.
	Team members distanced themselves from cover-up responsibility by holding the VP responsible for breaking the cover.
	
	     And they distanced themselves from any responsibility for continuing the cover-up of their cover-up.

3. Chose to focus on the manifest (surface) factors and to continue to suppress the latent (depth) factors.	Members distanced themselves from their decision to hide the latent factors and focus on the causal, manifest factors. They

Team Members' Actions	*Features of Distancing*
The surface factors could be altered by creating organizational rules that would reduce case team effectiveness.	also chose to hide the personal responsibility embedded in the latent factors.

The professionals report a high degree of pressure and tension related to client relationships. They accept these pressures as legitimate; however, there is a limit to how much pressure they can absorb. Hence, they habitually distance themselves from what they call "unnecessary and illegitimate pressures." Issues related to administration are viewed as unnecessary and illegitimate in the sense that they take too much time or get mired in long, tedious meetings. This kind of thinking evolves from the same reasoning processes that the team members used in this case.

What led the vice-president to make errors in judgment? One reason was that he had taken on too many assignments and was absent more than he should have been. But no one told the vice-president that the team needed him or why. Perhaps team members were afraid to communicate upward, being apprehensive about his reaction. However, this vice-president is one of the officers most concerned about human relationships. Indeed, the very act of holding such a meeting and opening up his own actions to inquiry illustrates his interest in personal and organizational learning. (Although such apprehension happened not to be a problem in this situation, I learned from subordinates that they would be careful in communicating upward with certain officers. Such information runs counter to the advice that a chief in unilateral control will solve the problem.)

Whenever people spontaneously act in a particular way—for example, withholding their views about the effective operation of the team—and later cannot explain their actions to their own satisfaction, it usually indicates that their actions are tacit and automatic. Tacit, automatic actions are usually actions learned long before entering the firm or, once in the firm, through the firm's own socialization process. Let us explore each of these possibilities briefly.

A little over a year before this case performance analysis, all the team members had participated in a seminar in which they wrote an X and Y case. All their cases were judged by the interventionist to be Model I. Several disagreed with this judgment, but after nearly four hours of discussion, all agreed that their cases represented Model I theories-in-use. An analysis of the tapes of the discussion indicated that most of the comments made represented attributions and evaluations, advocacy/no inquiry, self-fulfilling prophecies, self-sealing processes, and escalating error. Thus, when these persons were faced with judging and evaluating Y and then themselves (because of their disagreement), they created dynamics that were counterproductive to double-loop learning. Telling a vice-president that he may be erring, evaluating someone's withdrawal from team management, or judging a manager as not taking charge is precisely the kind of action that uses those Model I skills that lead to misunderstandings and escalating error, which not only take up valuable time and energy but can threaten the team's functioning.

What encourages such actions and reasoning processes is the Model I theories-in-use learned by the members long before they entered the firm.

Another set of factors is related to the company's socializing process. A clue to that process can be found in the transcripts. The consultants and managers believed that the responsibility of an effective member is to produce a high-quality product and to do it autonomously from the other members. An effective member, therefore, is an individual contributor. The corollary of this belief is that someone else—a chief—should be responsible for managing the team. Incorporated in these two beliefs is the idea that an effective team member is an autonomous chief for getting his or her technical job done and a dependent Indian for issues related to team effectiveness. This compartmentalization is dangerous to producing an effective team and client service, especially if a case cannot be easily decomposed so that the technical pieces can be produced by consultants acting autonomously. It also is dangerous in that it creates a gap between client and consultant.

Distancing will be especially counterproductive whenever it is hard to obtain client understanding of, and internal commitment to, the case team's recommendations. Distancing by the professionals will lead to distancing by the clients. Distancing may be less counterproductive (in the short run) when the client is a skilled strategic planning group that prefers to keep outside consultants at a distance or if the client is a senior line executive who intends to use the recommendations to accomplish things unilaterally that he believes his subordinates will resist. (In those circumstances, outside consultants usually find it difficult to get the data they need.)

Where does the predisposition for distancing come from? I believe that the professionals enter the firm with it and it is then reinforced by the internal culture of the firm. First, recall that an overwhelming number of consultants are people with very high aspirations for success and a high fear of failure coupled with a low degree of skill in dealing with failure. Their poor skills in dealing with failure are explained by the fact that the firm hires primarily from the top 5 percent of the top universities in the United States and abroad. Hence, these people have not had much experience with failure. Moreover, most of their university success came from working autonomously and producing high-quality individual products, such as term papers and examinations.

Second, the firm's recruiting procedures make it clear that people are being hired primarily for their proven ability to participate as individual contributors. And consultants enter the firm with just that intention. This fits with their success/fear-of-failure syndrome because these conditions are highly congruent with those under which they have succeeded to date.

Third, the financial rewards encourage this mentality.

Fourth, the participants at all levels lack skills in interpersonal relationship and team building.

Fifth, team building requires time and commitment; time is rarely budgeted for it, and commitment is low for reasons just described.

Hence, we have a pattern of factors that result in the professionals' feeling responsible when they are making individual technical contributions but not when dealing with team problems.

The notion of a "take charge" chief now takes on a meaning over and above the expectation that he will solve the problem. An added meaning is that a chief makes it unnecessary for the professionals to examine their automatic skilled reaction of distancing themselves from the client and from team responsibility. To the extent that the chief succeeds in this task, it becomes unnecessary to examine the firm's internal culture to identify how it encourages and rewards distancing (through reward systems and the like). The "take charge" chief is in charge of producing high-quality client service *and* of protecting the professionals from having to examine the consequences of these distancing forces.

There is another problem that is driven underground. If the consultants and managers knew that they were withholding information about the team's effectiveness, they also knew that they were violating the rules by facilitating poor customer service. How do people who value their integrity (and these people certainly do) deal with the fact that they are violating their values? One answer is "By believing they have to in order to honor a higher value." For example, they may believe that the team would be pulled apart and the customer service worse if they communicated their views. Hence, they may come to believe that they are violating their values for the sake of the organization and that being committed to the organization would mean that they place themselves in continual internal conflict.

One way to deal with this dilemma is to minimize interdependence. Members will then emphasize carving out a role on the team where they can work as individual contributors whose product can be integrated by the superior into a whole. So dealing with the problem by appointing a strong leader, and making many of the attributions undiscussable, leads the members to conceive of an ideal case team relationship as one in which they distance themselves from concern about the health of the case team as a team. At the same time, clients become the all-important focus; internal administrative matters become second-class issues.

Finally, such a context leads the participants to use Model I reasoning, such as creating premises about individuals or groups that are untested attributions, acting as if the premises were valid and did not require public testing, and building a self-reinforcing network of premises (for example, too many chiefs makes productive meetings unlikely, and this reinforces the factor of too many chiefs), inventing solutions that do not require them to explore these features openly, and inventing solutions that remain within the boundaries of Model I and O-I learning systems. When these reasoning processes are used, they necessarily set the stage for interpersonal difficulties. For example, making untested attributions about others will quickly lead to misunderstandings. If the attributions are valid, they may lead to defensiveness. To compound these results with self-reinforcing reasoning can lead to noncorrective, self-sealing processes—and worse, this is the type of causal factor that is undiscussable.

So we have a pattern of self-reinforcing factors which make it unlikely that the case team will go very deeply into double-loop case team issues, and which may also make it harder to introduce new concepts of team membership and role. For example, some of the practices the team members considered unacceptable were being used in another client situation to develop a closer relationship between case team and client team. The vice-president believes that future business will require larger case teams that will include several managers. But if the case team members are committed to a diagnosis that evaluates enlarging the team as counterproductive, then they may resist it or find it difficult to implement. And given the process of distancing, they will tend to hold their superiors responsible for implementing such practices.

Organizational Consequences of Distancing. The heavy activity in a consulting firm is in client work. This usually means participation in case teams. If the participants are embedded in the individual and group dynamics I have described, these dynamics become standard features of the organization in two ways. First, their very frequency and potency make them a central part of everybody's life in the living system of the organization. Second, these dynamics are carried from the case team setting to other group settings within the firm. Thus, people come to believe that responsible membership in the firm consists in producing first-class technical work for the client while distancing themselves from the problems of the internal system. They may decide that what the system requires is a chief to whom they can delegate these problems.

Office administrators in such firms can testify that their greatest dilemma lies in being charged with internal system cohesion by people who largely have distanced themselves from responsibility for it and who will not cooperate in maintaining it. If the firm is a partnership, and the office administrator cannot take unilateral action on important issues, he is forced to initiate cumbersome committee studies and to build a constituency that eventually will produce recommendations which he hopes the full partnership will accept. All this takes time, if only because the professionals spend most of their time with clients.

To make matters more difficult, the committee and partnership meetings will not be as effective as the attendees wish, primarily because they lack responsibility for building and maintaining groups (as did the case team members). This lack of responsibility and their practice of distancing themselves make it unlikely that they will have the skills required for effective committee and partnership meetings. To the extent that meetings are unsatisfactory, the members may reduce their private frustration by scheduling important client meetings on the days long before reserved for administrative issues. The resulting poor attendance not only frustrates those attending (those absent may later object or lack commitment), but it definitely frustrates the office administrator, who is concerned about internal commitment to the new rules.

So far I have described the situation as if most of the professionals fully distanced themselves from internal administrative matters. However, that is not the case. This firm, for example, includes officers and managers who are centrally concerned about such matters as career development, team effectiveness, and levels of trust and cooperation. These persons, interestingly enough, are often identified by those who have chosen to distance themselves as "liberals" and "overly concerned." Such critics argue that the liberals are too concerned about internal management and overprotect the younger consultants. These senior people say they seldom encounter the problems that the liberals keep talking about, but what they don't see is that the younger people realize that the senior people have distanced themselves from such problems and consequently do not discuss these issues with them. Moreover, whenever any of these senior people becomes difficult to work with, the younger professionals frequently react by expressing their frustration to someone else, whom they swear to secrecy. For example, they may decide to talk to the office administrator. In that case, the administrator is caught in a bind because he is being drawn into a secrecy that turns the information into gossip or worse and makes it unlikely that it will be used constructively. Soon the liberals feel that they are taking more than their share of responsibility for the human problems, that those who have distanced themselves from these problems are not fulfilling their responsibility. The office administrator is again in a bind because he would prefer to staff the committee with receptive people but he realizes these are the people who are already overburdened.

We have now come full circle to the individual reasoning processes described at the outset of this analysis. Recall that we identified manifest and latent factors. We can now see that the manifest factors are those that the individual/organizational syndrome of distancing permits to surface. The latent factors are those that, if surfaced, would call into question the extensive individual/organizational self-protective mechanisms.

We can now begin to see the paradox—namely, that actions that protect the system also harm it. The manifested reasoning and actions maintain the distancing syndrome. The distancing syndrome continues a particular set of organizational self-protective features and ensures that only certain skills will be rewarded. If the equilibrium of these factors is upset, the pressures on individuals and the internal system will increase. Because the distancing syndrome blocks consideration of the latent factors, they will continue to operate covertly to slowly but surely pollute the internal system with increasing tensions and pressures. Eventually, pollution will reach a saturation point so that even small increases seem to upset individuals and the organization. The protective mechanism of distancing will no longer protect individuals because now every little bit hurts.

The consequence may be legitimized distancing, which teaches people (1) to ignore that kind of reflection on their reasoning processes that will lead them to see the personal and organizational costs of distancing, (2) to press for organizational rules to overcome the superficial causes of ineffectiveness and, hence, (3) to make the firm more rule-driven, which (4) reduces the very autonomy that individuals seek to protect while it (5) increases involvement in administering and monitoring rules, which (6) frustrates people who prefer to focus on client demands and (7) distresses those who foresee that the new pressures and client pressures combined may make life unbearable.

A second-order feature of distancing is that people feel they must preserve themselves for client (and perhaps family) demands and are therefore justified in delegating pressures related to internal affairs of the firm to administrators. The firm must make a compelling case to obtain their involvement in administrative matters.

This results in yet another dilemma. The professionals "save" themselves for firm work by distancing themselves from dealing with the internal factors that are key to the organization's and their team's effectiveness. Consequently, the firm becomes increasingly rule-driven, which requires more administrative attention, precisely the attention that is hardest to obtain.

A third-order consequence is that people develop internal commitment to client work but only external commitment to the internal system of the firm. They will work hard to produce first-class client service. They will feel frustrated to furious with any internal factors that inhibit their client effectiveness.

Under these conditions, professionals who reject the distancing will feel unjustly overworked, underappreciated, and used by others who have distanced themselves but still receive high or higher financial rewards. It is the concerned professionals who find themselves in the awkward position of either resisting rules that cover up individual distancing or violating the rules that make distancing undiscussable.

Ironically, the professionals who see the danger of distancing also sense the importance of firmwide innovation. If they produce innovations, others may object; if they withhold new ideas, they are violating their own sense of responsibility. One way for them to deal with this double bind is to do what the more distanced professionals do—work hard with clients and give minimal attention to innovation.

Summary

When people are faced with double-loop problems in everyday settings and in classroom settings, they tend to act in ways that lead to escalation of error, double binds for self and others, undiscussability of both, and undiscussability of what is undiscussable and, hence, to act as if nothing were undiscussable.

There are three sets of causal factors for these counterproductive trends. First is the reasoning processes that people use to diagnose and take action. They tend to create and use incorrect and/or abstract premises that they believe are correct and concrete. They then reason correctly from incorrect premises, arriving at conclusions that are wrong. Because the premises are assumed to be correct, and because the inference processes of moving from premises to conclusions actually *are* correct, and because the premises and conclusions are seen as correct and concrete, the person tends to be unaware of the errors.

Second is the Model I theory-in-use that predisposes people to enact a world congruent with governing values of unilateral control, winning and not losing, suppression of negative feelings, and focusing on the rational aspect. Such a predisposition makes it highly likely that premises will contain error and that people will not be predisposed to test for error lest they lose control, express negative feelings, and so on.

Another important feature of a theory-in-use is the extent to which it permits self-reflection in order to detect and correct error. This feature is related to the face-saving strategies that people develop to protect their reasoning processes, their sense of being in control, and their capacity to produce intended consequences.

The third causal factor is the O-I learning system that reinforces a Model I theory-in-use. It provides societal support for people to reason and act in ways that have counterproductive consequences when they deal with each other, whether as individuals, groups, or formal organizations.

People dealing with double-loop problems will continually be embedded in situations that (1) are complex and contain influences from many levels of life, such as individual, group, intergroup, and organizational; (2) are dangerous to others because it is possible to upset people, harm relationships, and open up such a Pandora's box that the consequences (a) are dangerous to one's self—if I try to be candid, I may be evaluated as a nut (or a hopeless romantic); if I suppress my feelings and views, I may feel dishonest and irresponsible; (b) are dangerous to society because questioning the Model O-I learning system shakes the very foundations of social order; and finally, (c) are dangerous to all in that nonresolution of these double-loop difficulties will escalate self-pollution and the societally protective deceptions that make it even more difficult to enact double-loop solutions.

No wonder our primary response is to translate double-loop problems into single-loop ones—at least this provides a sense of being in control. But notice that this control is bought at increasing direct costs (for example, higher wages, benefits) and higher second-order costs (reinforcement of the factors that cause these problems in the first place).

Another evading approach is to distance one's self from having to deal with double-loop issues. People can use their reasoning processes in such a way as to be unaware of or to ignore these problems while holding to the belief that "you can't change human nature or organizations." Distancing one's self from responsible action now becomes an act of responsibility to the world. Concern for society now legitimizes the defensive social features that reinforce and protect the very factors that cause destructive social problems. Self-concern follows the same pattern. Individuals distance themselves from themselves in order to survive in a society where such distancing produces experiences of injustice and incompetence. Distancing requires a disconnectedness from one's own reasoning processes, a state that has heavy implications for the health and effectiveness of both the individual and the system.

7

Intervening
to Interrupt
Distancing

In this chapter, we learn more about distancing by interrupting it while it is actually occurring.

Case F

This case team meeting began with Nick (the officer) asking Harvey (the case leader) how he would prefer to begin. Harvey replied that he would like Don (consultant) to present his analysis of the client's cost system. As Don was preparing the transparencies, Harvey said that essentially the team saw three key issues to the case, one of which was the cost system.

The next 45 minutes was taken up with Don's presentation. He identified many inconsistencies and gaps in the client's cost system, believing that this was an important contribution to the case. It could also be a base from which to build other useful analyses.

The primary dialogue during the presentation was between

Nick and Don. At first, Nick asked questions for clarification. Although the overt message of the questions was one of seeking clarity, it appeared to me, the interventionist, that Nick was also indirectly communicating doubts about the usefulness of the cost analysis to the client. He asked questions that, if answered correctly by Don, would lead Don to realize Nick's doubts (the easing-in approach).

If Don sensed that Nick was easing into such communication, he did not act as if he did. He took the overt message in each question seriously and answered it as forthrightly as he could. Since he was in command of his analysis, he was able to respond to the overt technical inquiries promptly and fully. His success at this led Nick to feel increasingly frustrated because his left-hand-column concerns were not being dealt with.

About 50 minutes after the meeting began, Nick left the room with the comment "I'll be right back." Don continued his presentation to the rest of the team. Nick returned in two or three minutes. As he went toward his chair, he asked, "What are you planning to do with this stuff? How do you plan to use it?" Don responded that he wanted to show the clients that their cost system was full of inconsistencies and errors.

Nick: I don't know what to say. [Even if you proved their cost system is no good, I'm not sure where you go from there.]

Harvey: [If we can make the case that their cost system is bad, it could be powerful.]

Nick: OK, what would it take to make the case? What kind of effort would it require?

Don: [Describes that it would take three or four weeks.]

Nick: That sounds reasonable. I don't see that you can make much of a case for this unless you can get evidence that the client can alter the market. The client could argue that their cost system is adequate. But even if it were not, we would not have given them much help unless we can show how they can influence the market, based on the correct cost figures.

For the first time, Nick makes public some of the evaluations in his diagnostic frame. He believes the cost analysis will take too much time and effort, it may not be worth the cost to the client, and some other key issues are being ignored.

It appeared to the interventionist that Nick's comments focused on his concern about service to the client. But if his concern was valid, then he must, by definition, be concerned about the way Harvey and the team were thinking about the project. Why weren't they as concerned as he was? Were they aware?

Nick did not make this feature of the evaluation explicit; yet it was the key to his confidence in the team and to the probability that the team would produce a useful product. Why didn't Nick state his position more explicitly, even issue an invitation to challenge it? Nick's response was that he was trying to say that to the team, but he did not find it easy because he did not want to upset the team and harm its effectiveness.

But the attribution that their effectiveness would be harmed was never tested. Indeed, it assumed a further attribution, that some or all members of the team were so brittle that they could not be openly and directly challenged. However, this attribution was tested by Don's behavior and later by Nick himself (on Harvey). The responses of Harvey and Don indicated a considerable openness to learning, a willingness to be confronted.

Interventionist: Could I interrupt? Am I correct in believing that you are concerned about two things? One is the possible low yield of the approach in analyzing costs. The other is the way this group is thinking about the whole problem.

Nick: Yes.

Int.: Could you [Harvey] say what you believe he [Nick] has been saying to you during this meeting?

Harvey: He has doubts about this part of the analysis. It'll require going through two thirds of a lengthy analysis before we know if we have anything.

Nick: Yes, I'm also worried about whether, if you do this, when will you have the time to do that other stuff which is also murky [that is, industry profitability and so on]?

Int.: [To Nick] I don't know to what extent you think that they are taking a wrong path and you do not wish to upset them and to what extent you don't know [whether it is the wrong path] and you're caught.

Nick: The answer is that I don't know for sure [but I am equally sure that what they are doing probably has a low payoff for the client].

Int.: And you do know that they don't know either of these views.

and that's scary. If the only answer you get from them is that they are ready to run time-consuming analyses, then that's not helpful.

Also, it is not comforting to learn that one reason they are performing these costly analyses is that they will be needed sometime in the future.

Nick: Yes, and I'm not sure of that. We must return to that.

Here the interventionist introduced another possible source of Nick's concern. It is scary to have the kind of difficult, ambiguous client problem indicated in this case. It is doubly scary to sense that the team may not be aware of the low payoff of its present approach and hence may not have the client's real needs in mind. It may be triply scary if Nick attributes a brittleness to the team that makes it difficult for him to give his views.

It was important for Nick to state his views, for only then did he find out that the team could deal with such issues directly and forthrightly. Indeed, as we shall see, Nick was unknowingly setting the stage for a self-fulfilling prophecy, because the team sensed the covert, indirect message and was keeping that awareness covert lest they violate what they inferred to be the officer's rule, "Keep covert information covert."

Int.: As I hear it, Nick is asking you [team members] where you are going with this analysis, and you're responding, "We're not sure, but we need the data." Your response is not answering his concern.

Harvey: I'm thinking there are three parts to this problem [enumerates them]. They're all tied together.

Nick: Yes.

Harvey: My feeling is that I'm not real uncomfortable about being able to come up with a description of the leverage thing.

Nick: [Interrupting] OK, but I'm not sure I understand what that means . . . let's come back to that.

Harvey: The cost stuff . . . uh . . . uh-ev—I'm fairly certain that there will be something of value. The other stuff, [I'm not sure].

Nick: How does [such-and-such] differ from the issue of leverage? [Appears to doubt that there are any differences.]

Harvey: [It is important to ask how important scale utilization is. Theoretically, it should have been connected to . . .]

Note that Harvey's responses are at relatively high levels of abstraction. For example, he does "not" feel "uncomfortable"; he is "fairly certain." The fact that he is not uncomfortable or that he is only fairly certain is not adequate information to reduce Nick's concern.

Next, Nick candidly revealed what his thoughts and feelings were during the first 50 minutes of the meeting. He was straightforward and evaluative, expressing feelings and concern about the team members; yet his tone of voice communicated—as mentioned later by Harvey and Irving—that he was confrontable. In fact, Nick noted that they might neither agree with nor like what he was saying and openly invited them to respond.

Nick: I've got to tell you that you guys jangled my nerves by saying at the outset that there were three things that were important [cites them]. Then you [Don] got up and said that all we've done is to explore the validity of the cost system and that is incomplete, and that is all we've done because you can't do anything before you've done the analysis of the cost system.

Well, I could have said "Holy shit!" right there. I don't fully believe it. And furthermore, my immediate reaction to that was "Christ, all really important conceptual stuff and the real understanding of this thing, nothing has happened—all we have done is play around with the cost system."

At that point, you're going to have to convince me that we must understand the cost system [which you have not done], or I have some concern about the shape this thing is taking.

What it seems like to me [pause] . . . you may not like this, it may be negative to you, but let me say it anyway and you come back at me . . . but let me say it this way: You're working on the most detailed, and in some respects the least powerful, analysis first, and putting off the stuff that really explains how the business works.

Now that's what I was thinking and feeling while I sat here for about an hour. That's probably not a fair assessment of what was going on, but I still feel uncomfortable.

Int.: One more interruption? The message that you just revealed, which you said may be heard by them as unfair, I heard that at least half an hour ago [in other words, I believe you have been communicating what you believe you have been withholding].

[Harvey, Irving, and Don nod to confirm this.]

Nick: I don't know about hiding it. On the other hand, I wasn't very explicit about it.

Int.: Have you heard the message [that I suggested Nick communicated]?

Harvey: Yes.

Irving: Nick doesn't hide things.

Int.: I believe that Nick is trying to be supportive and helpful. But [as in all easing-in approaches] there may be undesirable consequences. I believe it would have been more effective to say to the group at the outset what rankled you during the first five minutes.

Harvey: [Nick didn't hide this, because] he wrote a memo to me telling me he was anxious.

Int.: Then, may I ask you something? As I saw the meeting, you [Harvey] began by describing the possible errors in the cost system which you believe would help Nick learn more about the client's problem. What I do not understand is your reasoning for organizing the presentation this way. . . . And if you knew that Nick was anxious, what was the reasoning that led you to the conclusion that this was the way to deal with his questions?

Nick: I might have asked that question if you had begun with those curves [that were presented near the end of the talk] and organized the problem in this way. I had the feeling most of the time that I didn't know where this was going to come out.

Harvey: I think that is right. Our presentation was structured around "Let us tell you what we have been doing." [As I see it now], this historical perspective is an easy way to do it but not as helpful to the listener. What we really need to do is to get in contact with the listener's thought processes. It would have been helpful for us to [describes what he might have done].

Nick: [Interrupting] Excuse me, but the other thing is that I think I understand a hell of a lot about what goes on [with our clients], and if you show me an outcome, I could guess the kind of analysis you went through.

Harvey: I'm sure if we had started at the end, you would have asked questions about our analysis.

Nick: I'm not sure. I might have, because of my skepticism.

Int.: I would like to add that Nick's request to start with the end result and then work backward if it is necessary is also a typical request of clients. Telling them where you are heading appears to reduce this anxiety, perhaps because it gives them a way to frame the analysis that you are presenting. If they don't believe you, then they can say so and you can dig into the analysis, but it is now at their request. So this is not only relevant for Nick but for clients.

Harvey: Yes, I agree. It would have been better for us to have this material up front.

Int.: I saw Nick as easing in; Harvey as not sensing or reacting to the easing-in; Harvey not having reached out to deal with the officers' anxieties. Harvey did not begin by recalling the memo, Nick's anxieties, and saying how he would respond to them during the meeting.

Harvey: What I could have done was start by saying what we intended to do. . . .

[Later]

Int.: It seems to me that Nick is saying everything you did enhanced rather than alleviated his doubts.

With this intervention, I wanted to explore Harvey's reasoning processes. Harvey and Don had a memorandum from Nick expressing his doubts. If we assume that they did not knowingly design the session to compound Nick's anxieties, then either Harvey had the erroneous idea that the cost-system issue would allay Nick's reactions or Harvey was blind to the impact he and his team were having on Nick (a blindness that Nick initially reinforced through his easing-in response).

Nick: We really could have started the discussion with what the client says about [that] because that will get at [this view of their business]. The cost stuff is primarily mechanical, which I'm sure that Don and you can deal with.

I don't know—why did you think that I needed to hear that stuff?

Don: I thought you might like to get at [certain assumptions].

Int.: I am recommending that you begin with the memo Nick has sent you. You could have said, in effect, "This is my plan of action and this is how I propose to deal with the questions raised in your memo." Does this make sense to you?

Harvey: Yes, I knew he was dissatisfied. I knew through the memo that he was skeptical. One of the things that we wanted to do was to convince Nick that this was a proper area to spend time and budget.

Int.: And what led you not to start out by making that explicit?

Harvey: I thought that we did that.

Int.: [Gives examples of Harvey's behavior at the outset], and from that I inferred that you did not wish to talk about differences in view regarding the use of team time and expense.

Harvey: I can see that one problem was that I did not address Nick's problems up front or at least tell him that I was aware of them and planned to address them. If I had done this, and Don started, then it would have allowed Nick to jump in and say, "You told me that you were going to answer my concerns. I do not see what is now being said that does that."

Int.: Yes.

Harvey: I can see even the formulating helps. I could say, "We're going to show you some stuff. I'm aware that you're going to be skeptical, but we think we've got a presentation to change your minds."

Int.: Yes, that advocates your position and invites confrontation.

Irving: It puts something on the table that was under the table.

Harvey: That's very helpful. I've got to treat him as a client. [I should add that] I didn't sense his impatience as I should have.

Reflections on Nick's Case Team

We now know that, after five minutes into the 45-minute presentation, Nick believed that the cost analysis was technically competent but misguided because (1) the client could argue many of the technical points; (2) the payoff in potential profitability was low. Yet, Nick's actions—that is, asking questions about the technical features of the analysis—did not match his belief. Further, the team members believed that Nick was not happy about the cost analysis and that Nick's judgment was misguided and could be corrected by presenting as elegant and compelling cost analyses as possible. Thus, they acted by making as detailed and thorough analyses of the cost system as possible and responding as competently as they could on the technical issues Nick raised.

The probable first-order consequences are, first, that Nick will feel increasingly frustrated because he is having difficulty getting the team to see what he believes to be its underlying error—namely, poor framing of the problem—and the team members will continue to provide support for their technical analysis but will be increasingly aware that Nick is not satisfied. Second, Nick will suppress his feelings in order to create a constructive climate for inquiry with the hope that the team will see the light, and the team members will suppress their feelings of bewilderment in order to create a constructive climate for inquiry with the hope that Nick will see the light.

The probable second-order consequences are that Nick's frustration will be reinforced and the team's bewilderment about how to reach Nick will increase.

So far we have a communicative process that is providing feedback that is not corrective. Technically speaking, the feedback is positive and hence could lead to escalating error.

To compound the problem, Nick may feel that the team is not as competent as he thought, or the team is competent but too busy on other cases to do a good job on his case. Either of these diagnoses would be as difficult to communicate to the team members as the original one (that their analysis was misguided). Nick now has created conditions for himself that may lead him to infer: "The team members will not correct this error because they do not see that the framing is wrong (because I am withholding a direct statement that the framing is wrong, because I want to create conditions for learning and cooperation)." A similar dynamic operates among the team members: They may feel that Nick is uneasy but is not saying so. Their diagnosis of Nick would be difficult to communicate because they would be violating the rule Nick has selected—namely, to keep his uneasiness undiscussable. The team members have now created conditions for themselves that may lead them to infer: "We will not be able to get Nick to correct his error of withholding his dissatisfaction (because we are withholding a direct statement that we believe Nick is withholding his views, because we want to create conditions for learning and cooperation)."

To compound the problem even further, Nick's withholding of his diagnoses implies either that Nick believes the team members are too brittle to confront or that he cannot communicate free from frustration and impatience. Thus, Nick is in a double bind. If he communicates directly what he thinks and feels, he believes it will upset the team. If he hides what he believes and eases into the problem, the team members will not get his message. Similarly, the team members' withholding of their diagnoses implies either that they believe Nick is too brittle to confront or that they cannot communicate free from bewilderment and frustration. Thus, the group members are in a double bind. If they communicate directly what they think and feel, they believe it will upset Nick. If they hide what they believe and think, Nick will never know their message.

We have observed several ways in which people deal with this problem. Usually those with power have the highest probability of making their strategies dominant. For example, Nick could—

Write a memo to the case team manager or otherwise communicate with him separately. Nick's strategy could range from easing in to being forthright. Empirically, we find that, in both written and spoken media, people tend to begin with easing in and gradually become more forthright.

Communicate to the team members that what they have produced so far is "very interesting," "shows they know how to make an analysis of a cost system," and so on, and that now he would "like to suggest an additional strategy."

Be more forthright and direct about his views and at the same time say, "I know this may upset you, but time is getting short and I must tell you what I think."

Tell them they are wrong and also tell them how to correct their errors.

Any of these alternatives could have been used during the meeting, thereby postponing action Nick considers undesirable. Presumably he can distance himself from a face-to-face discussion by writing a memo or temper the expected danger of speaking forthrightly about the issue by doing so only with the case team manager.

This means that whatever feelings of tension and frustration Nick had during the meeting, he will have to carry around with him and will rekindle during the meeting with the case team manager. It is my hunch that such feelings become excess emotional baggage and, depending on their intensity, can eventually exhaust the carrier.

The case team members, for their part, could continue to respond to Nick, pressing their views, until they hear Nick flatly tell them that they are wrong. They could then defend their position and/or react by asking for further information on what he would like them to do. They would, in all likelihood, withhold their feelings of frustration and anger, meaning they too must carry additional emotional baggage. Depending on how often such situations occur with Nick or other officers, the team members may conclude that the organization is unfair and uninfluenceable.

Additional Organizational Consequences

The team members may deal with these feelings by restricting their workload to cases they believe they can handle and by working with officers with whom they can work relatively effectively. The more often the consultants find themselves members of teams in difficulty, the more their tension will increase. It is unlikely that these tensions can be dissipated unless the consultants can influence the organization, especially the officers, to discuss the issues.

One way to do so is to talk with officers who are known to be sensitive and influenceable, even though these are not the officers who cause the problems. The consultants must hope that these "liberal" officers will communicate their views to the conservatives.

Note that we are now back to the conditions described in Chapter One. Recollect that the liberal officers did try to influence the conservative officers to be more concerned with morale and career development issues. The conservatives responded by agreeing to formation of a career development committee that would develop various policies, such as more frequent performance evaluations. Conservatives also volunteered to serve on the recruiting committee with the hope of solving all problems by hiring people with "the right attitudes and values." Creating the committee did have a positive effect because it showed that the firm cared. But many of the consultants reported they were "waiting to see" how well the new policies were implemented.

Part Two

Methods
for Producing
Effective Learning

8

Designing
Interventions
to Facilitate
Model II Learning

What have we learned so far that can be applied
to designing and implementing environments for learning Model II?
Two potential misunderstandings are hidden in this question and
should be dealt with at the outset.

First is the misunderstanding that the goal of learning Model II
implies that Model I is somehow bad or ineffective and should be
suppressed. On the contrary, Model I is the most appropriate theory-
in-use for routine, programmed activities or emergency situations
(such as rescuing survivors) that require prompt, unilateral action. We
must not forget that the strategy of all organizations is to decompose
double-loop problems into single-loop ones. The major part of everyday life in an organization is related to single-loop learning. Double-
loop learning is crucial, however, because it allows us to examine and
correct the way we are dealing with any issue and our underlying as-

sumptions about it. Therefore, Model II may be the appropriate theory-in-use for the nonroutine, nonprogrammed, difficult issues that cannot be solved unless we reexamine our underlying individual and organizational values and assumptions.

A second misunderstanding concerns the definition of *learning*. We are focusing on learning that includes, but goes beyond, discovery. We are interested in learning that leads to new action and new problem solving, which enable individuals and systems to continue to learn. One-process learning is not the goal.

Recall what happened to the participants trying to double-loop learn about X and Y. First, they had to *discover,* or evaluate, Y's effectiveness in the way he dealt with X. This was not an easy task, even though we made it simpler by providing them with only half a page of conversation. The next step was for them to *invent* a solution to correct the problem. They were then asked to *produce* the invention in the form of several pages of written conversation and to list any thoughts and feelings they might have that they would not communicate to Y. This material gave us the directly observable data from which to infer the participants' theory-in-use. The conversation could be used to infer the behavioral strategies related to advocacy. The "Thoughts and Feelings" (left-hand) column could be used to infer any self-censorship and hence face-saving strategies for self or others.

Finally, the interventionist encouraged evaluation of all actions, including his own, to assess the degree to which the actions designed (intended) were actually produced. This evaluation leads to discovery of new issues, and hence we have a cycle. The interventionist's design implied a learning process, as shown in Figure 3.

Figure 3. Learning Process

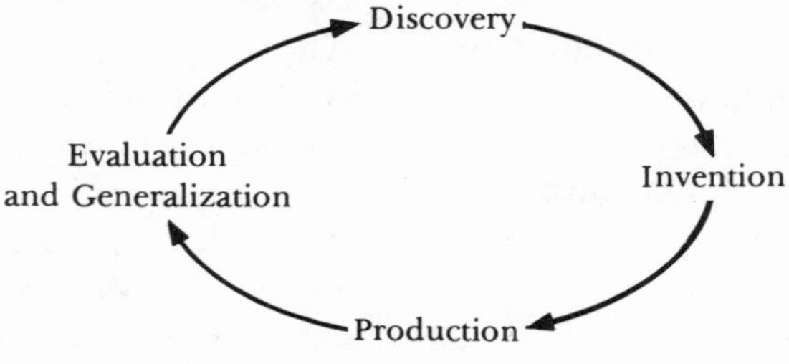

It is my assumption that this learning process used in the seminars is essentially the same learning process that people use in everyday life. Therefore, as the participants reflect on how they learn (that is, how they discover/invent/produce/evaluate/discover . . .), they will be learning how they would learn for any similar problem. The seminar focuses on helping people learn not only about dealing with Y effectively but about dealing effectively with all communication that is simultaneously important and threatening.

Ubiquitous Character of Models I and O-I

Donald Schön and I had difficulty accepting the finding that there was great variance in espoused theories and actions but almost no variance in theories-in-use. How could it be that everyone used Model I or the opposite of Model I? Surely, we thought, it must be our measuring instruments or the way we conceptualized the problem.

But by now the data appear overwhelming. We and others have given variants of the X-Y case to several thousand people. So far, almost all cases represent Model I theory-in-use, a conclusion confirmed by the case writers themselves. I have some speculations on how this situation came about. They are related to the nature of our information-processing capacities and our psychological processes for generating a sense of competence. I hope to explore these issues in a subsequent publication.

The point that the reader is asked to keep in mind is that there is variance—indeed, great variance—on rungs 1 and 2 of the ladder of inference. The variance practically disappears when we conceptualize the meanings embedded in the first two rungs into a theory. It may be that we have been fortunate in producing a theory that is generally applicable.

In any event, we expect most people who attend an X-Y seminar to be predisposed to create O-I learning environments and to resist Model II actions and O-II learning systems, even though they may value and espouse them. This incongruity does not mean that the participants are not credible or that they are confused. It is the very fact that they unknowingly tie up their sense of credibility with their competence that makes double-loop learning so difficult and so exciting.

People programmed with Model I theory-in-use are, as we have seen, unaware of their Model I-ness. They are usually blind to the counterproductive features of their actions whenever they are trying to double-loop learn or help others do so. This blindness exists mainly in the production of an action rather than in the consequences of an action. The blindness is designed, the result of a mental program that keeps people unaware of their Model I-ness. They are unaware of this program because it is highly skilled and hence tacit. They use it automatically. One reason they rarely reflect on it is that it is sanctioned by the culture. If the program fails, the predisposition is for the actor to blame someone else or to reduce the dissonance by saying, "That's life!"

People may be unaware of their Model I-ness and of the program that keeps them unaware, but they are not unaware of other people's Model I theory-in-use or of other people's blindness. This means that each of us will provide a great deal of data from which we ourselves and others can learn. It also means that other people will be crucial to our own learning.

Under these conditions, people who want to double-loop learn (1) do not know how to do so, (2) do not know that they do not know, (3) do not know that they have designs in their heads to ensure 1 and 2, and (4) do not know that they cannot learn to do so by using their present skills.

Unfreezing from Model I

As we have already seen, and as we will see in more detail in Chapter Twelve, learning about the ineffectiveness of their theories-in-use requires that people be helped to see that the actions they have considered competent and just are actually more incompetent and unjust than they ever thought those actions could be.

Figure 4 presents a model of the experiences that people go through in unfreezing their old theory-in-use in order to add (not substitute) a new one. We suggest that the longer people produce inconsistencies and unjust consequences and are unaware of why they are doing so (column 1), the more they will experience a decreasing confidence in their ability to act competently and an increasing sense of not being in control. As these consequences escalate, they will have increasing doubts about their ability to be in contact with reality (column 2). They will then feel varying degrees of vulnerability

Figure 4. The Unfreezing Process

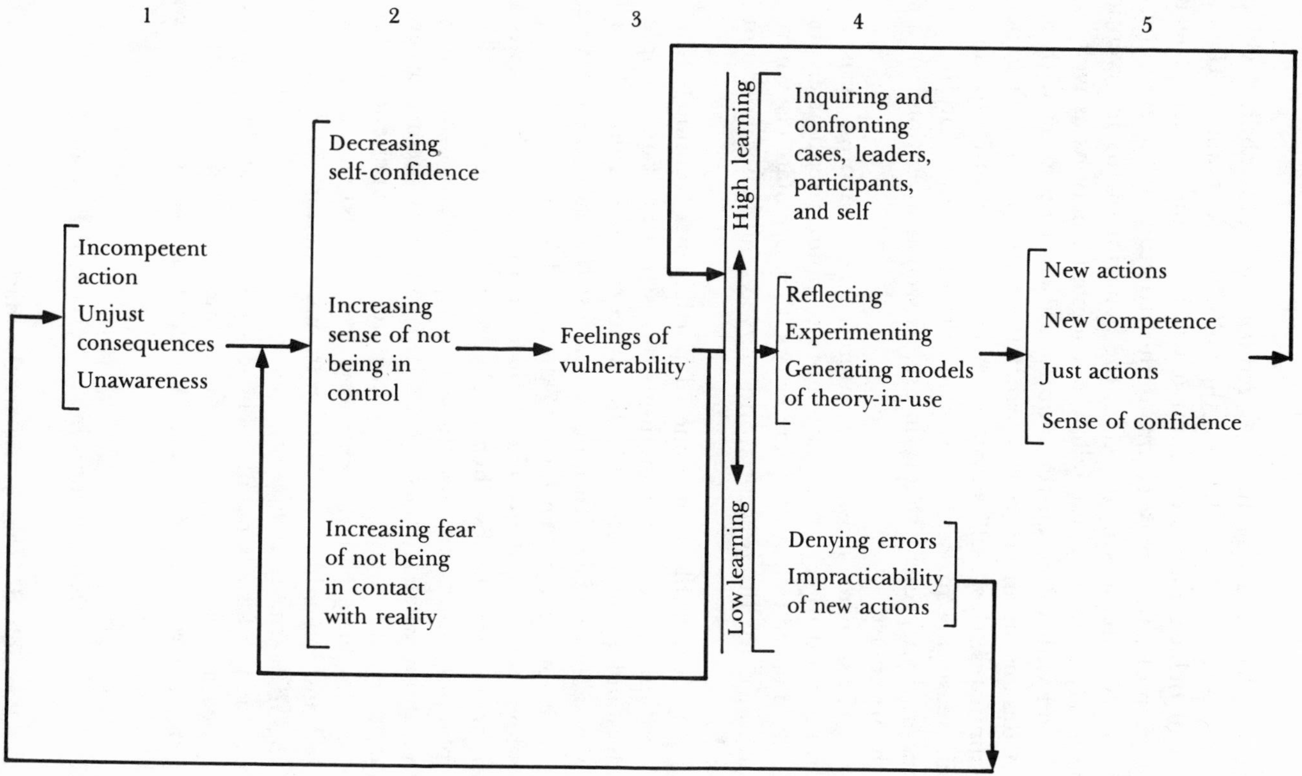

(column 3). Learning how to reduce the vulnerability will evoke varying interest, depending on the individual (column 4). High learners will behave defensively, but it will be in the service of learning. For example, they may confront the structure of the case, the validity of the sentences in the case, the behavior of the interventionist. They may also confront fellow participants' actions as well as their own and will follow up the inquiry and confrontation with new action designs in an effort to correct their errors. As their experience accumulates, they will reflect on their actions in order to understand their reasoning processes and will formulate rules for the propositions in their present theory-in-use, as well as inventions for a Model II theory-in-use.

Those who show little interest in, or express resistance to, learning tend to reject any attempts to point out their errors. They will emphasize that if there are errors, they originate elsewhere or are sanctioned by the present world anyway and hence need not be altered.

It is possible that some of participants' tension, failure, and frustration is due to our methods of instruction. For example, as we understand more thoroughly the processes of learning Model II, we may be able to design learning so it is less frustrating. We have experimented, for instance, with giving the X and Y case for shorter one- or two-hour sessions. Participants become intrigued, but few, if any, experience what is described in Figure 4. We have also noticed that, in planning interventions, these participants are significantly more naive about what it takes for a client to accept them than are those who have had the more extended learning experience. Moreover, those who have had the extended learning experience are less surprised and bewildered by the emotional reactions of others who are trying to learn, and they are therefore better able to deal with the frustrations of such people. Those who have had the extended experience appear to be better able to monitor their own actions and feelings and to manage them in ways that facilitate their own and others' learning.

Defensiveness in the Service of Learning

People's theories-in-use are the master programs by which they make sense of, and maintain some semblance of control over, their world. It makes sense for people to protect their theory-in-use by questioning the validity of any data or attributions that threaten it. Defensive actions serve learning when they lead to detection and correction of error. For example, a class member may deny that he created the same counterproductive conditions for Y that he asserted Y created for X. But if, after denying the assertion, he joins with others to publicly test the validity of his position, the defensiveness will facilitate learning. Or another student who asserts that the interventionist is wrong, or is manipulating, or is distorting, is acting in the service of learning if she is willing to publicly test the validity of these attributions.

People who protect themselves by denying the possible validity of the data and who refuse to create conditions in which to publicly test the validity of their denials are inhibiting the possibility of detecting and correcting error—that is, of learning. The refusal may come in the form of emotional outbursts ("I think this is unreal bull, and I see no way that it makes sense to continue this discussion!"). Or it may appear to be rational if the person makes assertions that neither he nor anyone else can confirm or disconfirm—for example, "I know plenty of Xs who would listen if . . ." or "If Y would handle X carefully, there would be no problem."

Let us call any defensive actions that facilitate learning, *Type A* defenses and any defensive actions that inhibit learning, *Type B* defenses. The interventionist should act to encourage Type A and discourage Type B. If Type B does occur, it should be respected though not necessarily agreed with. The person may be communicating that he does not want to be pushed further because public testing would be painful and upsetting. One might say, "I respect your rejection of these ideas, but I do want to note that your refusal to test your attributions makes it unlikely that I will know where you are correct and unlikely that you will know where you are incorrect."

Conditions That Facilitate Double-Loop Learning

What can the designers of learning environments do to facilitate double-loop learning?

1. Create conditions such that the data from which learning is to occur are at the first and second rungs of the ladder of inference. Observable data allow people to work to understand and confirm or disconfirm them. If people are provided with inferences based on the

leader's own theories-in-use, they are forced to accept those theories and to act as if they were true.

2. Use instruments that permit learners to design and produce relatively directly observable data (rung 1) and the culturally accepted meanings embedded in these data (rung 2). One such instrument is a tape recorder. Another is the X-Y case. A third is the X-Y format with the substance of the case designed by the participant. Another variant is for two or three persons to write about the same problem. For example, in one seminar a wife wrote a scenario about dealing with the loneliness she felt, and the husband wrote his version of how he would handle such a problem.

The interventionist can function in such a way as to facilitate the data gathering. For example, one could tape the actions of all the participants and ask questions that get at the automatic censoring that people do (for instance, "What is in your left-hand column at this moment?"). The interventionist can also help people reflect on the reasoning processes that led to their actions: "What led you to decide that the way to respond was to get angry at him?" or "What did she do that led you to decide that the way to reach her was to tell her she was all wrong?"

Whatever the instrument used, the person should be able to produce first- and second-rung data and meanings without being able to claim that the instrument induced or was biased toward such meanings. Second, whatever the instrument, it should produce data that are publicly testable and disconfirmable, without the challenger's having to accept any implicit or explicit theories of the interventionist's.

3. The interventionist should surface inconsistencies or incongruities step by step. Learning under conditions described in Figure 4 can easily trigger emotional tensions and an overload of information. It is helpful, therefore, if the counselor tests inconsistencies step by step. In the next two chapters, you will find examples of the interventionist asserting that he sees an inconsistency. He then acknowledges that his assertion is an attribution that requires testing. First he produces the directly observable data in order to test whether all relevant participants agree on the rung 1 meaning. He will do the same for rung 2 meanings. Then he will develop his inferences, making every step in the reasoning process (from premise to conclusion) as explicit and open to test as possible.

4. Communicate a respect for Type A or B defensive reactions whenever they occur. The interventionist's predisposition should be to seek to test any defensive reactions, his own or others'. Defensiveness does not necessarily mean resistance to learning. Type A defenses imply reluctance to accept a particular view *and* simultaneous willingness to make explicit the basis for the reluctance and to test the assumptions or attributions publicly.

5. Expect emotionality, beginning with bewilderment and frustration and leading to vulnerability, anger, and fear. The more effective the processes described in Figure 4 are, and the longer the participants are immersed in them, the more likely that they will feel threatened because almost nothing they thought was skillful appears to work. Moreover, the more people realize that they are unaware of why they produce counterproductive actions, the more frightening the learning experience is.

6. Empathize with the emotionality, but do not let it become an excuse for backing off. The counselor realizes that inherent in learning Model II is the paradox that experiencing failure (by realizing how little of what we do is effective) is also a sign of success. Chapter Eleven includes a transcript of a university seminar in which a frustrated student questions the sensitivity and motivation of the interventionist. She says that the students have been feeling "genuine confusion and frustration," and all the while "you have had a very big grin on your face"! The faculty member first empathizes with these feelings and then adds that the reason for his smile is that he is happy to observe people struggling to learn under very difficult conditions. In effect, most of the students were in a Type A defensive mode, and progress was being made.

Embedded in this approach are two assumptions about personal responsibility:

a. *You are responsible for the actions that create your feelings of threat and failure.*

The first requirement of a double-loop learning environment is to create conditions in which people can directly and unambiguously connect any feelings of threat and failure to their own theories-in-use and consequent actions. They are held responsible for their own discomfort. They are also encouraged to design ways to disconfirm that they are the cause of their own difficulties. It is assumed that (1) participants will challenge the idea that feelings of failure and threat are self-inflicted and (2) their acceptance of this fact is not adequate for bringing about change. In this process, they can be helped to make an informed choice about their personal responsibility. To the extent that they conclude they are responsible, they will be internally committed to redesigning their theories-in-use.

b. *You are responsible for your actions but are not responsible for the theory-in-use that leads to your actions.*

This statement appears to contradict the first assumption, but it does not. The first asserts that people programmed with Model I theories-in-use are responsible for the *actions* that lead to the sense of threat and failure described earlier. The second statement focuses on the fact that people did not choose the theory-in-use that guarantees that they will experience threat and failure. Models I and O-I are culturally taught, sanctioned, and maintained, creating a reality that includes threat, failure, and not being in control. If people are programmed for the possibility of failure, it is not because they made the wrong choice or because they are incompetent. They hold these master programs because they have been successfully socialized and continue to be so.

Understanding this paradox should help people see that their incompetence is not necessarily due to a lack of personal ability. Rather, their counterproductive actions result from highly skilled responses that are seen as competent by society and are common to all of us.

This means that, in order to learn Model II, people must set aside some very basic values and action strategies that are useful in routine, single-loop learning but counterproductive to Model II. It also means that extensive social change will not occur unless the culture and societal norms are altered so that people can learn both Models I and II, and O-II learning systems become culturally acceptable to the point of being integrated into everyday life.

Understanding this paradox should help people develop more realistic levels of aspiration as regards the speed and depth of learning. It should also make them realize that although double-loop learning ultimately requires societal learning and change, the individual learning must precede it. Awareness of this fact protects the society and culture against those who seek instant remedies and those who lack true commitment for changing features of the cultural fabric central to social order. As we learned during the late 1960s and early 1970s, nothing is more dangerous to a society than reformers who have good ideas (espoused theories) but who lack the perspective, skills, and commitment to alter their own theories-in-use sufficiently to build new learning systems that encourage orderly change.

7. Candor and openness are not the ultimate purposes of learning. They are conditions that enable people to reflect on the reasoning behind their actions and to design and execute mini-experiments so that they can test old action strategies and create new ones.

People enact their reality by creating premises and then drawing conclusions, usually in the form of causal hypotheses. The reasoning processes learned early in life are highly skilled and tacit. In diagnosing the X-Y case, people used faulty premises, rarely tested their hypotheses about what caused what, and frequently created conditions for self-fulfilling prophecies and self-sealing processes. In short, it was rare that they advocated their views in ways that encouraged disconfirmation. An environment for learning Model II requires that people have opportunities to slow down their actions and reflect on their reasoning processes.

As people begin to understand the errors they are producing, they can experiment with new designs, inventions, and productions. Such experiments are at the core of Model II practice. Practice in designing and producing Model II actions leads into the learning processes required to move from Model I toward Model II.

The interventionist must encourage a climate of experimentation and public testing for several reasons. The first is to help people assess the extent of their inability to produce double-loop learning as well as their unawareness of this fact. The second reason is to give people opportunities to become aware of the many tacit defense mechanisms against learning that they have, mechanisms that are activated whenever they question their values and basic assumptions. The third is to provide data for a genuinely informed choice about whether they really want to undertake double-loop learning. To the extent that the choice is informed, people will be predisposed to be internally committed to the choice, according to Model II. The internal commitment helps to ensure the persistence that is required.

The fourth reason is that the more people are aware of the factors that inhibit double-loop learning, the more they produce guideposts for what they have to change and criteria with which to judge their own progress. Without in-depth awareness, people may develop unrealistic expectations of how much and how quickly they should learn. Such expectations will compound their sense of failure and threat. Holding realistic expectations lets people be more patient with their own and others' progress.

Finally, along with reflections on their reasoning processes and experimentation, it is important for people to express their feelings because catharsis under prolonged states of failure and threat may act as a safety valve. Clearing the emotional air can increase the probability of effective reflection and experimentation.

Expressing feelings, however, uncovers more-profound insights. People learn that along with feelings go reasoning processes that are rarely understood, partly because they are tacit and partly because they are smothered by the feelings. In Chapter Two, we saw that participants felt the interventionist was manipulating them during the early phase of the X-Y case, and they became annoyed and indignant. Only after they expressed such feelings could the interventionist obtain from them data to illustrate their attribution. The discussions that followed led them to realize that they were not being manipulated. Some doubted whether they could trust the interventionist; others were confident they could. Once these feelings were expressed publicly, it was possible for people to examine their bases for trust or mistrust.

Another value of expressing negative feelings is that people collect evidence that expressing such feelings is not necessarily a counterproductive activity, as Model I would suggest. Instead of pulling people apart, it can bring them together to explore their differing feelings. This not only may increase their tolerance for their own and others' feelings, it may also allow them to be less threatened and overwhelmed by such feelings.

8. The interventionist provides appropriate theoretical concepts to help people make sense of their present actions and to design and implement new ones. Model I theory provides insight into

what is causing the unexpected inconsistencies, escalating error, and self-sealing processes. For example, a person programmed with Model I would tend to interpret a request to evaluate Y's effectiveness as being related to win/lose constructs. Hence, Y's actions will tend to be evaluated as plus or minus, good or bad. At the same time, the person may not be willing to subject his ideas to public testing for fear his inferences will be disconfirmed and his degree of unilateral control reduced. The same applies to attributions. There will be a tendency to create attributions that are consonant with the requirements of Model I or with those opposite to Model I. Hence, Y may be seen as striving to control or to fear controlling, as being rational or irrational, as being mature (by using face saving) or immature (by being forthright on issues that make others defensive). As with evaluations, people will not be predisposed to test their attributions publicly, because that increases the chance that error will be discovered, and (in a Model I world) that increases the chance of losing, not winning, as well as losing unilateral control.

If there is a predisposition not to publicly test the inferences made, then there will be a predisposition not to make the inferences public at all. And, therefore, the reasoning processes that people use to go up the rungs of their ladder of inference may not be made public. It should be rare to see someone give the directly observable data that she has organized (her enactment of the situation) and to see her test whether this organization of the conversation is agreeable to the other person. It should also be rare to observe someone making explicit the reasoning processes by which he moved from the first rung to any other rung on the ladder.

Another important feature of Model I is the self-censorship that occurs in order to remain in control and to win. The material in the left-hand column ("Thoughts and Feelings") is an illustration of the censorship. This is material that the person knowingly censors because of win/lose possibilities.

There will also be a predisposition to deny one's resistance to focusing on the data, making reasoning explicit, and subjecting inferences to public testing, as well as to deny self-censorship—in fact, to deny all face-saving actions. To make this denial effective, the person must also censor his denial. It is not possible to save face (one's own or others') if you say you are doing so.

The ladder of inference is another important concept. It helps people see that defining a problem is not really a concrete and simple act. To review: The first rung on the ladder is the directly observable data. The second rung is the culturally accepted meanings embedded in the data (first rung). At the third rung, we begin to get at the individual's meaning of the first two rungs (of data and cultural meaning). The definition of the problem begins on rung 3 and may be continued on higher levels of inference. As we will see, most people are not even aware of the theories of action that they use at rungs 3 and above. Most are unaware of the counterproductive features of their way of diagnosing a problem.

The ladder of inference can also be viewed as a normative model and as a map for effective action. Later in the chapter, I will give my version of how I would try to help Y in his dealings with X, beginning with the directly observable data and testing the meaning with Y. The next step is to coordinate my theoretical perspective with the meanings that Y confirms. In short, the ladder of inference suggests beginning with the directly observable data and working upward. This is the same strategy that is used to design the early sessions of the learning seminars.

9. Create opportunities to design models for action. A large amount of information is generated in the learning environment, and much of it is necessary if growth is to occur. But much of it may be unnecessary for designing new actions. For example, Chapter Twelve includes several cases of students reflecting on their learning. In one, after several hours of discussion and reflection, a student produced this heuristic: "Whenever I am about to deprecate someone, I deprecate myself first." This heuristic not only conceptualized the learning economically (after hours of work), but it could be easily stored and retrieved in future situations.

The students also created models of more complicated processes that actually escalated error. One person found she used a reaction pattern that prompted others to react counter to her intentions. She was able to revise that pattern to increase her effectiveness.

We know very little about the nature of these models for action. As we learn more, we will be able to design more efficient learning conditions and to help people package their knowledge so they can retrieve it quickly and use it even under stress.

10. The interventionist must be prepared to use his or her ac-

tions as a model of Model II theory-in-use as well as to have such actions confronted and questioned. Interventionists should, for example, advocate their positions and encourage inquiry; make attributions and evaluations but subject them to public test; make themselves vulnerable in order to learn.

But interventionists may not always behave in accordance with Model II. For example, when dealing with single-loop, routine issues, they may use Model I. Being human, they may also make errors and behave in ways that are counterproductive to learning Model II. However, there are two conditions that interventionists should meet when making errors: (1) They should monitor their own behavior and identify errors as soon as possible after making them, (2) they should be open to learning about their errors from others. It is comforting for participants to see that the interventionist can make occasional errors without losing his or her effectiveness. The word *occasional* is deliberately chosen. You cannot make frequent errors and still be credible. Some interventionists and organizational development practitioners believe they can make numerous errors as long as they are willing to own up to them. But making many errors—or a few flagrant ones—necessarily focuses attention on needs of the professional. It is not long before the clients begin to wonder about the credibility of their helper.

The objective in any setting is to increase the level of valid information produced by the clients (and the interventionist) and to do so in such a way that the clients can continue to produce valid information on their own in other situations. Valid information is information that can be subjected to test, to disconfirmation. There are many methods for disconfirmation. The interventionist may point out inconsistencies among propositions that a client assumes to be consistent. An interventionist may ask the client to illustrate experiences and conclusions by describing other situations and/or by observing his or her own actions within the learning environment. The interventionist may make predictions about what the client would do under similar or different conditions and test the client in action under those conditions. The interventionist and the clients may also design tests of their separate views by predicting how the clients will act under conditions that have rarely occurred but now could be designed to occur. In other words, the consultant acts to facilitate the testing of any proposition made during the learning seminar while teaching the clients, through modeling and explicit instruction, how to do the same.

Whenever the client—	*The interventionist—*
1. States unillustrated evaluations or attributions	Asks for the relatively directly observable data to illustrate the evaluation. When those are given, the interventionist asks the client to test the evaluation or attribution publicly.
2. Makes very high-level inferences and reaches what appear to be abstract conclusions	Asks the client to make explicit the rung in the ladder of inference that he or she used to arrive at the conclusion; then asks the client to go down the ladder of inference until the directly observable data are reached.
3. Asks for the interventionist's values and advice	Advocates his or her values (Model II governing variables) or provides advice based on the theory, combining either with a request for inquiry into it.
4. Asks for an evaluation of his or her actions	Asks the client to state his or her evaluation and the interventionist will immediately confirm or disconfirm.
5. Appears to become defensive	Strives to minimize any unilateral face-saving actions. The interventionist tries to be candid in such a way that the client can be candid if he or she wishes.

Redesigning the X and Y Case

In preparation for designing another way for Y to deal with X, let us review briefly the errors embedded in the meanings described in Chapters Two through Four, as well as some rules for redesigning that are congruent with Model II.

The most frequently imposed meanings were evaluations and attributions. Critical features of these meanings were that (1) they were high on the ladder of inference, (2) they were unillustrated, (3) they were not tested, and (4) the actors believed that testing was unnecessary because the evaluations or attributions were low on the ladder of inference; that is, they were concrete and obvious.

The most important single feature about the evaluations of Y was that they were negative. The most probable explanation for the negativeness was that Y's actions *were* negative. I would concur with the participants' negative evaluations. What is ineffective about communicating negative judgments if they are valid? The answer, from this perspective, is "Nothing." The problem is that negative evaluations should not be communicated by using the same features that the actors believe it is ineffective for someone else to use. To the extent that the way meanings are communicated contains the same causal theory the sender is telling the recipient is counterproductive, the sender will be experienced by the recipient as behaving inconsistently and unjustly.

The attributions had two major features. First, they were used to explain Y's actions by attributing motives "in" Y. For example, Y was protecting himself, was seeking to frighten X, intended to intimidate X, and was insecure. Second, the attributions placed the cause outside Y, in the role or the position that Y held. For example, Y was acting like a company man, like an authoritarian boss, like a superior identified with the hierarchy.

The attributions not only contain negative evaluations, but they imply that Y intended to make X defensive in order to protect himself or the organization.

If we combine the features of the evaluations and attributions just described, and if we keep in mind that the receiver is also programmed with Model I, then we have the basis for the predictions of self-fulfilling prophecies, self-sealing processes, and escalating error that were illustrated.

Turning to inventing and producing a different way of dealing with X, let us identify the key features of any intervention in which the message contains negative or threatening meanings although the intention is to facilitate learning.

The messages should be designed so that they are experienced as credible by the recipients. Recipients must have access to the data and the reasoning that the sender used to arrive at the evaluation or attribution. Hence, the evaluations or attributions should be illustrated and the reasoning made explicit.

The message should be communicated in ways that will minimize the automatic responses that people have to defend themselves. This means that the senders should state their messages in such a way as to encourage inquiry into or confrontation of their reasoning and meanings.

From the preceding it is possible to infer several rules for producing such messages:

1. Provide the (relatively) directly observable data (first rung on the ladder) that you use to infer your evaluations or attributions, and check to see whether the recipient agrees with the data.

2. Make explicit the cultural meanings that you inferred from the data and seek confirmation or disconfirmation from the other person.

3. Make explicit your judgments and opinions in ways that permit you to show why the consequences of the actor's action were necessary but without implying intentions to produce such consequences.

4. Help others to see that they are responsible for their specific actions (first and second rungs) in a given situation but that they are not held solely responsible for the meanings in rung 3 and above because they are not responsible for having been socialized into their theory-in-use.

5. Encourage others to express feelings or ideas that they may have about the process.

The reader might ask, "How efficient can such rules be? Can we get anything done under real-time constraints?" First, recall that these rules are for double-loop issues. Second, the question can be turned around—one can ask how much gets done with the present modes of communication. As we have seen (and as we will see further in Part Three), they actually cause more time to be expended, and worse yet, they generate a social pollution of misunderstanding and mistrust that gives people a sense of helplessness and hopelessness. As our world becomes saturated with this pollution, even a small incremental error can be the straw that breaks the camel's back. Finally, as we shall see, the process of designing and implementing meanings in accordance with Model II does not take much longer. When we have clocked Model I and Model II roleplays, the latter (when produced by actors who are moderately competent) usually occupy the same amount of time as the Model I roleplays or even less.

Moreover, as I shall show in Parts Two and Three, it is possible to organize Models I and O-I (as well as Models II and O-II) on a ladder of inference so that the user and the recipient can go up and down the ladder easily. Thus, the same ladder can be used to understand individual, group, intergroup, and organizational phenomena.

We now turn to an illustration of how the interventionist might deal with Y. Remember the ladder of inference and Y's statement that led us to infer the meaning "X, your performance is unacceptable." Whenever one makes inferences, they are subject to error and hence should be put to public test. Every move up or down the ladder necessarily means that inferences are made. The higher up the ladder of inference and the more abstract the ideas, the greater the chance of error, and therefore the greater the importance of public testing. Whatever theory one uses, it should make public testing as easy as possible.

To test an inference with someone else, it is necessary to make explicit both the premise and the conclusions drawn from the premise. The premise of an inference is always on the rungs below the inference to be tested. Hence, the inference "Your performance is unacceptable" is based on the premise that is (in this case) the words that Y spoke.

One can test by asking Y: "When you said, 'X, your performance is not up to standard,' did you mean that his performance was unacceptable?," or "When you said, 'You seem to be carrying a chip on your shoulder,' did you intend to attribute to him unacceptable attitudes?" If Y responds yes, then the meanings have been tested and it is possible to proceed to the next rung on the ladder.

If a participant in an X-Y seminar wanted to reveal his diagnostic frame, it is at this point that he would have to say something like "Well, I infer from these data that you prejudged S," for example, or that "you were too blunt" or that "you were insensitive." Such a response is likely to produce defensiveness in Y for several reasons.

First, Y may not agree with the evaluations/attributions. Y may believe that he had to be blunt or insensitive in order to get through to X. Or he may believe that he did not prejudge X, that X had given the organization years of data that led to the present judgment. Second, the evaluations not only attribute errors to Y but imply that the intention was to be blunt, to be insensitive, and so on. No one knowingly produces errors. If Y knew what he was doing, then he knew that he was being blunt and insensitive. There is an explicit negative evaluation coupled with an implicit attribution that Y intended these negative consequences.

Under these conditions, the act of testing by the interventionist is more of a trick than a strategy to help. He may have tested the first two rungs in order to nail Y with his third-rung evaluations and attributions, themselves difficult to test. Indeed, in our experience, not only does Y have difficulty in seeing and agreeing with the logic of inference between successive rungs, the participants also have difficulty. Recall how often in the transcripts the participants, when asked to illustrate their inferences, either were unable to do so or illustrated them with further inferences. If inferences are to be subject to test, then no matter how high on the ladder they are placed, it should be possible to go down the ladder and explicitly connect them with the first and second rungs.

To summarize, whatever the concepts being used, one should be able to order them on a ladder of inference, beginning with the relatively directly observable data and moving up to the culturally acceptable meaning and then up to the concepts used to organize the previous two rungs into the problem. It is at this point that interventionists are introducing their own (usually tacit) theory of help.

Let us return to the interventionist's two questions to Y. Recall that Y confirmed the meanings. But let us assume that Y said yes but was showing signs of impatience: "Of course I meant the performance is unacceptable!" or "Naturally I think X's attitudes are wrong! What are you driving at?" At this point the interventionist, using our theory of action, could say:

> I'll be glad to tell you what I am driving at. First I wanted to make sure that I had understood you correctly.
>
> I have a way of understanding the effectiveness of

the kinds of comments that you made. The first [repeats it] I call an "unillustrated evaluation." It tells the person he is wrong, but it does not include the data and logic of how that conclusion was arrived at.

People tend to react to these unillustrated evaluations and attributions by feeling bewildered and/or misunderstood. Depending on how free they feel, they may confront you or they may imitate your style and make their own unillustrated evaluations and attributions about you. If they state them in that form, without illustration, it is upsetting. It upsets the receiver, just as X was upset. Now if X acted on inferences that he is keeping secret, you would probably sense the secrecy because you would not see clearly the reasoning that X used to say whatever he did.

Let me stop for a moment. What is your reaction? Does this make sense? [or] Am I communicating?

Several features of this response should be highlighted. First, not only do the concepts of "unillustrated evaluation" and "unillustrated attribution" provide insight into a problem, but the insight is in the form of a causal theory:

> If you produce unillustrated evaluations, the receiver will not know the basis of your evaluations or attributions.
> The receiver will feel bewildered and misunderstood. He may therefore react defensively (unless he is afraid or prefers to be dependent on you).

The causal theory in these propositions has a logical validity independent of its empirical validity. If evaluations are unillustrated, it is difficult to understand the premises on which the evaluations are made. Moreover, it is possible to spell out the consequences of this theory. For example, some recipients of unillustrated evaluations may not be too upset, such as those who are dependent or withdrawn. Others may become quite upset. If Y accepts unillustrated evaluations and attributions as positive data, then he is explicitly accepting dependent-oriented or withdrawn subordinates.

The concepts used to describe the problem produce direct clues to how to correct it. For example, *illustrate the evaluation and illustrate attributions.* But another concept in the theory would say that this is not enough. Merely illustrating the evaluations and attributions will be experienced by the receiver as unilateral advocacy of a particular view. The closing sentences of Y's interventionist were intended to encourage inquiry and confrontation ("What is your reaction? Does this make sense?").

The theory states that asking for inquiry and confrontation is only one sign of openness to learning. Indeed, it may be the easiest sign to produce. A more important sign of openness to inquiry is how committed one is to going up and down the ladder of inference, making inferences as explicit as possible in order to test them. Another sign, of course, is willingness to recognize error.

Another correcting feature of the concepts is that they help clients to see their errors without encouraging the automatic reactions of bewilderment, shame, and guilt. It is one thing to tell people that they are insensitive, too blunt, and so on. It is quite another to say that whenever anyone uses unillustrated attributions or evaluations, they will have the consequences predicted earlier. Such a statement is a generalization that applies to the interventionist as well as the client; it indicates negative consequences that may occur whether the client (in this case, Y) intended them or not.

If the interventionist knows that the concept calls for inquiry and testing, he or she will be less likely to feel conflicted and anxious about advocating a position and simultaneously encouraging inquiry into it. Speaking in a manner that minimizes personal attack makes it more likely that the interventionist can utilize any defensive reactions for further learning. It is also more likely that the interventionist can defend his or her views, yet simultaneously encourage public testing of his or her Type A defensive actions. You may wonder whether it is possible in any given situation to produce all the testing and directly observable data required. We have learned several answers through observation in the seminars and in the everyday world.

First, as people become skilled, they may actually take less time to act, because they can be clearer, more precise, and less cagey. One reason is the lower utilization of the Type B defensive maneuvers identified in Model O-I, defenses that people normally use when communicating difficult information.

Second, significantly less information is considered undiscussable, and fewer games are played to keep the undiscussable undiscussable. Third, organizations in which double-loop learning occurs tend, as we shall see, to hold fewer or shorter meetings, because they can get to the difficult issues more quickly and because members do not need the meetings to keep one another appropriately informed (a euphemism for "I'd like no surprises").

It is important to remember that none of our participants had a relatively clear map of their theory-in-use, and hence they could not make explicit their steps of inference or the number of rungs on their ladder of inference. It seems plausible that a ladder of inference, like any good theory, is best when it requires the fewest rungs and when going up and down the rungs is easy. Neither of these characteristics can be developed if people do not even know their theory-in-use and the ladder of inference embedded in it.

Models I and II can be placed on a ladder of inference, as in Figure 5. For example, the third rung is related to such concepts as

Figure 5. Ladder of Inference

6	Model O-I learning
5	Model I
4	Combined action strategies (for example, advocacy combined with unilateral control)
3	Action strategies (for example, unillustrated attributions)
2	Culturally accepted meanings
1	Relatively directly observable data

unillustrated attributions and evaluations. Recall that all these concepts—testing, advocacy with inquiry, all behavioral strategies—have embedded in them causal theories about ineffectiveness and effectiveness. They tell you what behavior is effective (for example, illustrate evaluations and attributions) and what is ineffective.

The concepts may also give interventionists criteria for how to react when a relationship gets into difficulty. For example, if giving illustrated evaluations combined with inquiry makes the client defensive, that type of defensiveness is probably indicative of the client's problem. If the interventionist strives to minimize such defensive reactions, he will be utilizing a theory-in-use that is counterproductive for double-loop learning.

Returning to our ladder, the fourth rung is related to the combined action strategies, such as advocacy/no inquiry and unilateral face saving. Again, all those features have specified consequences—low public testing, defensive behavioral environment, and so on.

The fifth rung is related to the consequences of the fourth. As we have seen, Model I tends to create self-fulfilling prophecies, self-sealing processes, and escalating error. The sixth rung is related to the consequences of the first five rungs on the social system. It is at this point that we introduce the O-I learning system.

It is possible to help clients move to recognition of highly complicated systemic features of the environment. It is also possible to begin with a map of the learning system and to give a priori predictions of what is causing the learning system to operate as it does. Moreover, one could also predict to Y that if he (or anyone else) behaves toward X (or anyone else) in the way he did, it will have predictable consequences for the organization and its problem-solving effectiveness.

Illustrations of Movement Toward Model II

The next four chapters illustrate how these ideas can be implemented in individual learning relationships, in seminars (long and short), and in organizations. We will begin with an example of an individual being helped to gain insight into his problem in such a way that he can continue the learning when he returns to his organization. This case illustrates two of the most fundamental assumptions of this approach. The first is that increased awareness (discovery) is not adequate to make one a more effective inventor of new actions, and discovery and invention combined are not adequate to assure that the new inventions can be produced. The second assumption is that people require others to help them discover, invent, and especially produce new actions. It is not, for example, sufficient to help Dan—the client whose case is given in the next chapter—become aware of his counterproductive, aggressive actions. It is important to help him alter these actions. But this will not occur overnight; it will require many experimental tries; it will depend on iterative learning. Hence, learning is not an individual activity. Double-loop learning especially requires the help of others and a particular facilitative organizational milieu.

Next, we present the case of three partners who are in the process of helping one another. Robert and Bill help John become more aware of his behavioral strategy to "project" blame and responsibility when he feels pressured and believes himself to be in error. In the process of helping him, Robert and Bill learn about themselves, and all three develop a more effective team relationship.

Next, we turn to the X-Y seminar described in Chapter Three. We pick up the participants after they become aware of their Model I-ness. How does the interventionist help them go beyond their unawareness? Finally, the students illustrate the kinds of learning they believe they received, as described in their own analyses of the seminar.

9

Helping
an Individual Alter
Counterproductive
Behavior

The purpose of this chapter is to illustrate how individuals can be helped to solve important everyday double-loop problems in their lives.

I have little experience in individual consulting. One reason is that in my domain of work there are few solely individual problems. Indeed, as I have suggested, individuals may well be working social structures; individuals necessarily create learning systems that feed back to interpenetrate and reinforce their individual (though socially learned) theories-in-use. Hence, a diagnosis of an individual problem will usually require a diagnosis of a systemic problem.

Perhaps a more important reason is that our perspective assumes that people can learn to solve their problems by creating an environment where they can detect and correct their errors. But one of the most important barriers to overcome is individuals' unawareness of their own unawareness. As we have seen, this double-nested blindness is limited primarily to the actor. It is possible for any other person (stranger, friend, colleague, or someone else) to see errors the actor cannot see. This means that our learning depends on creating small groups in which people can learn. But in order for such groups to be effective, the members must also have learning and helping skills. Hence, our approach to individual help has usually required the creation of support groups. Not surprisingly, most of our work has begun with groups and larger systems. Once such groups are generated, we also necessarily generate the beginnings of systemic or organizational change. If a member of a group learns Model II skills, he will necessarily aid in creating O-II learning systems. If he can help create O-II learning systems, he will necessarily question and change such features of Model O-I learning systems as double binds, primary and secondary loops that inhibit learning, and games of deception and undiscussability.

In this chapter and the next, I present two cases of individual help. The first concerns a client, Dan, who comes for individual help with no thought of generating a learning group in his organization. By the end of the fourth session, he decides to create such a group, not only to continue his own learning but to help build a more effective department. The second case is an example of how a learning group helped an individual member deal with certain counterproductive actions.

Dan is an upper-level executive in a worldwide firm headquartered in the San Francisco area. His superiors consider him an excellent performer. With but one proviso, he has an open path to the highest positions available in the firm. The one proviso is related to the way he deals with people (especially superiors) when he disagrees with them or when they do not support him as he expects. Dan frequently "blows his top" and has other similar behaviors that bewilder those who fail to see the appropriateness of his reactions. Dan came to the interventionist to get help in reducing this counterproductive behavior.

The first step was to obtain from Dan some relatively directly observable data that would illustrate the problem he had with others. Dan said he had an excellent recent example. The interventionist asked him to write up the incident in the form of a case, containing a short description of the context and a description of the conversation as well as he could recollect it, as well as any thoughts and feelings that he had had during the episode but had not expressed. About four days later, the interventionist received the case in tape-recorded form. It contained all the data requested except that there was no information on thoughts and feelings withheld. The material was transcribed and studied by the interventionist before the first session.

Dan's "homework" was a specimen of conversation between Dan and his superior that Dan believed was an example of his problem. In other words, the first session (and parts of other sessions) was based on what Dan believed was a valid sample of what he was trying to understand and correct.

As has been stated, and will be discussed again in Chapter Ten, verbatim recollection is not a major issue. The important point is that Dan has committed himself to begin his learning by using this conversation. The conversation (first rung on the ladder of inference) may not be accurate or complete. But as we use it to infer the culturally understood meaning (rung 2) and then infer features of Dan's theory-in-use, we will have many opportunities to test the validity of the recollections. In addition, Dan may remember the conversation inadequately, but he cannot, according to our theory, create meanings that differ from his theory-in-use. We can design and produce only those meanings that are consistent with our theory-in-use. Only with the help of someone competent in Model II could Dan produce a Model II scenario. But if he made such an attempt—which was unlikely, given his anguish—the ruse would not last long, because Dan's Model I-ness would appear as he talked with the consultant.

The case concerned a meeting that Dan had with his superior, whom we will call Mike, and a peer of Dan's, Harry (who also reported to Mike). Apparently Mike told Dan that he was planning some organizational changes that included Dan's department. Dan became upset and accused Mike of acting unfairly and irresponsibly. Mike responded angrily and warned Dan not to talk to him that way. The meeting escalated emotionally and was terminated abruptly by Mike. Harry reported at a later date that he was surprised at how quickly the emotions had escalated and was so uncomfortable that he had not tried to help. He also added that he doubted he could have said anything that would have helped the situation.

All the consulting sessions with Dan were tape-recorded, as

well as the later session with Mike, Dan, and Harry. The transcriptions are edited to shorten the description and to illustrate the mode of intervention used with Dan. Sessions lasted an hour to an hour and a half and were scheduled no longer than ten days apart.

Session 1

The interventionist began by presenting his diagnosis of Dan's case. The interventionist stressed the importance of Dan's completing any homework assigned to him. He would make inferences about Dan's sense of responsibility and commitment from the quality of the homework. If Dan's commitment was to be tested partly by such criteria, then the interventionist's commitment to Dan should be tested in the same way.

A 20-page double-spaced transcript is rich with material for diagnosis. Both knew that they had only about five sessions. The interventionist therefore decided to begin with those diagnostic features that he believed were most important. He would present his views in such a way that Dan could confront them and thereby change the course of the helping relationship. Time was short, and the interventionist was assuming that he would probably get to the important issues more quickly than Dan could, because part of Dan's problem was his unawareness.

It was important for the interventionist to model his theory-in-use because that would give Dan the best opportunity to confront the interventionist as well as to test the usability and effectiveness of the perspective that he hoped to emulate. Note that the interventionist's opening comment shows willingness to advocate his position and encourage inquiry into it:

Interventionist: As I listened to your tape and reflected on it, there were many important points embedded in it. I would like to tell you several of them to see, first, if you agree that I understood the case, and second, to obtain any corrections that you may wish to give me.
Dan: Fine.
Int.: First, you diagnosed the problem as being Mike. You described Mike as being an insecure guy. For example, he asks for openness; yet when you are candid, he becomes upset. This, in your view, gives him low credibility.

Second, you believe, among other things, that he failed you as a boss because he did not stand up [to his superiors] when you and Mike felt the superiors were making wrong decisions. OK so far?

Dan: Yes, correct.

The interventionist presents his attributions with few illustrations. When people are in interaction with each other and plainly share the same data, then to repeat those data in detail could lead the client to feel bewildered, if not impatient. Hence, we have developed a category of tacit illustrations. This means that the evaluations and attributions are assumed to be illustrated; that is, they are tacitly illustrated because both persons have just lived the episode or, as in this case, both listened to the tape recorder and both have a copy of the transcript. However, the conditions of tacit illustration do not make it unnecessary to publicly test the evaluations and attributions, a test that the interventionist did perform.

Although Dan did confirm the interventionist's diagnosis, it does not follow that Dan's original description was valid. The interventionist may have based his diagnosis on invalid views. Hence, the next step is to test the validity of Dan's description, which means asking Dan to recall not what he had recorded but data that were tacit and missing.

Int.: OK. The next step is to test the validity of both our diagnoses. We cannot check with Mike or Harry because they are not here. So let's examine your reasoning processes. As you recollect it, what did Mike say or do that is evidence for your attribution that he asks for openness and then backs off?

Dan remembered that Mike had become quite upset when Dan leveled with him. He gave examples of Mike's responding emotionally. The interventionist responded that Mike may well have acted as Dan described, but how did Dan know that the reason Mike behaved that way was that Dan was candid and Mike was insecure? Dan gave some examples.

Int.: And [mentions some of the examples] this is evidence of—

Interventionist does not see what inferences Dan made or what conclusions Dan is communicating.

Dan: [Interrupting] This is evidence that Mike asks me to be open and candid, and when I am, he gets upset. Am I answering your question?

Int.: No, you are not answering my question, but you are focusing on aspects that are important to you. [Let me illustrate my reasoning] by asking you a few questions [to get at the information I seek].

Interventionist strives to make it clear that Dan is not answering his question; yet he still values Dan's response. He returns to his question and moves step by step through the reasoning process.

I can see how the quotes [mentions one] are evidence that Mike asks you to be candid.

Dan: Fine.

Int.: But you also suggest that when you became open, he became defensive. Can you illustrate that?

Dan: Of course. [Embedded in Dan's lengthy response were the following points, listed in the order spoken.]

I consciously or subconsciously challenged Mike.

For the first time, I told him that he did not back me up.

This [was] a devastating criticism against Mike.

I would never have made [such a criticism] before. It really goes totally against anything that had happened before in our relationship.

I have [always] avoided criticizing him.

We have a norm in our relationship. He does not criticize me. I do not criticize him.

He knows that I am very, very sensitive—oversensitive.

I am extremely aware that he is very sensitive when it comes to feelings about his supportive role with his subordinates.

I know that he feels that he is giving us his support.

Dan's responses contained many meanings, which could not be dealt with all at once. For example, the interventionist could have focused on the unillustrated and/or untested attributions and evaluations that Dan made about Mike. He could instead have focused on the assertions, such as that Dan had never confronted Mike before and that Dan has avoided criticizing Mike. Or he could have focused on the face-saving games that Dan described between Mike and himself. Finally, he could have focused on the attribution that Mike realizes that Dan is sensitive, even oversensitive.

The interventionist chose to focus on only one of these issues, the one that was most powerful in the sense of asking Dan to look at his own responsibility for the problem. This issue was the conditions of injustice and the implication of incompetence that Dan was creating if Dan's description was correct. Thus:

> Dan describes Mike as oversensitive, easily upset, and potentially devastated by candor.
>
> Dan asserts that these features are counterproductive to effective leadership.
>
> Dan acts toward Mike by using evaluations and attributions that, if Dan's diagnosis is correct, will guarantee that Mike responds defensively.

Hence, Dan is faced with a paradox. He creates for Mike the very conditions that he asserts are unfair and counterproductive if Mike creates them. The interventionist hypothesized that concentrating on the paradoxes and injustice produced would create in Dan a more powerful set of inconsistencies and, hence, would produce more energy for his working on his responsibilities than focusing on any other issue.

Int.: And if you were to charge him with not supporting you, then it would follow [from what you just said] that he would see that as an attack?

Dan: On reflection, absolutely. I didn't want to upset the guy. I didn't do it deliberately, but maybe I did. I can't think I did it deliberately—subconsciously, perhaps. It was the most devastating thing I could have done. Do you understand?

Whenever Dan (or anyone) states that he did not mean to act as he did, we can infer that he is probably correct at the espoused-theory level. However, at the theory-in-use level this cannot be true. It is not possible to design meanings that are not intended. What is possible is that the meanings that Dan designed were triggered automatically. The production of those meanings was beyond his control because they are highly skilled and are probably set off by cues of which Dan is only tacitly aware. It is important to understand the cues Dan experienced that led to his automatic response.

The next intervention was informed partly by this reasoning

and partly by the interventionist's attempt to illustrate, by what Dan had said, that Dan and Mike shared some characteristics. They were both "oversensitive" and "easily hurt" when they behaved toward each other in ways that understandably produced defensive reactions. The purpose of this intervention was to help Dan feel closer to Mike, focusing Dan's attention on the possibility that Mike and he had the same reasoning processes.

Int.: I also recall [from the tape playback] that he said, in effect, that you were acting immaturely by trying to score debating points.

Dan: That's absolutely not true, of course, and I resented that.

Int.: And I can understand how you could resent that. On the one hand, he was telling you not to attack him. On the other hand, he was, in your view, attacking and putting you down.

So the first thing that hit me was that each of you is doing to the other what neither of you wants the other to do to you.

Does it make sense to you that in this issue Mike and you are behaving in the same way?

After empathizing with Dan, the interventionist focuses on the consequences, that Dan (as well as Mike) is behaving in ways that he himself considers counterproductive. This paradox should help Dan examine his personal responsibility.

Another possible consequence of focusing on the similarities in the way Dan and Mike reason and defend themselves is to help reduce the predisposition, in most people who use Model I, to impute nasty motives to the other. The nasty motives may come from the following reasoning.

Mike knows me, Dan.
Mike knows what he is doing to me.
Mike knows that what he is doing to me is upsetting me.
Therefore, Mike intends to hurt me.

The logic is valid if it can be shown that Mike is aware of his impact and that he designs it in order to upset Dan. To question this inference process, it is important to help Dan see that he is not aware of the injustices that he himself created with Mike. If it is possible to help Dan see his own blindness, it is then possible to help Dan see that Mike may be equally blind. If Dan were to deny this possibility, then he would be asserting that Mike was either more competent than he (that is, more aware) or more vicious (or both). Neither of these two attributions made sense to Dan.

The next intervention moved from an awareness of injustices and blindness to the reasons that led Dan to respond automatically to Mike in ways that led to magnification and escalation of error and hence to Dan's reputation for overreacting. The intention was to move away from analyzing Dan's or Mike's motives toward helping Dan reduce his counterproductive responses and his unawareness that he was behaving in such a manner.

Int.: What do you think prevents you from saying that to Mike? For example, "Mike, I'm sorry that I have upset you. But I am trying to communicate something that isn't easy for me to communicate. I also feel that what I am trying to get across isn't being heard." Am I not right that you never said anything like that in your dialogue?

Dan: I would never, never have thought of saying that.

Int.: I agree. Your automatic response helped to escalate error. His was the same.

The point that I would like to work on is how I can help you to understand that, under these types of conditions, your automatic self-protective responses are similar to the ones Mike uses on you. I believe that you are unaware of this and unaware of how to design responses that do not escalate error.

Does this make sense to you? What is your reaction?

Dan: Well, it makes perfect sense. I can now see why some of the interpersonal problems occur. I can see why I react and why the others react as they do.

How does one go about seeing these responses as logical and applying them to himself? I could keep reminding myself, I suppose.

And that is my dilemma. How do I transfer the lessons learned from umpteen cases?

If I can't do it with Mike, for example, to express some of my inadequacy for a minute, . . . if I am totally incapable of doing that sort of thing with Mike, then how in hell am I going to do it with anyone else? Because I ought to have some rapport with Mike.

Int.: In fairness, Mike also behaves in ways that make it difficult. I do not say it to protect you, but to suggest that a diagnosis where you place all the responsibility on yourself may not be valid.

Now let's get back to your question. I'll start with the obvious —that you must first be aware of the problem. Next, I believe that we have to learn more about what pushes your button. What are your feelings about a superior who lets you down?

Dan: You mean emotional feelings?

Int.: Yes.

Dan: They are very profound. It is one of those things that I cannot describe. Not quite as strong as the death of a loved one—but pretty close. [My feelings] are out of proportion, and they become devastating. Now that's the only word I can use. The emotions appear to be devastating and appear to destroy me, or they seem that way.

Int.: If I understand you, you say that, on the one hand, the feelings are of being devastated; yet, on the other hand, the feelings appear to be an overreaction—so that the reaction is devastating and, if I have understood you correctly, inappropriate from your point of view.

Dan: Yes.

Int.: I believe that there is no such thing as inappropriate actions. Whatever action you design and implement is appropriate for you. If that is true, we then have to figure out what is appropriate about behaving inappropriately.

Again, the interventionist focuses on Dan's examining his theory-in-use, which will also mean that he examines his responsibility in the situation.

[One way to get at the question is to look at it historically. You may wish to explore it in terms of early childhood experiences and so on.]

Provides alternate avenues of help for Dan.

Another way to approach it is to find ways to correct the inappropriate behavior. You will need help from colleagues, including Mike. But in order to get help from them, you will have to learn

to say things that you presently
would   not—to   quote   you—
"dream of saying." [And they
must be interested in helping you
and themselves.]

There are several paths that Dan can take to be helped. One is
individual private counseling that uses such logic as that Dan distorts
reality, the causes for the distortions are "in" Dan, the causes are defenses, and the defenses were developed long before Dan worked
with Mike and Harry. The goal of such individual counseling would
be to give Dan insight into these early causal factors in order to overcome them.

The interventionist, in this situation, would agree that Dan has
defenses that lead him to add or subtract invalidly from his present-
day reality. He would also agree that these defenses were probably
created early in Dan's life. However, he would not agree that the
only or best way to help Dan is to try to identify the first causes and
the conditions under which they occurred. Using a theory-of-action
perspective, the interventionist conceives of Dan's defenses as presently held, presently operating, highly skilled actions. Although the
defenses may have started early in life, the reason they are still operating is that the generic meanings that led to their creation exist in
the present world. Hence, overcoming the counterproductive actions
can be seen as a problem of detecting and correcting their present
manifestation with people such as Mike. With the help of Mike and
Harry, Dan should be able to alter the counterproductive aspects of
his actions.

It is also true that Mike and Harry act in ways that reinforce
Dan's defenses. Hence, they have some responsibility for causing
Dan's reactions. If they choose to help Dan, they will automatically
be choosing to help themselves. If they do help him, all three will
learn that there are few "individual" problems, that most of these
problems are systemic, and that, as responsible executives, they must
learn to design and implement systems in which double-loop learning
is possible.

If Dan had selected the individual approach, the interventionist would have helped him find a competent individual counselor. If
he were to select a theory-of-action approach (as, in fact, he did), the

interventionist would eventually have to introduce Mike and Harry into the sessions in order to give Dan insight into his impact on them. But Mike and Harry have not asked to participate in these sessions. Indeed, they are not even aware that they are occurring. In this case, as we shall see, Mike and Harry willingly joined a long (five-hour) session with Dan.

But what if they had refused? The interventionist would have continued to help Dan by asking him to participate in workshops of the kind already described in this book. Dan would not have the advantage of Mike's and Harry's presence, but he would still learn. Often I have helped other individual clients design an approach to persons they believed were recalcitrant, with the result that these other persons participated in creating a new system. The appeal in these cases is not simply to help the Dans but to help them make their systems, and themselves, more effective.

The end of the session was approaching, and the interventionist wanted to create an opportunity for Dan to roleplay how he might now talk with Mike. The intention was to produce some directly observable data to see whether Dan's reasoning processes for diagnosing and implementing his actions with Mike had begun to alter.

Dan: [My reaction to what you just said] is that it will take a great deal of effort to do because I'd be admitting that I am immature.

Int.: Implicit in what you just said is that you have been successfully hiding the "immature behavior." I am willing to bet that many people see it, that they also see you as being unaware and are not telling you. [Hence, there may be many persons who tolerate you when you would not tolerate yourself; there may be more support available to continue your learning at the office.]

The interventionist is suggesting that people may be more tolerant of, and frustrated by, Dan's behavior than he realizes. Or if he does realize it, as he appears to suggest, then making it discussable may reduce the games he is playing to appear unaware.

Dan: [Yes, there is validity to what you are saying.] I have been sort of typecast as an emotive person. Perhaps another word for it is *immature*. Emotionally immature in this particular situation.

Int.: In those situations where you believe that your boss is letting you down.

Dan: That is absolutely true.

The interventionist returned to the idea that Dan might experiment with trying to design new meanings in his discussions with Mike. He asked Dan to make believe he was again in that difficult meeting with Mike and to try out a new conversation. What would he say? Dan included in his lengthy roleplay the following comments:

> Mike, I told you so.
> How many times did I warn you about . . . ?
> [Your reaction] was to go off on a tangent.
> Now you are left holding the bag, and you do not know what to do.
> I've been trying to tell you that.
> Unfortunately, you were off, and you were digressing, and maybe I did not press hard enough.

Int.: And what is different about this approach [from the one you used in the actual situation].

Dan: One difference is that I do not have the feeling that I have been hurt. I want to express my aggression, and therefore I use a different language. It is just that I would be relaxed.

Int.: [If I understand you], the difference is that you feel more attuned to your feelings, and so you are feeling less aggressive and angry. You are feeling somewhat more comfortable? [Dan nods.]

Feeling more comfortable is important, but it is not an adequate end result. The objective is to reduce the counterproductive actions and the blindness to such actions.

Int.: Maybe that is a problem. If I were Mike, I would be feeling, "There goes Dan again. He is still being disrespectful and self-centered."

Dan: You heard that?

Int.: Yes. For example, I heard comments such as "This isn't the first time" and "Perhaps if I were more aggressive"—which implies that Mike is so blind that, in order to reach him, you must hit him. Does that make sense?

Dan: Yes, yes, it does make sense. But you are putting me in a dilemma.

Int.: What is the dilemma?

Dan: If you cannot communicate with somebody in a civilized way, and you can't [do it effectively] in an aggressive way, how in the hell do you communicate?

Int.: That is an insightful question. I would also bet that others must be experiencing this dilemma with you.

The first meeting ended with Dan identifying an important dilemma. Again, the interventionist added that others must be having the same problem with him—namely, how to communicate with him. The interventionist asked him to think about this issue as part of his homework for the next session (in about a week).

Session 2

Session 1 exposed Dan to some of the major concepts for learning in the theory-of-action perspective—for example, the ideas of inconsistencies, injustices related to incompetence, unawareness, skilled reactions that mean automatic reaction to cues, the gap between invention and production, conceiving of problems of change as creating opportunities to continue to learn in the present context, the relevance of coming in touch with and expressing feelings in order to identify cues that automatically trigger counterproductive but skilled responses, and finally, the dilemma of knowing only how to be directive or how to ease in (Model I or its opposite).

It is doubtful that Dan has learned these concepts in the sense that he can act on them to produce new actions. He probably has achieved insight into the scope of the problem but has not clearly differentiated all the factors and their interrelationships. It is not likely that after five sessions of an hour or so Dan will be able to discover/invent/produce/evaluate double-loop issues effectively. But he will probably have a much clearer idea of what he must do to continue learning and how he can create conditions in the "back home" situation where he can achieve this learning. In other words, given the theory's predictions about the difficulties of learning to invent *and* to produce double-loop learning, and given its fundamental assumption that human problems (including those involving distortion of reality) can be treated as problems of detecting and correcting error, the goal of these few sessions is to help Dan generate enough skills to be able to manage and continue his learning with the help of a few persons whom he trusts and who have an opportunity to observe him in everyday life.

Obtaining the help of others also means that organizational learning will be enhanced because as the members of his learning group help Dan learn, they too will learn. Herein is one bridge—from individual to organizational. This learning process can be greatly facilitated by exposing the entire group to the kinds of seminars described in this book.

The next step in Dan's learning process was to help him become more aware of how to experiment with producing actions that are less counterproductive. In as rich a learning situation as the first session, there are several paths one can take. The interventionist began the second session by asking Dan to identify some of the ideas he had learned during the first. The answer would provide insight into how Dan had organized the complex and rich learning of the first session, what he had chosen to highlight, and hence what he had chosen to exclude. The interventionist could help Dan by correcting this first map, if necessary, and by helping him explore in depth some features of his map.

Dan identified his learning:

Dan: Do not try to hide my feelings that I am uncomfortable about certain issues [describes some, such as Mike's not supporting him]. If I feel I should say something, say it. And if I feel that I may not say it well, say, "Look, I'm not very good at this sort of thing, but here is my version, and let's have a go at it."

The interventionist confirmed the importance of Dan's expressing feelings, of advocating his views in combination with inviting discussion of them, and of making explicit when he believes he may not be able to communicate competently. He added a warning that if Dan did behave competently, that was no assurance that others would respond in kind. Dan said, "I know, but I think I will feel better and more confident in what I said and did." The interventionist confirmed that view and added one more learning that he wished Dan would also highlight. "You condemn Mike for behaving in ways which lead you to feel neglected, and yet you appear to act in the very same way with him."

Dan: I understood it intellectually. Whether I expected it emotionally is another subject. I just don't know.

[Returning to previous subject] What you are saying is, first, accept that certain situations are bound to upset me, for whatever reason. If possible, express my disturbance [points out that he tends to express emotionally]. I have a tradition of sort of shouting what I want. Yet after I clash—a debating sort of clash—afterwards I want to say, "It's just roleplaying, nothing personal."

If Dan had continued with this subject, the interventionist would have interrupted to say, "I cannot confirm it is not personal. I can agree, however, that the emotionality is an automatic response that you do not control as well as you wish." The interventionist would have been saying, in effect, that Dan's actions are highly personal. They are not consciously intended to upset Mike, but they do. The diagnostic and action frames that Dan is using are related to automatic responses to issues such as betrayal, and these frames began before Dan met Mike. Hence, Dan's actions are not personal in the sense of being fully deliberate attacks on Mike; rather, his lack of control is related to the automatic responses.

The interventionist illustrated a response that Dan might learn to produce that deals with both features of his learning—a response that would have the highest probability of being effective if Dan began to establish a learning relationship with the other persons.

Int.: Another response that you might learn to produce would be "I usually react strongly to these situations. And I am trying to control my responses more effectively." Another example might be "Sometimes my responses are experienced by others as a personal attack. I am not aware of this, so please let me know if it happens."

Dan went on to describe a new, important incident with Mike. This incident, about which Dan was quite upset, concerned a memorandum from Mike informing him that Mike was going to make further organizational changes in Dan's area. Dan was upset because Mike had promised not to make changes during the next three months; because Dan believed that he should have been involved, since the changes affected his subordinates; and because Dan was concerned about the impact the moves might have on his relationships with his subordinates. Dan's description of the incident was full of anger. The interventionist acknowledged Dan's anger: "I can well understand that you feel betrayed. However, I also see this as an opportunity for you to experiment with new ways to deal with such actions." Dan agreed. He said that his first reaction to the memo had been feelings of betrayal and anger. He also felt that his diagnosis of Mike had been validated. But he added that now he wanted to learn how to deal more effectively with this kind of event because it happened all the time in his work world.

Dan then produced several possible responses to Mike, including "If you promote or move people laterally when their immediate superior [like me] is not there, that is wrong" and "I'll be back from my several trips in a month; surely we can wait for a month." The interventionist then pointed out that Dan would be saying, " 'Mike, as the boss, you have the right to make these changes, but let me tell you my feelings.' . . . Instead of telling him your feelings, you then tell Mike not to do it." This response could upset Mike because he would experience it as an order from his subordinate. Dan agreed. The interventionist then used some of Dan's sentences describing what Mike had done as a basis for designing a response.

Mike, I understand you have the right to make these changes.

I am concerned about the changes made without discussing them with me, the messages that others may infer from the fact that I was not involved.

I would not like you to appear unconcerned about this issue.

It is difficult for me to see the dangers of waiting to implement the changes until I return so that we can discuss them.

Int.: If you were Mike, how do you think he would react to [that]?

Dan: In trying to be Mike, I would think about it. It is a very effective approach to getting Mike to rethink.

To review, the interventionist empathized with Dan's feelings of anger but focused on using the situation to learn to invent and produce new actions. He then asked Dan to invent and produce possible responses to Mike. Dan produced some responses. The interventionist identified some unintended consequences in the responses. Dan confirmed these consequences. The interventionist then tried to produce a more effective response by using sentences from Dan's description of the problem. In confirming the value of the interventionist's approach, Dan also had to realize that he had actually given a correct response but had done so when describing the situation, not when trying to produce a response to Mike.

Dan then added that he would have difficulty saying these things because he reacted so strongly when Mike behaved as he did: "I develop these feelings of being violently against that particular person. I say to myself, 'He is a bloody, stupid fool. An idiot.' How do I get over that emotional feeling [so that I can respond more competently]?" The interventionist's reply was "You are correct. It is doubtful that you can produce these responses if you feel about him the way you do."

In making this response, the interventionist intended to confirm the choice that Dan would have to make. If Dan feels that Mike is a stupid fool, then his anger toward Mike makes sense; that is, it is a rational response. If he behaves with anger, then he reinforces a situation that he wishes to change. But it may well be that Mike's actions were equally rational. For example, if Mike sees Dan as an angry, volatile reactor, he might postpone the changes until Dan is away and will have a week or so to calm down before he confronts Mike. The interventionist illustrated this:

Int.: Dan, would you please be Mike for a moment and let me ask you this: How do you think Dan would react if you tried to interfere in his work or pre-empt his authority?

Dan: As Mike, I'd say, "There would be a blow-up."

Int.: We know that Mike dislikes emotionality and subordinates confronting superiors. So Mike waits until you are gone.

Dan: [I can see that I have a problem.] I wish that I could design my words as you did. [As it is, I usually either shout, or I try to pacify the person and agree with him. In that process I destroy my own arguments.]

All I'm telling him [in my response] is "I know what your problem is. I may not agree with you, but in the state you are in, my God, I'm not going to say anything except that you're right, right, right, and the whole world is wrong. And that is wrong because I do not agree with you. [But since] I can't find a way of approaching you, I therefore agree with you."

[Another way I've been doing it is to confront by saying], "You should not have done that. You are not yourself. You just sit down and think for a minute, and listen to me. I am going to tell you what to do because you are not in the right frame of mind," . . . and that guy is going to reject me.

[The third way I have dealt with these issues is to listen, listen, listen, and when I have run out of patience, I'll tell him what I think.]

To summarize: Dan began the second session with some views about what he had learned. The interventionist believed that what he had learned was at the level of discovery, or insight. As a result, he might invent recommendations to himself for more effective actions. Yet, as in the X-Y case, it should not be possible for Dan to produce his own advice, and he should be unaware of this impossibility.

When the interventionist asked Dan to write a response to Mike's memo, he was creating an opportunity for Dan to experiment with producing new actions. The request was made in such a way that it could also be used as a test of the hypothesis just stated. Dan should not be able to produce the meanings that he might invent. Whatever meanings he produced should be largely counterproductive.

Dan responded according to the prediction. This helped him to see how locked in he was by his automatic responses, and the interventionist hoped this insight would reinforce Dan's desire to learn significant new ways of dealing with Mike and would simultaneously enable him to realize that this was not going to be easy.

Dan reviewed aloud the present action strategies that he would likely use and noted their counterproductive consequences. The session ended again with Dan in the dilemma that although he wanted to change, so far he kept producing action strategies that were not effective.

Session 3

Dan began the session by saying that he was trying to sort things out.

Dan: I've been trying to sort of classify the various situations that give rise to irrational behavior . . . in order to fulfill your suggestion to construct alternative ways of dealing with [irrational behavior].

First there are the situations where I have not communicated clearly. These are not difficult to deal with. I have to be able to admit that I am not clear or that I did not make myself clear.

Then there is the situation where I am sort of afraid for one reason or the other. I understand from what you said that one has to admit that one is afraid without saying, "You are threatening me." For example, I could say, "I just do not understand why you have done this or why I have done this to you."

Then we get to the difficult ones. These are basically the "ego-hurt" category. Your ego has been hurt for one reason or another. It is in this area that I have greatest difficulty.

The incident with my boss that we've talked about the last couple of times *is* an ego thing. He hurt me, hurt my ego.

These are uncontrollable. And it is the uncontrollability that I would like to correct with you.

Int.: [I would be glad to help. But I would like you to note that] you said that Mike hurt you. I did not hear that you also hurt Mike.

Dan: Maybe I'm not saying that because I can't accept it, I think. Probably we could talk about it.

Int.: Yes.

Dan: The only way I can accept that I hurt Mike is if he speaks to me. I'm sort of emotionally incapable of accepting it, although rationally I am accepting it. Maybe it's my temper. [I can blow up] and then it goes away, just like that.

Int.: Yes, yes.

Dan: [At the moment] I can't accept that he's hurt. It's incredible. I can see it. I can read it. I can listen to the tapes. [Gives several examples and concludes], I am now beginning to accept that I hurt him. I see the logic, and it is so irrational.

Int.: [I would like to tell you what I understand to be the logic embedded in what you said and did to Mike in the situation described in Session 1]:

I, Dan, criticize you, Mike, on a subject that I know will hurt you.

I am telling you that you have failed as my boss.

I realize that telling you that you've failed as my boss is going to hurt you; yet

I am upset with you because you do not want to listen and you respond with comments like "You are scoring debating points" while I am hurting you.
Does this make sense?

Dan: Oh, yes. That is what I mean by accepting it intellectually.

Int.: If I understand your position, it is that Mike should remain open and undefensive as you let him have it. You said that if someone spoke to you the way you spoke to Mike, you would blow up.

Dan: Yes.

Int.: But maybe Mike cannot be open because he has to protect himself from being hurt.

[Later]

Dan: What you are saying is that he was doing the same thing that I was doing. He was trying to cover up his hurt by camouflaging himself.

Int.: He was being hurt and covering up his hurt the way you were being hurt and covering up yours.

Dan: I see . . . we were both using the same defense mechanism. And, in fact, if we both were open, it would have been better all around.

Int.: Right.

Dan: We were both hiding [our feelings] and acting as if we were not hiding them.

[Later]

Dan: Looking back at it, yes, I was hitting him and hitting him hard.

During the early part of the session, Dan was able to accept intellectually that he hurt Mike in ways similar to the ways Mike hurt him, but not emotionally. One way to interpret this comment is that Dan understands the reasoning but does not accept it as a basis for action. The interventionist's response is to focus on the injustice of Dan's position *and* on the possibility that Mike is trying to protect himself as much as Dan is. Once both meanings were incorporated in Dan, he was ready to act. It may be that the interventionist's logic, once accepted, transforms the situation from win/lose (if Dan accepts the logic, he has been wrong and may also feel much guilt) to a situation in which Dan sees both of them as trying to manage their lives as effectively as possible. This view also transfers the attention to what each actor is doing to the other and points out that Dan can choose to alter his causal responsibility in the problem.

Int.: Let's add a bit more. When he responds by saying, "Don't try to score debating points with me," you respond by saying, "I'm not trying to score debating points with you. I'm merely pointing out the obvious." The logic of your response is, in effect, "Not only am I correct, but it is obvious that I am correct." That could upset Mike even more.

Dan: Yes. One question here. Don't you think he knows that his sarcasm hurts? Doesn't he know that he is using it as his ultimate weapon?

Int.: I'm guessing that what was going on in his head was the same as what was going on in yours. Each of you was feeling attacked, and you responded to protect yourselves.

The interventionist's interpretation is consistent with the perspective that actions are designed with the intent to protect oneself and the corollary notion that Mike does not have nasty motives. If Dan would accept these views, he might reduce his feelings of hostility toward and mistrust of Mike. He would see that Mike is acting with the same kinds of protective purposes and counterproductive actions that Dan uses.

Dan: In a situation like this, where the lid is coming off, where egos are hurt, and where you are in a state of emotional disarray . . . you don't want to admit that you are hurt, but obviously you should. [Looking back on the incident], I should have said at some stage, as early as I was aware that I was hurting him, that "I am terribly sorry," that I did not mean to provoke him. Is that right?

Int.: Yes, you are on the right track. [I would add one point.] You said that you did not intend to provoke him. From all that we have said, I infer that you did.

If you could become more accepting of the fact that when you are hurt, your immediate reactions are not as controllable as you wish, that would be helpful. Then you might say to Mike, in effect,

"When I am hurt, I automatically and unknowingly act in ways that are not as effective as I wish they were."

Dan then roleplayed how he might deal with a subordinate who was not performing effectively and to whom he might have to say things that would hurt. The conversation soon turned to Mike. Dan roleplayed several ways to communicate with Mike. Each roleplay began with some statement of his feelings but soon developed into an attributive conclusion ("I am trying to be open, it is not easy, and you are not helping by saying . . .").

Later, Dan addressed the issue of his angry outbursts more directly.

Dan: Do I need to blow up? That's what I'm really going to ask you. Is it inevitable? Can I keep the lid on?

Int.: I would not frame the problem as a need to blow up. I would say that you create, unknowingly, the conditions for your own blow-up. I would say that your automatic responses and ways to protect yourself tend to make others defensive. They, in turn, unleash their defenses, which may give you the cue that you need to blow up.

Dan: Then this is not an uncommon phenomenon?

Int.: It is a very common phenomenon.

Dan: [I think what is essential is if we could have this conversation with Mike and Harry.]

Int.: Yes, I agree.

Dan: I can see now that it is not a single-person thing. [Because of my pent-up feelings], I get in a cloud. I cannot see clearly; then I can't design effective reactions. If I ask myself, "How am I doing?," I do not see the situation clearly. So the question is, if I am in a sort of clouded position, what do I do? I can say that I am aware of it, but is this all I can do?

Int.: Another thing to say to Mike is that you are now aware that, because of the clouding issue, it is difficult for you to be aware of your impact to design appropriate responses. You can ask him for his help when he sees you being affected by the cloud.

Dan: Yes, that makes sense [if the others want to help and cooperate].

Int.: I agree. Everybody has responsibilities.

The session ended with Dan becoming increasingly clear about the degree to which he was responsible for the counterproductive features of the relationship with Mike. At the same time, the interventionist made sure that Dan did not hold only himself responsible. The interventionist kept introducing possible responsibilities that Mike had, as well as stressing that Dan and Mike might be in the same situation in that each was trying to protect himself from the other's attacks.

Session 4

The interventionist began the session by asking Dan about the possibility of meeting with Mike and Harry to discuss their relationships. He asked whether Dan could think of any reason that such a session would harm Dan in terms of organizational advancement and career.

Dan: No! No way. No, I think that it is an excellent idea. Basically, [as I see it now, it was my fundamental failure to appreciate Mike's position and his view of me]. It was a failure on my part to put myself in Mike's position. There was no attempt on my part to ask what Mike is thinking. Nor did I ask how he feels about me.

I know that he has been hurt as well as I have, but nevertheless I have nothing to hide.

I'm not ashamed of the incident, and I'm not ashamed of discussing it. I am sorry [for hurting Mike and myself].

Besides, if Mike, Harry, and I are going to work together, it's an excellent way . . . to understand each other. I do not mind being the guinea pig, because it happens that I was the person who failed to appreciate it.

Then Dan said that he had been working on how he would have dealt with the case if he could do it over again. He had given the idea much thought. The first conclusion was that he would not do it with a third party there and without Mike's having a choice about discussing the issue. "It was foolish of me to suddenly tell Mike that we had a terrible relationship in front of a person whom Mike had been telling that our relationship was fine."

The interventionist then roleplayed (as Mike) with Dan on his response to a hypothetical question raised by Mike: "What were you trying to accomplish that night when you confronted me?"

Dan (roleplaying as himself): I was trying to tell you [for reasons I now understand] that I did not understand why you didn't support me. I felt that you did not support me. Admittedly, I didn't think through why you did not support me.

Int. (roleplaying as Mike): The trouble with you, Dan, is that you do not know how to confront people. I think there are times when it is inappropriate for me to do what you want me to do.

Dan: Well, it is true. I have a tendency to confront people [whether they are prepared or not]. That is one of my weaknesses, which I recognize. But on that occasion I did confront you against a background of one year's frustration.

I think I now realize that if I have feelings of frustration, I should try to let you know sooner and talk them out. Also, it would be helpful if you tell me your feelings.

Int. (roleplaying as Mike): It is not that I did not think of my views. But the last thing I would do is tell you, because all you would do is blow your top.

Dan: May I again repeat that now I wish that you would risk my blowing up.

The interventionist then roleplayed what he would say to Mike if he were Dan.

Int. (roleplaying as Dan): I wish that you would take the risk. I would prefer that risk to the other, which leads to a blow-up. I can see how, in the past, I have behaved in ways where Harry and you would not want to take the risk. Now I hope you will, and I will try to respond more effectively.

Dan then explored what he now saw to be the ineffective advice that he had received from a senior personnel officer. The officer had told him, in effect, that Mike was one of his best supporters for a top position, and so if he ever felt anger toward Mike, he should forget it; if he could not, the company would find a different spot for him where he would no longer be reporting to Mike.

Dan asked how to deal with his other colleague, Harry, who became angry at him because he felt that Dan was wasting his time. The interventionist asked Dan what he was thinking and feeling while Harry was saying these things. The interventionist roleplayed a way of dealing with Harry by using Dan's comments:

Int.: (roleplaying as Dan): Harry, I am sorry that you feel I am wasting your time. I do see that you are upset. I would like to know what it is that you think I am doing that wastes your time. If it is under my control, I want to change it.

Dan: [Reflecting] Yes, [I see you are saying], "I want to understand why you are upset. It is not my fault."

Int.: Yes and no. I tried to say:

I sense you are upset and I am sorry.

It is not my intention to upset you.

What am I doing that is making the meeting counterproductive? Because I want to stop it.

Dan: I see you are recognizing his being upset, and you are saying that you want to change your behavior if that is what is upsetting him. [You do not hide the sensitive issues. You bring them up to discuss them.]

Int.: Yes.

The session continued with Dan experimenting, inventing, and producing different responses to several difficult situations that he experienced. None of the productions was fully correct, but each one had an aspect of Model II. Dan was beginning to build hybrids. He felt very good about his accomplishments and added that he was now ready to meet with Mike and Harry.

Session 5

Because of heavy travel schedules, the meeting with Harry and Mike was held about two months after the final meeting with Dan. Dan and Harry had worked cooperatively on their relationship because both had seen the interventionist individually and felt that they had a common experience on which to build (even though the interventionist was not able to be with them). Before and during the meeting, they reported specific actions they had taken with each other and with their respective subordinates to enhance the culture and the problem-solving effectiveness of their units. Each said that he had learned to utilize the other as a human relations resource. They hoped that they could expand the resource network to include Mike; they were doubtful.

As soon as Mike arrived, the meeting began with Dan making a short opening speech. (The report here is taken from the interventionist's notes because the tape recorder malfunctioned.)

Dan: I'd like to describe several things that I have learned. They include:

I am more aware that I must become sensitive to other people's feelings and take them into account before I react. In the past, I was primarily focused on how I felt.

I am also more aware that my actions that night were not helpful. I was not forwarding a rational argument. I was merely punishing you.

The main lesson, basically, is that I had not recognized what I was doing and the impact I had on you.

Also, now I see that I try to hide my feelings. I do it amateurishly. It never works, and all I do is blow up.

Mike: I would like to add that I have always been proud of my ability to communicate. But on the particular occasion that Dan refers to, I did very badly. I don't know why it was. But it took me a long time to realize that I had never communicated to Dan the reason for the reorganization and why it had to be handled this way.

Harry: [Asks what Dan believes triggered his outburst and what he, Harry, can do to assure more open communication about such matters.]

Dan and Harry urged Mike to be more forthcoming with his views, especially on the difficulties that he might be having with top management.

Mike responded that one reason he had not shared such information was that he did not want to burden them. He was also concerned that people like Dan would insist that he fight issues more aggressively, whereas Mike believed that such a strategy was counterproductive in this firm.

This led the participants to discuss their preferred strategies for dealing with policies and interdepartmental conflicts. Mike downplayed the amount of conflict and hostility that might exist in the firm. Dan, and less so Harry, magnified the conflicts and emotions. Dan and Harry withheld their feelings but found themselves blowing up at small provocations.

The participants began to evolve the following picture: The preferred strategies of Dan and Harry created the very conditions that Mike strove hard to suppress. Mike reacted by withholding information ranging from what was going on upstairs to his own doubts and ambivalences. Dan and Harry interpreted this strategy as Mike's unwillingness to share important information and attributed that to his predisposition to control. Mike's view was that he was trying to protect the company, as well as Dan and Harry, from getting a negative reputation with the top.

The meeting ended with the participants planning next steps to reduce miscommunication while building a more cohesive management team.

Summary

We began with a frustrated and hurt Dan who believed that Mike was an "immature, ineffective, overly submissive" executive who espoused openness and candor but summarily suppressed it when it occurred. Mike felt that Dan was the immature, ineffective subordinate who confronted superiors on any of their actions with which he disagreed and who became inappropriately emotional when he did not get his way. Neither felt that the other was influenceable, and each felt that the other was at fault.

In the five sessions, Dan was helped to see the degree to which he created the very conditions that he criticized. He was also helped to identify the automatic responses that made it very unlikely he would be aware of the self-fulfilling prophecies and the self-sealing features of his actions. Dan moved from a position of being certain that Mike was out to hurt him and that his feelings of betrayal and rage were valid and uncontrollable to the position that Mike and he had similar automatic reactions to each other's behavior, that neither he nor Mike wanted to hurt each other but their counterproductive actions were related to their lack of competence in dealing with these issues.

This made it possible for Dan to ask for a meeting with Mike and Harry, a meeting that, at the outset, he had considered foolhardy and dangerous. During the meeting, Dan was able to say many of the things he had feared telling Mike and to do so in a significantly more effective manner. Both Harry and Mike attested to this evaluation without being asked. Mike was especially strong about his views that Dan's actions were changing, and, more important, "I think Dan and

I can talk more productively in areas that I would have thought not possible before." Mike added that another sign of progress was that he was able to identify some of his own shortcomings and, together with Dan and Harry, could develop plans to correct them. Harry, who was not a focus of this story, also showed important changes in his awareness and actions.

10

Promoting Learning
in an Executive Group

The second example of individual help is more typical of an action approach in that the individual is a member of a learning group embedded in a larger system. John is a partner in an organization that will be prominently featured in Part Three. Robert and Bill are the other partners. They began to learn the theory-of-action approach about ten years ago.

John, who entered the partnership after Robert and Bill, began to have second thoughts about it. He doubted that he would ever become an equal member of the group and felt that Robert was dominating and overcontrolling.

The episodes in this chapter occurred early in the relationship. They no longer reflect John's feelings. The partners were eventually able to resolve many of these issues and, at the same time, created a problem-solving process. John, as we shall see, not only feels fully

Note: The material in this chapter is taken from a previously published paper, "Psychological Defenses, System Intervention, and Preventative Mental Health," in Clayton Alderfer and Cary Cooper, eds., *Advances in Experiential Social Processes* (London: Wiley, 1972), vol. 2.

integrated now, he also feels that he is a very important resource to the partners as they each continue their own growth, to the development of the partners as an effective group, and to the constructive confrontation of difficult issues. These experiences, John will say, have led to a personal learning growth that he had never even imagined before he entered the firm. They also have led to the creation of a culture within the firm that far surpasses the level of humaneness that he experienced in any other organization.

In this connection, some of the data here come from sessions in which the partners included their wives in discussion of the growth of the firm and the impact it would have on the families. The focus is on John because his case illustrates how the psychological defense of projection can be dealt with using our approach.

The substantive issues during the first session relate to ownership and compensation of the partners. John begins by stating that he doubts that Robert and Bill want to involve him as an equal in a genuine partnership. A long, intense discussion results about what, in John's view, Robert and Bill did to lead him to infer that he will never become an equal partner. During the discussion, a theme of inconsistencies appears in John's position. These provide the data from which his defensiveness is inferred.

The remaining three episodes occur during the two-day session with the partners and their wives. In Episode 2, John displays similar inconsistencies, now when dealing first with the interventionist and then with his wife. By Episode 3, John has received adequate data to suggest that the pattern of defensiveness is real and not random. This leads him to self-inquiry. The first step is to develop a "thought experiment" that, if his hypothesis is not disproved, would prove that he should not change. John carries out his experiment, and his hypothesis is disconfirmed. He concludes that the next step is to begin to alter the defensive reaction. At this point, he not only designs rules to keep himself aware of his learning in the future but becomes more open to feedback from his peers (partners and wives).

Episode 1

The first episode (excluding wives) occurs during a meeting to identify and correct long-range problems of the firm. One of these problems is the growth of the firm and the integration of new partners into the "Executive Office," or top officer group. John, who has been a member of the Executive Office for about a year and a half, begins by describing the difficulty he is having integrating with the other two partners, saying he has concluded that the firm is a two-person firm: "It is very difficult to break into the relationship between you two" (Robert and Bill).

John: I'm wondering if this firm will ever be something more than a good little company. Robert and I have started to have some real problems in the last few months. . . . Also, the way compensation and ownership are handled, I wonder if newer partners like myself can break into the inner circle of you two.

Robert: I don't understand that. I don't think we're having real difficulties. I think we have a couple of personalities that can go "bang." I think that's inherent in very strong characteristics that each of us has.

Robert appears to play down the personality and interpersonal issues. If John continues with his view, how will Robert react?

John: Yes, you like to control. You like to be in control, and the easiest person for you to work with is somebody that will be controlled. I don't want to be controlled. We can't have equality among partners if you are in control all the time. I know that you think this is my problem, but I do not think it is only me.

John is correct. Equality is not congruent with unilateral control. Is he implying that Robert is unaware of this? If so, it would not be confirmed by the data all of us have about Robert's confrontability. I predict that Robert is feeling hurt, bewildered, and probably angry.

Bill: It is the characteristic of our jobs that we deal with people who desire to have control. We need to be in control.

Bill finds causes for interpersonal problems which are valid *and* which distance people from their personal responsibility. As Bill has pointed out in the past, he dislikes interpersonal hostility.

Interventionist: Would you like to respond, Robert?

Robert: No, I'm more interested in hearing Bill's views.

Robert seeks data from Bill before he responds. Later we learned that Robert felt very angry and he deferred to Bill in order to calm down. None of us detected overt signs of anger in Robert.

Bill: Well, yes, let me back into it. I would agree that all three of us like controlling the situation. . . . We never give up anything among each other without a difficult fight.

As Bill has often stated, he hates interpersonal conflicts. He is now able to "back into" them.

The dialogue continued with John giving examples of how oppressive Bill and Robert had been during certain meetings. Bill confirmed John's interpretations but questioned whether John had not magnified Robert's oppressive behavior. He then added:

Bill: I think that, during the first two years, Robert was oppressive. Starting the company caused him a lot of emotional problems. . . . Robert may have thought that he had to make it work but could not admit his uncertainties to others.

I can confirm Bill's evaluations, partly because Robert has stated that he was anxious and kept it to himself during the early years of the firm.

John said he sought a relationship in which he would not be continually checked on by Robert or Bill. Robert listened attentively throughout the dialogue. He spoke several times but only to ask questions about John's description.

Int.: Robert, how did you react to John's comments?

Robert: I was angry—a flush of anger that I have not felt for a long time. I felt that John's description was really unfair. [He

Robert appears to be describing his feelings candidly; he is stating his desire not to have his motivation and behavior distorted; he is

selected specific things, seen only from his point of view, with no consideration for others' views.]

I think you're angry that you're not getting paid what you think you're entitled to. But I believe that you are earning more than we committed to you.

accepting some of the responsibility.

How does he know this is true? Is he going to test this attribution?

John: Money is not the issue, Robert.

Robert: But you keep coming back to the same scenario: I am so controlling, and I take unfair advantage of you. It's articulated in terms of last-minute changes, unfair expectations, perfectionism, unbelievable demands, et cetera.

I don't see [the problem] as me; I see that as you *and* me. I don't see you as seeing it as you and me.

Again, Robert accepts responsibility, asks John to accept his part of it.

John: You don't see it as just my problem?

Robert: Absolutely not.

John: I don't see it as your problem alone either. I see it as *our* problem. So I see it the same way.

Nothing said so far indicates that John is accepting a share of the responsibility. I am glad he owns up to the mutuality of the problem, because that increases the likelihood of learning.

Robert: OK. Because I hadn't heard you say that before.

John: I see it as together, both of us.

Robert: My concern is if you can't see that I was making [financial] contributions to you [and my trying to help you],

Robert is becoming more candid about his despair over the number of times this type of episode has been repeated. Are his acthen I despair if you will ever [understand me].

[Gives examples of ways that he helped John. Bill is able to confirm most of them.]

Yes, I do like to be in control of things, in a way of a defense. I think you, John, also like very much to be in control.

tions also punishing John?

Robert admits he is controlling when he feels defensive and attributes the same to John.

John: Um-hmm.

Robert: And personally, I find you much more controlling than I find myself [gives examples].

There is a quality of counterattack. But the examples were confirmed by Bill and largely agreed upon later by John.

[Later]

[What it all adds up to is that] we don't care about the money; our passions come from [the feeling] that you value me and all the work I put into [the firm].

Robert agrees that he wants to be valued and attributes the same desire to Bill and John.

This discussion leads the partners to conclude that, in order to be valued, one must be successful in the business *and* not ask for help. All agree that they hate to ask for help.

John wonders what concrete action they might take to stop these job pressures from recurring. He guides the conversation to solutions that are mechanical (such as being on time for meetings and keeping to the agenda), which do not deal with all the inconsistencies just produced.

After they have agreed on the "solution" of scheduling meetings more effectively, the interventionist mentions that they have made such promises before. Bill then says that he can see how a new partner might come in and say to himself, "Look, I'm as good as they are. I'll show those sons-of-bitches that I can produce as well as they do. I'll never ask for help."

John: Yes, as soon as I say to myself I can't do this and I can't do that, I am afraid that you

John describes his fear of being seen as a failure.

guys will say that "he can't make it."

Robert: I wish we could figure out a way to resolve this issue. [We think the world of your performance. You keep underrating your performance and competence.]

As Robert points out, they have repeatedly told John that he is highly valued. Robert has described John's performance in glowing terms to the board, in John's presence.

John: I am reluctant to ask for help because I was afraid that you, Robert, would see that as *really* weak. . . . I'd rather not do that.

There is plenty of evidence that Robert has made himself available to help other partners when they are pressed. In addition, a fourth partner who had not been producing well was kept on longer than John thought appropriate because Robert wanted to give that partner ample opportunity to correct his performance.

Int.: And what has Robert said or done that [showed] he would interpret such a request as weak?

John: [Pause] I guess it's a standard of the firm. If you can't [do it], that's defined as a failure.

Note that, in describing organizational issues, John also makes public important personal feelings. Bill and especially Robert respond to John's feelings about the organization and about them. Simultaneously, they express their feelings about John, feelings that are not superficial or trivial.

A few minutes later, John mentions that maybe he is not appreciated "on a sustained basis." The interventionist wonders whether such an idea will lead Robert and Bill to see John as "weak" because he needs to be complimented all the time.

It appears reasonable to hypothesize from the foregoing that John is feeling pressed, frustrated, and fearful of being in a situation in which he may not succeed. He is in a double bind. If he asks for help, he will feel like a failure. If he does not ask for help, he runs the risk of failing.

Int.: It may be, John, that Robert is not your only problem. You seek to be successful and you make commitments that overwhelm you. You then hate like hell to ask for help—because of the attribution you make about Robert and Bill's reactions to such requests. But you may also get angry at yourself for placing yourself in a position where you will see yourself as weak.

John: Say that again?

Int.: You do not like yourself when you place yourself in situations where you have to admit you are overcommitted and need help. You get anxious when you are not in control.

John: Yes. I don't like to ask for help.

Bill: Me, too. It drives me up the wall.

John: [I believe when you are under pressure, you should] grit your teeth and run through the line, and hope you don't get your ass busted. So [I blame others] when I'm really overloaded, because I don't know how to ask for help.

Int.: Or you do know how to ask for it but are embarrassed to do so.

John: I hate to look weak. Who the hell wants to look weak!

Robert: I wonder if we have created a group norm for hours and volume of work which is too high. And secondly, a norm of never asking for any help.

John: "Never show weakness" would be the general statement. Asking for help would be an expression of that.

Robert: If so, our organizational norms will become rigid because they are undiscussable.

Bill: And the people in the firm use the same rules and demonstrate the same rigidities.

We may note the following themes:

John asserts that Robert and Bill distance themselves from him. Their actions prevent him from feeling that they want him to become a fully integrated partner.	*Yet*	Robert (and later Bill) recommended these sessions to help develop genuine integration among the partners.
John says that Robert sees his sense of being left out as being only John's problem.	*Yet*	On several occasions, Robert acknowledges that he tends to control and to pressure, espe-

		cially when he is tense and anxious about the quality of their service to the firm.
John states that Robert controls and pressures others through his high standards and a compulsion for work.	*Yet*	John also states that he, too, has high standards and that he is often blind to the effect that his constant work has on others.
John asks for greater autonomy.	*Yet*	John asks to be appreciated on a more sustained basis.

The interventionist's strategy throughout the episode was to focus on the quality of the learning processes that the participants were creating. For example, he notes Robert's downplaying of the interpersonal issues and wonders whether John will become angry. Both these activities would inhibit learning. He notes that a series of attributions John makes about Robert are accurate but also describes "negative" features that apply to John himself. (The interventionist is able to make these evaluations of John's attributions because he has observed the partners during their everyday business meetings and during board meetings.)

As the inconsistencies develop into a pattern, the interventionist places more attention on keeping the problem-solving process facilitative of learning. He notes that Robert does take on a measure of the responsibility, as do John and Bill. The episode ends with John saying that he hates to feel weak and hence rarely asks for help. The others agree that this is true of them also.

Throughout the dialogue, the interventionist tests the validity of the participants' assertions about one another against his own directly held knowledge. He also attempts to test his inferences publicly. Such tests serve two purposes: to encourage confrontation of his views and to provide a model for the clients.

He is prepared to intervene whenever he sees actions that would inhibit learning but waits to see whether the participants themselves take on this responsibility. Because they do, the interventionist does not have to intervene as much as he might in groups where the problem-solving process is less effective. In the few times that the interventionist takes action, it is to give Robert an opportunity to respond to John; to ask for data he needs but has not heard ("Robert, how did you react to John's comments?"); to ask for data to illustrate a key attribution that he is making ("What has Robert said or done that [showed] he would interpret such a request as weak?"). All these interventions help to inform the partners, too, and hence to build an effective problem-solving process.

The same interventions also help the interventionist to realize that John is adding and subtracting invalidly from reality and that these invalid additions and subtractions appear rational to John if he can blame the other partners or the organization for weaknesses that he himself holds and reinforces. These are, in effect, second-order invalid additions, which, for John make the first ones rational. But because the second-order additions are disconfirmable by data jointly held by the interventionist and the partners, and because John espouses that he wishes to learn (and to behave in ways that support his view), the interventionist is able to deduce that the second-order additions are covering up information John holds about himself that is tacit and not in his immediate awareness. Hence the interpretation that the interventionist makes ("It may be, John, that Robert is not your only problem. . . .").

Episode 2

John, Robert, and Bill and their wives (Mary, Jill, and Judy) dined together before their first session. The objective of the session was to discuss interpersonal problems they were having, especially those related to the dominant role the firm played in their lives.

John said during dinner that he would begin the session early by raising a serious question with the interventionist. "Four months ago you asked us to complete a case. Then three months ago you asked us to write another case. Tonight I thought that you were to start the session during the meal, and now you seem to be uncertain how to start it. I'm beginning to wonder about you. You have our lives in your hands, and I'm not sure that you can be trusted."

The interventionist asks how others feel. Mary (John's wife) expresses annoyance at having to write another case. The others do not agree with John. They present data to illustrate their disagreement. For example, they recall that the request for the different cases was made three months ago and that the interventionist had told them that they could, if they wished, use the original cases. They recall that the interventionist suggested the new format because recent research had showed it to be more productive. John agrees with these recollections. The interventionist then adds that the reason he does not want to begin the session during dinner is that the dinner started late. The working style he planned would be counterproductive under the circumstances, and he was concerned about how tired everyone was (because of travel tie-ups and so forth).

This appears to be another example of John fearing that the interventionist is incompetent. Assigning "weak and confused" behavior to the interventionist makes it possible for John to express his fears because he is not aware that these characteristics can be attributed to him.

The interventionist may test this attribution about John. He finds that his own view of reality is supported by the others (and is subject to test later by having an independent observer listen to the tapes). He does not proceed further because the hour is late and it is the first session with this group. He wants to assess the capacities of the group to learn so that he can decide whether further discussion of the issue will be fruitful. The group is quite able to deal with this issue, and discussion is continued the next day.

Episode 3

John is describing the goals he set for his wife, Mary. He wants her to prepare herself for an increasing autonomy as the children grow up.

John: [To Mary] Look, your major job now is to pour into the three children all the good things [that you can]. You can't change adults. But you have a real opportunity to change three young children. You ought to pour it all in, and you shouldn't be diverting your activities to other things. But that's a definite period of time. It's going to be over. And you want to make sure during that period that you're building something, so that when they grow up, you're not feeling lost.

Int.: Do you feel that Mary would not grow unless you put the pressure on?

John: Yes. . . .

Jill: What's the evidence for that?

Mary: Yeah, why would you think that I wouldn't grow unless you prodded me to grow?

[Short silence]

Judy: Maybe you want her to grow in a different way?

John: No, I do not wish to control her. . . .

The purpose of the interventionist's question about Mary is to generate data on whether Mary is as dependent and helpless as John's strategy implies. If not, then the hypothesis that John is being controlling will not be disconfirmed. If so, then the interventionist himself may be distorting, and that will require exploration in the group setting.

John appears to be controlling Mary but to be blind to this fact. Is this another example of John being controlling because he is frightened? He see his wife as weak, as needing to be controlled and managed. One way he can prevent being in a situation he dislikes (having a wife with nothing to do, without interests) is to try to design parts of Mary's life. "What is it that suggests to you that Mary would not grow unless you keep a kind of optimal pressure on her?," the interventionist asks. John says that he is "planting seeds as opposed to pressuring. I don't think that I am turning the screw down." Mary says, "It is stressful, though."

Int.: [To John] Could you be unaware of the stress that you are creating?	If he is willing to own up to this unawareness, I will ask him to surface what his feelings would be if his wife "failed."

John: OK.

Int.: How would you feel if 15 years from now Mary turned out to be like her mother?

John: I would feel very unhappy because I'd know my life is going to be tough. I know it would be stressful for me. I wouldn't like that one bit.

Int.: [Recalls Episode 2 and describes it quickly to the wives.]

This appears to me to be like the previous case. When you get anxious, you place the blame on others and see them as weak.

Mary: Yeah, I'll agree with that.

John: Got that. Is there some learning I can get from that now that you've clearly identified the way I act?

Is this interpretation that new to him? Did I state it incorrectly? Does he hear it but not believe it?

Int.: Well, first, does all this make sense to you?

John: Yes, it does.

Before the interventionist can respond, a long, involved discussion occurs between John and the three wives. They see him as controlling Mary. John thinks out loud about the possibility that the wives also hate to admit that they have inadequacies and that it would be especially difficult for them to admit this to husbands who dislike weakness. The wives agree with his insight.

Int.: A while back you asked me what can be done with the insight. What is the insight as you now see it?

John: Whenever I get anxious, I look for some factual information [I can use] to pass that anxiousness to somebody else. Then I can cleanse myself of it and don't have to get uptight myself.

Mary: He passes the responsibility on to somebody else.

John: So that I can abdicate the responsibility. So what you're saying is that one of the characteristics is to systematically screen out information . . . for my benefit.

Int.: When you are anxious—not in every situation.

[Later]

John: Let me tell you another insight I am having. When I want an issue discussed and I am not sure that it will be, I add to it—magnify it—to make sure it is difficult to ignore.

John now appears to recognize some new inconsistencies. On the one hand, he describes himself as "willing to get his ass busted while plunging through the line." On the other hand, he acknowledges that when he gets anxious, he strives to pass the responsibility on to someone else. Further, he now appears to realize that he magnifies problems so that the others involved will find them harder to ignore. However, if the others do not agree with the magnification, then he only creates new problems for himself.

Some readers may point out that John is not really learning, or if he is, it is at the intellectual level, not the emotional. John deals with interpretations that he accepts as valid by immediately asking for action recommendations. This too quick agreement can be a sign of resistance to learning.

But our perspective suggests another interpretation. John values his theory of effective action. He is not going to make paradigmatic shifts in this theory until he is relatively certain that his present theory is inadequate. His behavior is similar to that of most social scientists dealing with evidence that appears to disconfirm their theories: He resists altering the theory until he has tested it further.

John conducts a series of thought experiments to disconfirm the new information. If he succeeds, then he will not have to make a paradigmatic shift in his theory. If he does not, every experiment will provide insight into the aspects of this theory that require changing. Let us look at an example of such a thought experiment.

Episode 4

After the third episode, John explores various implications of the insights with his wife. He designs a thought experiment that suggests to him that the insights he is getting may be counterproductive to his effectiveness.

John begins by repeating what he has learned about distorting reality and by simultaneously putting the blame elsewhere. He is not coming into contact with his fears of probable failure, his desire for help, and his possible weakness, until he says:

John: I guess that I'm the kind of person who likes to win and doesn't like to lose. I don't like to admit that I'm weak, and I don't like to admit that I might lose. And the actions that I take are predesigned to reduce the chance of losing.

If I lost, that would lower my self-esteem. Hence, the solution is that I have to lower my self-esteem. And there's going to be some benefit to that, which is ill defined.

I have trouble in seeing the benefit of losing more often and reducing my self-esteem.

Mary: You see why I wanted him to bring this up. I've been sitting here for an *hour* hoping he'd bring it up!

Robert: I don't think you appreciate yourself as much as others do. You have a nationwide reputation in your field. If you felt as confident about yourself as others do, then I think you would be able to take the defeats or losses *in stride*. No problem!

Don't reduce your self-esteem. Let it rise to a realistic level.

Jill: You ask what you'll get out of it. Well, you won't require other people to take on your anxieties. People will feel less defensive with you, and that will enhance the relationship.

Bill: The only person you're protecting on that scoreboard is yourself. You've lost with the other person [if you continue your present defensive strategy]. If your only strategies are either to win or to lose, I would accept neither.

[Later]

Int.: You started by saying that you hate to lose. We are not suggesting that with your old strategy you will only lose. The other person may not tell you that is the case.

Also, you say that you do not want to appear weak and frightened. Yet [in all the previous sessions] I experienced you as frightened and so weak that you were distorting reality. You speak of self-esteem. One criterion of a person with a high self-esteem is that he can create conditions for others to enhance their self-esteem.

Your old strategy did not help you or the others. Your new projected strategy would be equally counterproductive. To use your language, you would be playing a losing game.

John: I guess I see. I'm pretty slow in this area. I have a lot to learn. Is this something I have to solve by myself, or is this something [on which] I can expect and ask for help from others?

The group members respond that they all feel they have much to learn. The interventionist agrees it will take time; it *should* take time. The key is to be open to learning and to have resource people. One purpose of the group is for the members to become resources to one another. For example, Bill and Robert could alert John when he was going into a counterproductive cycle, and Mary could help in the home setting.

The Established View of Defense

A defense is usually defined as "a protective action or attitude directed against danger," whereas a defense mechanism is a specific technique used by the ego, such as projection, denial, or repression, to ward off inner or external dangers.[1]

According to Kroeber,[2] defenses have been viewed as having adaptive as well as pathological features. Freud spoke of the difference between "moral" and "pathological" defense mechanisms, but as Anna Freud pointed out, his primary interest was in the pathogenic features of defenses.[3]

Kroeber[4] viewed the pathogenic and adaptive features as part of the ego mechanisms. He described the pathogenic features as defensive and the adaptive as coping. Defensive behavior is rigid, compelled, channeled; is pushed from the past; essentially distorts the present; involves a larger component of primary process thinking and partakes of unconscious elements; and permits impulse gratification only by subterfuge or indirection.

John's behavior before the interventions began approximated the defensive features of being rigid, inflexible, pulled from the past, and distorting the present situation. The interventionist's task was to help John shift his behavior toward coping behavior. Although John's behavior may have been pulled from the past, it is not necessary to identify it as partaking of primary process thinking and unconscious elements. Another possible explanation, as we shall see, is that it involved secondary process thinking and preconscious elements.

A fundamental assumption of much of present counseling practice is that the maladaptive aspects of defenses can be corrected if insight can be obtained into the distortive processes peculiar to each defense. Another basic assumption is that a dialogue between

---

[1] Mark Kanzer and Harold P. Blum, "Classical Psychoanalysis Since 1939," in B. B. Wolman, ed., Psychoanalytic Techniques: A Handbook for Practicing Therapists (New York: Basic Books, 1967), pp. 109-110.

[2] Theodore C. Kroeber, "The Coping Functions of the Ego Mechanisms," in Robert W. White, ed., The Study of Lives (New York: Atherton Press, 1963).

[3] Anna Freud, The Ego and the Mechanisms of Defense (London: Hogarth Press, 1937), p. 4).

[4] Kroeber, 1963, p. 184.

client and therapist can give insight into the distortive processes.[5] The paradox in this assumption is that the therapist must depend on the reconstructive capacities of the client even though those capacities involve the very inference processes that are distorted, including the processes that keep the client blind to how the distortions operate. When people remember, they are reconstructing what they have already constructed. Hence, the recollections tend to be removed from the action that the therapist and client are trying to understand.

Therapists recognize this problem. They strive to create conditions that can surface these distortive capacities, as well as insight into when they may have begun. For example, transference is used in this manner. Transference is "the experiencing of drives, attitudes, and defenses toward a person in the present which do not befit that person but are a repetition of reactions originating in regard to significant persons of early childhood, unconsciously displaced onto figures in the present."[6] The therapist's task is to surface the issues and objects that act as symbols to trigger the defensive reactions and divest them of their anxiety-producing potential.[7]

Four features of John's actions are relevant to the concept of defense: (1) He added to and subtracted from reality. The validity of his additions and subtractions was publicly disconfirmed. For example, his attributions that Robert and (less so) Bill were responsible for his failure to feel included and that they saw him as a failure were disconfirmed by data that Robert, Bill, and the interventionist produced. (2) John made requests that were contradictory. He asked for more autonomy but also for sustained signs that he was appreciated. (3) John surfaced needs that were unacceptable to him but were necessary for his effective performance ("I hate to ask for help"). (4) John appeared unaware of the disconfirmability, inconsistency, and contradiction of his actions. These four features acting in unison made it highly unlikely that John would be able to detect and correct the error caused by his behavior or be aware that he could not do so.

[5] Kanzer and Blum, 1967, pp. 109-110.
[6] Ralph R. Greenson, *The Technique and Practice of Psychoanalysis* (New York: International Universities Press, 1967), vol. 1, p. 171.
[7] Nicholas Hobbs, "Sources of Gain in Psychotherapy," in Emmanuel F. Hammer, ed., *Use of Interpretation in Treatment* (New York: Grune & Stratton, 1968), p. 17.

Defensive action may be defined as any invalid addition or subtraction from concrete reality that inhibits detection and correction of error as well as detection of the unawareness that the actions are defensive. Defensive actions are therefore error-enhancing, learning-inhibiting actions about which the person is usually unaware.

Some defensive actions do not inhibit learning or enhance error. People may differ with others; they may strive to correct incorrect attributions about their views or their psychological motivation. As long as these defensive actions are implemented in ways that preserve valid reality, and the actions do not block learning, they may be viewed as protective coping actions.[8]

Robert exhibited coping behavior when he maintained that he was not the only major cause of John's problems; when he provided data (concrete examples) to illustrate his views; and when he deferred to Bill in order to restrain his anger with John. I would prefer to call these actions defensive. This would reverse the present extensively accepted meaning of *defensive action* (a switch in meaning that might only create confusion).

As is the practice, I view defenses as reactions to danger or vulnerability, and I infer that vulnerability must exist when people behave in ways that inhibit effective learning.

It is not necessary, for our perspective, to discover the origins and ideology of defenses or to categorize them according to their specific mechanisms. For example, John could be projecting or displacing past feelings. All we need to show is that his actions invalidly add to or subtract from reality and that they prevent awareness of this fact.

It is not necessary to view defenses that inhibit learning as unconscious ways to deal with anxiety. People may be unaware of their defenses simply because they are skillful, complex microtheories-in-use and effective execution requires that they be tacit. This does not mean a defense could not also be associated with trauma. The rule is to first consider the "unconscious" factors as factors that are simply tacit. If they are tacit, they are part of skillful behavior. Skillful behavior can be surfaced by interrupting it. John's defensive behavior (which I am calling skillful behavior that invalidly added and subtracted from reality) was interrupted because he was in a learning

---

[8]Kroeber, 1963.

environment where he was trying to acquire an additional theory-in-use.

Keep in mind that we are not dealing with pathological defenses. All our clients are operating relatively effectively in their everyday life. John's case illustrates how nonlearning behavior can manifest both maladaptive and adaptive features. To use Kroeber's terms, John's actions led to defensive and coping features. The former are related to the lack of learning, the latter to John's superior performance. It may be, for example, that John designs his life to reduce the probability of fear. He therefore works very hard to be a superior performer and is highly successful at his job (which, however, does result in his resisting asking for help).

We obtain information about John's defenses as he is presently manifesting them and do so with relatively directly observable data. Hence, we are not dependent on his reconstructions. Nor do we require transference-type relationships, because we are able to observe firsthand any invalid attributions of motives, feelings, and values by the actor toward others. Or, to put it another way, we are able to observe John participating in a transference relationship with Robert. Robert, being the president, could be an authority figure, and thus an appropriate target for transference, to John.

In our approach, we seek—

1. To place clients in situations that approximate as closely as possible the conditions under which they appear to get into trouble.
2. To observe the conditions and the problem with minimal dependence on the client's recollections.
3. To examine and reexamine these conditions by repeated replay (for example, tape recordings).
4. To invent and produce new courses of action, which can then be tested for their effectiveness.
5. To have the situations required for the repeated tests created in noncontrived events.

These conditions imply that (1) the actor's capacity for learning is not so distorted that he or she cannot learn from colleagues; (2) the actor is motivated to learn and to experiment; (3) the critical situations required for the tests are repeatable in noncontrived ways; (4) opportunities can be created to reflect on the experiments; and

(5) the interventionist has models of inquiry and action that the client finds easy to understand and is capable of learning to use.

If clients are so vulnerable that they cannot permit themselves to learn, then perhaps the "deeper" therapies are required. But before this conclusion is accepted, we must be aware that the "deeper" therapy is constructed with the same Model I theory that the therapist uses to construct his or her own private reality. The deeper features of the client's problems may appear because of the self-fulfilling processes by which they are discovered. The unpeeling process is a function of the theory of therapy used and the learning conditions created.

For example, Fenichel[9] differentiates between transference resistances and character resistances. The latter are "deeper" and more rigid than the former, and they occur in many different situations. One could make the case that John's defense was a characterological one because it appeared in many situations over time and it resisted change. But the surfacing of the defense was relatively easy and straightforward. What about the resistance John showed to changing defenses? It is possible that the resistance was due less to threat and more to the number of thought and action experiments John wanted to create in order to validate the insights and make a paradigmatic shift in his theory-in-use. People without any signs of deep emotional problems have taken two or three years to make such transformations.[10] Reasons for the extensive time may be that learning these activities is inherently difficult, others do not know how to help the actor learn, and opportunities for noncontrived experiments where reflection is possible immediately afterward are infrequent. Another reason is related to the primitiveness of our learning technology.

To the extent that the conditions we seek to create hold, learning about psychological defenses will occur through the use of skills we already have to build and test theories. These skills, therefore, may be more easily taught than the skills involved in traditional therapies, an advantage that allows others to eventually become on-

[9]Otto Fenichel, *The Collected Papers of Otto Fenichel* (New York: Norton, 1954), p. 138.
[10]Chris Argyris, *Increasing Leadership Effectiveness* (New York: Wiley-Interscience, 1976).

going resources for learning. This assumes that clients can work through their anxieties and make their defensive responses less automatic by means of learning experiences in the present. If John requires more approval than Robert and Bill can give, and if John can see that this need is inconsistent with his need for autonomy, that it can inhibit his effectiveness as an executive, or both, the hypothesis is that he will alter his behavior without having to work through the original causes of the defense.

We can predict that John (with the help of others) will decrease the number of times that he automatically distorts reality (denies, projects, or displaces); that he will design and use new behavior that is effective; and that if he returns to defensive behavior, he will be aware of it and can admit it. These predictions are subject to disconfirmation because we have continued access to John's work and home life. If the predictions are not disconfirmed, then our belief that John is indeed working through "deeper" defenses by more socially available and usable educational techniques would not be disconfirmed.

To illustrate, we turn to Albert (in a different seminar), who presents the case of Joe (his subordinate), a poor performer. During the discussion, Albert becomes aware of his suppressed anger with Joe. In the next session (one week later), he realizes that he has also suppressed feelings of anger toward himself (for not confronting Joe with his poor performance and lackadaisical attitude). He begins to see that these are related angers.

"I now recognize," he writes in his analysis of the tapes, "that I was angry at myself. I wrote down a heuristic: When you experience anger, you are often angry at yourself as well as the other person."

Several weeks later, Albert becomes angry at his wife. He remembers the "automatic angry response" and the heuristic. For several days, he tries to figure out what he might be angry about in his own behavior. He finally recognizes that he hates to have his competence questioned.

He explores with his wife what it was about her questioning that led him to interpret it as questioning his competence. He concludes that he holds an unrealistically high expectation of his performance. Indeed, if he followed his expectations, he would have to be perfect; anything else would be failure. Under those conditions, even innocent questions are experienced as threatening.

Albert then reports that he developed two heuristics that he has found helpful in other situations: "The anger you experience at yourself may be related to (1) an unrealistically high sense of personal expectation of yourself or (2) an unrealistically high sense of personal responsibility to the system in which you are involved."

Here we see a person becoming aware of his anger toward others, relating it to anger at himself, and relating the self-anger to an unrealistically high sense of responsibility. As he begins to develop a more realistic level of aspiration, he becomes more accepting of himself and of others. He finds it easier to confront poor performance in himself and others more effectively.

The sequence of events in these cases might be described as follows:

1. The actor constructs reality and makes public the assertions that follow from his construction. The presentation is usually about a central, rather than a peripheral, problem.
2. The problem is stated in front of the people involved. The statements are tape-recorded so that the same relatively directly observable data are available to all parties.
3. Several directions then become possible:
   a. The others disconfirm the actor's assertions. They then present additional data and/or show the actor that he is interpreting the data incorrectly.
   b. If the actor does not agree, they enter into a joint process of inquiry that produces more data and/or leads to an agreement on who is or is not making correct interpretations.
   c. Assuming that inquiry leads the actor to become aware of his share of the distortions, he must be helped to see that the responses to the stressful situations are not only defensive, they are automatic. Automatic responses indicate behavior programs or rules that are so well learned that they are tacit. Responses informed by tacit rules cannot be corrected until the rules have been made explicit. For a while at least, the actor will be in the situation of responding incorrectly and becoming aware only after the fact.

Relating the Theory-of-Action Perspective to Other Perspectives

We now relate our perspective to some recent work by clinical psychologists who share our information-processing bias. Wexler[11] suggests that people may be vulnerable when they have no rules to organize information and they lose it in their short-term memory (denial) or when their rules are not adequate to organize all the information they have (distortion).

This means that reducing defenses will require that people become aware of the rules they use to make automatic responses that are counterproductive, the rules they use to hide the first rules from their awareness, and the consequences (the inconsistencies) of holding such rules.

For example, John may be said to have two rules in his head: (1) Ignore my feelings of weakness, which would make me angry with and fearful of myself should I become aware of them, and (2) remain unaware that I have such a rule. But John is not willing to hold rules that put him in a position he cannot knowingly defend to himself or to others. He holds a third, more general rule, (3) that his reality constructions cannot be either inconsistent or counterproductive, and he should be able to advocate his position to others successfully as long as they, too, hold the rule that they do not wish to be inconsistent or counterproductive.

The first two rules violate the third rule because John is unlikely to be consistent and to create valid information if he ignores important and relevant information.

To continue with the sequence of events:

4. With his new awareness, the actor has now differentiated his life-space to include more information than was previously acceptable. He now needs rules to integrate his information.[12] But integration is a slow and difficult process.

    a. The initial steps are usually designed to maintain the old

---

[11] David A. Wexler, "A Cognitive Theory of Experiencing Self-Actualization and Therapeutic Process," in David A. Wexler and Laura North Rice, eds., *Innovations in Client-Centered Therapy* (New York: Wiley-Interscience, 1974).
[12] Wexler, 1974.

rules. For example, as soon as John becomes aware that he distorts reality, he asks the interventionist for solutions. John's request makes sense if we keep in mind the old rules. For example, if John's rule is "Do not accept weakness," and if the new awareness leads him to feel weak, then if he can correct the awareness, he will no longer be weak. But the difficulty is that John not only doesn't have a solution, he cannot even invent one, because he is operating under the old rules.

b.   A next step is to conduct experiments to try to disconfirm the consequences that the actor must change. For example, John blames the organization for his fears. Part of the blame is accepted and corrected by the partners, but that does not solve John's problem.

The person may also conduct private thought experiments. For example, John develops an analysis of how he would lower his self-esteem if he reduced the defenses. As a result of inquiry, he learns that his analysis is faulty and that continuing the present strategy would be counterproductive.

John's experiments designed to delay integration also create the conditions for integration. The experiments provide new information, and every one of John's experiments proves that it is in his best interest to integrate the new awareness. Moreover, every experiment provides information that can be used to design new cognitive maps of integration.[13]

5.   The next step may be called active, or planned, integration. It can occur privately or publicly. Albert developed two rules: (1) Don't trust your existing construction when you get angry at others who appear to you not to be performing adequately, and (2) if you become angry at others, ask privately what the other person said or did that might have been a threat to you (as Albert did with his wife). Do it privately so that you are not seen by others as incompetent, because that would trigger the old rules.

[13]Wexler, 1974.

Once Albert is able to see that he is angry at himself for not performing effectively *and* for having unrealistically high aspirations for his performance, then he can go public and discuss the episode with his wife. He is now able to be aware and in control. This reduces the likelihood that the old rules will operate.

The time it will take to internalize the new rules—to make them tacit—varies with individuals, with the intensity of the threat, and with the context. One can facilitate the learning by increasing the number of private and public experiments in two of the most important segments of life—namely, work and family. The experiments will not be contrived but will come naturally. In John's case, this will happen whenever he is under stress or pressure. But now he has the resources to help him interpret data correctly and to develop and practice new skills.

A second research program from which we can learn is the recent work by Havens[14] on therapeutic intervention strategies. Havens reexamined the interpersonal perspective of Harry Stack Sullivan. He not only has developed new theoretical insights about personality theory but has connected these to clinical practice. A key strategy in the new perspective is to help clients look at their defenses by the use of a "counterprojective" screen. The purpose is to move the clients' projections "out of the medium between therapist and patient onto the space on the screen before them." The goal is to encourage clients to see their distortive processes.[15] The second key strategy is to create conditions in which the clients can share their feelings and can acknowledge the reality of their distortions. The goal is to reduce or disavow the distortive actions.[16]

The conditions illustrated in John's case do create the screen that Havens recommends. First, the organization became a counterprojective screen for the partners when they were talking about their human problems. They could surface and project the causes of distortive processes partly because they could blame the organization. For example, John's defensive actions became apparent as the part-

---

[14] Leston Havens, *Participant Observation* (New York: Jason Aronson, 1976).

[15] Havens, 1976, p. 101.

[16] Havens, 1976, p. 103.

ners were trying to discuss ownership of the firm and the structure of the Executive Office. Bill created a screen because he hated emotional conflicts. Every time John attacked Robert or owned up to his feelings about admitting weakness, Bill was able to show that the same feelings were also caused by the requirements of starting up and maintaining a highly competitive business. The wives helped John by exploring the way their husbands pressured them. Finally, the interventionist created appropriate screens by relating John's actions to organizational dynamics within and outside the firm. Diagnosing systemic defenses may make it easier to reflect and own up to one's own defenses because one can see that the organization is partly responsible *and* that, in surfacing systemic defenses, one helps the organization. Finally, any diagnosis about systemic defenses that is confirmed by others makes it easier for individuals to explore the personal defenses that appear to be triggered by systemic issues.

11

Teaching
Action Strategies
in the Classroom

The university seminars of Chapters Two and Three began with the interventionist feeding back a collage of the diagnoses made by the participants. After any questions are answered, the interventionist asks, "Does anyone see some important part of his or her diagnosis that I have omitted from this pattern?" The intent is to have on the blackboard a pattern that represents as many of the views held by participants as possible. The interventionist adds any further contributions suggested by the participants and says, "As I understand it, all of you believe that the important features of your respective diagnoses are represented here?"

The intention is to build up a diagnosis that the majority confirm as a valid representation of their individual contributions. The interventionist does this by presenting the collage, or pattern, advocating and encouraging inquiry into his diagnosis. The interventionist modifies the pattern that he is placing on the blackboard until no further disconfirmations or additions are forthcoming.

Next, the interventionist surfaces the predominant causal propositions that are embedded in the pattern. You may recall that in all examples presented in Part One, a causal view was embedded in the pattern. For example:

> Y was unilaterally judgmental and evaluative, authoritarian, unconcerned, and insensitive.
> Therefore, X will feel unfairly judged, misunderstood, and rejected.
> Therefore, little learning will occur on the part of X or Y.

The interventionist asks for confirmation or disconfirmation of these causal propositions. To date, participants overwhelmingly confirm that the causal propositions given represent the causality they believe exists in the relationship between Y and X. Again, the interventionist models advocating his position and encouraging inquiry into it. Because it is publicly tested and confirmed, the participants' internal commitment to the diagnosis and its implicit causal perspective is reinforced.

The interventionist then applies the group's causal proposition to their diagnosis of Y. He points out that their diagnosis of Y contains untested, unilateral attributions and evaluations. Hence, they framed their diagnosis with the same features that they inferred Y used in dealing with X. The causal microtheory embedded in their diagnoses of Y's actions toward X should also hold, therefore, if their diagnostic frames were to be communicated to Y. The interventionist then asks the group for their reactions: "What do you believe would happen if the diagnostic pattern on the blackboard were communicated to Y?"

Participant 1: He'd get upset.

P2: I can see that he might react negatively.

Interventionist: OK. Does anyone have any idea as to what would lead this group to frame their diagnoses so that they contain counterproductive features that are similar to those that they identified in the way Y acted toward X?

[Silence]

P1: Would you please repeat that?

Int.: Why is it that you've framed the problem in a way that is congruent with the way you believe that Y framed his problem with X? A way which you have diagnosed as counterproductive to learning?

P2: Well, don't we all bring a kind of subjectivity to our diagnoses? We begin subjectively, but then we will go beyond that in our intervention.

P3: It seems to me that there is a distinction between framing the diagnosis and communicating it.

Int.: And what are you predicting about the communication?

P3: I'm predicting that the communicating better take a different form than the diagnosis.

Int.: Some of you acknowledge the inconsistency but believe that you will solve it by not communicating directly what is in your diagnostic frames. Is this a valid inference? [Several respond yes; several nod affirmatively.] Does anyone have any ideas as to what would lead you to frame problems in ways that you do not intend to communicate?

P4: Because it is pragmatic.

Int.: I do not understand. What is pragmatic about it?

P4: If I were a doctor and you had cancer, I do not think that I would tell you at the outset.

Int.: So you have the expectation that eventually people will tell their diagnostic frame to Y, but they will do it later?

P4: Yes, probably.

Int.: We have talked about the idea of behaving congruently, or authentically. We have defined these terms as stating your feelings and views candidly. Would it not be correct for me to infer that we are now witnessing conditions under which you would choose not to behave congruently?

P5: Well, yes, if you want to put it that way.

Int.: I am trying to follow the group's reasoning. If you believe that I am distorting your views, please tell me. I want to learn that, because it is not my intention to do so.

P6: I think that you are confusing minimal correlation here with causality.

Int.: I do not see any correlation here.

P6: You may have given me some confusing information, then, in your question. I think that you can decide that Y has been judgmental and threatening, and degrading toward X, but you don't have to approach Y that way.

Int.: And what is OK about that? Are you implying that the diagnoses that we hold about Y will not influence the way we talk with and listen to Y?

P6: No, obviously not, but . . .

P7: I think my diagnosis was different. I see Y as a fundamentally insecure person.

Int.: Yes.

P7: Y dealt with X the way that he did because he was afraid of confrontations.

Int.: Two reactions. I believe that your diagnosis that Y may be insecure fits with the judgments already on the blackboard. If not, please help me to see why not. Second, I believe that you are saying that it is possible to judge Y as insecure and approach him in ways that this view is not communicated. If you agree, what is the evidence that this is possible?

P8: I don't think it is OK. I feel lousy doing it. But it is the only thing that I have to work with. . . . All I know about Y is this conversation.

Int.: Are you saying that the class dealt with Y in this way because they lacked information about Y?

P8: Yes, they did not know him personally. If you don't know a person, then you have to act that way.

Int.: What data, theory, perspective, do you have to present to make that assertion compelling? I, for one, doubt that knowing him would alter your diagnosis or strategy. And we can test out my hypothesis in several ways. One, I can give you more data. Just tell me what it is you want to know. Second, we can observe how we deal with the case over time.

P9: Well, I'd want to know what's behind what he's saying.

P10: You may be able to empathize.

Int.: What does that mean, "to empathize"? Why not roleplay whatever you would do in order to get behind what Y is saying?

[Silence]

P11: I think that what she [P8] said was important. If you could see the whole case and know more about the relationship between Y and X, you'd have a better understanding.

Int.: I have several reactions. One, let us try it. I'll be glad to supply you with whatever data . . . I have. Two, we have tried it, and with a greater amount of information, people embellish but do not change their diagnosis of Y. But that may not be the case this time. Finally, I am interested in teaching you a perspective which may not need more data, one which will allow you to act in helpful ways with this amount of data.

P12: I'd like to go back to the distinction between our diagnoses and how we would really approach Y. I agree that our frames are full of assumptions and attributions that have not been tested. But one reason that we want to hide the diagnosis and ease in is to test these attributions.

Int.: In doing so, would you tell Y what you are doing?

P12: Obviously not—not at this time.

Int.: Hence, your mode of testing your views requires that you keep the testing procedure secret from the client.

P2: Is it possible to keep it secret? Won't he [be able to] tell?

P10: I'm not convinced that the implications follow in that causal sequence that you described previously.

Int.: Fine—what are the inconsistencies or problems that you see in my formulation?

P10: Well, first of all, [I do not believe that Y created a sense of mutuality with X. If he had, then some of the causal sequence might not hold.]

Int.: Right on. How might Y have acted toward X to create more mutuality?

P10: Just by setting up a common goal from the start.

P13: It seems to me [that our having] made a diagnosis at the outset doesn't preclude . . . modifying it once we talked with Y.

Int.: I have my doubts, but I may be wrong. We can try it out in at least two ways. One is, we can examine the scenarios that you have written. Secondly, we can go beyond the scenarios by roleplaying.

P5: Are you saying listening will not lead us to change?

Int.: I am saying that our listening—what we hear—may be influenced [without our knowledge] by our diagnostic frames. I am also saying that other groups who tried it did not change. And finally, I would like to encourage that we try it.

P6: Telling us that other groups have tried it is not encouraging.

Int.: How else could I have said it? I do not want to hold [this] back, . . . because if I told you later, you could point out that I was easing in with you.

Let us pause to summarize the participants' primary responses and the interventionist's replies:

Participants:	*Interventionist:*
1. We do not intend to communicate the content of our diagnoses.	What would lead you to frame your diagnoses in ways that you do not intend to communicate?
2. Our diagnoses were pragmatic.	What is the meaning of *pragmatic*?
3. The reason we will not communicate the content of our diagnoses directly to Y is that doing so would upset him.	What would lead you to frame your diagnoses in ways that would be upsetting?
4. If our diagnoses were inadequate, it is because we lacked the whole picture.	I would be glad to provide you with all the information that I have, but I doubt that this is an important issue.
5. We are not communicating the content of our diagnoses directly until we test them.	How will you test them?
6. We will test our diagnoses without telling Y. We will ease in.	The strategy that you have selected requires that you keep the strategy secret from Y.
7. The gaps the interventionist is stating are not compelling.	I would be glad to try to make them more compelling or to see the holes in them. Help me by illustrating a gap, and then I will try to fill it in.
8. We know how to listen and modify our diagnoses.	I believe that your listening will be influenced by the way you have diagnosed Y's actions and intentions.

The participants reacted to the awareness that their diagnosis might contain the same counterproductive features as they believed Y showed toward X by a series of logical counterarguments. The interventionist was able to show that every counterargument contained further inconsistencies. For example, the response that they did not intend to communicate their diagnoses directly appeared contrary to their espoused theory of consulting, which said that effective interventionists should behave congruently with their diagnoses. The response that their diagnoses were pragmatic was countered with an inquiry into the meaning of *pragmatic,* which they could not decide to their own satisfaction. The response that they intended to test their views before communicating them to Y was countered with the observation that, in order for their strategy to work, it would have to be kept secret. Such unilateral censoring would violate their intention of candor and nonmanipulation. In other words, the interventionist was able to show that every response contained nested inconsistencies. As a result, the participants began to see that their arguments did not withstand the very logic that they espoused.

The participants' response may rightfully be viewed as defensive. But it is a type of defensiveness that, from a theory-of-action perspective, is productive of learning and hence should be supported and encouraged.

The interventionist, in effect, is generating data that lead to the inference that the participants hold diagnostic frames that are counterproductive. If this inference is not disconfirmed, the participants' helping abilities can be seriously questioned. Hence, it makes sense for the participants to seek every possible gap and inconsistency in the interventionist's reasoning processes. They are using with him the same process of inquiry that he is using with them—namely, identifying inconsistencies and gaps. In responding to the interventionist, they can watch how he deals with attempts to disconfirm his views. In striving to defend their views, they produce responses that make public the nested defenses with which they protect themselves. Becoming aware of these nested defenses helps the participants become aware of the pattern of their defenses.

To the extent that these conditions hold, the defensive reactions introduce more learning into error-producing thoughts and actions. These are Type A defenses. Type A defenses are any attempt to protect one's paradigm (that is, one's theory-in-use) carried out in such a way that learning continues. Whenever the defensive reactions reach a point at which detection and correction of error are no longer possible, then Type B defensive reactions can be said to exist. The interventionist strives not to create or reinforce Type B defensive reactions. If they do occur, it is important that the participants be helped to see how such reactions are closing off learning.

The first phase of Type A defensive reactions focuses mainly on the participants' defending their actions and reasoning processes in response to the interventionist's inquiry. A second phase eventually begins when the participants move toward confronting the interventionist. Previewing the results for a moment, this phase of confrontation is very important for several reasons. First, the strategy of easing in assumes that people like Y are too defensive to learn from interventionists who advocate their positions, even though they may encourage inquiry. This theory of help implies that all defensiveness is counterproductive to learning; it follows that effective interventionists must not produce defensiveness. Our view, however, is that effective interventionists encourage Type A—not Type B—defensiveness. This issue will surface when the participants begin to question the interventionist's actions.

The second reason that confronting the interventionist is important is so that the participants see how he deals with it. If they see that there are ways to react constructively to Type A defenses (namely, to produce Type A defensive reactions that facilitate learning), then they have generated further data to question their previously held theories of help as well as data for inventing new responses.

Let us return to the session and note how this phase began and its consequences.

P14: Well, I'm having trouble with seeing what is different about the way he analyzed the case and what is happening right here in this class. We made judgments about Y, and you made judgments about us. [Other participants agree.]

Int.: Fine. Let me characterize how I believe that I have acted during the session and get your reactions to my view.

I collected data—namely, your cases. I analyzed the diagnostic frames into simple patterns. I identified a causal theme in the frames. All these were judgments.

I came to this meeting and began by presenting my pattern and testing its validity with you. I then showed how I inferred a causal sequence that was embedded in the pattern and again tested it with you.

Hence, I stated what was in my frame and tested it as I went along. So I believe that I am advocating my position and encouraging inquiry into it, especially ways that may disconfirm it.

I honestly doubt that it will be disconfirmed. But I also believe that I am open to, and encourage, the design of any valid test that may disconfirm it. If disconfirmation does occur, I believe that I will be shaken, that I will feel good about having participated in the design of the experiment that produced the disconfirmation, and that I will start to reexamine my theory.

P8: Yes, he's being consistent.

P10: Yes, damn it [laughs].

Int.: My position, therefore, is not that we should not make evaluations or judgments. It is how do we frame them, and test them, and utilize them to help others. I do not believe that this class, so far, has emulated such a perspective, although almost all of you espoused it in your cases.

P2: Well, I still believe there is something here not being examined. It seems to me that I can make judgments and evaluations about a person and still respect that person—not evaluate [him] as bad—and therefore not have the counterproductive consequences.

Int.: I hear you. Let us call that an invention to dealing with the problem. Do you, or does anyone else, believe that [he] produced this invention in [his] case? [Several persons say no.]

This is an important issue. We find that many individuals are able to invent valid solutions, but they are unable to produce these solutions and are unaware of this fact. One thing that we can do here is to try to produce the invention.

P15: Looking back on our diagnoses and what is happening here, I see that we have no information from Y about how Y sees his own performance.

P12: The way the [interventionist] has dealt with us is that he gave us this sheet of paper with a collage of our statements. Then he asked us to confirm or disconfirm, to add or to change.

Int.: And if you were to use that model with Y, what might you do?

P12: I would begin with the conversation.

P11: Yes, I am sure that if he heard the two consecutive sentences "Let's discuss your feelings" and "We do not have time to discuss your feelings," he would say, "Oh, God, how could I do that!?"

Int.: Or he might react the way this group is reacting to the inconsistencies that I believe you have produced. You are expressing your doubts and seeking gaps and inconsistencies in my views. And I hope that I am acting in ways that provide us an opportunity to test your views and mine.

P16: I think that one of the problems here is that we play with your rules. In my judgment, the problem is not Y and X, it is the organization. We had to do a dialogue; hence, we were forced to deal with Y and X.

Int.: Fine. Let us assume that the issue is really an organizational problem. What would you do?

P16: I don't know.

Int.: I do remember your case. You did identify it as an organizational problem. Would you please tell the group what you advised?

P16: I suggested that we change the hierarchical relationships to more equal relationships.

P12: I think it is sort of a defeatist proposal because consultants can't go in and say that.

P7: They can say that, but how far will they get?

Int.: Those of you who know my writing know I do value structural relationships of the kind that you suggest. But I believe that what my data show, and what I believe this experience is showing, is that people are programmed with theories-in-use that will eventually make more equal hierarchical relationships unequal. Each will strive to unilaterally control the other person.

For example, in your scenarios many of you controlled the client unilaterally. You [P16], who suggested more equal relationships, created in your case top-down relationships with Y [and we can test that attribution with the class]. Finally, [P12's] assertion just now that your ideas are defeatist could have been viewed by you as unfair or incorrect.

To summarize:

Participants state that:	*Interventionist:*
1. Consultant is behaving toward us the way we behaved toward Y.	Describes his actions and asks for disconfirmation or confirmation.

Participants state that:	*Interventionist:*
2. We can make judgments about Y and still respect him.	Asks for data to illustrate their position. This leads to the possibility that people cannot produce what they invent.
3. We have not asked Y for directly observable data about our judgments.	Illustrates that it is possible to do this by the way he is acting toward the participants.

Next, a return to the first-phase defenses:

4. The problem is the organization.	Asks if that were the case, what the participants would recommend.

Then back to the second phase, only this time the confrontation is of each other's views. For example, P12 doubted the validity and practicality of P16's invention.

The first phase of expressing Type A defenses, and the second phase exploring more of what is going on in the here-and-now situation, are followed by a third phase, in which the participants begin to look inward. They begin to explore feelings and thoughts that they have generated but have kept to themselves.

P12: I am glad to hear the others also feel my confusion and frustration.

P14: I think this whole thing is so puzzling that I have spent most of my time trying to figure out what you were up to. I do not think that I have listened to much of what you were saying.

P17: What I feel uncomfortable with is [that] our genuine confusion and frustration seem to be coupled with your obvious delight.

Int.: When you say "delighted," what is it that I said or did that suggests to you that I was delighted?

P17: You have had a very big grin on your face.

Int.: How many others saw me as delighted? [Many raise their hands.] OK, let me tell you. I *am* delighted. I am delighted with the way you are digging into all the issues, with the way you are trying to learn. . . .

P17: But I would be more comfortable had I perceived your smile as not being connected with my discomfort.

Int.: But it *is* connected with your discomfort. Because you connect your discomfort with all sorts of productive confronting behavior. If this group responded in ways that were designed to shut off inquiry, then I would not be delighted.

To put it another way, one of the puzzles of this learning experience is that the types of failures that you produce, which lead you to feel confused and frustrated, are signs of learning.

P18: Well, I, for one, do not feel uncomfortable. So far I trust you because you are pointing out errors and you're doing it in ways that you make yourself vulnerable.

Int.: What is it that I do that suggests that I make myself vulnerable?

P18: Well, you build up your case, step by step, with our data. You are up front with your views; yet you encourage us to disagree and disconfirm. Now I'm waiting to see how you react when you make an error. [Laughter.]

Int.: I am, too. I hope that I will accept responsibility for it. But I can become defensive and hope that you will help me in seeing that.

P19: I'd like to say something about how I feel. I feel that if my case is discussed, I will be scrutinized, that the focus will be on me.

Int.: Yes, there will always be a focus on you, on me, on everyone. That is the purpose of the class. My hope is that we do it openly and that we test it, because as consultants you, too, will be scrutinizing clients.

P (unidentifiable): That leads me to ask, are you saying that everything you do here is a model of what you would do elsewhere?

Int.: Yes.

P (unidentifiable): Would you, for example, ask clients to write cases?

Int.: Yes. I have asked clients to write Y and X cases as well as cases that illustrate problems that they have experienced. But whatever vehicle I use, the actions that I have been taking in this class—for example, of advocating, testing, inquiring—I would use in any situation.

P (unidentifiable): So you don't ease in.

Int.: Not knowingly. Unless I do not trust the strength of the client. And that is a difficult attribution because it is so difficult to test. In any event, when I am in doubt, I focus on testing with the client.

P20: I'd like to go back to the power issue. Y has power over X, and that cannot be denied.

Int.: Have I acted or said anything to suggest that I want to deny the power?

P20: Well, you don't discuss it.

Int.: My recollection is that I did. I believe that I said that when people use their organizational power to make untested attributions and evaluations, and to act as if they are valid, they are acting in ways that are counterproductive to learning. I believe that I also said that you people would tend to make untested attributions and evaluations, even when you do not have formal power over the other. So I believe that you are predisposed to create the dysfunctional impact of top-down power even when you do not have it. If I can help you to alter that predisposition, then I can help you to deal with the formal power issue.

A Second Illustration

To date, we have identified empirically three different and interdependent phases. In the first phase, the participants explain the inconsistencies in their diagnoses and actions by, on the one hand, accepting responsibility for them. On the other hand, they say (1) they were not given enough data or enough time, (2) they did not intend to upset Y, and (3) they were striving to test their diagnoses carefully before they took further action. Every explanation was considered by the interventionist as a hypothesis to be tested. He brought to bear whatever data were available to the participants or suggested ways to collect more data.

As each of their explanations resulted in their digging deeper holes for themselves, they turned to the second phase, which was to question the interventionist. They advocated that he might be the cause of their inconsistencies through the use of the data that they produced. For example, if the interventionist behaved toward the participants the way the participants behaved toward Y, the interventionist would be unilaterally controlling the class. Again, these hypotheses were disconfirmed by the participants, and the dialogue continued.

The third phase began with the participants examining their here-and-now behavior and feelings. This led, more often than not, to reflections that identified, as one participant called it, "my stuckedness." Two consequences resulted from this reflection. First, the participants produced something that accurately expressed how they were presently thinking and feeling. Second, the participants began, on the one hand, to feel success instead of failure. On the other hand, the information gave them insights into specific actions that they would have to change.

The third phase contains a paradox that is an important one for participants to learn to accept. The paradox is that they will feel and be successful only to the extent that they can identify and accept their failures. This is difficult because people believe they should hide their failures. More important, they believe that the natural and inevitable consequence of identifying failure is to feel failure. How is it possible to feel successful while experiencing failure? It is possible if the person can successfully identify the cause of his or her failure. For the seminar participants, it means identifying (1) errors (such as inconsistency) and (2) what prevented them from being aware of their errors (usually the reasoning processes they used, combined with any automatic responses designed to hide the unawareness and the errors).

A second illustration is included because the participants[1] were more confronting of the interventionist and they also began to produce more constructive reflections about their own actions.

The session began with two participants roleplaying their suggested solutions (they had had a week to prepare their roleplay). Both produced the inconsistencies that they had thought they would not produce.

Then a participant said:

P1: We appear, in some of our roleplaying, to be forthright, and the reaction has been bullshit. Then some we used tried to be diplomatic, and then we saw that we were not communicating honestly and people become defensive—so what's left?

Int.: I am suggesting that, given your individual theories-in-use, the members of this class will always vacillate between easing in and being directive. This does not mean that we cannot learn a new theory-in-use. But to repeat, you are pointing to a key issue. Although easing in and being directive are significant actions, they lead

---

[1] A class of graduate students in a counseling and consulting psychology program ($N = 80$; 55 percent female and nearly 20 percent minority).

to the same consequences—that is, client defensiveness. This, in turn, creates a dilemma. You, as consultants, are advising Y not to create defensiveness; yet you create defensiveness in Y.

P2: So is there another way? Can you show us?

Int.: Yes, there is another way, and if pressed, I promise to show you.

But what I think is more important for your learning is to reflect on the way you frame and reason about these problems so that you can make explicit why you create this dilemma in the first place. If you know what it is that you do to create this dilemma, then you will have gone a long way toward correcting it. Moreover, the reasoning processes that you presently use so automatically, that create the dilemma, are kept hidden from your awareness by your own design, of which you are unaware. If I provide you with a new model, it may well trigger off the same automatic reactions, and we will get into a competitive win/lose situation. Hence, I would like you to become more aware of these reasoning processes before I try to roleplay. However, if you are not able to do so, and/or if there is not enough time, I will roleplay an alternative solution.

P3: I feel we are going around in a vicious circle. I don't understand where you are taking us. I feel that I am on a merry-go-round.

Int.: That is where I am taking you. I am trying to show you that you are programmed to create a merry-go-round.

Moreover, I am also saying that you will probably not be able to get off this merry-go-round.

Finally, I am saying that I have done nothing to place you on, or to create, the merry-go-round. If someone can point to any action on my part that makes me responsible for the merry-go-round, please do so. As I see it, I have been, and continue to be, responsible for helping you to reflect on your actions.

P1: Do you think it is possible to get off the merry-go-round?

Int.: Yes, I do.

P4: Can you do it?

Int.: Yes, I will try to illustrate it now if I am forced to do so. But I repeat, the important issue at this point is for you to reflect on the ways you frame the problem and your reasoning processes.

P4: Are you off the merry-go-round in real life?

Int.: Sometimes yes, sometimes no, but hopefully on it less often. And when the former occurs, I should be able to acknowledge that, to listen to feedback, to strive to correct the situation.

P5: Is this new theory-in-use that you are getting at something that some of us have used once in a while?

Int.: If my research is correct, you may have espoused the new theory, but you should never have produced it. If you were able to produce it, I should think that you would have produced it here during the last three sessions, or even several of you might have produced it outside the room and could tell us what you said and did.

By the way, if you look at the collage of the advice that you gave Y, you do espouse much of the so-called new approach.

Your problem is not that you do not have the correct espoused theory. It is that you cannot produce what you espoused, and whatever the reason is, it cannot be overcome by simply having this awareness. The reason, by the way, is the present theory-in-use that you hold.

P6: But if I am unaware that I am unaware, could I not be using the correct theory and not know it?

Int.: I doubt it. Recall that the data show that although the actor is unaware of the discrepancies, others [for example, observers, recipients] are highly aware.

To put it another way, if you are producing it but you are unaware, someone in this room should see it and identify it.

P6: But you have set up this system. You are responsible for what is happening.

Int.: I believe that I am not responsible for the inconsistencies that you people produce. If you and others believe that I am, I would very much like to hear what it is that I have been saying and doing to create the inconsistencies.

P7: But you are creating this by saying that we have the same theory-in-use and that is what is causing the inconsistencies.

Int.: The theory-in-use is a concept that I introduce to explain what has been going on in the class. Let me put it this way. This class, for the past three sessions, has vacillated between easing in and directive action. The class also has found all such attempts to be counterproductive.

I do not believe that I am responsible for these inconsistencies.

P6: But the reason why our roleplaying has not worked is that you are roleplaying Y.

Int.: That is important. If my doing the roleplaying is causing the inconsistencies, then my position is refuted. But let me review—I have done the roleplaying and asked the class to keep track of whether I appear to be trying to make it tough on the roleplayer. So far the class has not found me wanting—or at least they have not said so.

Second, I believe that I have been roleplaying a more supportive Y than many of you might be, as indicated by your written scenarios. Third, and more important, we have had several roleplays with students only, and they have created the same dilemmas. Finally, recall that all of you wrote a case with a scenario—and presumably you did that alone and with plenty of time. All the cases contain the same dilemmas.

P6: But you have reached a conclusion that we are inconsistent.

Int.: I believe that you are inconsistent. But more importantly, this class has time and time again reached the same conclusion.

P7: What are the inconsistencies?

Int.: Well, recall the collage that you have in writing. First, I asked the class if the collage represented adequately their individual diagnoses. The answer was yes, from everyone.

Next, I identified a causal microtheory in that collage. It went like this: If Y is blunt, insensitive, dominating X, then X will feel defensive, and then learning will be minimal. The class agreed.

I then said that the class produced this very causal theory in their actions toward Y (as illustrated in their scenarios).

I also said that the class will create the same causal theory in every roleplay that they produce, even though they wish that this not be the case.

P7: I think what you are saying is this: This class has eased in, and that did not work. The directive approach, which seems the only other approach we know how to take, has the same defensive consequences.

I agree with this. And I can't find another way except ease in and directive. I can point out the flaws in everyone else's roleplay. But when I point out the flaws, I either ease in or become directive.

Int.: Yes, what he just described is what I am also experiencing. And note, he does not need my theory to describe the experience. You do not [need it] to see if I am manipulating.

If I have a hidden agenda, it is either unconscious or it is part of the gaps in my theory-in-use of which I am unaware. And I am willing to explore these and other alternatives in any way that the class can think of.

P10: I think that you know what you are after. But I do not know. And you move so fast.

Int.: You are correct. I know exactly what I am after. That is one of the advantages of having a theory. Second, I have made explicit, in writing and in every class, what I am after. Third, the feature that I may move too fast or talk too fast—I acknowledge that as my problem. As I have said before, whenever I appear to be moving too fast, please tell me. Finally, at the beginning of today's class I asked P8 if she wished to roleplay with me or someone else. She chose me.

P8: I wish that I had said someone else.

Int.: Fine. There is no problem. We can do it again with someone else.

P5: Let's try it again.

Int.: Fine. May I repeat again that what I am saying is that the roleplays should oscillate between easing in and directive.

   I think that what may be troubling you is not that I have a hidden agenda but that you have a theory-in-use that is hidden.

P9: I think that I have a different approach, and I would like to try it.

Int.: Fine. Would you like to choose someone to roleplay with?

P9: I'll do it with you.

[After the roleplay]

P10: [I think that I know some people who would have responded more favorably.] You [interventionist] seem to be uncooperative.

Int.: I am trying to mirror Y. But let us try it again with someone else who would be more cooperative. I may have been too tough—but I do not believe this is the case.

P (unidentifiable): I don't think you have been too tough.

[No one volunteers to roleplay again.]

P7: What I saw [P9] do is a very fine combination of directive and easing in. He would say nice things about you in a directive manner, but when he started to criticize you, he switched to an easing in. So I have not seen anything different. But his has been the best combination.

   What sticks me is how we do this. [I might add] that he appeared motivated to help you.

Int.: I, too, felt that [P9] intended to help me. I had not realized the pattern that you pointed out [that is, plus feedback was directive and minus feedback was easing in]. But that makes sense.

I had two problems with [P9's] comments. One, when he was critical of me, he was implying that I was motivated to make X defensive. He said, in effect, "You made X defensive," or it was my responsibility that X would not hear.

If somehow he could get across these dysfunctional aspects of my actions [in roleplaying Y, about which he is probably correct] without imputing that I was motivated to make X defensive, it would have been more effective.

[Later]

P8: Looking back on my reasoning processes, what I was thinking was "This guy Y is a jerk." But I did not want to express that.

Now what I see is that [kind of frame] isn't good enough. I gotta not think that he is a jerk. I gotta change the way I think about thinking about Y.

Int.: Yes, indeed, I would say that if there is a way to help people by disliking them in our thoughts and suppressing those thoughts, I do not want to invent it. That would lead to 1984.

Come to think of it, there is a way to do the above, and you people know it. I call it Model I. But you see that it has its problems.

P7: What I'm wondering now is, OK, I don't want to think of him in that way because I want to help him.

Int.: I am suggesting that those of us who automatically think of Y as a jerk have a frame that is counterproductive to helping Y.

Now, to blue-sky a bit. You say you were motivated to help Y but you thought of him as a jerk. I just said framing Y as a jerk is counterproductive to helping him. You said, in effect, "I knew that. That is why I hid my feelings [had them in the left-hand column]."

But what we have seen is that we use the left-hand-column material to evaluate Y's responses. So if he responds in ways that we interpret as noncooperative or resisting, we see the response, judging from what many of you have written in your cases, as evidence that he is a jerk.

So framing Y as a jerk and combining it with our present reasoning processes helps to assure that we will not become aware of our own incompetence in this setting.

The first step now is to ask the question of why we even frame the problem as we do. What is it about our theories and reasoning processes that tells us that it is valid to frame Y as a jerk [or its equivalent]?

P10: When [P7] said that he now realizes that if he frames a person as a jerk, he will not be able to help him, is that not a sign that we need unconditional positive regard? You can't go in and help Y and think negatively about him.

Int.: I think my dilemma is that I do not have unconditional positive regard for Y because I do believe that he behaved incompetently. Somehow I need a language and skills where I can express my evaluation of his incompetence, of my conditional regard for what he said or did.

Now, some might say that if I evaluate Y negatively but do not dislike him as a person, then that is unconditional positive regard. This distinction requires another, one frequently made in helping theories—namely, that one can value the human being but not his or her actions. I like that distinction as long as it is not used to blunt my evaluative views. Too often unconditional positive regard has been interpreted to mean to minimize evaluations [indeed, I wrote such a view about 15 years ago]. Often we are in situations, as in the case of Y, where, in my opinion, it does require judgment and evaluation. I might add that I have experienced many situations where clients have been greatly relieved that I do not value them when they are behaving in certain ways because they do not value themselves [although they may hide that from others and initially from themselves].

P7: This leaves me stuck. I don't know why I think of people as jerks, but I do. Yet I know if I do, I cannot help them. But if I feel they are jerks, then I'm stuck.

Int.: One way to get at this issue is to try and gain insight into why we frame Y as a jerk. This insight perspective requires that we gain insight into the needs and defenses that may be operative.

Another way to begin is to ask, is there a way that I can communicate my evaluation of Y's counterproductive actions so that (1) if he becomes defensive, it is his responsibility, and (2) we can learn from his defensiveness? It is the latter approach that I believe I can help you with.

Such sessions usually end with the participants beginning to assess the extent to which the interventionist would use a similar strategy in his interventions. This is a sign that they are beginning to explore the interventionist's strategy as a possibly effective one. To the extent that this is happening, the interventionist will find himself being questioned about his theory of help. It is at this point that he provides his map of effective intervention. It is also at this point that he can expect a repeat of the first-phase Type A defenses. The difference is that the participants will now do their best to find inconsistencies and gaps in his theory. To the extent that the interventionist has a relatively clear picture of his theory, including its gaps, and to the extent that he is able to articulate it, his actions will help to facilitate a crucial testing process. It is during this phase that participants assess the extent to which the interventionist "knows his stuff." If he appears to be able to respond effectively, the participants learn the value of becoming aware of, and having a relatively consistent theory of, intervention that they can state as theory.

The participants may voice admiration for the interventionist's knowledge of his theory, wondering how long it will take them to develop their own theory of intervention. My response has always been that such an exercise takes several years and is a never-ending process. Too few interventionists do reflect on their own practice. The interventionist may use this opportunity to recommend that the participants use tapes, and one another, as resources for theory building. It is my experience that many professional consultants resist developing a theory because the only models they have been taught are the positivistic approach and the humanistic, existential approach. Elsewhere[2] I have tried to show that neither is adequate.

Often, some organizational development consultants resist the idea of generating theory as "too much headwork and not enough attention to feelings." This response echoes what has been taught to many practitioners through various forms of experiential learning. I have dealt with this issue by illustrating that, basically, "to the head" or "to the gut" is the way human beings enact their world and react to it. That choice, in turn, is influenced by the way they reason. The many feeling- or gut-oriented practitioners in the group described in Part One were no more effective than their clients. Having feelings may be an emotional response, but paying attention to them and learning from them require skills in discovery and a mapping of one's theory-in-use.

Reflecting on the Experience

One of the strategies the interventionist used was to continually reflect on the experiences that participants had during the ses-

[2] Chris Argyris, *Inner Contradictions of Rigorous Research* (New York: Academic Press, 1980).

sions, as well as the reasoning behind their thoughts and actions. One of the most powerful Model I automatic reactions is unilateral self-censorship. There are many thoughts and feelings on the left-hand side of almost every X and Y scenario participants write, which provide important insights into their reasoning processes and theories-in-use.

The same holds for understanding the "here and now" seminar situation. It is useful to ask participants to reflect on their thoughts and feelings about the first several phases that they have experienced.

The group described in Part One were asked to keep short diaries of their thoughts and feelings. These diaries were given to the interventionist, who then developed a collage of the class. The following five comments are exemplars of varying subgroups within the seminar.

1. "I was *shocked* [participant's italics] as I saw the parallel logic between my own strategies and Y's. My response was to defend [rationalize] my approach . . . a *drive* to *prove* that mine was different than Y's." (Represents 70 percent of participants.)
2. "I was genuinely surprised at the similarities between our approach and Y's. I immediately felt manipulated having unknowingly placed myself in a group which appeared all too predictable and wrong." (Represents 49 percent.[3])
3. "What is he driving at? What does all this add up to? It is not the material that he's approaching, it's *us*." (Represents 70 percent.)
4. "I am wary, feeling argumentative. I am not going to let him get away with this without some fight. After all, my confidence is on the line. I try to create a solution. He asks me to produce it as a dialogue. Three minutes later I am stuck. Damn. Nice try anyway . . . the frustration is creative for me anyway." (Represents 62 percent.)
5. "He kept pointing to our data and consistently asked us to analyze ourselves. He dealt with the resulting defensiveness by remaining accessible while acknowledging his role of power, and not making false or connived alliances with us.

    Although I doubt my ability to refute his evidence, I felt that if I could accumulate my own and present it convincingly, he would acknowledge his mistake. This failed to alleviate my defensiveness but I didn't feel helpless." (Represents 30 percent.)

---

[3] Individuals may have more than one reaction.

The first three comments suggest that the automatic reaction of the participants on becoming aware that they had behaved inconsistently and incompetently (by their own standards) was to strive to prove that the interventionist was responsible for manipulating them into the situation. These responses are consistent with Model I win/ lose responses, in which people hold the other person responsible for their own errors.

Comments 4 and 5 also indicate automatic responses of competitiveness and fight. However, considerable attention is given to how the interventionist is behaving. Although he is seen as winning, he is also seen as open to acknowledging error and not trying to manipulate or make false alliances.

The emotional reaction tends to be, so far, more intense among consultants and counselors, perhaps because the exercise raises doubts about their professional competence. For example, the participant who wrote comment 1 believed that he had established a caring, trusting relationship with Y. When he realized that he had not, he stated, "I *fought* for my view and grew angry at the 'putdowns' of our various attempts to support our respective methodologies." When asked to illustrate what the interventionist had done or said that led him to feel "put down," he could only say, "Every bit of data we brought up seemed to disprove our view." Those represented by comments 4 and 5 were quick to describe actions that allowed them to infer that the interventionist was not "putting down" the participants. As one of them said, "If we are feeling that the hole is getting deeper and deeper, I agree, and believe that we are digging it."

Another interesting reaction was to focus on the interventionist's intent in terms of the ideas that he was trying to communicate. "I was feeling that you knew something that we did not, and instead of telling us, you were attempting to tease it out of us." As the discussion continued, one person said that she had at first felt that the interventionist was doing something to the participants. She still felt that he was, but her conception of what he was doing had changed. She concluded that he was successful in helping them to surface the feelings they have when they see that they are making errors.

The interventionist supported the idea that his intention was to be candid about what he was doing. He reviewed what he thought his actions had been during the past several sessions:

1. Collect the participants' diagnoses of espoused theories about how to help Y.
2. Collect as directly observable data as possible about how the participants acted toward Y when they were helping him.
3. Present the data and ask for confirmation or disconfirmation.
4. Once confirmation is achieved, infer the meanings embedded in these data.
5. Test publicly the meanings inferred.
6. When these meanings are confirmed, infer the consequences and test them.

The evaluation of inconsistency and the sense of incompetence occurred as a result of processes which were public, in which reasoning processes were subject to continual test, and in which evaluations originated from, and were confirmed by, the class. In other words, the interventionist was using an approach that made it highly likely that inconsistencies in the participants' actions would be surfaced only if they existed and only if the participants had the skills to identify them. The technology used by the interventionist could as easily have led to disconfirmation of his expectation that the participants would behave consistently with Model I. The technology had the features of any experiment: a hypothesis about the participants' theories-in-use and an environment where data could be produced that could either disconfirm or confirm the hypothesis.

In contrast to a typical experiment, however, the interventionist did not keep any of the design or his intentions secret. He described what he was doing and why, so that unilateral secrecy was not a feature. If he had kept his intentions and design secret, he would have inhibited the learning of several important ideas. These are ideas so powerful that participants cannot alter the data they produce even when they are aware of the limitations and inconsistencies of those data—for instance, the idea that one can genuinely test without having to hide the purpose of testing (a typical Model I strategy) or that advocacy and inquiry can be combined to produce valid information and at the same time to give people informed choice under very different conditions by questioning their competence. If the interventionist convincingly illustrates these ideas to the participants, he has illustrated how Model II can be produced and the consequences it can have for their learning.

As the participants became aware of and accepted these lessons, some tried to produce them in their interactions with each other. They found that their automatic responses were still consistent with Model I. They also learned that collecting data, inferring meanings, testing the validity of the meanings, and organizing the meanings into patterns required a theory, or framework, because the moment they tried to perform, they were faced with too many choices of what data to collect, what meanings to focus on, and so forth.

Finally, participants realized that it was not enough to learn the new action strategies of advocating with inquiry, of public testing. It was important to use them in the service of Model II governing variables—producing valid information, informed choice, and internal commitment. Initial attempts at Model II action strategies were often accompanied by attempts to win and not lose. For example, participants would inquire and, after receiving a set of responses, would "nail" the respondent. This activity, which was termed "lawyering," became common. Such activities also provided important illustrations of "gimmicks," attempts to use Model II action strategies in the service of Model I governing variables.

Gimmicks can be viewed as actions that people produce when they feel vulnerable and do not wish to lose. The interventionist's theories of learning and intervention require that the actor be as subject to vulnerability as anyone. It must be genuinely possible for the actor to make errors so that they can be discovered and corrected. If vulnerability is not there, it is likely that the actor is utilizing a Model I theory-in-use.

By exploring the participants' feelings, we were able to surface their automatic responses to the learning that was going on and to see how these automatic responses were Model I reactions. This was important in helping them see their predisposition to hold to Model I theories-in-use and to realize the danger of producing gimmicks. Going through these experiences enabled them to see how the consultant dealt with such actions. Such experiences provided public tests of the efficacy of the interventionist's views, as well as illustrations of how participants themselves might deal with clients when they are acting as consultants.

Toward the end of this phase, participants usually reflect on their anxieties in order to better understand their emotional reactions. At the outset, the insights they produce are consistent with the previous ones—namely, that they may not be as competent as they thought in helping people deal with threatening, double-loop issues.

But there is another insight that is important to surface at this time. The participants now see that they had produced important errors. None of them intended to produce, or were aware of, these errors. Hence, errors existed precisely where they were confident no errors existed. Recalling the axiom that no one can unknowingly design error, it follows that the participants have designs in their heads that they use to produce error *and simultaneously* to be unaware that they are producing error. They are error-producing persons, are unaware of this fact, and hence are not likely to correct it. Yet, as consultants and counselors, they are describing themselves as persons who can help others overcome errors.

To compound the problem, many realize that they have been taught various theories of defense that lead them to produce easing-in strategies. These easing-in strategies, as we have seen, were not effective in solving problems. At best, they created conditions that suppressed knowledge about the errors.

So we have error-prone persons holding a theory-in-use that blinds them to the errors that they produce, creating and then becoming embedded in a learning system that encourages the suppression of error.

These conditions penetrate deeply into reasoning processes. They influence what people see in the environment and what environment they construe or enact. They influence the premises that people create, the inferences made from these premises, and the conclusions that they reach. These conditions, therefore, influence people's most fundamental ways of construing their world and then taking action, including producing feelings related to (as well as maps about) what is happening to them.

The task of any consultant, therefore, is to help clients become aware of (1) their skilled incompetence and unawareness; (2) the reasoning processes that produce these; (3) the learning systems that reinforce 1 and 2; and (4) the ideologies (ranging from theories of defensiveness and help to unilateral hierarchal power in systems) that are reinforcing 1, 2, and 3. The first step toward taking corrective action is to become aware of the incompetences. The second step is to become aware of the cues that trigger the automatic responses that produce the unawareness. A key means of becoming aware of the cues is to surface feelings and to explore the meaning that they have for the actor.

12

Dealing with the
Failure Cycle
with Donald Schön

The living environment described in Chapters Two, Three, and Eleven is designed primarily to help people become aware of their espoused theories, their theories-in-use, their actions, and any discrepancy among the three. We left the participants of Chapter Eleven in a situation in which they were encountering multiple dilemmas that created feelings of failure. However, we said that such feelings were actually a sign of successful learning.

The next step is to design and implement Model II actions. This is much more complicated than we thought it would be, precisely because of the feelings engendered by failure and frustration. These must be worked through in a way that encourages learning.

We have been experimenting with several learning environments. One is a series of seminars (described later), and another is using as learning environments actual settings of the client system. For example, performance evaluation sessions in a consulting firm became a learning environment for both officer and subordinate. I met with officers before the session to help them design their actions, participated as a facilitator in the actual session, and afterward critiqued the entire session with the officers and/or the managers. When asked to do so, I met with an officer or manager who had listened to the tapes and wished to reflect further on the session. Other examples are acting as facilitator in the regularly scheduled officer meetings, in team meetings, in sessions preparing for difficult client interactions, and in actual client encounters. (The story of these learning experiences will be the subject of another publication.)

The seminars on which I will focus were developed by Donald Schön and me, initially as advanced seminars for doctoral students and later as workshops for anyone interested in learning to produce Model II actions. The particular seminar described here consisted of 20 advanced graduate students in consulting, planning, and management at Harvard and the Massachusetts Institute of Technology. The participants wrote cases describing (in the X and Y format) an incident that illustrated a key area in which they wanted to enhance their competence.

One or two cases were the subject of each seminar. The writer of the cases managed the session. He or she would begin by emphasizing the kinds of learning sought. The class members would then act as consultants to help the writers rework their cases and to generate the desired learning. All sessions were tape-recorded so that the participants could listen to them later. They reported that the tape listening was a revelation because they had had no idea of how much they had missed during the session.

It is possible to present their experience as a five-stage process:

Stage 1. Students encounter multiple dilemmas that interact to create a failure cycle.

Stage 2. Interventionist responds to the failure cycle by decomposing and slowing down the process, surfacing and discussing student fears, formulating heuristics for the transition, and stressing the experimental atmosphere of the seminar.

Stage 3. Students begin to produce elements of Model II responses without being able to string those elements together, and they evince theories-in-use for reflection, as contrasted with theories-in-use for action.

Stage 4. Constellations of meanings, inventions, and productions begin to appear, which we call "hybrids" of Models I and II.

Group norms and interventionist/student interactions begin to show significant changes.
Stage 5. Postseminar learning.

We will begin the description with Stage 2 because Stage 1 has already been described in the previous chapter.

We begin with two students, A and B. A has been roleplaying how he would implement a Model II interaction with B, who is acting as the client. The roleplaying has finished, and A says that he has not acted in accordance with Model II because "I was thrown by B right at the outset."

The interventionist asks, "A, is there anything that B did or said that made it difficult for you to say you were thrown?" A's response is "I was very concerned about being seen as good, competent, helpful. So when he said [what he did], I felt lost. It just didn't occur to me to say that I was lost."

This comment elicits intense discussion because the students identify with A's dilemma: How can you appear competent when you do not feel you are and at the same time encourage client reactions that enhance your probability of being effective? If the client reacts candidly but you are not competent to deal with his reactions, how do you reinforce suitable behavior while hiding your own anxieties? Won't a client in real life become anxious under these circumstances? And if so, are we not back to the original problem of dealing with anxiety—but with the problem compounded because the client's anxiety is due to the interventionist's action?

Here are some of the students' suggestions:

Students' Suggestions	*Other Students' Reactions*
1. Say you're lost, because B's behavior was violating your view of the consulting contract. Ask B whether there is a discrepancy.	1. Why ask B whether there is a discrepancy when you believe there is?
2. Say, "I don't know much about you, B, or your subordinate. But you know quite a lot. Together we can work it out."	2. It sounds as if we did not have much information. But we believe that we do not need the information that B believes necessary. Together we can come to *my* conclusion.

Next, the interventionist raised some possibilities.

Interventionist's Suggestion	*Students' Reactions*
1. How would you react to saying to B, in effect, that "your strategy is one way of dealing with the situation; it is not mine"?	1.1. I don't feel that I have only one strategy. 1.2. I do not feel that I have any strategy that I am sure of. 1.3. Maybe if I am open, he can show me a better strategy.

There was much disagreement with the third reaction. "After all, why are we consulting if the clients are to tell us our strategies?" The key to success was to be confident in our strategy so that we could use it effectively under some degree of stress; if we succeeded, we would reassure the client that we are competent. "But none of us has a strategy that we feel good about and competent [in]." Hence another dilemma: Having several strategies about being open to the client's recommendations may be confusing to the client. Not having one strategy in which we have confidence can be disastrous.

Interventionist's Suggestion	*Students' Reactions*
2. When the client raised the other strategies, how would you feel about saying, in effect, "I believe that I can show you that having such a strategy illustrates one of the problems in the way the case was handled"?	2.1. It would appear too convinced. I don't go into the situation that convinced. 2.2. I would not wish to put myself on the line like that. 2.3. I'm not sure that I could back it up.

Some students believed that because they were not very competent, it was best to be flexible. There are several problems with this position. In every roleplaying episode, the student interventionists were as rigid as A had been. The students were unknowingly placing themselves on the line; they were simply unaware of the judgments the clients were making. And in all the roleplaying, the student clients judged the student interventionist low in competence. As we shall see, flexibility may require having a clear map and a well-formed program in our heads. Keeping one's options open, listening accurately, responding immediately require complex skills that the students did not as yet have. Therefore, the students are not able to behave flexibly; they will fail to achieve their own goals, and this experience will reinforce their sense of failure and incompetence.

It made sense for the students to fear that they could not back up a strategy such as the one suggested by the interventionist. The difficulty was that the strategies the students had were all Model I. But the client had gotten into trouble because his strategy was Model I. If the students used their "strengths," they would probably create failure conditions for themselves and their clients, and it takes a great deal of confidence and competence to fail without jeopardizing the consulting relationship.

Another dilemma surfaced when several students said that their preferred strategy would be to make sure that the client was internally committed to their own strategy. The aspiration to create internal commitment was unrealistic because no client could become internally committed to a strategy of which he was unaware and, worse yet, which he would probably reject if he understood.

Most of the students knew this before the seminar. Why would they use a strategy that they knew had a very high probability of failure? One reason is that they "knew" this information at the level of espoused theory only. They sought early client commitment so that if the strategy did not work, the client would share the responsibility or at least not get angry. We are now back to the purpose of preventing client anxiety. But, as many of the students also knew, such a purpose would lead them to design strategies on the basis of what they perceived to be the clients' fears and anxieties. They would then find themselves being managed by the anxieties of the clients.

The discussion turned to still another dilemma. A student said that the consultant should start out by making his theory and biases clear to the client. Another student responded that he had tried that, and it created difficulties: "I had in mind that I had to disclose my invention strategy so that the clients could make a more informed choice. But that led me to control the dialogue so that I could say what I wanted to say. I was so convinced about being Model II that I controlled my conversations with the clients. . . . Behaving according to Model II is not my normal behavior. So I have to reverse it. I evolve a pattern that I think is going to work. [This leads me to go into a client situation] with a hidden agenda. I keep pulling back to my agenda. Hence, I control these [agenda items] in order to create free choice!" The first student disagreed that this had to be the consequence. But when he was asked to roleplay his scenario, he was unable to avoid such consequences.

These incidents lead to another puzzle. Students seemed to react almost automatically with suggestions that, on reflection, they "knew" were unlikely to succeed; yet they appeared to be unaware of this. Their awareness came not in the process of invention but when they tried to produce the scenarios they had invented. To put the matter differently, the students were very often able to *recognize* a production as ineffective (certainly those of others but often their own); yet they were unable to *produce* an effective intervention. They seemed unable to coordinate their after-the-fact, external view or feeling with the before-the-fact, "inside" cues that would enable them to avoid error.

Reflections on Stage 1

Complexity

As the students sought to produce Model II responses, they also tried to leave behind their old Model I skills. But without the tacit and automatic Model I responses, they found the new situation unmanageably complex; there were simply too many things to pay attention to at once.

Each intervention involved many purposes and values and seemed to lend itself to many Model II "rules," which turned out, on the slightest consideration, to conflict with one another. When students became aware of these multiple conflicting norms, they generally focused their attention on one such norm, acted from it, and discovered to their chagrin that another equally important norm had been violated.

Thus, A, intent on "setting the contract for the session," unilaterally controlled the contract-setting process—for the sake of granting freedom to the other person within the frame of the contract. Students who advocated "openness to the other's input" were faced with the unanswerable question "Why are you in the consultant's role?" Those who wished to "surface their problems and feelings" focused attention on themselves rather than on the client. The student who wanted the interventionist to "start out by being clear about his theory and his bias" found himself paralyzed when he tried to produce his invention, because, as he said, "I want to figure out how to be helpful to him. But I do not want to take all the time on explaining my view of the problem." When others suggested that this student might feel freer if he could tell the client "I might make mistakes, so let me know," he was helped to see that this might make the client anxious about his competence. The student found that the resulting conjunction of relevant norms left him no space for action.

In the transition from Model I to Model II, awareness of complexity may be taken as a sign of progress. However, the first encounters with this complexity seemed only to lead to paralysis.

As students learned that Model II norms could conflict with one another, they also became aware that "rules" such as "Give directly observable data," "Surface relevant feelings," "Couple advocacy with inquiry" were useful heuristics, or rules of thumb, that held good in some contexts but not in others. The descriptions of the relevant contexts were too complex to be remembered and even if they were learned by heart, too burdensome to use.

Fears, Unrealistically High Aspiration Levels,
and Competitiveness

As we reflected on the student who became upset the moment he tried to produce his invention and on the other who clung rigidly to his ineffective program, it occurred to us that the students' otherwise puzzling mistakes might be understood as natural defenses. We asked the students to list the intervention situations they feared the most, and they willingly produced a set of rather elaborate papers in which they mentioned fears such as these: "An inability to answer a legitimate question," "Becoming paralyzed—drawing a blank," "Losing objectivity," "Satisfying the 'wrong' demands of the client in order not to lose [him]," "Anger toward myself for not behaving competently," "Required to deal with clients that I do not like," "Fear of hurting them," and "Making someone defensive." Most of these fell into a few major categories—fear of manipulating or hurting others, of failing, of being incompetent, or of not being worth a fee.

As one student put it, "I recognize intellectually that I am incompetent to intervene in a Model II manner . . . [but] I am having difficulty in dealing with the feeling that I *should* be competent and on top of every expectation [—it] is unreasonable. I have an image of being almost paralyzed before a client. . . . Experiencing that feeling of helplessness with a person or group of people I don't know very well is very scary to me. Part of my concern, it seems, is a fear that the situation will get out of control, that is, will go in directions that I had not anticipated and consequently am not prepared for."

These fears are quite understandable as responses to unmanageable complexity. The students' fears are natural consequences of their attempts to make the transition from Model I to Model II.

In a Model I world, we are well defended against incompetence and uncertainty. We have well-established skills for being diplomatic and roundabout so as not to provoke anger, for withholding negative information so as not to give offense, for softening our advocacy and our skepticism so as not to reveal our ignorance, and for suppressing our feelings to maintain the appearance of objectivity. We do all this tacitly and automatically, without having to think ahead. At the same time, these tactical skills keep us from attending to our own feelings of threat or anger and from recognizing data that would disconfirm our attribution to others and lead us to awareness of inconsistency and incongruity within ourselves.

As we try to move from Model I to Model II, not yet having learned to create Model II meanings, we seek to act from Model II rules that make us abandon our defensive strategies. We try to give disconfirming data, to express feelings, and to surface dilemmas, but we continue to create Model I meanings. And we continue to be plagued by the "automatic intercepts" triggered by our Model I meanings. For example, an executive who is about to fire a subordinate may formulate a dilemma, which he nevertheless automatically withholds; the subordinate may express his need for help but automatically chastise the superior for *his* defensiveness ("getting the other guy before he gets me"). Under these circumstances, it is understandable that students produce interventions that they "know" to be ineffective or that they find themselves paralyzed at the moment of production.

Such fears are exacerbated by unrealistically high levels of aspiration ("I feel I should be competent and on top of every situation"). For example, students aspired at the first try to produce Model II and then to take responsibility for their failure—aspirations that fostered unfounded claims to competence, which, in turn, fueled fears of incompetence.

To compound the difficulties, the students' interventions and criticisms often had the quality of a contest. While they competed with one another and feared failing in front of one another, the interventionist's ability to produce Model II meanings "awed" them and invited dependence. We can begin to understand the sense of frustration, failure, and withdrawal that occurred in Stage 1.

The Failure Cycle

To create an environment for the transition from Model I to Model II, both interventionist and students must experience paradox and dilemma. So that participants can first experience their natural predilection to create counterproductive, disorganized, mutually contradictory responses, the interventionist must design an environment for the meaningful surfacing of confusion and non-sense. The initial conditions for learning will be suboptimal, yet are necessary for learning.

Those who wish to learn to generalize Model II actions must learn how to discover, invent, produce, and generalize Model II responses. They must also discover that they do not already have these skills and will not be able to exhibit them. On the contrary, they will be placing themselves in situations in which they experience unmanageable complexity and hence uncertainty and confusion. They will feel frustration and impatience, loss of competence and embarrassment.

Because they enter the learning environment with Model I theories-in-use, they will tend to see and act on the world in terms of Model I meanings, thereby creating O-I learning systems, even if they are encouraged not to. One consequence is that whenever their understanding of a double-loop problem is vague, ambiguous, inconsistent, or incongruent, the tendency will be to make it even more so. This self-reinforcing, error-escalating process we call a "primary inhibiting loop."

As a result, people experience uncertainty and loss of competence—feelings they have learned to fear. They will respond, tacitly and automatically, with Model I skills. And these will yield results that people learning Model II can recognize, after the fact and much to their surprise, as errors. Students form more accurate, more complete pictures of others' impact on reality than of their own, and they are better at recognizing their own impact after the fact than at anticipating it.

Because students hold unrealistically high levels of aspiration for their own performance and feel competitive with (yet dependent on) the interventionist, their frustration and bewilderment can escalate into anger, despair, and disbelief—feelings exacerbated by their discovery, counter to the conventional wisdom of Model I, that progress lies in expressing these feelings and testing their validity.

Students will also be unaware that the early help they get from fellow students tends to be highly inefficient, if not counterproductive. They soon realize that (1) understanding and believing in Model II is not sufficient; (2) the feelings generated during the early stages of learning are counterproductive to experimentation; (3) to overcome these problems, they must begin to behave contrary to their socialization; (4) their colleagues, even though they mean well, will not be able to help them very much; and (5) these factors produce fears that inhibit learning. Under these conditions, practice is the recipe for failure.

Stage 2: Redesign of the Learning Environment

The learning cycle of discovery, production, and generalization is common to all of us. We have learned skills appropriate to each phase of the cycle, and as their use has yielded experiences of short-term effectiveness and success, these skills have become tacit. Hence, behind participants' Model I skills lies an entire process of socialization of which the limitations are initially hidden and initial difficulties have been forgotten. The task is to reduce the negative impact of the failure cycle while creating a new process of action that places Model I in proper action perspective.

What is needed is an interventionist who can help participants to emerge from the failure cycle and reflect on their learning, to identify the smallest signs of progress, and who realizes that one sign of learning is that participants persevere when their instincts suggest withdrawal. The interventionist must be able to create contexts that will help people bypass their automatic defenses and must teach them to make the many small experiments essential to practicing Model II. The paradox here is that an interventionist who exercises such control over the situation is behaving according to Model I. The interventionist can make the paradox a transitional one by accepting unilateral control for the purpose of generating valid information, free choice, and internal commitment while inviting confrontation of his or her action in terms of its effectiveness in satisfying the governing variables of Model II. As this occurs, the participants will experience the modeling of Model II behavior.

One way to help participants make a more informed choice about relinquishing control is initially to allow the failure cycle to develop freely. This surfaces the kind of learning environment the participants would produce if left to their own devices, helping them overcome the ensuing failure cycle and at the same time correcting their misperception of its value. In short, the interventionist must initially create bypass interventions in order to set the stage for more comprehensive ones.

Surfacing and Discussing Students' Fears

The students reacted positively to the discussion of their fears. Some felt that a burden had been taken from their shoulders; others were relieved to learn for the first time that fellow students they considered "strong" had fears similar to theirs. Most important, perhaps, students were encouraged by articulation of the realistic basis of their fears: that skills considered productive can be counterproductive; that we seldom have a back-up strategy to place in the gap; that skills now seen as counterproductive are usually judged by most of the world as productive; that exposing others to Model II action may bewilder them as much as the actor is bewildered; that bewilderment and frustration tend to be undiscussable and are used by people as indexes of incompetence or immaturity; and that attributions of incompetence and immaturity are also undiscussable. The discussion also led to an awareness that if it was difficult for students to learn Model II theory-in-use, then it would be at least as difficult (if not more so) for those who are not aware of Model II or who believe it to be counterproductive.

As the students became more aware of their own fears, the

causes of their defensiveness, and the automaticity of their defensive responses, it became easier for them to lower their unrealistic level of aspiration—thus, we believe, reducing their propensity to compete with one another and enlarging their time perspective for learning Model II skills. All these factors increased the likelihood that they would learn more effectively in subsequent sessions.

Responses to Unmanageable Complexity

When skills are tacit and automatic, participants are able to whiz through the learning cycle. Our task, however, was to help participants learn a new set of double-loop skills, which were neither tacit nor automatic.

When we asked the students to roleplay their interventions, we were asking them to suddenly discover/invent/produce double-loop interventions. When we became aware of the consequences of this method, we decided both to decompose the process and to slow it down. We wanted the students to see practice not as sheer repetition but as experimentation.

We proposed, therefore, to separate out experiments about discovery, invention, and production, allowing participants to work separately on each. Over the course of several sessions, we tried several versions of this approach. At first, we preserved the roleplay format, asking the roleplayer to think out loud about the meaning of the situation, the proposed invention, and its production. We learned, however, that it was difficult for participants to move readily from roleplay to reflection and back again to action. We tried next to elicit group discussion of alternative meanings and inventions. This procedure yielded a multiplicity of meanings (we will see an example in the following section), thereby raising the issue of "completeness" of meaning and the problem of selecting particular strategies. The method tended to remain stuck at the phase of meanings. Our final approach was to ask each student to write privately the meanings he constructed for a commonly agreed-on event in a case, the invention he proposed, and his production of that invention. This was the method we retained throughout the rest of the seminar.

As we were trying these approaches to "slowing down," we offered the students several heuristics for the problem of unmanageable complexity. One of the most important of these became known as the "incompleteness theorem." It said, in effect, "Interventions need not be complete, in the sense of taking into account *all* relevant meanings, honoring *all* pertinent norms. It is enough if the intervention takes off from one relevant meaning." Thus, for the student who felt he had no space left for action, it would not be necessary in a single intervention to honor all relevant norms—"Be clear about your theory of intervention," "Be open to client's input," "Leave him free to choose," "Keep the focus on him," "Voice relevant feelings." It would be enough to select one or two such norms (for example, "Create a choice about how to proceed without sloughing responsibility onto the client"). An example of a production might then be "Some clients prefer that I begin by identifying the problems I see, others by formulating the starting problems themselves. Which do you prefer?" Such an intervention need not be perfect in the sense of optimal precision, for precise descriptions tend to be long and complex. And meanings omitted in the initial intervention, leading perhaps to a perception of error by interventionist or client, may be added later on. The interventionist ought then to be willing and able to make immediate corrections of any errors implicit in his first or later responses.

The students professed to find these heuristics helpful, particularly in defusing the loaded situations of Stage 1. As one student noted in his postseminar account of the experience, "I think writing down my interventions gave me a chance to invent in a more Model II fashion and then later begin to produce a few Model II responses. I think the 'you don't have to be complete and perfect' heuristic helped me on this."

Just as the public discussion of fears led to more realistic levels of aspiration, so defusing the assumed requirement of being complete and precise relieved students' fears. The shift to private writing of meanings, inventions, and productions (to be discussed later) publicly reduced competitiveness; students could then practice without having to look good in front of their peers and could experiment and reflect on their experiments.

The slowing down, the public discussion of fears, the heuristics all sanctioned the difficulty of double-loop learning. Students could then develop more realistic time perspectives, and this further lowered their unrealistic levels of aspiration.

As it became more vividly apparent to the students that the

interventionist was prepared to experiment with the seminar design—indeed, wanted and needed to do so—there seemed to be a further defusing effect, as though the students were confirmed in feeling that it was all right for *them* to experiment, to make and correct errors.

Stage 3: First Reactions to Redesign

The following encounter took place in a class four sessions after the first encounter.

The students selected an episode in a case written by a class member, one in which the case writer tries to induce his client (the manager of a unit) to meet with his immediate subordinates, especially with one who seemed to be key to the organization's problems. Each student wrote down the meanings he attributed to the student interventionist and the client. These are examples of meanings attributed to the client: "She [the subordinate] is not a person I can reason with," "She is an obstruction," "I do not want to take your suggestion to talk with her," "I hate to deal with her negative feelings," "I am taking charge," "You [interventionist] cannot be very competent if you propose that I talk with her." Meanings attributed to the student interventionist included "This is a critical issue in our relationship; I cannot trust my client," "I got shot down by my client—and now he has slammed the door in my face," "My client is attacking me," "My client sees me as all fouled up."

In both sets of meanings, there is an underlying theme. Each actor believes the other is wrong, each believes he has the correct solution, and each is striving for unilateral control in order to implement his own solution.

The students agreed that most of the meanings were validly attributable to the actors. They also recognized (quite explicitly, by reference to the incompleteness theorem) that they did not have to define precisely all the meanings in the situation, nor did their intervention have to take account of them all. It would be sufficient for the design of intervention if one or two meanings were selected.

In their productions, the students were now able to include Model II components—for example, "What has she done that leads you to believe that she should be excluded from the meeting?" However, they were not able as yet to string these components together, nor were they able to avoid Model I components, which seemed to come up often as afterthoughts or add-ons.

"I'm puzzled by what you just said. One way to take it is that you do not wish to hear from your staff. Another is that you question the validity of my suggestion. Is either of these correct? [and then a Model I add-on] If so, you're making my job more difficult [you are to blame]."

"You say that I have created a bad situation and that I'll compound the error if we bring her into the meeting. I doubt if this is true, but we should test it. [and then] The only way to test it is to bring her in! [as though there were no other way to test]"

The interventionist suggested that if the client was indeed resistant and defensive, it might be premature to invite him to publicly test his views. Moreover, if the client had doubts about the interventionist's competence, would he be likely to trust such a test? Instead, the student interventionists might ask, "What do you see in the situation that suggests an open discussion is dangerous?" Such a question would give the client an opportunity to focus on factors beyond his difficulties with the subordinate, perhaps even to focus on his views of the interventionist.

The class then turned to another episode in the same case. Here the client ordered the student interventionist to turn in a report to him alone and again rejected meeting with his subordinates. Some of the meanings attributed to the client were these: "You [interventionist] are not very competent," "Get off my back," "Stop trying to threaten me—I am the boss." Some meanings attributed to the interventionist were "I do not want to write the report and give it only to you; I could get in trouble with the others," "I do not wish to write the report without your participation and the participation of your staff," "If I comply with your order, I will lose my effectiveness in the situation."

This episode represents a difficult situation, for an error could lead to dismissal. These were the students' principal strategies: (1) refuse to write the report under the present condition, (2) bargain with the client, (3) comply with the client's demand. The underlying assumption appeared to be that when a client refuses to go along with us, we are in a crisis that calls for Model I. Another underlying assumption was that it is not legitimate for us to be angry at a client.

But why is this a crisis? And why is anger not legitimate? Doesn't the client have a right to protect himself? The students began to see that they had defined the situation as a crisis, legitimizing a return to Model I, because they had few skills for dealing with strong client resistance. Moreover, their anger toward the client might be due not simply to his resistance but to its meaning for them. The more he resists, the more they are apt to make public their inability to deal with him except through Model I skills (skills he already has).

The students seemed able to create "hybrids" of Model I and Model II only where they felt relatively low levels of threat and defensiveness. But as they made progress in learning double-loop skills, they also surfaced new and more difficult problems, thus raising the ante for learning.

Stage 4: Later Consequences of Redesign

In the next-to-last session of the seminar, two months after the previous encounter, certain changes appeared in the pattern of students' interactions. But these changes contrasted with the students' responses to the case situation.

In his case, participant 1 tries to gain the cooperation of a school principal for a research project on student "tracking" that the superintendent has asked P1 to carry out. In their discussion of the case, students give one another disconfirming data, show less competitiveness and defensiveness than in earlier sessions, and display in their exchanges a higher level of interest in inquiry and greater additivity. The interventionist is far less active in making the limited, bypassing interventions characteristic of earlier sessions.

Participant 1: Well, [P2], if that's true—that grouping is necessary for teaching and learning—I'd certainly want any data that you might have to bolster your point of view that I could include in my report. [P1 is trying to revise an intervention that he had included in his case.]

Interventionist: Does that seem like a good answer to you?

P1: Right at the moment, I think it's better than what I had.

P2: Yes, it's better. But I think there's some "win/lose" in it. You talk about "data to bolster your position" as if his position is weak.

P1: Hmm.

P2: But I do think it's better than the first one.

P3: What I heard was something more like "If you think that ridiculous thing is *true.* . . ."

P1: Again! I've done the same thing a second time!

P2: It's fascinating that you've done it again. Because I think [the interventionist] has a point, that there's some constructed meaning, some assumptions which lead you to do that.

Students were now more willing to challenge the interventionist openly and directly, and their challenges were, on the whole, less competitive and more interesting than in previous sessions.

Int.: [He has just given his version of an intervention with the principal.] I empathized with the dilemma he was experiencing, not with the position he held.

P4: Why?

Int.: I saw this person who didn't particularly want this research, but I needed him. I empathized because I thought this might lead to greater cooperation.

P4: Where does that fit into a theory of intervention—"creating empathy?"

P5: I thought [the interventionist] said he wants his cooperation. And that if he empathized, he'd likely get it. In the intervention, [the interventionist] said, "I want your cooperation," not "I'm going to empathize in order to get it." He made the objective explicit.

P6: If he really disagreed, he should have made his disagreement explicit.

The students' competitiveness had lessened and at the same time their awareness of it had increased, perhaps because as their competitiveness decreased, so also did their need to protect themselves from awareness of it.

The students' Model II interactions contrasted with their initial responses to the case. Sometimes meanings and inventions were Model II, while productions contained mixtures of Models I and II. Participant 1, for example, framed this problem: "How can I ask someone to produce data without making that person presume that I oppose him?" He then offered this invention: "Demonstrate that I'm open to his point of view among others; that as a person who's going to write a report, I have an obligation to look for data to substantiate a number of possible positions." But P1's production was the one quoted earlier:

> Well, [P2], if that's true—that grouping is necessary for teaching and learning—I'd certainly want any data that you have to bolster your point of view to include in my report.

In another instance, participant 7 delivered the following meaning, invention, and production:

> *Meaning.* [P2 sets up an external straw man and presents not only their case but also the problems with their case. They don't understand the problems; resources are too limited for what they want.
> This simplifies and undercuts the case for individualizing—all without providing any evidence in support of his statements. He portrays this group as advocating an impossible situation for teachers. [P1] acknowledges [P2's] point, and provides some personal support of it, but also some personal, unspecified support of individualizing. [P2] and [P1] seem to be testing one another's attitudes and beliefs through broad, abstract generalizations.
> *Invention.* [P1] should minimize the reliance on abstractions and generalizations and should maximize valid information through the use of, or at least acknowledgment of, directly observable data to support his conclusions.
> *Production.* [P2], what evidence do you have to support the belief that teachers would have an impossible time of it?

P7 did not disagree with others who described his production as one that would promote defensiveness. He himself said of it, "I seem to be advocating by asking." But he was shocked, as were many others, to discover that not only his production but his meaning and invention were already full of language such as "external straw man," "their case and the problems with their case," which framed the situation as an adversarial one. When the interventionist noted P7's pervasive use of the metaphor of the courtroom, P7 said, "What surprises me is the connection between what I said and an underlying belief which I may not have stated." P7 was surprised to discover that he could not help creating Model I meanings, which revealed themselves in his language.

One explanation for the difference between the theories-in-use brought to the class interactions and those brought to replaying the case is that by this time the class had become a setting in which the dominant theme was reflection. The slowdown and privacy described earlier helped to create an "inside" culture in which reflection *about* intervention was the focus. When the students shifted to the context of action, however—as they did when they put themselves in the position of interventionists acting in outside situations—their theories-in-use reverted to the Model I/Model II hybrids.

We believe that some students brought to the seminar a capacity for behavior high in inquiry, provided the context was one of reflection. When the context shifted to action, Model I came into play. In this session, the students' hybrid productions revealed how far they had come and how far they still had to go. We became aware of the value of such hybrids and of the students' initial capacities for reflection.

Stage 5: Postseminar Learning

After the seminar, we asked the students to write papers on their attempts at double-loop learning. Judging from these, such attempts continue outside the seminar. One paper throws an interesting light on an aspect of skill development central to the transition from Model I to Model II. It was initially surprising to us that students could often *recognize* the Model I errors in a production and yet were unable to produce an intervention free of such errors. Later we became aware that production also involves a kind of recognition. The actor has an "inside" view of his situation just before and during action; after his action, he and others have an "outside" view of the production. To say of someone that he cannot convert his recognition skills into production skills is to say that he cannot map his outside views onto his inside views of his action.

Student P5 describes in his paper a view of the process by which he became capable of coordinating inside/outside views. He focuses on the development of one particular skill: "the ability to recognize and deal with my own negative feelings, particularly anger, in my relationships with others." P5 describes his initial situation as one in which he was virtually blind to anger in himself: "It seems fair to conclude that, initially at least, if I experience anger at all, I report it as a different emotion, for example, helplessness, loss of control, or fright; and I may well have projected my own feelings of anger on others . . . to Joe, for example, in my case." P5 had tried to confront a subordinate, Joe, who had let him down by failing to prepare for an important meeting. In his case, P5 had expressed fear that the preparations might not be made and concern that his interrogation might be making Joe angry, but he had registered no awareness of his own anger. In a class session devoted to his case, P5 "began the session seemingly unaware that I was feeling angry. Midway through the session there is evidence that I acknowledged my anger but doubted the wisdom of expressing it. Finally, I seem to acknowledge that I should express the anger in order to become more effective."

Thus, P5 describes himself as having been helped by both students and the interventionist (1) to move from their outside view of his action to a new inside view of his own feelings, (2) to recognize from an outside view that the object of his anger was not only Joe but himself, (3) to see the situation as one in which it is legitimate to feel and express such anger. What is remarkable in P5 is that, having formulated a heuristic derived from this particular situation, "Pay attention to unexpressed anger, and make differentiations, distinctions, and connections relevant to it," he went on to try to apply it to other situations and to deepen his understanding of his own unawareness. In one such incident, P5 gets angry when his wife asks him to put away some equipment she thinks may be dangerous to their children. He reflects on the incident: "Wondering if perhaps some of the anger I experienced toward [my wife] was not anger at myself for not having thought of putting the sections away myself. . . . The fact that I didn't [put the sections away] reflected on my competence as a parent and as 'protector' of my children. I found questions of my competence in this area . . . very threatening, and I reacted defensively. . . . I converted the defensive reaction into anger at my wife, which may have accounted for the highly volatile reaction I had initially."

P5 then asks, "What happened during the class session which

led to my recognition that I was feeling angry toward Joe and should express it? . . . First, the class, with [the interventionist's] help, kept the focus on anger, a focus which I would not have maintained on my own. Second, the class made it legitimate for me to be angry—as [P8] said, in essence, any reasonable person under those circumstances would have felt angry at Joe. I had been able to project anger to Joe but unable to allow myself to experience it. Finally, the class analyzed my behavior, via the roleplay, to indicate that I had in fact expressed anger whether I experienced it or not. When I roleplayed me in the situation, [the roleplay] came out essentially where I had—expressing fright in a way that conveyed anger." Later P5 describes how he realized that he was angry both at Joe for failing to perform adequately and at himself for failing to monitor Joe.

Then the interventionist produced an intervention that included the following: "I've got two feelings. One, I'm scared as hell that when the teachers are here, the tables are not going to be set, and if I find myself in that position, I'm going to feel angry both at you and at me for not monitoring you." P5 responded by saying, "I think that's an accurate description . . . I think that's what I really was feeling." Later, after discussing the incident with his wife and reflecting further, he created a new heuristic: "The anger you experience at yourself may be related to (1) an unrealistic expectation of yourself or to (2) a high sense of personal responsibility and commitment."

P5's story suggests the following generalization of what may be involved, at least in some instances, in the coordination of recognition and production skills and in the overlay of inside and outside views of action.

A person's inside view of his action may be subject to systematic error. Displacement and projection are mechanisms of such distorted perception, triggered by automatic defensive intercepts. By attending to others' outside views of his action, the person may recognize his blindness to this sort of error. To detect and correct such errors before he acts, he must construct a heuristic mechanism that initiates with a cue—a feeling, an inside view—and points to an error. An example is "When you are suddenly unaccountably angry at someone else, test for anger toward yourself." In a more general form, "When you experience the cue, look for the distortion."

By attending to the cue, the person is better able to recognize (and correct) the distortion, thereby enhancing his ability to feel the cue—attending to his anger, for example, rather than making himself unaware of it. As he becomes a better observer of such internal cues, he can more easily correct his perceptions of a situation. But for this, he needs outside views of his behavior. With practice—a term whose meaning now extends beyond repetition and even beyond experimentation—the person can become less dependent on, though never wholly independent of, outside help in testing his perceptions.

A Student Reflects on His Learning (by Gerry Garnett Ward)

In the preceding analysis, we reflected on students' actions and thoughts in order to infer what they were learning. The case that follows is a lengthy quotation from a student's reflection during a similar class. His case provides insights into how students begin to reflect and analyze their own and others' actions as interventionists. This student is the same person whose case was described in Chapter Six. The following material is his reflections on the seminar discussion of his case.

Reflection 1: Evaluating the Effect of a Strategy—John

John provided the first of many interventions that the class would provide during the session. Its brevity and relative simplicity in design lend it to an easily constructed analysis.

Excerpt from Tape of Session

John: (1) Well, as I told you [before class], I see this case as similar to mine. (2) The impression I have is it's some kind of an "easing-in" approach, some kind of a high-level abstraction. (3) You both talk about "proposal." (4) You ask about "proposal" and about his commitment. (5) You discuss it from this high level, "proposal" and "commitment." (6) So if you ask him about "commitment," he could say yes or no, and it's very [tape inaudible] and good. . . .

My initial reaction at the time was that no learning or insight into my behavior could be derived from John's intervention. As he spoke, I agreed with what I thought was his general observation, which was that I was not revealing my actual thoughts to T. Yet

John's attribution that this behavior consisted of an "easing in" approach ran counter to my understanding of the concept of "easing in." However, as client I chose not to confront him on that labeling question, since I thought perhaps that his intervention would be developed further (my behavior in that moment came close to the "easing in" concept).

In the present analysis, I infer the major thrust of John's observations to be somewhat different. That is, he was primarily attributing that my statements to T were not designed to actually exact from T a concrete indication of his intent, which therefore would allow T to provide a simple yes or no to my request for tangible indications of commitment. The cause of my confusion at the time, and my present criticism of John's intervention, can be traced to its design.

Line 2 of John's intervention (as numbered in the tape transcript) was an attribution that was not limited in its scope; that is, he referred to "it." "It" could cover any one part or all parts of the case. The effect of this nonspecificity is that an open field of data is offered to the client, who must then, on his own, work or guess at identifying the actual data that justify the attribution. The second effect of line 2 is that it introduced the concept of "easing in," which in most cases demands a case-data-supported tracing of a behavior pattern that proceeds as follows: The actor holds a key piece of information which he intends to reveal to the other and which he fears will incur the other's negative reaction; the actor initially presents nonnegative information with the intent of establishing a positive rapport with the other; the actor then presents the negative information to the other. Line 2 created in me, the client, the expectation and interest of having the consultant present specific data from my behavior in the case that would illustrate the pattern of easing in.

The end of line 2, and lines 3, 4, and 5, do not present data that validate the attribution of "easing in," but instead equate the "easing-in" concept with speaking in abstractions and provide data to support the revised concept. At that point, confusion was effected in me, the client, concerning the consultant's knowledge of the concept as well as the nature of my behavior in the case.

Lines 5 and 6, by their design, did offer help, though in a limited degree. They are, in terms of attribution (that is, speaking in abstractions) and in terms of data (that is, citing the specific words of

the client—"proposal" and "commitment"), both logical and validated. Thus, as an intervention, they offer the client the information
that the behavior referred to is counterproductive to the objective of
gaining a tangible indication of T's commitment. Yet, given that this
is the extent of the effect of the intervention, it remains within the
framework of my approach in the case, which is to move T to my
position without telling him of my suspicion of him, which I will
maintain.

The potential of the intervention for helping the client to revise his behavior is limited to changing his strategy for the approach.
It does not bring the client to examine the governing value and objectives in the case, nor does it lead to an examination of the inner
logic that guides the observed behavior. As a client following that intervention, I would therefore continue to hold the same assumptions
about T and aim toward the same objectives that I had held in the
actual case. My operating framework would remain intact.

It should be acknowledged that it is obviously unrealistic to
expect one intervention by a consultant to change the framework of
a client's understanding of his behavior or to change his disposition
toward behavior in a similar situation in the future. However, a realistic expectation or evaluative guide is the degree to which an intervention focuses on the critical or causal factors in a client's counterproductive behavior. John's intervention as it is analyzed above is held
to that standard.

It should also be acknowledged that the process of consulting
by a group holds a dimension that John, as the first contributor, was
not able to draw on. That is, as each class member/consultant intervenes, he or she provides direction, focuses on data, voices inferences, and elicits new data from the client. Most of this intervention
provides a foundation for subsequent interventions to be more effective. The group consulting process thus functions to supplement the
individual effectiveness of each member of the group.

Reflection 2: Clarification of a Goal: Exposure of an Ineffective Strategy—Martha and Jim

John's focus on the nature of the commitment that I was asking of T was continued by Martha. Her questions elicited data from
me that provided a base for Jim to offer an analysis that proved most
effective as an intervention.

Excerpt from Tape of Session

Martha: (7) What were you asking him for when you asked for commitment? . . . (8) What would he have to do to demonstrate his sincerity?

Me: (9) I'm not sure. I'd have to come clean to do that—tell him what I suspected of him and then establish just a basic level of human trust. (10) The discussion would have to focus on that directly.

Jim: (11) Martha asked how could he prove his sincerity. (12) You say, "He couldn't unless I revealed my left-hand column."

Me: (13) Exactly.

Jim: (14) So then the conclusion would be that, by making your choice of not to level with him with your left-hand column, you created the situation in which it was impossible for him ever to disconfirm your attributions or to demonstrate his sincerity.

Me: (15) Uh-huh. I agree. (16) But the other side of that is the fact that when T was dealt with directly, he shut people off. . . . (17) So in order to keep his ear, I made the judgment that I could not share the suspicion I had of him.

Jim: (18) It seems realistic that if you told him your left-hand column, he would get upset.

Martha's initial questions in lines 7 and 8 elicited some critical data that I, the client, had not provided to my consultants—namely, that T had to demonstrate an explicit good will toward me in order to provide the commitment that I was seeking. As basic an intervention as her question may seem, its effect was critical in that it demanded of me further clarification of a standard (that is, commitment) which I had privately devised and which I was using to measure T's personal and professional worth as well as my own professional effectiveness. In providing the data to Martha, I gained a recognition that surprised me and directly brought me to face the personal nature of the demand that I was making of T. Before the clarification, I was assuming that my demand for T's commitment fell within the "conventional" realm of our shared professional concerns about the matter of change in staff responsibilities. With the clarification, I recognized that T's demonstration of commitment was, as I framed it, far more sensitive, personal, and difficult than I had realized. In the present analysis, I make the inference that the implicit personal nature of the demand may have been an additional factor operating within me to induce my avoidance of discussion.

Martha's effectiveness as a consultant rested in her going outside my frame of mind, which was to remain unclarified on the issue. The intervention that John provided in lines 5 and 6 pointed to my nonclarification but did not use inquiry. Martha's intervention used immediate inquiry to gain new information that was also "new" to me, the client.

The intervention that Jim provided in lines 11, 12, and 14 proved at that point in the session to effect the most progress in my understanding of the case. Through a direct restatement of fresh data, Jim, in lines 11 and 12, reemphasized through the client's own words the necessity of my taking initial action if T was to demonstrate commitment. Then in line 14 he established that the direct effect of my stated decision not to take action was to create the condition that I defined as noncommitment in T, for which I held T accountable.

Jim's intervention contained two elements: (1) newly exposed data from the client and (2) logically framed effects of the client's behavior. By placing the purified data (commitment equals basic trust; exposing left-hand column creates trust) with existing valid data (my decision to withhold my left-hand column; my holding T accountable for commitment) into a causal framework, the intervention illustrated the inconsistency of my behavior. I held T accountable for the condition of noncommitment; I directly equated noncommitment with a lack of trust; a lack of trust was derived from my decision to withhold my feelings. Thus, my obstructionist role in the relationship and my unfairness in holding T accountable for my actions were both explicitly established.

Within the Model II mode of consulting, the design of the intervention in line 14 had all the essential elements of a heuristic in that it described in a logical framework both the directly observable behavior and the causal effects of the behavior that could be inferred. So presented, a client's behavior appears before him in a form that is outside his own system of viewing it, which often contains unclarified data and gaps or inconsistencies in logic. In the heuristic form, the presentation of the behavior and its effect is simple for the client to understand and is open to testing for correctness of data and logic. As such, it is an effective device for bringing the client to see his behavior in a different light as well as for monitoring the accuracy of the interventionist.

The heuristic that Jim offered provided the first step outside my reasoning processes in that it showed an alternative line of logic concerning my interaction with T. In grasping that alternative ordering of my behavior, I understood the contradictory nature of my general approach to T. However, as a client who had learned of the inconsistent nature of his approach, I did not understand a way outside the behavior that I had chosen, in that I felt compelled to avoid leveling in order to keep T's ear. Thus, in lines 16 and 17, my explanation of the behavior was offered with apparent acceptance of the necessity of contradictions.

The limits of the effect of Jim's intervention could be seen in my responses to it. My learning about my behavior in the case was restricted to identifying illogical reasoning. A basis was thus established through which I could understand the explicit illogic of my behavior and inferences. Yet the dilemma still existed for me in that I still regarded T as a force operating to coerce me into contradictory behavior.

Reflection 3: Suggestions for a Production—Martha and Bea

Excerpt from Tape of Session

Bea: (1) Did you have an experience on your own that showed you that you had difficulties in dealing with T?

Me: (2) There were staff meetings where opinions were voiced that were counter to T's. (3) The pattern established was that they were unilaterally shot down by T. . . . (4) So there was a lot of data there for me to say, "Well, look, T, you've done this kind of thing in the past; how do I know you're not going to do the same in this instance?"

Bea: (5) Right. Well, that's what I'm wondering. Why hadn't you asked him . . . ? [She suggests a production congruent with the design of line 4.]

Me: (6) Uh-huh.

Martha: (7) [Building on Bea's suggested production] . . . where you say to him, "We don't trust you for reasons of X, Y, and Z. And if you feel that you would like us to work on a proposal for change, you can demonstrate this by X, Y, Z. (8) And if you don't want us to work on it, I'd like you to tell me so and maybe to clarify the reasons why."

Me: (9) Well, T's in a dilemma. If he gave an open refusal to the assistant directors' request, he'd be denying the process that he brought up to boost morale. (10) So I don't think that position for him was a viable one. (11) Does that help you at all in giving you the context?

These two productions of Martha and Bea, in their basic design, were essentially like the final productions that the class offered near the end of the consulting session. Both productions advocated sharing with T my distrust concerning the issue, based on past observed data. Martha's production advocated in line 7 an approach that involved T partway through the planning process. Her production in line 8 allowed T to indicate his actual position and had built into it an inquiry about his rationale for a possible rejection of the proposal for action at hand.

As consulting interventions, however, both were flawed by their timing, which was premature. As evidenced in line 6 and more blatantly in lines 9-11, I (the client) remained in a framework of thought that led me to deny the effectiveness of the suggested productions. At the stage of awareness in which I functioned at that point in the session, the conditions of not alienating T and unilaterally protecting him from a dilemma were part of my tacit framework. Those assumptions, or governing variables, shaped my critical ability so that the productions offered seemed ineffective or inappropriate to the situation. At that point I needed a piecemeal demonstration of the ineffective and contradictory nature of the individual components of my theory-in-use before I would be capable of logically considering valid productions. And as the interventionist explicitly stated later in the tape, for a client to actually learn to examine the reasons for his behavior and to learn to create effective productions on his own in similar situations, he must be shown the inner logic and functioning of his theory-in-use.

The intervention that Jim provided, in which he explicitly showed the contradictions of my strategies for action, has been identified as the first effective consulting intervention. As such, it was the first step in the examination of the internal nature of my theory-in-use. The second effective step was the following intervention by Julio.

*Reflection 4: Exposure of a Strategy for Action and
Evaluation of Its Effect—Julio*

Excerpt from Tape of Session

Julio: (1) You've mentioned that, with regard to another party, at least on one occasion, the effort was made to be direct with T, but this was met by losing T's ear.

Me: (2) Uh-huh.

Julio: (3) And you mentioned on your page of comments that one possible merit of your approach may be to allow the individual some freedom, enough to move toward your position.

Me: (4) Uh-huh.

Julio: (5) I don't see much movement here, and (6) I'm wondering if it's your assumption that while one party may have lost T's ear by being direct, you have some part of his ear by not being direct—that is, that you would have something to lose by being direct. (7) I am making an attribution, which is: I attribute that assumption to be hidden.

Me: (8) Yeah, that's fairly stated. I hadn't identified that as an assumption. . . .

The importance or effectiveness of Julio's intervention in lines 3 and 5 lay in the explicit exposure of my action strategy juxtaposed with the effect of the strategy. As a client, I was shown the data that proved that my strategy of nondirect communication, meant to allow T to move toward my position, had instead the same result as a direct approach, a result I saw as being ineffective—namely, that T did not move. Both pieces of data were known to me but had not been framed within my rationale as an inconsistency.

In lines 6 and 7, Julio's intervention built on my new recognition of the ineffectiveness of the strategy and identified a hidden assumption that was critical to my theory-in-use: that I had something to lose—that is, T's ear. In acknowledging that keeping T's ear was an operating factor (as yet not identified) in my behavior and that it had been exposed as not accomplishing my espoused goal of allowing T to move toward my position, I had to suspend my previous understanding. My previous understanding was that I was guided by one objective in my theory-in-use, which was to effectively communicate to T the option of approving the assistant directors' proposal. Keeping T's ear previously had been identified as a means to an end rather than an implicit end in itself.

Table 7 shows, in Model II terminology, what Julio's intervention as a whole illustrated to me. The end point of the espoused

Table 7. Exposure of an Action Strategy

	Behavior Strategy	Effect of Strategy	Goals Achieved
Espoused theory	Don't confront.	Keep T's ear. Preserve relationship.	Open communication. Potential movement toward approval.
Theory-in-use	Don't confront.	Keep T's ear. Preserve relationship.	None.

theory is different from the end point of the theory-in-use. The critical question for the client, which at that point in the consulting session I was only beginning to frame, was: Which objective is the ultimate objective (that is, governing variable)? An effective approach to T would have to effect the specified objective.

Reflection 5: Inferences About the Client's Reactions—Interventionist

Excerpt from Tape of Session

Me: [In reaction to Julio's observations on my strategy and some probing by interventionist] (1) Well, what you [interventionist] are saying is that there's a broader context here [previously defined by me]—that is, my relationship with the individual. (2) What you [Julio] are saying is that, given just this one case, if this was solely my objective—to bring T's movement to the proposed change—then I wouldn't have anything to lose by bringing it up. I walked away with nothing accomplished except that I walked away with my relationship with T preserved. But if you remove that broader context of preserving the relationship and just look at this case [of presenting the assistant directors' proposal], I don't think that I do have anything to lose in taking a more confrontive approach.

Interventionist: (3) There's something about that reasoning. It says "Julio, you're right if we narrow the case down in a way that's unreal. . . ." (4) You've created a condition where if it's right, it's trivial. . . . (5) So I'm attributing to you that your response, if we're not careful, is the kind of response . . . that says, "Gee, I'm really open . . . I realize I could have done these nasty things . . . what's next?" (6) [Speaking to class] And if we continue, he may be as uninfluenceable as T is in this case. . . . (7) So if you want to reach this guy, don't tell him what to do with the other fellow. Focus on what he's doing . . . in the present case and in this room.

In this intervention, which was discussed mainly in the context of group process, the interventionist asserted that there was a directly observable similarity between my unawareness of my behavior in the case and my unawareness of my responses to the group's suggestions during the session. His subsequent advice that an effective intervention would focus on both behaviors implies that the same reasoning processes were present in the client in the two situations.

The interventionist's observations in lines 3, 4, and 5 appear valid, as my in-class behavior and my case behavior were alike: I was unclear on what the governing variables of my behavior with T actually were. The rationale that prompted me to choose a nonconfrontive, noncommunicative approach in the case was based on the belief that holding T's ear was not a governing variable of my theory-in-use but only a means to the aim of open communication. The rationale that prompted me to choose to trivialize Julio's analysis was based on the same belief.

In spite of Julio's careful intervention, which brought me to focus on the priority of maintaining a relationship with T (as shown in my behavior), I could only recognize it as an isolated phenomenon. Similarly, the previously identified internal inconsistencies of my theory-in-use appeared to me to be flawed reasoning or behavior but to be isolated from the larger system of behavior that was taking place. Thus, as a client, I could acknowledge that the immediate behavior described was illogical or inconsistent by itself, but I was not able to recognize its place in the larger system of counterproductive behavior. Accordingly, I responded, "Yes, you're right, but I'm not sure [the inconsistency] matters."

Within the present role of writing this reflection as a consultant to the consultants studying my case, I would advocate that they label each identified inconsistency with a term that indicates its function in the overall theory-of-use. Therefore, Julio's intervention would also involve explicit identification of my behavior as an ineffective action for the stated goal, or governing variable. Through that label, a client—at least one who is familiar with the framework of Model II—can place the identified, flawed behavior in the context of the larger system and thereby understand the exact nature of its counterproductive effect.

Reflection 6: Identifying Inconsistency Between Assumptions and Strategy of Espoused Theory—Julio

Excerpt from Tape of Session

Julio: (1) I had underlined two things on this sheet of comments. (2) One was "assuming that [T's] hidden interest [which you, Gerry, attribute to him and which you seem to have some data for] will be protected by him at all costs." (3) And then leaping to the judgment that your [approach] "has some merit in that [T] may actually move toward your approach"—(4) that seemed inconsistent to me. (5) And then also, using the data of your case and what I was interpreting within the field of data in your case, I did not see that your approach had the merit that you claimed it had, insofar as it did not achieve the results that you desired.

The data that Julio cited in lines 1, 2, and 3 of his intervention were observed strictly in the espoused theory provided to the consultants in a one-page statement by the client. In writing that statement, I was not aware of the inconsistency between my attribution that T would protect his hidden interests at all costs and my strategy to move T toward my position. As a client who absorbed the data that Jim presented in a revised order, I was forced to confront the fact that either my assumption about T's defensiveness had to change or my goals for the interaction had to change. As I had designed my behavior in theory, it was doomed to failure or it was based on erroneous information. Obviously a clarification had to be made in my espoused theory.

Within the scope of his intervention on the illustrated discrepancy between the assumption and goal of my espoused theory, Julio did not follow up further. He reemphasized in line 5 that the effect of my actual behavior was not congruent with my goal. However, he did not ask for a clarification of my theoretical position.

One possible continuation of Julio's intervention would be as follows:

> Well, you agree that the view that you hold of T—that he'll defend his hidden interests at all costs—is inconsistent with the goal that you set, which is to allow him to move toward your position. As you frame the situation, either you have set an impossible goal for your intervention with T, or you have made a mistaken attribution about his probable behavior or his actual intent. Which of those three components would you choose to reconsider?

In so presenting the client with the contradictions of his espoused theory, the consultant would lead him to revise either his goals or his attributions about T. Either revision would warrant a change in the espoused theory's strategy for action.

It should be noted that such an intervention would not necessarily create Model II behavior in the newly produced strategy for action. The client would have to be guided by specific Model II values and strategies in order to achieve that change. Otherwise the client could as easily remove his contradictions in the espoused theory by, for instance, attributing that T could be moved and then devising a strategy to unilaterally achieve his goal of moving him, a goal that would be Model I by design.

Reflection 7: Exposing Inconsistency Between Governing Variable of Espoused Theory and Behavioral Strategy of Theory-in-Use

Excerpt from Tape of Session

Int.: I've taken his [Julio's] comment and turned it into the form of a heuristic, a proposition, which is: "When I'm dealing with someone who is so defensive that he will protect his hiddenness at all costs, I, too, will act in the same way."

This intervention was submitted as a follow-up to Julio's reference to my failure to achieve the goal of allowing T to move. Stated in heuristic form, the action strategy of my theory-in-use was explicitly illustrated. The corollary that acting in a covert manner will not encourage openness in another person seems reasonable, given the general data of one's life experience.

At that point in the session, I, as the client, still had not integrated the effects of my inconsistencies. I was aware that I could not act covertly if I hoped to achieve openness in T. And at an earlier point, I had been made aware that I was acting covertly to keep T's ear. But I could not explicitly or consciously identify the connection between the implicit governing variable of my theory-in-use and my strategy for action in my theory-in-use. Identifying the congruence of those two elements of my theory-in-use might have created a powerful realization. It would have centered on the opposing nature of my general espoused theory and the effect of my general theory-in-use. I would have realized that although I espoused a goal of creating open communication with T, I functioned to create closed communication, since that was congruent with the goal of my theory-in-use. To maintain a relationship with T (which I believed was necessary for open communication) was the observed goal of the theory-in-use.

Reflection 8: Identifying an Implicit Governing Variable—Julio

Excerpt from Tape of Session

[Julio produced a heuristic based on Dotty's observation that I refused to give T any details of the proposal despite his request.]

Julio: (1) I'd like to see if the proposition I've come up with matches what you think you're thinking, which is: (2) "T wants data; if I don't give T data when he wants data, I am more likely to achieve my aims than if I give him data." (3) And that would seem to me to be inconsistent. [Explains the data from the case and from the session that justify the heuristic.]

Me: (4) Yes, I am saying that. (5) The reason that I am saying that is that . . . giving T data . . . would be such a long process that would make me . . . and the rest of the assistant directors vulnerable. . . . (6) So, yes, it would be to my advantage not to give T data unless I got some real commitment.

Julio: [Soon following up on my response] My thought is that I still see an inconsistency. (7) But what you're saying is that, well, there was an inconsistency, but . . . it was an inconsistency of logic. (8) But it wasn't really an inconsistency with your total aim, which was to communicate with T and achieve some assurance from T that he would listen to the proposal that you and the assistant directors had. (9) Either that or simply go through the motions of discussing the proposal and simply maintaining the relationship with T and not getting anything done.

Julio's heuristic in line 2 made explicit my conscious strategy and executed behavior with T as well as my conscious defense of both my behavior and my strategy. The critical effect of that intervention for my learning was that I became aware that I saw the action, in spite of its apparent contradictory nature, to be correct. Thus, in lines 4 through 6, I presented a defense of the approach.

As a client presenting an apparent inconsistency between the strategy/action of my theory-in-use and one of my espoused governing values (namely, possible movement of T to my proposal), I sought to clarify for myself and the group a previously implicit governing variable of my theory-in-use. In line 5, I identified that aim, which was to avoid vulnerability. Thus the aim—protection of self—was consistent with the strategy of denying T's requests, which, however, acted to prevent his movement. At that point, it became apparent to me that one of the governing variables of my theory-in-use was at odds with those of my espoused theory. I could not create a situation that allowed T's movement to the proposal if in action my governing variable was unilateral protection of myself and the other assistant directors.

In line 8, Julio, as a consultant, remained within the explicit data that I had provided concerning my stated aim. In line 8, Julio appeared to be accepting the congruence of my previously stated aim and the strategy/action that he illustrated in the heuristic. In fact, they were incongruent.

At that point, Julio did not draw on an inference from the new data that I had just provided in lines 5 and 6 in response to his earlier intervention. Redesigned to include an inference based on the new data, line 8 would have been something to the effect of "So then your strategy and action were not inconsistent with the aim or governing variable that you've just identified, which is to avoid being vulnerable. That aim could also be labeled unilateral protection of

your position." In spite of that missing element, Julio's intervention had brought to the surface an aim of my interacton with T that I had not consciously identified. Direct comparison of the newly identified aim with my other espoused aims was a subsequent step to be taken in my understanding of the contradictions between my espoused theory and my theory-in-use.

Excerpt from Tape of Session

[Julio continues to clarify his observations of my behavior.]

Julio: (1) It occurs to me that . . . I made another attribution to you about what I thought you were really doing in this case. On two bases, I'm going to say this. (2) One is that I don't see you having accomplished the aim that you state, which was to receive assurance from T that he would think about your proposal. (3) The other is that, given what, in your mind, is data that T in the past had not considered your proposals whether they were expressed directly or indirectly, (4) you were really going in with the thought that "Well, it is very unlikely that I will achieve the aim that I've stated here, and . . . my best hope is to simply go through the motions of discussing the proposal that really, in fact, is never going to come into being. (5) And my best hope is to simply maintain rapport."

Me: (6) So you're saying that I don't have the expectation of getting anywhere toward my aim. . . .

Int.: Now I'm Julio [roleplaying]: (7) Gerry, all that I'm doing is telling you the inferences that I'd make about your theory-in-use from your behavior. (8) And I'm not trying to infer what your motives were.

[Later, summarizing one of my inconsistencies] (9) I think he [Gerry] said, and I'll add what he said in class: ". . . I won't give T data when he wants it, because I'm more likely to achieve the aim that I did not clearly state in my paper but which I will now clearly state in class, which is: (a) not to be vulnerable and (b) not to get this thing . . ." [tape ends here, but I recall that the words were "sandbagged by T"].

The further clarification of Julio's observations of my behavior drew on data and inferences that he had established with me earlier in the session. He then used those established data to draw a direct and forceful inference that was next to impossible for the client to deny logically or misunderstand.

In line 2, Julio reasserted that the strategy and action of my theory-in-use were ineffective for my espoused aim. Line 3 reasserted the inconsistency of a guiding assumption and my strategy for action. With the establishment of the critical inconsistencies drawn from the session's data, Julio produced in lines 4 and 5 the logical inference that my observed behavior would lead to. That logical inference about my aims or governing values was explicitly different from my espoused aims.

As a client who tended to have difficulty accepting the assertion that I held the aim of simply maintaining rapport with T to the exclusion of my espoused aims, I reacted with confusion. The interventionist's line 7 clarified that Julio's inference was not about my espoused aims but about my accomplished aims. That final clarification allowed for a fairly clear understanding on my part of the opposing nature of my theory-in-use and my espoused theory. That understanding was gained through a gradual comprehension of the internal inconsistencies of my theory-in-use.

Further inconsistencies between other governing variables of my theory-in-use and the governing variables of my espoused theory were reasserted in line 9 by the interventionist. Having stepped out of the framework of my original behavior, I, as a client, began to understand more easily without resistance the contradictions of my behavior in the light of my desires.

Part Three

Applications
to Organizations

During the past ten years, I have studied several internal and external consulting organizations. The studies have led to programs ranging from two to eight years' duration. In each case, we tried to introduce Model II actions and O-II learning systems at the upper levels, then helped the top to educate the next level below, and so on.

    The material in Part Three is taken from our data on a firm with which we have worked for eight years. The criteria for selecting the episodes were that (1) the issues being dealt with had to be exemplary of those experienced in growing firms; (2) the issues had to be difficult ones that involved tough double-loop problems, problems that are rarely dealt with directly and openly so that a culture can be created within the organization that enhances double-loop learning; and (3) the issues had to illustrate how distancing and disconnectedness can be reduced in organizations.

The examples are taken from tape recordings of meetings held in a consulting firm (about 75 employees) that in less than ten years has become the top firm of its kind. Tape recordings of the monthly meetings of the Executive Office (that is, the four partners), of the partners and vice-presidents, and of the partners, vice-presidents, and managers together were sent to me.

The partners had only two one-day sessions to learn Models I and II. They discussed the X and Y case as well as cases that they wrote describing problems that they had with one another. They also had a two-day session that included wives, discussing cases relevant to family and family-related business problems. The only other education the partners received was that which I was able to give them while participating periodically in their Executive Office meetings (about three times a year, for one or two days, over a period of five years). The emphasis has been on working with the partners because it is my strategy to work with the top people until they are able to produce hybrid Model II actions or better under zero to moderate stress and/or until they can be confronted on any discrepancies between their espoused theories, actions, and theories-in-use. Once this point was reached, and Model II had passed the dangerous stage of being a fad, I began to work with the vice-presidents and managers.

In listening to and analyzing the tapes, it became evident that the criterion for what was discussable continually changed. At the outset, many topics were undiscussable. As the partners' competence and trust increased, they continued to up the ante of what issues could be discussed among themselves and with the vice-presidents and the managers.

For example, Chapter Thirteen deals with several problems related to integrating new partners. How does an already cohesive partner group integrate a new member? As we shall see, John, then the new partner, despaired that he would ever be genuinely integrated. Another difficult problem that arises frequently is the misunderstandings new members have about expected financial earnings and how soon they are to be introduced to profitable clients. In Chapter Thirteen, we discuss the problem of building a collegial group. For example, there is the problem of the senior partner who manages his work activities as if he were in one crisis after another. Not only does this create tensions among the partners, but it also creates difficulties with the lower-level employees who must adjust to these crises. Still another problem is the fear that one partner may take away lucrative clients from another partner. Another is the problem of meeting commitments to the new vice-presidents so that they are brought on board as soon as possible.

The originator of this firm, Robert, was well aware that one of the most distressing problems of new organizations is that they may hire, early in their history, people who are soon outdated and outdistanced by the firm's growth. Robert wanted to create a climate where such issues could be candidly discussed among the partners, vice-presidents, and managers. He sought a culture in which, if someone was not performing adequately, the others felt a responsibility to help him or her redesign the job in order to correct the situation. He was quite prepared to provide the additional financial resources that job redesign might require.

As we shall see, Robert and the other partners continually worked to create a climate where subordinates could confront superiors, especially on the matter of providing them with adequate learning and growth opportunities. This was so not only because individual development was valued but because only if the subordinates had genuine control of their jobs, with genuine financial and peer support, could one justify removing those who did not achieve the job performance that they designed.

Finally, we will illustrate one of the most difficult issues that plague new firms: what to do with the partner who originated the firm and who appears unwilling to let go, who strives to dominate others while espousing the value of individual autonomy and growth and a cohesive collegial group.

Throughout Part Three, we will find people struggling to state their thoughts and feelings in a way that allows others to do the same. At first, candor is relatively high compared with other organizations, but the competence is not as high. At times, people do make untested and unillustrated evaluations and attributions; they advocate in ways to win; they sometimes create self-fulfilling prophecies.

Even though the problems become more difficult, I believe the data illustrate that the clients were learning to act in accordance with Model II or to produce hybrids of Models I and II. We describe several episodes in which someone acting in accordance with Model I is confronted (often by a subordinate) and consequently strives to change his actions or at least is open to the possible validity of the challenge.

Work with these clients continues and is expanding. More and more persons are learning to produce Model II actions. More and more, they use one another as resources toward this end. There appears to be almost no forgetting curve, although competence to produce Model II actions may vary, depending on the degree of stress involved.

Model II action does not mean being soft with people and their performance. As an organization develops an O-II learning system, its members are able to talk together about very difficult issues so that excellence is not sacrificed. The involvement required makes it likely that people become more connected with their reasoning processes and less distant from their personal responsibilities to themselves, to one another, and to the organization.

13

Integrating
New Group Members

Robert, Bill, John, and Don are partners in a fast-growing organization whose consulting services are considered by most knowledgeable officials to be superior, if not the best. Robert, the founder of the organization, not only was determined to create an organization that would provide superior services and be profitable to all employees, but he also wished to accomplish these objectives in a firm where the quality of work life was superior. Robert recruited Bill at the beginning of the firm's history. John was recruited about three years later, and Don about three years after John's arrival.

Creating a cohesive partnership is a difficult task. Creating one that is able to produce Model II features while building and maintaining a young organization is even more difficult. One of the more vexing problems is how to acquire senior partners and integrate them genuinely with the original partner group. You may recall that Robert and Bill had this problem with John (Chapter Ten). They dealt openly with the issue. In so doing, John not only began to become more integrated but learned some important lessons about his ways of defending himself. If space permitted, we would see that Robert also learned about his acts of unilateral control, of which he was unaware. Bill learned about his withdrawal from conflict. They all learned how all three defensive patterns interlocked and reinforced one another. Thus, when John would accuse Robert of unilaterally controlling or not meeting commitments, Robert would become upset and respond in ways that partly confirmed John's fears. But one reason for Robert's response was that he knew he would not get valid support from Bill. Bill would withdraw, leaving the responsibility to Robert. This, in turn, would increase the likelihood that Robert would take the responsibility, thus reinforcing John's view that Robert was overcontrolling.

These and other defensive reactions operated whenever the partners were dealing with difficult business as well as interpersonal issues. The reason is that, as we have seen in Chapter One, people dealing with substantive issues make attributions about each other's motives and competences—attributions that, though untested and often wrong, influence the way they deal with the substantive problems.

Robert, Bill, John, and later Don became committed to solving these age-old problems in a way that helped to build a more cohesive partnership and a more effective organization. The latter meant that they wanted to work with the people below them as well as with one another.

In this chapter, we continue with the integration of John into the partner group. In Chapter Ten, you may recall, the three partners (Don had not yet been hired) explored their difficulties and agreed that although John brought up the issue in terms of financial promises made to him to attract him, the underlying issue was that he felt undervalued by Robert and Bill. They felt that John was distorting reality about the financial issues and that he undervalued them. These feelings led them to explore the puzzle that each of them would feel valued by the others to the extent that he was succeeding *and* not asking for help. All agreed that they hated to ask for help from one another. They felt close to one another when they were able to feel "I'm as good as they are. I'll show those son-of-a-bitches that I can produce as well as they do. I'll never ask for help." The puzzle is that cohesiveness is connected with competitiveness and with distancing from one another.

Distancing may be connected with cohesiveness by a process of *discounting*. For example, John's unilateral attributions that

Robert and Bill reneged on their promises did upset Robert and, less so, Bill, because neither believed that the attributions were valid. But they recognized that John was expressing ideas and feelings that new partners might have but rarely would state to the old partners. Thus, they saw that John's intent was to create a more open culture, even though his (and their own) actions were not as consistent with Model II as they wished. In essence, they all discounted the negative impact of the Model I actions as much as they could because they knew the intent was to generate an O-II learning system.

Such discounting also occurs frequently in a Model I world. People often say, "I didn't get upset because I knew he didn't mean what he said" or "I ignored the needling and listened to his ideas." But there are at least two important differences between the two discounting processes. First, in a Model I world, discounters act as if they were not discounting. Second, they rarely, if ever, expect to reflect openly on the discounting. Discounting is not discussable. In an O-II learning system, the discounting is discussable either as it is occurring or relatively soon afterward.

Episode 1

The next episode occurs about two years later, during a meeting in which the partners are designing the ownership of the firm. Robert begins by stating that he wants to clear up his relationship with John before they talk about ownership. One of the issues troubling Robert is that he feels John acts significantly more out of self-interest than out of interest for the firm as a whole. This concerns Robert deeply because (1) the concept of the firm is that the partners manage it equally, (2) Robert is emotionally committed to a Three Musketeers relationship among the partners, in which it is "all for one and one for all," and (3) Robert fears that because the present compensation scheme rewards partners for sales, attention to the organization depends more on partner loyalty and commitment than on financial reward for it.

Neither Bill nor Don agrees that John is motivated mainly by self-interest and ignores the company. They see John as being firm-oriented in the partners' meetings. If John has not carried his share of the firm's responsibilities, Bill and Don attribute that to his newness in the firm. They believe John is working very hard but, admittedly, not hard enough on certain firmwide responsibilities. John agrees with Bill and Don. He also believes that the doubts he expressed two years ago (see p. 215) were based on misunderstandings that have now been overcome. Robert is still convinced that John believes the firm made pledges it did not keep.

Bill believes that Robert will not bury the past until John admits that Robert did not mislead him about financial arrangements. "That," says Bill, "is a win/lose thing." John agrees and adds that he has no evidence that Robert misled him, but "I would have real difficulty saying, 'Yes, I was *completely* wrong.'"

Robert: I am reluctant to express my view at the outset because I feel it would be better for me were John to go through a change in his assessment of his experience of coming into the firm, changing his assessment from negative to positive, which is what it should have been. John's negative assessment hurts my feelings. So I'm reluctant to go ahead unless that's cleared up. Another thing is that I perceive that you, John, are more concerned about your self-interest than about the firm as a whole, while for me, it's the opposite. Your perception has been from your own point of view rather than from the point of view of the firm as a whole. I impute a selfishness which I see as diminishing in you. But I still feel hurt.

Robert expresses his belief that he should not state his view of how he might transfer equal control to all present (and future) partners before resolving John's attitudes toward the firm. He expresses his views and feelings but does not illustrate them.

Interventionist: Before John responds, what do Bill and Don think? What data do you have?

Bill: I'd probably agree—not to the extent of Robert's reaction, but I do feel in agreement with the first half of his statement. John's entry into the firm wasn't

Bill confirms Robert's diagnosis only partly and illustrates his attribution that John is concerned about the firm. Bill, as we shall see, often takes on the role of

a bad deal for him. On the question of selfishness, I don't feel quite as strongly as Robert does. The only time I work with John is in the partners' meetings, and I see him as taking a corporate orientation in these meetings. I guess that Robert's attribution of selfishness on the part of John must be based on other data.

Robert: I mean self-interest rather than the selfishness of a teenager.

Bill: It has to do with anxiety, too. If I see our system as a sales system with the reward as the number of sales on the books, and I feel anxious about achieving it, then you'd err in that direction [of self-interest].

Robert: I see John as being concerned with self-interest. [I hold his quality in high regard.] But if we shift from a Three Musketeers orientation toward getting paid for our own work and competing with each other, that concerns me.

Int.: How do you see this question of John's self-interest, Don?

Don: I want that [corporate interest], and that quality is a fragile thing. We'll be hard put to maintain it, especially with more people. I think the accommodation process has been extra effective. I don't see the self-interest thing Robert sees in John, but I don't believe I would see it if it were there.

balancing any polarization that Robert and John might create.

Bill notes that the compensation scheme, which places a premium on client sales and contact, applies pressure on the partners in the direction of self-interest.

Robert wants to see whether a compensation scheme is possible that rewards partners for client sales and yet does not encourage destructive competition among the partners. This recurring problem is resolved only after much discussion and continual monitoring.

[Later]

Robert: But what difficulties do you see? I can't see any for myself over the past year. I'm afraid I'm carrying forward my bad feelings about a past experience [John's feelings of kill-down and so on].

Robert begins to wonder whether part of his concern about John is related to the difficulties they have had in the past in which John felt that the firm had not met its commitments. This had upset Robert because he believed the firm had more than met its commitments.

John: I'm trying hard not to get back to the old issues.

[Later]

Robert: ... I don't have anything I can point to as John being self-interested rather than interested in the firm as a whole.

Robert also believes that John still feels somewhat wronged. He notes that although he feels that John is self-oriented, he cannot point to data to illustrate the attribution. This is a sign that Robert questions the basis for his attribution.

[Later]

John: ... And I've been trying to make a transition to saying, "Look, you can't just look at it from your own point of view because Robert continues to make propositions or attributions about how this is going to work out ... and not only on compensation, but he's done it on programs and on sales and on report writing and data process, and all those other things." And whenever I've heard the attributions, I've always said, "Boy, you know, I really have trouble believing that that's going to be that [great]." But so far, everything has come out as you said it would. Robert,

John then adds that he has been doing quite a bit of reflecting on the issue and believes that most of the promises made have been kept. John now questions the basis for his early attributions. He does add that the firm ought to be careful in the future.

John reflects on his reasoning processes, the inferences he makes, and that frequently they have been wrong.

keep telling me that really it's going to be this way. Because every time he does it, it does come out right. And I really value your keeping [on] doing that.

So then I say to myself, "OK, what you've got to do is get yourself above yourself and look at it from the company's point of view." The one thing I still have going on is, I keep saying, "Look, I don't see anybody representing the VPs or the new people coming in." And I'm concerned that—I've never said this, and I guess it's good to get it out. . . .

John admits that he should take a more positive view of the company.

John warns the partners that he believes the new vice-presidents will have some of the same problems of integration as he has had.

[Later]

John: There are things that are going around that I should get out, I guess. You said before, and I think we've talked about it before, that you and Bill feel that I don't highly value that wonderful opportunity that has been given to me by this company. And I see now how you feel that. I had expected to earn more dollars than I did in the first two years. You have told me to relax, I would earn the money. And as I've said before, every time you've made propositions about the future, you've been right. And so I'm becoming relaxed that those are going to be right.

John now expresses his fear that he may not be as highly valued by the partners as he wishes he were.

These feelings appear to continue for many months and are not easily dispelled. John and the partners will discuss them several times before they are resolved.

As we shall see, one of the payoffs is that John takes the lead in helping new vice-presidents and managers who may have these feelings by reflecting with them on the problems he had with Robert and Bill.

Robert: I hear you attributing to me that I made promises to you about the future and your income in the first two years at the time

Robert returns to his concern that John believes the firm broke its promises.

that you were talking about joining the firm.

John: We had some perceptions
that were—

Robert: That were not fully met.

John: Well, the compensation, I
think—

Robert: Is that attribution correct?

John: The compensation system
that we had was not—before I
joined the firm, I don't think it
was.

Int.: It was what?

John: It was formalized in terms
of the point system and the
amortization of points. And so
my assumption was that current
profits would be shared on a current basis and that there was not
going to be a deferral of profits.

Robert: That was your assumption.

John: Yeah.

[Later]

John: I . . . I'm not going to be
very skillful. I'd like to go past
those differences. Let's forget
them. Call that partly my problem and maybe partly yours—but
not try to identify who's the
problem. Because in the future, I
can see it's going to be substantially different than that. And to
try to keep going back to that
would be, I think, a mistake, to
try to identify what it was and
what was wrong and can we
change that. I'd just like to put
all that behind.

One reason Robert returns to
this issue is that he believes commitments made are sacred and
cannot be broken. Thus, he believes that his integrity is in question. If that is not clarified, John
and others may not provide the
mutual support they may need in
case of misunderstandings with
future personnel. Moreover, Robert may be reluctant to turn over
control of the company to the
partners (which eventually is
done) if he believes feelings of
mistrust exist among them.

Robert: Why?

John: Because I don't think it's relevant and productive to continue to go back and discuss it. The only thing that I would like to say is that I have the feeling that you and Bill attach relatively marginal value to my coming to the firm three years ago, and the contributions that I have made in the last three years have been—I sense that you don't value them very highly. And I have some problems with that. And that you feel that the firm would have been just where we are today if I had not joined, and that my coming along was a good stroke for me, but it wasn't particularly helpful to the firm.

John attributes that Bill and Robert only marginally value his coming to the firm. He does not illustrate the attribution.

Robert: What's the evidence?

Instead of becoming angry, Robert asks for data to illustrate the attribution.

John: [Pause] I'm not sure I can articulate the evidence.

John is unable to provide data.

Bill: I would have a hard time with that one. I would consider that that's absolutely wrong. I'd go back to, I think what was said before . . . where I get upset is [that] somewhere along the line is "Look, I made a mistake to come with the firm because it was harder and less financially rewarding the last couple of years than I expected it to be. And that's you guys' fault, and I will continue to hold that against you."

Bill, whom John views as more understanding of him, does not support John's attributions.

Bill expresses a fear he has that John will hold grudges against Bill and Robert.

Robert: I can go further. What I hear you saying is "But I'm man enough to let bygones be by-

Robert adds another lingering fear. It is important for these attributions to be tested and

gones. Provided only we don't examine it, because it might turn out that I made a mistake on my own, by myself, in attributing to the firm a behavior as to the economics . . . then I can hold that as still legitimate for my anger, but I'm big enough to go past it. And then you guys can never get it because I will [hide] it."

worked through if the partnership is to be genuinely collegial and have high trust.

Bill: And the only problem with that is, if you let it go by, won't you still be wondering if you got screwed? As you were talking, I was looking for the slightest slip. While you were talking, I was not so much listening to what you were saying, which was correct about the VPs; I was saying, "Now, I know he thinks he got screwed, and I know he's going to think it's going to screw him again. So let's watch for that very carefully." So even when you're not, and it's past and everything else, if it's not clear, it'll get attributed to you every time and you won't be looking for it. [And people may be suspicious of your motives.]

Bill illustrates that during this conversation he was looking for any slips by John that might reveal his feeling of being screwed. Again, inattention to such issues can inhibit trust.

John: I guess one of the pieces of evidence I would have taken—again, I didn't confront, so this is a good example of how you don't communicate—that my contributions would not have been particularly valued in the first three years. The nature of the company has really changed, and because [of what you've said], we should have a high

John communicates some data and admits it was his responsibility to air these thoughts when they first occurred (many months ago).

value on ownership. Have a high value on ownership that we had not discussed before. "And the system that we're going to have is going to be a five-year wait. And so, John, you're not going to be able to participate in that for two more years." And what I impute to that—and again, I should bring all of this stuff out —was that, really, the nature of the change in the company to cause ownership, to create value, has been what Robert and Bill have done, not what I have done. Therefore, Robert and Bill should participate, but I should not. In fact, I should not for the next two years, because I haven't been part of that change in the nature of the company. I guess, now that I think about it, that is what was going on, but . . . at such a subconscious level.

Robert: Yes.

John: . . . That a minute ago, when you asked me, I couldn't come up with it.

Robert: But as it comes up now and it surfaces, how do you handle it? I mean, putting it against evidence, for example?

John: Well, the evidence now is that that was wrong.

Robert: You have tested that assumption.

John: . . . That I tested it . . . in the form of "Maybe we should change the approach," and that the approach has changed, and I was —"OK, John, you were wrong." I have never articulated that before, but I wanted to get it out, because it has been something I guess I felt.

Robert: . . . And so your personal experience will be, assuming the five-year wait, that you get a stockowner's interest in the sixth and seventh year, which I will not experience, even though as I perceive it, I took a substantially larger risk and made a larger contribution to the development of the firm . . . and so I didn't see it as being a negative between us.

John: So you would say that my attribution that the contribution that I have made—that you do not highly value [me]—would be wrong?

Robert: I would say yes, but that's not important compared to how you see it. I would say that evidence that we value your joining the firm would be that we gave you an equal vote in the control of the company, so you became a one-third controller of the decision-making process. That I gave you clients that were important clients. We gave you a going concern to work with without charging you for it. [You get all of your sales value.] Help you in any way you want help. If you want me to travel with you instead of working on my self-interest and my sales, sure. You want me to spend days and days and days with you, going to see your clients, sure. [Do you want me to give you my clients? Sure.] I would say those are all kinds of evidence of a very substantial commitment to an individual and an expression of the importance [of that person to] the firm.

Robert believes that John's view is incorrect but encourages him to hold it until it is disconfirmed to John's satisfaction.

Robert then provides data to illustrate his view that John is valued highly.

John: Yeah, I agree with that.

To summarize so far: John asked that the discussion move beyond the past. Robert was not willing to do so. This led John to assert that he felt that Bill and Robert placed only marginal value on his joining the firm. Robert asked for data to illustrate this attribution. John was unable to give any. Bill told John that although he espoused "let bygones be bygones," that was not how he was behaving. Robert agreed, and Bill continued by saying that they all should be alert to this issue to see whether it gets in their way.

Don: [You're both right], but I can see why John would feel that way and could interpret it that way. I think that's a fairly normal reaction for a thoughtful man, which does not deny *at all* what you said about things that you guys did to make him feel welcome.

[Later]

Int.: If Don's reaction is valid, then it has an important implication, because if Don feels this way, and John did, it means that future partners may in fact feel that way.

[Later]

Int.: . . . I thought John said, "When I heard the five-year deal, that cue led me to feel that my work was less valued." So far?

John: Yes.

Int.: What's the data that says that this issue is not discussable or influenceable?

John: There isn't any.

[Later]

Bill: But does each person incrementally that comes in feel less influenceable?

Bill relates this problem to the introduction of future partners and officers.

Int.: Well, that's the kind of thing we have to keep an eye on.

The interventionist does the same.

Robert: [Let's get back to what John and I were discussing.] In fairness, John, I think it's because I think I can show you that the difficulty you have is a man-made difficulty made by yourself.

Robert returns to his concerns because he is not satisfied that John and he agree.

Int.: The difficulty being?

Robert: That John has a set of expectations with regard to his income in the first year or two in the firm that were not—that were above what he experienced . . .

and I believe that that was not at any time made by me, that there were no statements made by me that I would have been able to understand to be delivering that information.

[Later]

John: What I hear you say is "I think if we talked about it, I think I could change your mind, John. Because I could bring up some facts." And I think that that would be productive. What are the facts?

John states an attribution and encourages Robert to illustrate his views.

Robert: And I think you would change your mind, and as you change your mind, your emotions would be changed substantially over time as a consequence. And I'd love that. [They discuss different views.]

[Later]

John: No, what I say is that I'm willing to go past all that and bury it. Robert is unwilling to let me bury it and keeps bringing it up. . . .

Int.: Could you tell Robert what it is that leads you to be willing to bury it?

John: . . . Because it is in the past, and it was something that is no longer an issue, no longer relevant to my position, to my problem, to my difficulty, but it may have been earlier, but it is no longer relevant to anything about the company, about myself, about my relationship with my wife.

John makes a clear statement that he no longer considers these negative feelings relevant.

Int.: It may be in the past for you; it's still not in the past for him. We also have some pretty good data this morning that when you confront Robert on something that is his error, he'll not only own up to it, he'll pile up more evidence. So you've got a guy who's willing to be confronted [if he feels strongly about it, and you also have evidence that he's confrontable].

The interventionist is concerned that Robert also express any of his reservations about John's charges and attitudes.

Bill: [I think John feels that the only way to bury it in Robert's eyes is to say John is the one responsible for the error. Robert appears not to trust what John is saying and seems to feel the only way he will trust it is if John says that Robert didn't mislead him and that John was wrong.] That's a win/lose thing.

Bill suggests that John feels Robert is trying to make John accept full responsibility for the misunderstanding. If so, that would be counterproductive.

Int.: What I hear now is that [John] does accept some responsibility, much more than I've heard before. And what else I hear him saying is that he cannot be placed in a position—because it would not be true—to say that it was *all* his error.

The interventionist agrees with Bill.

John: I'm not questioning the motives. I don't have any evidence that Robert has ever tried to do anything with malice. Ever. [That's true for all of us.] But I would have real difficulty saying, "Yes, I was *completely* wrong, and it was all my fault, and there was never any possibility that you ever said, or didn't say, something that would have misled."

John then says that he is not questioning Robert's motives but that it would be difficult for him to say that it was all his own fault.

Int.: Robert, do you believe what he's now saying?

Robert: Yes.

Int.: If you believe that is true and reasonable, what is it that you'd like more from him?

Robert: I'm not sure.

[Lunch break]

Int.: I don't know if this is valid or not, but I'd just like to throw it out as a hypothesis . . . that the issue between Robert and you is not simply what was said during those early days. I believe that Robert wonders how grateful, in a genuine sense, do you feel for what he did after you joined the firm. [Robert had to educate you, give you some of his clients, and so on.] Or to put it another way, do you recognize Robert's actions, in his eyes, to more than meet the commitments made to you?

The interventionist believes that Robert is seeking from John not only an admission of error but an expression of genuine gratitude, if he feels it. The interventionist also believes that Robert would have difficulty asking for such an expression.

John: That's a good question. I have seldom talked, I guess, publicly about it, so let me do that, because I think it would be a perfect thing to do. As I look back over the past three years at my growth and development, I was in a position in my previous company where . . . my growth was coming to an end soon, and I thought I could grow quite a lot more.

John responds to this inquiry with a lengthy, at times emotionally punctuated description of how grateful and lucky he feels to be a member of the firm. He provides illustrations that establish that his words are not said simply to pacify Robert or Bill.

I had no idea how much I could grow, and this company has shown me that I can do *lots* of things that I never thought I could do. The freedom and flexibility to do things on my own time, at my own pace, and have the freedom to go anywhere, at any time, has a *very,* very high value to me.

Being associated with a firm that has the reputation and the credibility in the market, largely built by Robert and Bill . . . whenever I talk with somebody about our firm, [he has] great things to say, and it's wonderful to be able to say that you've been a part of that. Robert has taught me an awful lot [illustrates]. His willingness to share and to be confronted, and to be right down the middle on it, as long as I could come up and produce to the level he expected. . . .

Robert has an unbelievable ability to be both conceptual and detail-oriented. And I know of no other human being in America that does that as well as you do. It's wonderful to watch you conceptualize overview and bring basic things together, which I would really like to learn how to do. You also come right down to detail, and do that, too. And I love to watch both of those. In terms of a person to be, if you will, modellike, you're the ideal. And the experience of being able to work with you has really been something for me.

And my ability to grow, as I would see it, in the last three years, has been *way* above my expectation. [Continues genuine appreciation, stressing "wonderful experience" of being with the firm.]

The reduced tension that we've had in the past year and two years has been unbelievable. And I feel very comfortable—although I don't do it still as often as I should—[to] bring things up and as quickly as I should. I continue to wait on some things, looking for the time and place, and I need to stop doing that as much. But for me, this has been an unbelievably attractive experience, and the only thing that has not come in has been the money. And I'm relaxed about that now. I was not. And the major reason I was not relaxed the first year is that I was going into debt every month. [Now that is solved.]

I really don't want to get into a position of being a subordinate. I really want to come up and be head to head with you as an objective, and to be able to give you good ideas back so we can both play back to each other. That's what I'd like to do. And so I will exert myself over and above, to try to make sure we don't get into one of these [tape inaudible]. But compared to my expectation of what the company could be . . . that's also unbelievable, too. [The only limits we have are finding the right people to work with us.] . . . My outlook on life has improved a great deal. The structure here fits my temperament perfectly. And my wife has grown a lot in this experience, too.

Episode 2

In the next episode, Robert and John advocate how much each is entitled to claim of the earnings from a particular client whom Robert had transferred to John. Robert maintains that he turned over to John a client with strong commitment to the firm, and therefore he should get a high percentage of this year's earnings from that client. John, however, asserts that the client's commitment was so weak that he had to start the client relationship all over again. Robert believes that if the client's commitment was low, it was because John did not make appropriate client-building visits during the year. In effect, Robert is attributing negligence to John.

The session begins with each participant asserting his judgment. Note that Bill is again able to facilitate the discussion between John and Robert.

John: [Client A] should be 100 percent mine.

Robert: [Client A] should be 70 percent mine and 30 percent yours. It was a strong transfer. I established the foundation.

John: [The client] said they did not use our stuff last year.

Robert: That surprises me. Merv found out from our work that the customers were not as upset as he feared.

John: Merv and others did not give me the impression that your efforts paid off that much.

Robert: I have given you the pick of my best clients so that success can be relatively easily achieved. I'm not going to do this if you're going to say to me two or three years later that the client didn't see any big value in what I did and if it wasn't for you, the sale would not have been made.

John: I was given the wrong advice by the chairman of the board, and we lost the sale for that year. Then I was able to get them back. So I figured it was my sale, especially given the representation by the top about Robert's previous impact.

Int.: Did you communicate these representations to Robert to test them out?

John: No.

The discussion continued with each partner illustrating his view with whatever data he had. It appeared that Robert was correct that John had contacted the clients at the wrong time. John, however, was able to document that the chairman of the board of the client company had suggested the time that John used. Robert appeared to want to make the point that if John had kept up the regular service calls, he would have realized that the chairman's advice was wrong. As John agreed that this was an important lesson for him to learn, Robert began to state a somewhat different position.

Robert: The client didn't sign up because John visited the wrong offices at the wrong time.

Int.: So, in your view, John did fail.

Robert: In my view, the above is a failure. [But] all I've said is I don't think he should cause me loss of participation . . . not that John has to be penalized.

Robert differentiates between identifying John's action as a failure and punishing him for it (although the others felt that 70/30 would be a punishment).

Bill: John, if you had known that Robert's view was a 70 percent transfer price, would your actions have been any different?

John: I admit I chose to take what turned out to be poor advice. But when Robert said, "You're fumbling it," that really hurt me. [Now to your question], would I have done anything differently? I don't think so. Because I would have seen something different as being pushy, and they would not like that. So I backed off. I lost.

John expresses his anger over Robert's attribution that he fumbled the ball. He also says that he would not have handled the case differently because he did not want to be seen as pushy.

Bill: [Cites example in which he lost an account for not being pushy.]

Robert: I chose the word *fumbled* carefully because it implies that you did finally get the ball. All I have said is I don't think I should have a reduction in my participation.

Bill: I agree with that.

Don: No one is arguing against that. John isn't arguing against that.

Int.: I think the others are saying if "fumbled" is not failure, then 70/30 is too high.

Bill: That's what I'm saying.

Robert: I don't think that 70/30 is too high.

John: If we look back at last year's and the year before's division, . . . 70/30 is a higher price for transfer.

Robert: I don't think so.

Int.: The impression I get is that Robert feels that he has been wrongly accused by you [for example, of making commitments to attract you that the firm did not keep], and that he has given, given, and given, and he has reached his limit.

The consultant believed that if the transfer price is usually 50/50, then Robert may be holding out for other reasons. He recalled a conversation about an hour earlier in which John had initially accused Robert of not meeting his commitments but later had said that the attribution was wrong.

John: And I feel that I haven't got what I thought was fair.

Int.: If by some objective criterion we can establish that Robert is asking an unfair price, maybe his price is less related to this particular case and more to the previous poor relationships between the two of you.

Robert: No, I am looking only at the merits of this case.

Int.: But, Robert, it is rare to see three partners agree to disagree with your judgment. If John screwed up, then maybe 70/30 is too lenient. If he lost the account because he listened to the client, then maybe 70/30 is too high.

Robert: If John had been attentive to this account, and had actively sought to connect with others, and then lost it, I would not see it as 70/30. But my view is that for six to nine months he did not contact them and was not informed as to what was going on in the organization.

Bill: Then you are penalizing him.

Int.: I wish that you took the position that John screwed it up. Then the 70/30 makes sense. You keep saying that he did not screw up, yet when you describe the data [illustrates], do they not add up that you believe John screwed up?

Robert: I can understand that John listened to the chairman, but I believe that John lost the momentum with the client. [If he had kept close touch], it would have prevented the false signal that they sent.

Robert appears to begin to change his mind and seeks a solution without saying so.

Bill: How would John's lack of bird-dogging the client have prevented the chairman from saying what he did?

Robert: Well, I think we're taking too long. [The time has come] for you guys to tell me what you think the numbers should be.

Asking the partners to make the decision may be a face-saving device. Bill and Don report later that they did not raise that issue because they were feeling the pressure of time.

Bill: Sometimes you say that 70/30 is a transfer cost, no matter what John did. Sometimes you say 70/30 is a fair price for John's errors.

Robert: My view is that John fumbled it and recovered the fumble and should not be penalized, nor should I be penalized for that process.

John: I believe all other transfers have been at 50/50. 70/30 is a higher price for simply a transfer.

Robert: Well, maybe I'm uninformed.

John: We can look at the records.

Bill: I thought the reason that you suggested 70/30 is that there was an implicit penalty.

Robert: No penalty intended.

Int.: I cannot agree to that. You have said that John has gummed it up. Someone then asked you how much, and then you said 70/30.

The interventionist was not going to collude in a face-saving device in which Robert denied that he had intended that John receive a penalty. This was important for this case and also for the way future cases are handled by the partners.

Robert: I think your view is correct. I hope that my argument was that I think there was a fumbling and I don't want to be penalty-payer for that fumble. Yes, [John is right] that it was a hard sale, but that was because the momentum was lost.

I don't want your loss of momentum to lead to my getting less than I would have received if you had done a good job.

Bill: I think that's a legitimate statement.

John: If the issue is transfer value, then I think we need to go to the record. There are two issues. What have we done in the past? And what should we be doing in the future?

Later the partners did obtain the necessary data and solved the allocation problem to the satisfaction of all.

Episode 3

About a year after the meeting described in Episode 2, every one of the partners states that the relationship between Robert and John has improved considerably. Each appears to be more aware of what might upset the other. They not only alter their actions but increasingly confront each other when they have questions or doubts.

One day Robert comes across some data that suggest John may have tried to covertly take away one of his clients. Such action would violate the most fundamental policies of the firm as well as the "all for one and one for all" culture that they are trying to create.

During a partner meeting (without the interventionist present), Robert decides to raise the issue. In an O-I world, if such an issue were raised at all, it would be raised only between John and Robert, and conceivably the discussion could culminate in John's termination. But Robert raises the issue openly in the partners' meeting, before all partners. It is discussed candidly, and the negative attributions are disconfirmed. Several factors of the discussion work to strengthen the partnership. First of all, the discussion raises the ante on what subjects they can deal with as a group. Second, they are all pleased that the discussion focuses both on learning and on justice. Third (as usually happens), the discussion reveals that John had experienced some of the very concerns that Robert is surfacing and had actually acted in the interest of the firm, given the conditions at the time, or at least had intended to do so. Fourth, as another partner stated, it makes it easier for him and future partners to believe that the discussion of such difficult issues not only is possible but can be done in ways that enhance the cohesiveness of the group.

Robert: I would like to surface something that is not well thought out. And it's—it's to me very delicate and tentative stuff, but I'd like to put it on the table and talk about it. I think I see a pattern. I don't remember the data well enough, but we did, a couple of years ago, have several different times in which you [John] had a need to get an exception to a company policy in closing down some sales. We made those exceptions, in my view, several times when I really didn't think we should. But we'd gotten into it far enough so that to reverse would be worse than to go ahead.	Owns up to the fact that what he wishes to discuss is delicate and not well thought through.
John: Yes.	
Robert: [Gives data that suggest to him that John closed a deal that should have been given to Robert.]	Data are given in a relatively straightforward description.
John: [Gives his view. He responded to a request from Robert's client because he knew that Robert could not be in town and	John does not appear upset. He begins his description by saying, "I'm glad you're bringing it up."

he wanted the firm to appear responsive.]

And so I made the judgment that because it was a short period of time, and I could do the luncheon, and I wasn't sure whether you could, and he was calling and saying, "I'm setting up my schedule right now because I have those meetings in New York next week," that if we slipped a day or two, that meeting would slip. So that was the basis on which I made the judgment "OK, let's go ahead." But if he'd have said, "I'm coming to New York in the next month," I would not have acted the way I did in that case.

Robert: [Says the irony of the situation was that he had lunch free that day.] The note that I got from John, as I read it, was "A decision has been made by me to meet with this fellow because I've got such a strong relationship with him that it is really my sale. And I'll turn the relationship over to you afterwards." In subsequent conversations, with the client and with John, I hear it differently: The client had a strong regard for our company and that he knew of John as the individual [to contact].

And it bothers me—if you'd left a note, "Robert, please talk to me today because I want to set up a meeting," I would have gotten back to you, and it would have been easy to do that day. I would not have said to the guy,

Again, the emphasis on presenting the relatively directly observable data so that each actor can see the first rung of the other's ladder of inference.

As the description continues, gaps and misunderstandings appear which begin to document that John did not intend to take away a client and which emphasize how important it is for the parties involved to contact each other in such situations.

"Delighted to meet with you." I would have turned that over to you because that's my understanding of divisions of responsibility.

John: Even if he said he was coming next—

Robert: I might have said, "I'll cover for you." Unless you couldn't meet and he had to have the decision then, I would have found a way for you to meet with him. I don't see that in your [behavior]. And I don't like being in a situation of [*John:* "Yeah."] "Robert, this is the decision that's been made" without our best efforts to get us involved.

Bill: Is what you're saying that you believe that John has a pattern of being soft on certain policy things? [I don't understand the "pattern" you mention.]

Robert: I'm concerned, I'm trying to reach forward without saying something that I think is wrong or inappropriate. But it is —I would like to know that each one of us has really bought, and would hold out for till death do us part, the principles that we articulate together. And that financial influence would not cause us to behave differently. And what I am afraid of is, to get the sale, you accommodate to their problem. You and I talked about it once, John.

John: That's interesting, because when I was having that conversa-

Note that Robert appears more aware that he could unrealizingly distort or polarize a very difficult situation.

Robert again repeats his concern that money never come between them.

John supports Robert's view and describes the thoughts and feel-

tion with them on the phone, what was going through my mind, and this is where I have a real problem, because what I was saying to myself is "Look, this guy's pushing right now. He's obviously setting up a schedule. I can meet with him, I don't know if Robert is . . . Robert, I know, covers him. If I do the hard policy, and Robert can't meet with him, he may drift away. And for the firm to capture that sale, I really should meet with him, although that's not the proper approach." And what I hear you saying is "John, don't make those judgments. Let the chips fall where they may, and if Robert can't meet with them, and they do float away, that's tough, because the policies are better." Is that correct?

Robert: Maybe the way to clarify that would be to have a decision rule that would be if you decide you'd better do it for the firm, you don't get paid. But I would be concerned about— you're talking about something like four or five thousand dollars.

Bill: It's not the money.

Robert: It is, but—

Bill: Yeah?

Robert: It's not the four of us. It's when there are eight guys here as VPs who've been [*Bill:* "Oh, I see, OK."] with the firm for a year and a half, and they say, "My family needs a vacation." I'm not worried about us and the money.

ings that led him to do what he did.

John states an attribution and tests it.

Robert relates the need for a decisive rule to the future when the officer group will be larger.

Bill: I can just see—I can see a parallel on the way I acted in the sense of—I think you're right, it can come up a lot. I mean, that never even crossed my mind. I thought I was just doing the firm work. Parallel would be this: [gives example].

Bill illustrates that he may have committed a similar error without ever thinking about it.

Robert: I just—the evidence is— you get accident prone, it's a funny pattern, my guess is there's something that you're doing that is leading to your having several of these difficulties. And I don't find anybody else having these difficulties; so I want to send a signal. One, John, you seem to be having difficulties with client perception of your representation of our policy. And I see that as a significant item. And finding a way to not have those problems. And I want to assure you that, as one partner, I'm going to insist on the company policy which we defined.

Robert identifies a pattern that he is attributing to John. He defends the present policy and is seeking a way to prevent the problem from recurring.

John: OK. Take this case as an example. [Goes on to examine a case in order to develop the rules clearly in his mind.]

Robert: I want to say something. I realize that I have been talking about something challenging and threatening, that I could be misunderstood as my giving John a hard time. I just want you to know that it's my trust in you as a person that allows me to talk about something that I think is important and not do it with a lot of softness. That's something I value very much in you, that I

Robert speaks of his basic trust of John and how much he values John.

could say the things that are in a deep part of my mind straight on out. [*John:* "Um-hmm."] I see it as being a measure of the goodness of our relationship.

John: Well, let me add one thing on that: that I feel an interest in trying to do what's right for the firm rather than for myself. And I've made an effort, although it's not still on the right ground, I guess, to try to find a way to do that. And I am reluctant, as a person, to do something that will not help the firm but follow policy. I emotionally react against it.

John confirms his commitment to behave in ways that do not harm the firm.

14

Building a Cohesive and Effective Executive Team

Episode 1

Bill wonders whether Robert wants input from the other partners as much as he says he does. On questioning from the interventionist, Bill states that the reason he is not doing his share of the internal management activities is that he knew that the decision that he take on such duties was wrong for him in the first place. "As an individual, I had absolutely no desire to do it. I knew it would cause my left [that is, thoughts and feelings] to be really difficult. I got caught between saying no and loyalty to the firm. . . . I did it for the company because I thought it was the right business decision." The interventionist points out that if Bill accepts the decision but then does not implement it, the other partners could justifiably feel confused because he accepted the duties but is not fulfilling them.

Bill responds that he is aware of this and wants to correct it. The first step is to learn not to "cave in." "Eventually I'll cave in if there is enough pressure. I look at that as [my] weakness, and I say

335

to myself, where do I eventually stop? And I have not been able to do that yet."

Robert gives examples in which Bill has started to say no and has received support from the others. Another partner says that he had no idea Bill was feeling pressured. "Of course not, because I do a good job of hiding it," Bill replies. But now he believes he will no longer hide it.

Robert supports Bill and then repeats his preference for a group of partners who are "one for all and all for one." He wants to create an organizational design that encourages this active "shoot for the moon" collegiality. But if that is not realistic, he is willing to explore other alternatives. However, he is getting impatient to settle the choice of direction. Bill wonders whether Robert wants input from the other partners as much as he says he does. This leads back to Robert's being asked how he believes he is taking more responsibility than the other partners. Robert responds with concrete illustrations regarding the partners' relationship with the managers. The interventionist confirms Robert's views.

John then explores how he made a "private" decision to focus mainly on his programs and less on his organizational responsibilities. "I made the decision that I'd work with my clients first, my programs second, and the company third." Don agrees with John and states that he has done the same, partly because he is new in the firm and is developing several new programs.

This discussion continues with partners sharing views. Robert introduces another personal concern: He is tired of being the one who takes risks with the managers in order to build the open organization that they all espouse.

Robert: I don't like being in those managers' meetings where, over and over again, being the one that has to take the risk of being—"Oh, shit, I said it the wrong way" . . . being kind of at the front edge, that's tiring.

Bill: [Admits that he lets Robert get out on the front line and does not help him.] I am not afraid of [confronting] Robert and him being upset. I think [his ideas] are testable. Maybe I feel—I don't want to cause these managers to see that I'm really very critical of the way [Robert] just said that.

Interventionist: But if you disagree with Robert and the managers believe that you disagree, then if you say nothing, won't they infer that you are afraid to disagree? Could you not [state your differences]?

Bill: Yes, John has done that fairly effectively.

Int.: Otherwise it seems to me that you may be seen as little boys who don't dare [interrupt], and therefore Robert becomes more feared.

Bill: Not only more feared but [something that], of course, taps into the syndrome we were talking about before, which is "He has the answer, and these guys will go along, so why talk to any of the other guys?" About an important problem that relates to the company because . . . they'll have an opinion, but it might get overruled, or maybe it's off the shoulder, and you'd better know it's from Robert because at least if it's from Robert, it's the ultimate.

Robert: What I would counsel is please don't sugar-coat your counsel. Don't give the impression there's nothing to worry about, we're all going to make it. Express that you've got a concern so that people who are not sure that they can make it all the way will hear something more valid and—

Bill: But see, [the interventionist's] point is, if I had challenged you because I was sensitive to the way your views were coming across, you could have expressed that.

Robert: That's correct. Apparently everybody saw it the same way you did.

Don: I did. Yup.

John suggests a technique they might use: ask Robert to hold back his contributions during the early phases of a meeting so that the partners take the initiative. Robert responds that he has tried that and it did not work. Bill and later John advise against such a mechanistic solution. "I don't believe that you should be silent when you disagree. You should speak out, and so should we."

The compensation scheme is designed to reward each partner for his ability to attract and keep client business. The scheme also rewards for cooperation to some degree because each partner is paid an additional sum based on how well all the partners have performed. In this episode, Robert asks how the partners can be induced to share more information about their respective programs so that each can benefit from the experience of his fellow partners. Robert believes that this not only would inform each one what the others are doing (thereby making the demands on the firm more explicit) but could increase the degree of innovation in the services being offered by the firm. Although all agree that these objectives are desirable, the other partners admit that they are not acting in accordance with the firm's policy or with the norm of "one for all and all for one." Bill notes, for example, that it is still more lucrative to focus on his own programs than to spend precious time discussing someone else's.

After a lengthy discussion, the interventionist suggests additional causes for the partners' reluctance to act cooperatively. Bill, it appears, would not wish to discuss his programs with Robert even if he had the time. Robert senses that Bill feels that way. Bill confirms that he is resisting such talks and says that his resistance is not based on financial considerations. Robert believes Bill must feel that he and Robert cannot problem-solve effectively. Bill denies this attribution and responds, "I am willing to discuss [these issues]. The only trouble is that . . . they are [usually discussed] at the eleventh hour." Robert responds, "Maybe we do [that] to each other."

Bill: My personal interest is to make my sales easier. That's my [interest] as a project manager.

Robert: The company's interest is to allocate its resources in a way that maximizes the company's interest.

Bill: If I think as a partner, I would carve out as many pieces of as many programs into separate items . . . the more the merrier because that leverages the profitability of the firm. But as a program manager, I'm nervous about the total number of sales I'm going to get in a particular year in a particular program. As a result, I want the perfect questionnaire that makes sure I get the sales.

[Later]

Int.: My experience in going back and forth with you on this is that you really *are* uncomfortable about the process of reducing the amount of time available to your personal program.

Bill: As a program manager, I am. You're working as a program manager, trying to squeeze more value into your programs, and I'm working as a program manager, trying to squeeze more into my program.

Robert: But what determines the resolution of that is how do we do in negotiating.

Bill: That's right. I'd agree with that.

Int.: But let me ask you . . . I'm attributing that Robert, when he discusses this issue with you, . . . can't go as far as he would like because he gets cues from you that the discussion is uncomfortable for you.

In previous discussion Robert has suggested to Bill that he hesitates to be as candid with Bill as he is with John. The interventionist takes the opportunity to surface this issue during a discussion in which Robert and Bill are exploring candidly the way they operate and defend themselves.

Robert: Yes. For example, I feel that if I push you harder to have more of [such-and-such resources] allocated to my programs, you will perceive it as [that] I am taking something *away* from you for my benefit, rather than you and I as partners are maximizing the value of the firm. And I perceive you to be in a position of defending as much as you can, pretty much in whatever way you can, the amount of time you've got available against my incursions or efforts.

One of the dilemmas is a compensation scheme that rewards partners as individual contributors, contrary to the partners' desire to become a highly interdependent group.

Bill: Yeah, what I am defending is a program. So I say, "Look, I see these resources as valuable to my clients and leveraging my sales," and if you're going to take them away, I'm insecure that it's going to affect my client relationships, either in sales or in value added to them in the program. I'm not involved in a *financial* reaction to it. Maybe on the side I'm worrying. But I'm not saying, "Geez, that's going to cost me $20,000."

Bill confirms the problem and describes that it goes beyond money.

Robert: But implicit in that viewpoint, it seems to me—I don't know how to test it, it is an attribution— . . . is that if we

Robert makes an attribution about Bill's view but is careful to admit that he is unable to illustrate it or test it.

were to have a candid, open examination of the cost, trade-off, benefit, and so on, to the best of our knowledge, that you and I would not come out with comparable views . . . and that to protect the integrity of the program from my making a faulty judgment, or a judgment adverse to the program, you better not discuss that.

Bill: No.

Bill disagrees with Robert's attribution.

Robert: Because if it gets really open and discussed, it's going to lead to a conclusion that you would not consider valid for the firm.

Robert makes an untested attribution.

Bill: I don't think that's true.

Bill could have asked Robert for the reasoning behind his attribution.

Robert: Then why wouldn't you be interested in discussing it?

Bill: Well, I am willing to discuss. The only trouble is that when we're doing those discussions, they are at the eleventh hour.

Here we see both partners identify a common distancing practice in many busy organizations: People contact one another to discuss different issues under very tight time constraints. Usually nothing is resolved; yet each participant can say he did bring it up.

Robert: That may be part of the strategy . . . it may be a part of our corporate strategy. We may do it to each other.

John: What I sensed you were saying was "If I give up this feature, I may lose a client, and a client loss is $20,000, and so I really want to protect as much area as I can because . . . I see losses starting to build up, and I can't see what the gain is that I might share in."

Bill: I can see what the gain is. That's easy. Every dollar that comes to the bottom line for the next couple of years is to my benefit. My concern is more of a long-term concern. I want you to keep the program viable because that is where my compensation is, long-term, coming from.

[My problem is how am I, as a program manager, who is only one partner, going to communicate his judgment to his fellow partners of what features are important in a way that they can judge whether he is right or wrong?]

Robert: [We could have you rank the features by their order of importance in your mind and then circulate that to your better clients] and say, "Here's my assessment of the priority valuation. Do you concur with it? Would you change any of these priorities?"

Bill: Then you get six guys who say it's important and fourteen who say it isn't. Do you say to the six, "You guys lose"?

The interventionist suggests that every partner appears to want space for free movement within his program area, and perhaps Bill is worried about his freedom being curtailed.

Robert is bewildered about how to deal with the problem. All the partners appear to agree, but they do not take the initiative to implement any decision. Robert asks what else he can do. He wants to be of help to them, and he wants their help too. Bill then responds, "I hear you saying that you have the time, but I don't believe it." Robert asks for the data that Bill uses to conclude that he, Robert, is not interested. Bill gives several examples, which Robert asserts are highly distorted. Robert states that he is very upset, and Bill responds, "OK, let's discuss it." The discussion that follows is mainly between Robert and Bill. However, John and Don say that the examples Bill gives illustrate some of their own problems with Robert.

Note the increasing ease with which the partners are able to make discussable what is usually undiscussable. Robert expresses his view that his competence is not being used adequately by the partners. Bill responds directly with his feelings of guilt and cites examples. Robert does not become angry, nor does he dismiss Bill's attribution; he asks for data on how he communicates these meanings. When Bill provides data, Robert is able to confirm some of them. The data lead John to surface an inconsistency in Robert's views, using Robert's own words. Robert expresses his appreciation for the discussion. Bill asks how he could have communicated with Robert more quickly and effectively. These interactions not only begin to solve the problems, they also build a partner team whose cohesiveness is not based on group-think.

Int.: I don't know if this is a metaphor that communicates, but if you think of the space of free movement, each partner must have some free movement, and you get some of that free movement by defining these features. . . . And the question is how discussable is the free movement. I would think an alternative *might* be that for certain periods of time you say, "I don't think I can make a valid case except that that's part of the space of free movement that I want for another year or two." But then it's up front. . . . It also puts you on notice that uncontested space of free movement is an expensive thing.

Bill: I'm not arguing against the thing. I think it's a good process to [use]. I'm just saying let's not say that the customer is going to solve the problem. . . . I'm just raising the flag that the customer reviewing it is not going to be the full solution of the fact that I'm either good or bad at communicating what's important to Robert or Bill.	Bill identifies ways that the partners might distance themselves from their responsibilities.
Robert: My proposition is that we're not aggressively trying to maximize the value of those minutes to our clients and therefore to ourselves. We do tend to maximize the probability of protecting what we've already been doing.	Robert also focuses on further games of distancing.
Bill: The problem that we've had so far is that each program manager has been protecting his own markets.	Bill confirms the evidence of these games.
Robert: [We are each feeling that we don't want to discuss it because each feels that if we discuss it, he will lose.] I really don't	Robert surfaces an important problem that he has with Bill. Robert believes that Bill is difficult to reach because he is always

know how to handle this kind of process, but I think it's important. You [Bill] have a pattern that I find pretty well closed up, self-sealing kind of thing where, because you're fully booked and because you've got tremendous strains and don't have discretionary time, you tend to do whatever is most time-urgent and not to do things in advance, and therefore by the time you're involved in something, it's terribly time-urgent, and therefore it's not realistic for me to try to have an influence on what you're doing. And I see you not being influenced by what I *do* do—a very time-consuming effort that doesn't seem to pay off very much, and I find myself saying, "Screw it, I'm not going to be able to do very much as long as things continue this way."

At the same time, I'm saying, "Boy, you just wait until there's another partner, and then you will have free time, and then I'm going to come and say, 'Wait, this, that, and the other thing has got now to be discussable.'" And we may be in for a hell of a confrontation.

Bill: I see it differently than that, because what I see is there's not time . . . to have those kinds of discussions.

Robert: But why is there not time?

Bill: Because I don't find you really interested in—I hear you

going from one crisis to another.

Robert warns Bill that when Bill has more help and less objective reason to be in a continual crisis mode, then Robert intends to confront him.

Bill tells Robert it is not only time that is the problem. He does not

saying, "And I have the time." But I don't find you interested in going through the nits and picks that go into the creation of the end. And that's my problem with it.

contact Robert because Robert seems to be interested only in the end product.

Robert: I don't see evidence that I [am not interested].

Robert asks for data that he is not interested.

Bill: Well, things that come to you in rough form, you say, "Geez, I'm not really interested in looking at that in rough form until it's further down the line." And I find that hard, because I say, "What I need to do is to really spend half a day talking through the rough form."

Bill illustrates the attribution and tells Robert some of the beliefs and feelings in his left-hand column.

Bill and Robert now dig deeper into some very important counterproductive features of their relationship.

Robert: I resent receiving a pile of paper in a very rough form and [your] saying, "Robert, would you take a look at it. . . ."

Bill: No. What I'm talking about is three or four months ahead saying, "Here's a paper. Can we spend some time really going through that?" And you'll say, "I'll look it over [by a certain time]." And I'll get it back with nits and picks all through it. So I get a signal [that] you're really not interested in sitting down and really going through conceptually on that on a very rough form. That's the signal. May not be what you're trying to say, but the signal I get is "The detailed stuff is really kind of a bore on that."

Robert: I think that that's a terrible [misrepresentation].

Bill: OK, let's discuss it. I may be wrong.

Robert: I don't think that's fair, and I'm really upset.

Bill: Well, we both are, because I don't think your attribution is accurate either.

It is possible for Bill and Robert to communicate feelings of unfairness, of being upset, and of misrepresentation without blowing up. Both are able to express their views and reflect on the processes going on between them.

Robert: I'm not making an attribution—I'm describing. Maybe I am making an attribution. . . .

Bill: I think you are.

Robert: My intention is to describe.

Bill: That's what my intention is, is to describe.

The foregoing episode is important because Robert and Bill are discussing a very difficult issue. Bill is the partner who in the past ran away from any difficult discussion. Here we have seen him state his views, listen to Robert's anger, and respond with an invitation to have his views tested. Note that Robert is able to see that he may be making an attribution when he intends to describe, and Bill confirms that this is also his own intention.

[A few minutes later]

Robert: [I got up at 5:00 A.M. to answer your question, Bill, and did it.] Took an hour and a half and made what I perceived to be a good value that would increase the ability of somebody to understand what you're getting at. [I felt it was a good use of my time.] What I got back was "No, Robert, it was not a good use of your time because I'm not using it. Not only am I not using it, but I'm not going to tell you I'm not using it, because I'm going to the printer's, and so it's not a discussable item."

Bill: Let me tell you the signals I heard. I said, "Final draft's out. I could have it to you Sunday night . . . to look at it or not. Will you have any problem with that?" He said, "No . . . I've got plenty of time, and if not, I can do it in the morning."

Int.: Is there not also the following problem? When Bill is swamped, very busy, he is also uninfluenceable, because when Robert and others see you as swamped and spinning around, they make a decision not to add any more pressures to your life, which makes you then an uninfluenceable person.

Robert: That's a much better way of saying it, because that's what's going on.

Int.: Robert, part of your theory-in-use, therefore, is to protect Bill, or to support him, because you do not tell him about the negative impact he had on you.

[Later]

Robert: . . . I have a real problem. I don't feel you guys value my time. And yet I want to be open and responsive to your using my abilities. And so I'm working back and forth . . . what I got back was "Didn't see value in what you suggested, didn't *ask* [you, Robert] whether I was seeing it fairly or not, made judgment to go ahead."

Bill: The problem is, I think—and I don't know if John has this problem—is what's Robert's role in this situation. If he says to me, "I've got a stack of an hour and a half's work to do," I know that that's there . . . I have a problem with the open-ended commitment to be helpful, and I know it's not true. I *know* that [Robert] does not have an open-ended commitment to be helpful. And I have a real problem dealing with that because . . . I'm not too sure it is deliverable without adverse effects on [Robert]. On you putting aside an hour and a half of work that you really think you should be doing.

Robert: Well, I'm free to make that choice.

Bill: Yeah, but I don't think that you make it in a vacuum.

Int.: But isn't that his responsibility to decide?

Bill: The price I find myself paying is a real guilt at asking him to be involved in it, because it is subtracted from his work to make him productive, or from his family, or from his sleep. That's the message I get [though not in this conversation].	Bill agrees that Robert should be held responsible if he decides to take work from Bill. However, Bill also speaks of the guilt that he feels when he makes demands of Robert.
Robert: That's not what I mean to be sending at all.	Robert does not confirm that he is angry at Bill for making the demands.

Bill: I know, I know it isn't.

Robert: Do you know?

Bill: Yes, I do, because you're saying it. But what I'm saying is, when it's prefaced by "I got up at five to do this," that sends me guilt.	Bill gives Robert an example of a cue that leads Bill to believe Robert is upset, although he himself may not be aware of it or aware that he is communicating such feelings.

Robert: I guess you are right. It must have been intended to cause you to pay attention—[that is], be guilty about it—or else what's the point of saying it?

Robert owns up to his intention to get Bill to pay attention to him by making him feel guilty.

Bill: Yeah, and maybe I'm super-sensitive to this, but I get signals like that in—I can't give you the examples, but other things that preface those kinds of piecework, that makes me feel enormously guilty that if I ask Robert to do something. . . .

Bill continues to describe the depth of his guilt feelings when he makes demands on the others.

[Later]

Robert: [And are you saying that] there is a cost always to me of doing anything for you? My offer is: You can have access to my good time provided you use the results of it in a way that I can see the value of that time.

Int.: And that's the price? That's an enormous price for somebody to pay. I wouldn't want to pay that price.

Robert: Why not?

Int.: Bill is saying, "I valued what you [Robert] wrote [for] me, but I made a decision that I didn't want to include it. Now I hear, in some form, that I should have told you I valued it but I don't want to include it, and I assumed that you know that. I don't have to tell you that. In fact, I feel so badly about asking you to use an hour and a half . . ." Am I misinterpreting you?

The interventionist wants to communicate that the price Robert apparently wishes to "charge" for his help is felt to be too steep. This leads to an exploration into the price that Robert appears to charge for his help and the price that John and Bill are willing to pay. As a result, they develop a much greater sensitivity to each other's autonomy.

Bill: No, that's right.

Robert: I don't see why you [interventionist] advocate that.

Int.: You can provide me with alternative choices, different views, and so on, but if you tell me that the sign that I value your help is to use your ideas, then I will get into a guilty position if I don't use them.

Something you said before was another cue. You said, "I don't think you two guys value my time the way I value it." That could be interpreted by the others as an assertion that they are blind, and all the data that I've heard from these two fellows is just the opposite. In fact, all the data from the three of you. [Each of you—Robert and Bill—takes responsibility for the other.] But if he hears "Hey, Bill, you don't value my time," then it does become his business, because there's a price. And the cost is "I've got to explicitly and repeatedly tell you how much I value you and your ideas."

Interventionist connects Robert's previous statement that he wants to be used more as a service with the price that he may charge for such service.

John: There is another cue that's conflicting. Because on the one hand, it says, "All the time that you need," [and on the other hand, it says], "You really don't value the time that I use, so be really careful not to use [too much]." And I guess . . . another way of saying what the price would be is, I would feel it would be that the price is "You ought to use every suggestion I have or have a damn good reason why not." Be able to answer articulately what the reasons are. And there's very little space of free

John then adds further dilemmas, citing other prices that he does not wish to pay.

movement created in that environment. And I find that hard.

Robert: I don't see why. . . . I've tried to make a consistent offer: I
will provide all the time that you can use in a way that is valuable to
the company, and I will make that time available. But I feel entitled
to have some validation that the commitment of time that I made,
and my ability, is in fact being valued. And I didn't see . . . that I
should be in a position of being [asked], "Robert, will you do this?"
[and then] I do what is wanted and then turn it back in and the
other person unilaterally decides which will be used and which will
not, without taking the time to find out why those things [that are
valuable to me do not show up]. It shouldn't be [that] I make my
best effort and then someone else decides without discussion, without my being able to make an appeal, what will be accepted and not
accepted. I see that as being really a cruel process.

John: What are the standards that you use to measure whether your
work is highly valued?

Robert: Well, the easiest one is: Is it used? The second one would be:
The things that are not used, is there some discussion as to why they
were not used? Can I understand why the judgment was made? And
is there opportunity for me to say, "You didn't see something that I
could add that you might change your mind on"? Is it fully discussable?

Bill: That really sets up a very—*difficult* is not the word. [On this last
proposal, I used all your suggestions except one, and I gave you two
reasons why I didn't. And you reacted that you were uncomfortable
with that. . . .]

    If [my suggestions to you] have come back, though, and there
has been something that I've crossed out, I have not expected you to
come back to me and say to me . . . , "Bill, the four reasons why I rejected this are these reasons."

Robert: I am not looking for "You are damn well accountable for
any way that you use any of my precious time. . . ."

Bill: Well, that's what it sounds like.

[Later]

Bill: But what I got back from [what you, Robert] said before was
"Boy, you really bagged me by making me do it that night." That
then puts me under a guilt situation which adds to the pattern which
I have . . . attributed to you . . . which is really a desire to be helpful,
an open-ended commitment that turns out to be nondeliverable, not

in the data that comes back but nondeliverable on how much of an imposition it was on you, and that's the price I pay.

Robert: . . . I should not have said to you anything about the cost to me of getting the time because I was easy on that issue.

Int.: Another possibility is that indeed you *did* mean to focus on "How much do you [Bill] value me?"

Now we get back to John's question. If they do know that there are these pressures and . . . all that, now what kind of communication do you want to hear from them that they value your time?

Robert: [I'd] like not to get rough material. "Robert, would you please go over this and give me your suggestions and ideas, and see if you could set it up pretty well," which to me has always said, "I don't have enough time to do this kind of work; you have a facility for this kind of work; you have a way of organizing things, and so I see you as being good at this. But I'm not going to take the time to work my ass off in doing this." And also implicit is "I'm not going to have to learn how to do it. I'm going to get you to do the rough work. Then I will take it from there." And I get that from *both* of you. And I get it, in my mind, *all* the time.

Bill: That explains a lot. OK. Let me tell you the other side of what that is. What I attribute is, look, Robert can't work with rough kind of stuff. . . . Robert has an inability to work with the preamble kind of a process where you really want to put the foundation together. The only thing that Robert can work with is a final, perfectly typed [piece] which I consider final. By the time I get from [putting] in an enormous amount of time to get it [to what Robert calls] kind of rough, falling-apart stuff—by the time I get there, I've got five weeks of time in it. And what I want to make sure is, if there's really something wrong in there, if I've missed something, I want to see that now before I go to final drafting. Because I can change it now.

What *I* hear in that working process is "Look, give me your complete effort, and I will start with your complete effort. Because if you haven't put a complete effort into it, there's no value with me putting any effort into it." What happens to me then is to say, "Damn, I have now spent all of this time to get the completed effort, and what's frustrating to me is I missed three or four really important things that cause me to go back from the twelfth step to the fifth step, and I'm already there."

So it's interesting the way you describe it. I can see how you can get that impression really clearly. And so I say . . . , "You can't work with the stuff unless it's final." And what you're saying is

". . . If you don't give me final stuff, it must be because you are lazy or you haven't thought about it." And my time's less valuable than your time. So I can see how we have it, because what I'm saying is "Look, I've got to give it to Robert or he'll tear my original apart, and I'll have to go back to step one." Not negative tearing it apart, [I mean constructively].

But what I'm trying to protect against is that when I go to production, [where I get] really uptight about typing up a final and then having to redo 80 percent of it, . . . that's got to be done tomorrow at nine o'clock. Yet your reaction when you see it in handwritten or not final-form tables [is] "Look, Bill hasn't had time to do this, and obviously it's [tape inaudible]." So it's an interesting thing that we're working within. I say you can't work with conceptual stuff; you're saying, "You're giving me sloppy work." I'm saying, "I'm not going to give you the final, because you're going to find some good ideas and I [will] go back to step one." And we're going around in a pattern.

Robert: How do you deal with it?

Bill: I don't know.

Robert: What I do with you fellas is, I work until I think I have got a really good piece of work, and I don't expect you to have any substantial changes, structural changes. . . . But if you have any, I expect to use them. But my intention is to work on it until it, in my judgment, is ready for final typing. That is, it's been typed on the typewriter but not on the composing typewriter. All the tables are right, the tables are laid out right, they're in the right order. And if you *now* look at it and have some real difference of structure or something, I'll respond to that. But [I don't give you] an in-box full of stuff that you then have to . . . sort out, and you tell me what you think is good and if I like it, I use it.

[Later]

Bill: . . . I think that that's correctable and should be tried on that basis. The only thing is that *ideally* we should be doing that on everything. . . . We hit each other all the time with these overnight turnarounds. And what it causes us to do is to say, "Let it go," where, in reality, we should say to each other whenever it is applicable, "Look you did not give [me] enough time on that." Yet the problem is the emotional penalty when it happens is still there. . . . We're still penalizing each other for the process on it.

John: We're also creating a reward system for being late and keeping [track of] time—

Bill: Sure. Sure it is.

John: Because then you don't get the rigorous analysis. Then you don't want to go back and rewrite.

Robert: It's a very short-term reward because it does reduce the opportunity to learn to upgrade the value of the work and increase the stature of the firm and other things.

[John and Bill agree with Robert. Conversation turns to a technical discussion of prices.]

Robert: I think we're getting into some pretty heavy stuff. . . . I really don't know how to do this, but I have a question with regard to what is your responsibility to me, your responsibility to John, as partners to be sure that we do in fact understand something, that we give you evidence we're not paying attention to a situation if it would have significant consequences. And if you don't oblige us to understand it, is it right for the firm and for the quality of the relationship to say, "Fellas, you did have an opportunity. In fact, you had a couple of opportunities. And you didn't move on those opportunities. And frankly, that's your own tough luck"? I have a hard time with that's where we as a firm ought to be.

Bill: Yeah. How would I, over two years, have gotten your attention better?

Robert: Just sort of the same way we've done it today . . . "Do you realize that you're talking about something on the order of $20,000 that you're not paying attention to?"

Bill: No, I didn't know—until we worked this out, I had no idea what that differential was.

John: What, in a sense, we didn't understand was the dynamics of the system. And I keep coming back to, you know, don't understand the dynamics of our bonus system, and is this going to create a situation where in a steady state we're OK, but if something goes one way, we don't understand the dynamics? And are we locking ourselves out of being able to go back and rethink what [effect] *dynamic* changes have on the system? Yeah, that's the thing I worry about more than [the] money.

Robert: I worry about two different things. One is, how could we as a group of people make this particular demonstration of incompetence somewhere along the way? And secondly, I don't

The discussion illuminates the cues that each partner gives, the untested attributions that each one makes that inhibit the creation of the cohesive partnership they all espouse. But it is this

see this as a unique problem . . . a failure to communicate really effectively . . . if you would have said, "Robert, did you understand my message? Can you *tell* me—demonstrate that you understand?" That would be something I would like you to do more of.

candid exploration of these hitherto undiscussable features that builds a cohesive group. Robert then presses Bill on his responsibility to make sure Robert understands him.

By this time, you have probably identified a theme that now will take on increasing importance. Robert (the founder of the firm) increasingly feels that he is the only partner who worries about the internal management and health of the firm. He believes that the other partners are performing effectively with clients, but they are not fulfilling their responsibilities in managing the firm. They appear to Robert to espouse a "one for all and all for one" theory, but they are not acting to make this part of the firm's theory-in-use.

Episode 2

This episode begins with the partners agreeing that Robert is doing more than his share, but as Don points out, this makes sense because "the strongest element is helping the weakest." Bill and John accept this formulation as being only partly true and a temporary state. Bill, however, points out that the issue is not sheer work because all of them work very hard. The issue is how much the other partners are giving and receiving help from one another.

John: [Robert is ready to] help us, but we remain noncommitted. We are not saying, "I won't do it," but neither are we saying, "I will do it." There's some game that we must be playing of holding back because if we just hold back long enough, he'll withdraw.

John is able to accept personal responsibility for the fact that he (and the others) may be playing a game that inhibits creation of the interdependence they espouse.

Robert: I will accept the idea that I'm a very productive person. I've worked my ass off to be productive. I am not going to, I am *not* going to . . . continue to be the workhorse of the firm. "Gee, Robert, you're so good at writing, why don't you write this?" "Gee, Robert, you can do questionnaires better than anybody else, why don't you [do this one]?"

Bill: I don't think that's the issue.

Robert: It could turn into that. Wait a minute. What is it that you see, Don?

Don: I think the strongest element is helping the weakest, and that is logical to me.

John: But I think I hear Robert saying we ain't that weak.

Don: "Weak" sounds bad. I don't mean weak. Talking about an experience curve or something.

Robert: "Weak" doesn't sound bad to me.

John: I think Robert works too hard, I agree, and you make too many sacrifices. I think we all work hard.

Bill: That's what I'm saying. That's why we shouldn't get into the working hard. I don't think any one of us works less hard than anybody else, and we work harder than 99 percent of the people in the country.

Robert: Yeah, and I think that's a problem.

Don: That's important, OK? But that's a different issue, so I don't want to get polarized around who's working hardest or not working hard. I mean, it's something—and that's as far as I can go, that's all. Because we're going to get all defensive, and John is going to say, "Well, I work just as hard as you do, and my kids are going to get—" we all do that, so let's get back to the process.

I think you're right to have interrupted on that.

John: Maybe I muddied the water. I meant to put another aspect on it which I think is quite clear. . . . How does a . . . firm . . . operate most effectively and efficiently? And then . . . , well, what price do you pay for that, and does it all make sense, and all that.

Robert: Yeah, it's also the commitment that you make when somebody comes in.

Don: Which is a compliment to the firm and a compliment to you, et cetera.

Robert: I said [to John], "You have not committed yourself, you have not gone to Don and said, 'Don, I'm anxious to be helpful. What can I do to help?"

If you said, "Look, Robert, you can do this faster than other guys, and therefore we'll ask you to do more pages of it," or more proportionately, I'd say "Fine." I think that makes sense. But I don't like being in a position of feeling "Well, I made a commitment to Don that I'd work with him until he's fully established. Nobody else is making any commitment to work with Don, so I guess I have to do all of it." Don is damn near dead on too much work. Don is also doing a crummy job of consulting letter follow-up, and probably not doing enough sales and not doing enough consulting—Don's in trouble because he doesn't have the resources to do this work. If Don's in trouble, and there's a new market and a new series of programs, the firm is in trouble . . . therefore, for the good of the firm and also for my commitment to Don, I've got to go. Someone's got to deliver, and I'm responsible for that delivery. Who will help?

Bill: Yeah, I think in the beginning stages, I think certainly two or three years ago, I started to understand a little bit of that, which was . . . sort of ancient history with the way Robert and I worked, which was, Robert would come to me and say, "Do you need any help?" And I had two reactions. First reaction was, "I'm not going to say yes because that's a sign of weakness, and I'm not going to say no because I know his intent is good, and I don't want to hurt his feelings and say to him, "Geez, I reject that help," because I really appreciate the intent. You see me in trouble and you help me. And that gave Robert . . . neither . . . a yes nor a no. So he was in a bind, right?

[Later]

Bill: I think that every principal that's come in the firm has done just what Robert described, OK? And I think this comes back to the counternorms that we have. I think the key, however, is, at least I hope, in the way I've been trying to change in the interrelationship with each principal is not to impute to [him] the reasons why I shouldn't ask [him] to do something. . . . I'm trying to get to the point where . . . I'll [just] ask Robert to do something. If he wishes to tell me he's not going to do it, that's his responsibility. If he says, "I will do it," the only thing I ask of him is not to come back three days later and say, "This caused me to. . . ." And I've tried to catch him on that when he's done it, and he's tried to catch me on it when I've done it. . . .

[Later]

Robert: I would not like to be in a position that we as a firm have agreed that there's some work to be done and [then] to have it imposed on me to have given you enough strokes, in areas where you wanted to have strokes, that you didn't tell me you wanted to have the strokes as a precondition for your being willing to go ahead and do what I see as a legitimate fair share of the work that had to be done by our group. I would not like to have to go back and think through, "Now, let's see. John is very sensitive about what he might have done. What is it that might be representative to him . . . ? Let me give enough strokes there, because if I give enough strokes—which I won't know for sure I'm not stroking the right place—but if I stroke him enough and it is the right place, then maybe John would feel that I was no longer the inhibitor, and then he would come forward." I do not like to be put in a position to be saying, "John, I'm your president and I tell you to do it." We've all agreed that's not what we're trying to design in the firm.

John: I agree with that. I hear Robert, he's built up—unless you say otherwise—a relatively clear picture of how he's struggling to try to get me to voluntarily say, "I'll help," . . . and he's also going on the assumption that all of us don't like the idea of Robert ordering us to do it.

The reason for the noncommittalness thing, it has not been a saying, "I won't do it," but it has been a *not* saying, "I will do it." That's really where it's been, I think. And I think there's two different things. One is, I can't see where I can get into the process and make a productive contribution that's not going to hurt me and the firm in what I have to do in the next four or five months. Now, what I sense—what I hear you saying back is "Look, John, you may consider yourself really busy, but you're really not. Because compared to what I'm doing, you're really not very busy. And you really should sign up for more and come on up."

I believe that if I sign up for a heavy part in Don's area, we're going to have delays in my area, and then we're going to be right back in the soup you and I were in last year. And I really don't want that to happen. I want to get those programs out nicely, smoothly, and I don't think I can take a big chunk, and I can't see a smaller chunk that I can take that's going to be productive to the effort.

Robert: I've got a concern that you [Bill] are putting in a lot of time and effort on Program A. Sales are very rewarding. Don, an equal member of the firm, working his ass off on a very unproductive program in terms of profit contribution. I'm working as hard as you, but I feel responsible for helping Don.

My general concern is that it would be a shame if our economic incentives were to do the things that were the easiest way to make money, and you guys wouldn't do the old "We're all in it together, what the hell, let's row the boat." If it won't work among the four of us, it sure as hell isn't going to work with new officers who come in and say, "Listen, what's this stuff you guys are all talking about? I don't buy it." I would not like to see our financial system overwhelm our value system, and I'd like not to have to go through creating a new value system.

Robert has now returned to the role of the financial system in facilitating competitiveness and self-centeredness among the partners. The partners will eventually be able to manage the financial system pressures that decrease interdependence. A greater problem is the degree to which they may prefer to be dependent on Robert, even though they may espouse the opposite view.

15

Educating
New Officers
and Managers

Episode 1

A perennial problem in consulting firms is the education of new consultants. This problem is especially acute in a successful and expanding firm. Because of rapid growth, the consultants' time is usually overbooked. As soon as they are convinced that the expansion is "solid," they hire new people to absorb the overload. The dilemma is that their own work pace allows them little time to break in the new officers who are supposed to ease their work load. Introduction of new consultants requires considerable time and effort to educate them and generate client confidence in them so that they can take over the caseload for which they were hired.

The dilemma may be aggravated by compensation schemes. In this situation, the more work the senior consultant carried, the greater his financial gain for the current year and for the following five to seven years. There was an economic incentive, therefore, for the senior to work himself extremely hard for "one more year." But if he did so, the education of the new consultants would suffer. The problem was especially acute in this company because the new vice-presidents were carefully selected for intellectual capacity, track record, reputation, and business acumen. Because they came into the firm with already outstanding ability, it was easier for the partners to limit the amount of time they spent with the new consultants. Moreover, the new consultants were also more likely to prefer operating on their own as soon as possible.

However, it is not a simple matter to introduce new consultants into an ongoing client relationship. The partners were well aware of this difficulty and were deeply committed to plans for educating the new vice-presidents.

During the meeting, it became clear that Jack and, somewhat less so, Parker (both new vice-presidents) were not getting the quality of training that the partners had promised. This upset the partners more than the vice-presidents. The new officers observed the busy, harried life of the partners and minimized asking for their time. Moreover, they felt that because they themselves were relatively experienced, they could function independently to a great extent. They further reasoned that if they kept the partners informed, the latter would alert them if they appeared to be heading into serious error.

Robert saw several dangers in what was happening. First, some of the clients were not being well served. Second, the education of the new vice-presidents was being delayed.

Beyond these two immediate concerns were some longer-range concerns. What kind of internal culture and norms would be created if partners made commitments that they did not keep? If the vice-presidents filled in the vacuum by going off on their own, would that accelerate the forces that propelled the professional group to function as individual contributors, with little or no sense of interdependence? If so, how would the partners and vice-presidents learn from each other? Moreover, how could the firm continue to produce major product innovations when development of these innovations depended on exchange of information within the firm?

Furthermore, if the consultants became entrenched as individual contributors, wouldn't their success, reinforced by the compensation scheme, create a firm where the top people were concerned primarily with their own narrow interests? And wouldn't this lead to a culture of distancing and indifference, with competition among the professionals for material gains?

Inherent in the firm, therefore, were forces that could lead to a living system and a culture remarkably different from those that the partners were espousing. Those familiar with the history of new firms are aware that the original aspirations of the noble founders slowly but surely degenerate, and a much lower level of aspiration is eventually accepted as proper.

The meeting opens with Robert expressing concern that the firm is not training the two vice-presidents as promised, and the vice-presidents are not confronting the partners on this issue. Toward the end of the first episode, Bill concedes that he has been negligent in the matter. But he also notes that the problem began when he accepted the responsibility of having Jack and Parker on his programs. Looking back, he wonders out loud whether he should have discussed the group pressure he was experiencing.

It is important to add that the pressure from the partners came from a genuine concern for Bill as well as for the firm. Bill appeared to be "running all over the place." The partners feared he might burn himself out. The outside board members had reached a similar conclusion and virtually ordered the partners to hire help for Bill. Hence a dilemma: To reduce Bill's work pressures, those pressures would have to be increased temporarily. This had been discussed, and Robert and John had promised to help. Bill chose not to express his feelings of being pressured. He felt that because he had made the commitment to train Jack, it was his responsibility to fulfill it.

Robert: I'm really concerned. I hear a very clear complaint being subtly presented, understated, not brought to the surface, and being smothered with generalities like "We're working so hard we couldn't do much about the problem." All kinds of combat war stories, lots of good-guying, and things that will allow us all to go back home after this meeting and talk to our wives about how the company is all messed up—and not how to talk with ourselves about the problem.

The reader familiar with consulting firms may recognize the tendency of these firms to be full of war stories about how hard people work and how unmanageable the firm is. There is no record of any firm's successfully coping with these problems. Robert does not intend to let the firm fall into these errors.

Bill: I don't hear it being so subtle. What I hear Jack saying, and Parker may also be saying, [is] "Look, given the sales territory, and I did not get the support from the partners to be successful in that sales territory—"

Bill confirms Robert's fears even though he is aware, as we shall see, that he is a major cause of the problem.

Robert: I would also say that you, as the guy in the front office who is responsible for teaching them how to do sales in that program, didn't do your job properly.

Robert evaluates Bill firmly and negatively (tacit illustration).

Bill: Yeah, I think—I think there's something to that.

Robert: And if you didn't do it because you couldn't do it, maybe you should have grabbed one of the partners and told us that you can't do it. What prevented you from doing so?

Robert suggests that Bill should have asked for help if he needed it and asks why he did not.

John: That's a private decision, isn't it? As opposed to being a partners' decision?

Robert: Yes. That's one part. Second part of it is [laughs], how can my beloved friend be trusted if he is not going to surface these issues? Also, is it fair to say to a vice-president, "Don't worry about it, you've got our favorite partner to work with you," and then wind up underdelivering? And Jack goes through a bad experience rather than a productive one.

Robert relates this example to his previous fear that Bill makes promises he is unable to keep. He is being very tough on Bill's habit of underdelivering on his promises.

Bill: Yeah, and I see it going back to the beginning where we had a really hard conversation in this room between the four of us

Bill accepts the responsibility. He traces the root of the problem to when he agreed to help educate Jack and succumbed to group

about Jack's involvement. I see now that I caved in to the Executive Office pressure to get him in. I did *not* say, "I cannot train him in that area." Once I experienced the overwhelming pressure of the Executive Office, I said [big sigh], "OK, I'll try to do it the best I can." I did not say to you, "If you guys, as Executive Office, want him to cover that Southeast, then one of you guys figure out who's going to train him into doing that." What I did is say, "I've got five bricks to carry. I'll carry the sixth one." Because I know when we had that discussion, I was really strong about not having him involved. The argument the Executive Office made was that I would screw him from a career. So somewhere [in] the confrontation with Executive Office, [I should have been] saying, "Look, guys, if you want it to be done, as program manager and as mentor, I can't handle it. And if you want that for the firm, and if you want that for Jack, somebody stand up and train him and monitor him through that geographic area."

pressure instead of confronting the issue. Note that the first step is to accept partial responsibility for his actions.

Next, Bill raises a question that is usually very difficult to raise publicly in most consulting firms. He asks to what extent Jack ignored certain clients because he could see that they would not be as profitable for him to handle as others. The fact that Jack is able to say that he had such intentions, and that it was one reason he moved away from certain client commitments, shows the degree of candor that was possible.

Bill: I would like to test something with Jack, too. I'd like to test to what extent did you feel that Parker had a lucrative program, that you should try and get a piece of it? And that you were stuck with a slow program? Therefore, maybe you found yourself doing the slow and the good program.

Jack: I think it's fair to say that there was some of "I've got to do this if I want to be part of these programs." I was also saying to myself, "Well, I took a good shot at letting everybody know I was having trouble with [the slow program]. I guess they know and nobody's doing anything, so I guess I'll continue on."

Jack (the young vice-president) is surfacing information that he withheld, as well as the reasoning behind it.

Note the distancing from his responsibility to contact his superiors.

Robert: This is an important issue. One of the questions that Bill's raised is the possibility that you have, in trying to think out how you can have your success curve go at the right clip, look to move away from a slow program and pick up on a more lucrative program. And making that decision essentially privately. Nothing malicious involved, you're just paying attention to yourself, which, in any other firm, is the right way to do it.

Robert does not agree with Jack's private decision and asks how Jack and the partners can work together so that Jack will feel his career is on a success curve.

We would like this to be a firm in which you don't have to kind of watch out for yourself, that we could figure out and find strategies jointly, and if the strategy at the end of the first year

Robert indirectly states that the distancing Jack showed (by making the decision privately) was not going to be acceptable action in this firm.

Robert requests candor from everyone on issues of career and success.

isn't right, then we can talk about it and shift it. John and I were talking just last week about maybe shifting some responsibilities from me to John because it looks like our mix isn't quite right. And we're going to constantly be doing that, and you guys will be involved in the same process.

We see ourselves as being changeable, we always can rebalance, and let's be open as to what the name of the game is and succeed, and let's be sure that your strategy isn't, in fact, as you see it, the same one that we would see it, and not get caught after the fact saying, "Geez, I wish we'd done it differently," which I think may be a separable issue but certainly one we care a lot about.

Robert asks for candor about the games that members play to succeed so they can either accept them (as a group) or do away with them.

Bill: Because we've been through it individually ourselves. . . .

Bill supports Robert and Jack's interaction by saying that the senior partners have experienced the same dilemmas among themselves.

Robert: Frankly, I hear we are providing you with all the help, and we're not. And if the latter is the case, that should be changed, and we should address that and find a way that it doesn't happen, not only now but for the future.

Robert asks Jack to confront the partners if they are not meeting their responsibilities toward him. The request for confrontation implies that distancing strategies are not acceptable.

Jack: Well, you've asked me a question, and the question, I think, is, am I attempting to move away from the slow program?

Jack does not ignore the question asked him.

John: Or are you trying to move to domestic because that's where the bigger plums are in the short run anyway?

Jack: I don't know the answer to the question. I really need to think about it. I don't think I have, but I've certainly gone to John a number of times and kind of tried to understand better about what I'm supposed to be doing in International, and I don't understand it very well because I've been saying, "Geez, I'm not going to meetings and things."

Jack admits he is not clear on the matter. He describes some of his thoughts.

Robert: Let me provide you with a backup insurance that may be helpful. It will be the responsibility of the four of us [partners] not only to keep our opportunities even—and we once a year go back over it to be sure there are opportunities—but to provide even opportunity for all vice-presidents coming in. And if one guy gets in 1986 a better meld of opportunity, in 1987 that will be attended to by providing opportunity to other guys. And while we can't claim to be able to offer even opportunity every single year, over any reasonable time period each guy joining this firm is going to have the same opportunity. And even shifting back and forth among ourselves to make sure that happens.

Robert gives assurance that Jack will have the best possible mix of lucrative and less lucrative programs, that the senior partners will not keep the best programs for themselves. This assurance is given in front of all the senior partners and is publicly supported by them.

Bill: I guess where I'm concerned is both in working with you and Parker, you know, you're really strong people in the sense of convictions in your own abilities. And my tendency is to let some-

Bill warns Jack that he tends to ignore the vice-presidents unless they pressure him.

He also notes that he had difficulty in going to Robert during the early years to ask for help.

body go until [he] really [yells] for help hard. And that may not be fair to you. OK. So that I guess that I had some—I knew that you didn't get the sales help, as an example. And I know Parker hasn't gotten the consulting help. And what I don't know—where your individual concerns are. And . . . we had this with all of us in this company, that we're all motivated and we're all good guys and we do A-plus work . . . Robert and I had this in the beginning, with just the two of us. I just wasn't going to Robert and say, "Damn it, I cannot do this piece of work." Because my attitude was, look, I'm a big boy, if I'm going to be successful in this firm—if I can't do this work, I should get the hell out of this firm.

And that, I think, has affected everybody in this room, and it has been uniformly a negative across the board. Because what it does is, you go home and you say, "Damn it, it's running out of control, I'll never get up on it," and then you have self-doubts: "If I can't do this work, what the hell is wrong with me?" The whole thing gets left-sided all over the place.

Jack: But the situation just seems to continue to run right now—as we're going through this conversation, I'm thinking about that memo I wrote on case management and said, "Here's my understanding of everybody's consult-

As a result, he felt highly pressured and unfairly treated by the firm.

Bill, in effect, acknowledges his predisposition toward distancing and asks Jack and Parker to call him on such actions. This may imply that Bill will also do the same for them. Further, Bill states that the original partners did (and still do) the same thing, which should help make distancing more discussable.

Note that in discussing his reflections on distancing, Bill also recollects his reasoning processes. This activity will reduce his disconnectedness from his reasoning processes.

Again, making public his reasoning processes.

Jack reflects on how he distanced himself from fulfilling his responsibility in a task assigned to him. Note that he was unaware of his distancing until he now thinks and reflects on the incident.

ing assignment in case management from the program managers." I sent it out to the four guys, and nobody's ever said anything until I went back to you and said, "Hey, Bill, remember the memo? Are you happy with it, what do you think?" And we got it out, and we've sort of gone through that. But I haven't taken the memo to Don yet. We've talked about doing that, but we still haven't done it, and . . . I see Don as an international program and now I'm thinking about this conversation, am I moving away from International? Maybe I'm not doing it myself, maybe I'm letting it happen. And if I am letting it happen, as I've listened to the conversation, I'm trapped now! I'll have to tell Don I can't do anything in International for four or five weeks. And you're not screaming about it [said to Don].

Don: Yeah. Because I understand it.

Bill: But I think that the thing is that we should not get into these binds.

Don: Yeah, I figure I'll take it on the chin again. I don't think it's Jack's fault.

Bill: But that's not the point, Don. The point is that the four of us have the individual responsibility to yell because there's so much going on now. On the consulting memo, I would have said

As Jack becomes aware of his distancing, he also reflects on his reasoning processes as well as the unintended consequences of his actions.

Don may be trying to support Jack, but as Bill notes later, that type of support is not needed for reducing distancing.

Bill explores his distancing, and what he could have done, and what Jack or Don could have done, to make certain the consulting memos were produced on time.

we've got time, OK, to make that decision. You may have said no, we don't have time because of these three reasons. And that would be input to me to say, "Hey, Bill, that's not as easy an item as you're making up, it's got to be decided right now." I think that the end result that we came out with—Don should not be involved—which I've communicated to Don, but that I think the point that you make is that there's so much going on—it's like balancing your checkbook.

Jack: I've been operating on a basis—I think incorrectly, now that I'm seeing it—of you keep everybody informed, like in the Navy. You tell them all what you're doing, and then you go off and do it. And you know, you always used to send down a message in the Navy—"No negates." And this meant as long as there were no negates that things were OK. And I keep telling Don, I tell you, everybody nods respectfully, I send you a memo and nobody says anything, so I make the decision. And then I'm looking back at some of the decisions I've made in Program A and said, "I don't know whether I made the wrong decision or didn't have the input to make the right decision."

[Everyone talks at once.]

Robert: . . . John, are you as terrified of what's going on in your company as I am?

Jack realizes that the age-old practice of "no negates" may be a device that permits both parties to distance themselves from their responsibilities on important issues.

Robert expresses his fears.

John: I'm becoming more re- | John feels more relaxed because
laxed as we're having these con- | the fact that these subjects can
versations because I think this is | be discussed will make them more
the only way that you guys are | discussable and manageable in
going to get involved in the shar- | the future.
ing. Because if we're all making
our own private decisions, which
is essentially what's happening,
you guys are seeing a series of
things going across your eyes,
say, "OK, I'm going to do this
and this," and never check, then
we're going to get in a real mess.
But I think this kind of conversation is very productive.

[Later]

John: I'm not at ease about where | The partners have been able to
we are, but I'm at ease about the | identify and analyze a cancerous
process of what we're doing. | activity in their firm without the
usual punishment and recrimina-
Robert: Yeah, my reaction is, | tions, discussing it with an intent
thank God we're having this con- | to cure the problem.
versation because this is like find-
ing cancer. And if we didn't get
... gray things on the X ray, we
wouldn't even—at least we can
talk about it, but I don't think
we're solving the cancer now that
we've got it on the X ray.

John: It's a very classic reaction.
These people that you bring in,
and you have a history in the
background and the teaching that
they've learned in the institutions that they've been in. . . .

Robert: Let me be very direct
about it. It's my belief that when
you join a firm, you've got substantially more hands-on, direct,
day-to-day conceptual explanations, strategizing, and so forth—

Don has gotten more from me, Don's gotten more coaching and counseling and bird-dogging and strategizing and stuff like that than I hear going on.

Parker: Robert, one thing that I wanted to make sure in your mind [is] that you aren't generalizing from one instance about Jack's experience with Program A vis-à-vis my total experience within my area for a year. Because I have traveled quite a bit—wrongly, as we discussed before—for the first three or four months of my involvement with the firm. And I have an excellent involvement and understanding of the client-based organizations and players, and all those types of things.

Robert: Could I summarize your position thus far? It would be that you've had all the back-up and support and help that you would like to have? And that you would recommend that we match that in any new vice-president joining? [Laughter]

Parker: I think there would be certain aspects in the consulting area—as specifically as I can, I would like more specifications. But we haven't been through that. It's slated for this month and next month. But I would say no, not all. But in substantially larger part than the experience with Jack in Program A would indicate. I was getting the sense that you were generalizing more

Parker assures Robert that he has received some very good help from Bill and Don.

Robert maintains his position that Parker did not get all the support he should have.

out of that as opposed to, in fairness, what Bill's done with me.

Robert: I would have hoped that you come to the meeting of this kind saying, "I'm not able to get satisfaction on the basic direction that we're going in terms of responsibilities. I'm not getting the help that I need on how to make presentations." So what you're saying is different from what I would have expected because I have only heard from you, in meetings of this kind, dissatisfaction in how much you're getting and how easy it is for you to get resolution of issues. And I would have thought you'd say, "I'm not getting the kind of feedback that I would like to have. I don't feel that I'm getting as much teaching as I would like to have." If I'm wrong on that, I'm really glad to learn.

Bill: I think you're polarizing—I think the problem—I'd rephrase that, Robert. . . .

Parker: There is no question that . . . one of the issues that I continue to feel as a problem is the scarcity of time and face-to-face dialogue in terms of training. It's the note-leaving . . . our institutional training is notes and carving things up and so on, and all the terrible left sides that you can have when, you know, you say you do good work and you want to do A-plus work, but when you see it come back through the

Robert again encourages Jack to confront his superiors when he is not getting the help he needs. If he does not get success in a one-to-one relationship, then he should bring the issue to the larger meeting.

shredder, it sure doesn't appear
like A-plus work.

[Later]

Parker: I, in my own assessment
of my ability, have not been as
demanding as I should have been
in saying I'd like two hours of—I
don't care if it's a Saturday morning or anything, any convenient
time. Because . . . to the Executive Office, I, as an individual
vice-president, have stopped short
of saying, "Here, call you at
home and we'll talk about this
for two hours, we'll get together
later." I've just said no, I won't
do that. Perhaps wrongly. Perhaps
I should have.

Parker realizes that he has not
been adequately demanding and
begins to identify actions he
should have taken.

Bill: I think it goes back to that
thing we talked about of . . . not
making decisions for others. I
know that John is really overworked. So I'm not going to ask
him to meet on Saturday, which
we've all gone through with the
Executive Office situation. So I
think that that may be something that's going on. You know,
the assertiveness with which to
say, "I need X, Y, Z."

Bill identifies an additional action that results in distancing—
namely, making decisions for
others about how they will react.
In effect, Bill is asking everyone
to reduce these untested and covert attributions.

John: That's an assumption that
I had said I wanted to test earlier.

Robert: I don't want to put
words in your mouth, [Parker],
but I still don't understand what
you really are saying. I'd like to
get to the understanding. If I understand correctly what you're
saying, it is that there have been
occasions, and I would guess that

Robert appears concerned that
Parker is not surfacing clearly the
situation in which he did not receive the help that he should
have.

you're talking about somewhere between five and ten occasions, where it would have been helpful to you to have had an hour— maybe half an hour, maybe two hours—but once every other month, roughly, there's been an occasion where it would have been a good idea if you had sat down with Don or Bill or possibly John and me and gone through some particular example and really talked quite thoroughly about what it's all about so that you would have gotten more training during the last year than in fact you have gotten. If that's an accurate assessment, and there aren't other elements that would be added to it, then I would come away from the meeting saying, "Son of a gun, that's awful close to right." That's a minor adjustment, and we ought to include an underlining in the memo you two gave to us saying that the vice-president is responsible for asking for help on . . . but that you're talking about a pretty minor adjustment.

Bill: I think it's more than that. If you're characterizing it as five or ten times, I think it's more—let me give you an example. [Does so, then adds] So you really missed the learning process off of that. I think it's a significantly greater amount than what you just articulated.

Parker: And that's where the time element becomes involved in Bill's personal time, where unless I went with him and traveled with him on that particular business meeting, I wouldn't have gotten that unless I was in the Chicago hotel room.

Robert: . . . So what I'm afraid of is guys who are trying to be helpful, supportive and kind and gracious and low key will never come together. . . . You could take the draft [*Parker:* "Yes, I could"] and the revisions and find an occasion now, in the spring, summer, some other time, when you can learn what it's all about.

Parker: You're absolutely right, Robert, and again, we've had this conversation between you and [me] several times. There are now 72 other things that need to be done that are all more pressing. . . .

Robert: And watch what will happen. Two things. You could get caught in this "working hard, good selling skills, really likes working with clients," after four years is asked to leave the firm because he never really mastered the research skills. And the principles of the firm are pretty strong-minded. If you can't master that area, you'll never be able to do the rich and in-depth consulting, and you will feel screwed. That's a possibility of what could happen by not being able to get to it by doing the things that are time-urgent. So we lose Parker and the firm suffers and you suffer.

Robert is forthright about the dangers that the vice-presidents face if they do not get all the instruction promised them.

[Later]

Bill: I guess the one thing you do is you put the requirements on at the same time—we used to say in the Executive Office meetings, well, how the hell can you meet for two days a month when we've got all this client stuff going on. And it really is something that's under our own control. But it's got to be two-way control. . . .

Robert: One of the questions I keep asking at the end of this is, what should I be doing differently with Parker than I did with you guys?

Bill: Praying? [Laughter] The other key is what should we be doing differently as the four of us.

Jack: It tells me that I think we need [another view]. I think that somebody in the Executive Office is going to have to go to Bill and keep debriefing every two months, like "Is it happening?" and "What went on?" It's so easy for me to say—I don't mean a big debriefing, but somehow—it's not working now, and it's easy for the vice-president to say, "I guess if that's the feedback I'm getting, it must be right, and on with the show!"

It's a process of what do you guys do, what was the last . . . transaction you had with Jack other than taking him down to _____ and showing him a briefing? What—what do you do with the specs? What are the five things you did at the last meeting? A half an hour debrief, a 20-minute debrief, not a big formal process, but something that—

John: What is the progress you're making, is it right, or not the right kind of thing?

Jack: Yeah. In fact, I was a little surprised. Parker and I were talking about, as part of this feedback process and evaluation—I guess what I was thinking about was, when we had the review, I didn't know where I stood on some of these issues. And we thought we'd dove into that vice-president thing for a six-month review, and lo and behold, we went back the other day and got the memo out and found out we hadn't. And I was feeling some discomfort on these issues.

Bill: I guess where I am is, if there is discomfort on an issue, that rather than have another member of the Executive Office asking the questions so the discomfiture comes out, what is wrong in the system that says that you say to me, "Boy, you're really screwing me on these things." And then, well, if I say, "Tough, Jack," [then maybe we go to the Executive Office].

Again, Bill encourages Jack to confront him if Bill is not meeting his obligations.

Jack: My problem was, I didn't know I was being screwed. I didn't know.

Here is an excellent example of the consequences of distancing. Jack now realizes that he was never aware the situation was so serious and that he may therefore have been harming himself.

Bill: And the process then means—

John: Yeah, that's the kind of thing that you ought to test.

That's the private decision making. "This signal means this to
me; therefore I'm going to act
this way on it." And my concern
is, you'll never get out [of your
mouth]: "Is that the signal you
want to send?"

Bill: And I'm guessing if you don't create that between yourselves,
the other person is not going to do it either. And so that if you don't
open that up—I mean, if you and I are working together, and . . . you
test—and I say to you, "Yeah, Jack, that's right." I'm not going to
tell you that because I'm going to hold all these relationships for myself, that's when the Executive Office comes in. But if you feel that
way, and you are only comfortable having it with a third party in
there to surface that, then your and my working relationship is really
very bad.

Robert: I agree with that, although I think you're virtually untouch-
able. I watch these two fellows coming in to talk to you, and what I
experience as an observer is that you can keep it up.

Bill: Well, that's what I'm saying. If they feel that way, then they
should confront me on that right then and there.

Robert: I hear Jack trying to do that within the bounds of naval
training [laughter], and I hear Parker trying to do that within the
bounds of being a terrific good boy.

Bill: Well, I guess where I'm going is that I have not been confronted
yet either.

Robert: Is that valid?

Bill: I mean, I haven't had anybody say, "Hey, you know, you're
really doing a number on me." Which I'm hoping to—

Jack: No, really, I haven't had that problem, but as I've been sitting
here listening this morning, I keep thinking about those specs on cash
management, and I keep wondering, "God, I wonder if those things
are *right*???" And I don't know, I'm assuming, because nobody's told
me they are wrong, they must be right. And we presented them to a
bunch of clients, and I'm not uncomfortable that you haven't told
me anything until I started thinking that this morning, and then I
thought, gee, you know—

[Later]

Robert: In the memorandum that you drafted, if I recall correctly, it says that it is the vice-president's responsibility to be sure that he is going at a good clip, that he's learning all the stuff, and if he's not satisfied, he should come to the Executive Office and say so. I've got several things I want to kind of put out. You drafted with me a list of factors—checkpoints—where a vice-president coming along at the end of year's review would say, "Yes, I've done that, that, and that. And here's where I'm going." I suspect it would be a good idea for all of us to see that on a checklist, which I've not seen confrontable. You went through and then I added some things, but I haven't seen a final one.

Episode 2

As in any organization, there are times when policies are not followed and mistakes are made. In this episode, Robert was very upset with Parker because he had asked him several times to read the background file on each client before sales visits. Robert believes that a key element of a successful sales effort is to be as completely informed about a client as possible. When Robert asked Parker why he did not at least check with John or himself about certain clients before he visited them, Parker responded that Robert was swamped and John was not in the office. Robert says that he cannot accept that as an explanation. Parker could have scheduled a meeting with John, or he could have telephoned him.

Parker: [Agreeing] Maybe I should have made better use of the time between 8:00 and 10:00 at home with John on the phone —that I did not do—OK? I probably could make better use of that time in better preparing.

[Robert apparently hears Parker's response as only halfhearted agreement.]

Robert: [Visibly emotional] Let me tell you something that I believe, and I hope you will believe. Preparation homework is the essence of good selling. If you do

Robert is again being tough with anyone who does not produce the best possible service for clients. You may recall that he has done this with all the partners at

not find time to prepare, I think you'll have a very substantial lack of success.

I'll tell you, Parker, I would never let you have a client of mine if you take the attitude that I realize I am attributing to you, which is "I couldn't find the time to do my homework."

Parker: I don't think that is a fair assessment of my attitude.

Robert: But you said, "I'm not sure I could have conducted the sales campaign I've conducted if I'd taken the time to get fully informed of all the knowledge our firm has about my clients."

---

various times. He becomes very emotional because he is committed to providing the highest-quality service. He warns Parker of an attribution that he is making about him.

Parker rejects the attribution.

Robert provides the directly observable data (the conversation) from which he made the inference.

Jack cites several cases when he, too, did not get all the information available but says that he did do extensive research. Robert is firm and adamant. He feels that he must bring up these gaps because otherwise the vice-presidents are doing only a partial job.

Robert: ... And if you guys can't get the message with the kind of emotion that I am conveying, then I'll find other ways to get the message across. [Illustrates with examples of Jack's not obtaining all the important information available.]

And when I've asked something as fundamental as "Did you do a thorough job of homework?," there is nothing wrong with saying, "No, I didn't." There is something dreadfully wrong with "No, I didn't, and I don't see any reason why I should."

Robert differentiates between honestly admitting that a thorough job was not done and admitting the fact while acting as if that were not a problem.

Parker: That's your interpretation of what I said?

Robert: There is the tape.

Parker: Yes, let's play it back. There is no question that I could have talked to John. I'm not disagreeing that the best preparation makes all the difference in the world on sales. No one is questioning the fact. That's a given.

    You know, I sort of don't like the attack, personally.

Robert: In a way, I really don't care if you don't like the attack nearly as much as I care . . . whether you got the message.

Parker: I got the message.

Robert: I'm glad, because I thought I heard you say, "I don't have to take that message."

Parker: I didn't say that. I'd like to know how you interpreted that—how did you get that out of what I said and did?

Parker does not agree with Robert's interpretation and says so.

Parker tells Robert he does not like the personal attack.

Robert continues to be firm and unilateral about the issue of standards.

When Robert makes what Parker considers a wrong attribution, Parker is able to ask for the data.

This is an example in which Robert behaves toward Parker in a forceful, unilaterally controlling manner. It is not consistent with Model II. Robert reports later that he realizes that. However, he was very upset over Parker's apparently sloppy standards for dealing with clients. Robert is also upset because he feels that it is Bill's responsibility to train Parker, and he is not doing that adequately.

    Note that Parker is able to accept the validity of the substantive points made by Robert while simultaneously questioning the necessity and advisability of Robert's personal attack.

    Now John enters the discussion, identifying for Parker the cues he gives that upset Robert. Note how John communicates the important difference between a commitment of "I would like to do it better next time" and "I *will* do it better next time."

John: [To Parker] I can put myself back in exactly your position because these are very close to conversations Robert and I used to have. Robert would assert something that he would like me to do. I would respond, "Gee, I tried, I did the best I could, and I don't think I could have done any more, or I wouldn't have been productive if I'd have tried to do any more." And Robert, I think, and properly, hears that as "I wouldn't do it differently the next time." Which says that you haven't learned anything, and I think what he wants to hear is "I probably didn't conduct as effective a campaign as I could have. I thought it was a pretty good one, but it probably wasn't as effective." And what I heard from you is "Next time I do one of those and go to a city that I haven't been to, I should talk with the people more carefully who have been there," and I don't think he's hearing that come back as much as he would like.

Parker: I just said that. Well, what I thought I said was, yes, I would like to talk to John.

John: And that you *would* do that—

Parker: I said I would like to do it . . . to do it next time.

John: And that you would do it? Or would you just like to do it?

Parker: No, I *would* do it.

John: If time happens to be there, you will?

Parker: No. . . .

John: Be more assertive in that "I *will* do it."

Parker: I'm a little shell-shocked. I've already said that.

[Pause]

John: Well, what Robert's saying, . . . I think, is "I'll wait to see some evidence." And I would like to see some evidence, too . . . from both.

Robert: The way to do the most effective industrial selling is to do homework, and when you join a firm that's already been doing work, to take full advantage of what that firm knows before you go out as an individual . . . and to say that "I was working hard," very hard, super hard, doesn't happen to relate to [my concern that you are] doing homework as a high priority before you're going out and doing fieldwork, and whatever homework you can fit in is being done. And it's my strongest belief that successful industrial sales is primarily a function of homework.

Parker continues to confront Robert about his actions toward him. Robert now explains more about his impact on Parker; yet he continues to assert the high standards of performance that the firm expects of its officers.

Parker: I personally found the manner in which you delivered it was hard. You know, I personally didn't like the way you delivered it, as an individual. It just put my defense mechanisms in overdrive.

Robert: What didn't you like about it?

Parker: Well, it's again perhaps a difference in personalities between the two of us, but I thought it could have been delivered perhaps . . .

Robert: Softer?

Parker: Well, not necessarily softer, but I mean it was rather vituperative in its . . . vehement in—which you intended, from your later statements. I find that personally—

Robert: Only after the first time when you said no.

Bill: OK, but I think it still goes to what John said. Parker took your comments as categorical . . . you said, "Everything you did over the last six months has been absolutely wrong because of this instance." I think that his reaction to this is "Now, wait a minute . . . perhaps it could have been done better, but let me—," boom! He got caught in the bind of starting to get defensive because he knows that a lot of good things went right, and in a lot of instances he did do well.

Parker: Plus the record of sales would indicate to me that I couldn't have been that bad if, in fact, I did a relative—

Robert: Let me show you where I get polarized. That's the fourth or fifth time in a row that I've heard you say, as I hear it, "I, Parker, know more about this than you or any other person outside of this firm. I have success, I am being a clear-minded observer, and I am able to critique myself, and I therefore do not have to pay deep, close, serious attention to what is now being said." Or something around that. . . . And I'm very uncomfortable with . . . seeing a guy who wants to be successful in this firm . . . not able to get feedback, and reach for it, and want to use it, and instead, rationalize or defend or shift the subject away from the feedback dimension. And it's that pattern of behavior which I saw that caused me to lift the adrenalin level very fast. And I don't know how to get some communication process going that. . . .

John: This starts it. Because as soon as you go to the end, and don't talk about the means, you will close down your ability to learn, because you'll basically reject Robert's suggestions . . . by coming and saying, "Look, the end result was OK. Look at all the sales that I got."

Parker: But I also admitted that it would have been better to have—that's where I differ, you know, in a sense, because I admitted that it would have been better—I might have gotten three more sales if I was a little bit more attuned to my clients.

John: Yeah, but the way you said it was . . . "Well, if I had the time and had the chance, I'd do that, but of course, as you guys know, I don't ever have the time to do that," so next time we'll go through this same game again. And we'll play out the same record, and . . . next time. . . .

Parker: The one point of Robert's directives has been quite clear, in that it's unacceptable.

Bill: Yeah. Yeah, but what John just said is really important because we've all been through—we've been all through this ourselves. That's really good insight. And that's what I used to do too, so. . . .

[Later]

Robert: You're both developing, as I perceive—I may be dead wrong on this, but I perceive a point of view or perception of what role I have toward you as individuals, and within the firm, that I don't think is correct.

Parker: What is that view?

Robert: I don't know. Something about distance. Something about lack of trust. . . . I think you think I don't trust you, and I don't think you trust my feedback to you, and I think that you feel that you're getting unfairly treated somehow, that I keep coming at you in a way that isn't quite right, and that you don't fully respect some of the things that I say, and [you find] the way I say them as being inappropriate or out of line.	Robert attributes to Parker that he may mistrust Robert, that Parker thinks Robert treats him unfairly.
Parker: Confrontation, Robert—and I'd make a point on this—the confrontation aspects in the way	Parker responds that Robert's initial confrontation was an edict. He, Parker, has difficulty

that you first delivered the edict to me—and it wasn't a discussion, it was an edict in terms of "You will do this next time or it doesn't fit a part of our firm," is very difficult to take, and . . . I don't learn from that. I don't know that Jack does or anybody else. . . .

The way we're having the discussion now is very productive, and I think that I acknowledge I should have called John and you about sampling. That's, to me, important learning because I've admitted I could have done it, . . . and I do think I did a good job, but it could have been a better job. And I'm not just saying that as a platitude. And I understand the directive that you've said correctly is what should be done 100 percent for every client.

John: But the real learning, then, is to say that . . . the next time, I'm going to do it differently. You can see it in my behavior.

Parker: That's right, yeah.

learning under those conditions.

Parker identifies the present dialogue as very helpful; it makes it possible for him to acknowledge his errors.

Episode 3

In Episode 3, the focus is on the managers who are responsible for the internal services that produce the product and maintain the internal systems (personnel, finance, data processing, and so on). The partners are dedicated to a principle of exceptional freedom for the managers, intending that they will manage their jobs, and one another, so that they become a top operations group. The partners are also committed to providing the necessary financial capital to ensure that the firm will have the best people and material resources that the managers can envision.

In the eyes of the partners, however, the managers are not taking enough initiative in designing their jobs and organizing themselves into a top collegial managing group. Nor are they producing
proposals for improvement of operations. Robert and John are especially concerned about this lack of initiative. The managers are aware
of the discrepancy between their output and the opportunities available to them. It is their view that the discrepancy exists because they
are swamped by the everyday pressures caused by the firm's phenom-
enal growth. The partners agree that growth does present problems,
but they are willing to invest in new people, computers, and any
other resources that will free up the managers. Because the managers
are not taking advantage of this offer, the partners are beginning to
wonder whether they are capable of doing so. It would not be the
first time that a fast-growing organization outgrew the capacities of
managers hired during the early years. Usually such organizations
keep secret the fact that these early managers are a deficit. They
either slowly shunt them off to one side or, worse yet, "promote"
them to responsible positions where they eventually block younger
and more capable subordinates.

The partners had decided to talk about this issue early in the
history of the firm. They wanted to encourage the managers to do
everything in their power to grow with the firm. They also wanted to
be free to demote or even to dismiss managers who were not able to
grow, *and* they wanted to do that openly if possible, with all the
managers involved in the decision. If the partners felt that a manager
was not producing adequately, they wanted to be able to help him or
her (with the cooperation and help of the other managers) to redesign the work, to get additional help if necessary, or to plan to
leave the firm for a job that better matched his or her capability.

In this episode, we focus on the partners' attempt to communicate the initiative they expect from the managers and their willingness to give financial and other support to make this expectation a
reality. In the next chapter, we see how they actually deal with a
manager whose performance is inadequate. Episode 3 begins with
Robert describing some of his aspirations for the firm.

Robert: We talk as though we really want to keep on going, and I
think we do. At some point along the way, we're going to stop our
progression. It's very clear that there's nothing external to the firm

that constrains us. We've got good economics, with very strong needs and demands among our clientele, a beautiful reputation, all the characteristics you'd look for to be able to shoot for the moon. So if we fail to shoot the moon, in my view we will have failed to do that because of our own shortfall.

It's my belief that we are now strategically limited by the competence of the company internally and that that's partly staff, numbers, and competence, and it's partly managers' competence and experience, and that we will this next year be deliberately not expanding our external activities, partly because we don't have enough professional people working with clients. Simultaneously, for reasons of inadequate capacity internally, . . . we, as a firm, are certainly shifting into neutral gear so that we can take the time to improve the efficiency of our organization internally. When we have developed the internal capability, we would be very likely to put ourselves back and expand in volume.

I want to surface that it is my driving ambition, and I'm amazed at how much this means to me, that we as a firm will become truly excellent, not just pretty damn good, not just pretty profitable, but in every dimension really superb.

I observe what we're doing in the company, and I have to say to you in candor that I think we run the risk of putting more burden and strain on the managers as a group, and as individuals, than you are prepared to handle, not just in terms of volume but in terms of growth and competence required. I'm anxious to do whatever we can to make it possible for you to succeed during this, which I believe is a very difficult situation for you. To develop that experience and competence base that will allow you to become managers of a larger, faster-moving, more skillful, more complex, more responsive, more adaptive program . . . I have some real doubts about whether human beings can make this kind of transition. The strain, I think, is very, very high.

Carol: It's twofold. It's frustrating . . . [on the one hand] you work your brains off and mistakes start happening, and [on the other hand] you know, the challenge of the future, and—you remember that poster of "Hang [in there], baby!" You're just hanging on, and then on top of it there's this voice, "We're gonna go ahead, are you ready . . . ?" [Laughter]

Robert: I am prepared, certainly intellectually, to wait a year, to stop expanding, hold where we are, take that lack of change in the things that we do as an opportunity to create change in the way in which we do it. To bring people as needed into the firm. Develop staff people, and I think we need to upgrade staff right across the board. To have the educational experiences, to make that kind of a "Hey, guys, this is the time when we cool it in the marketplace," but I'm only prepared to make that decision for a while.

Vince: One of the problems I have with your depiction of the reality as it is is that you relate to change only as it is outside, whereas I maintained certainly a lot of things that I had planned and a lot of things other people have planned, and there are a lot of changes going on all the time. A typical example—

Robert: Where does that lead you?

Vince: Well, I get a sense that you detect change only in relation to competence, changes viewed from the outside.

Robert: That is not where I am.

Vince: All right. For example, in my area there are changes we are constantly involved in which, for a number of reasons, one of which [is that] there just isn't enough time, are just never communicated. That's just an ongoing process. There is a desire to do that, to be on the lookout for different ways, better ways. . . .

Robert: If I have given you the impression that I don't think there's tremendous progress . . . and capable change taking place at the initiative of managers within the firm, that is not so. I see a lot of very big changes. My concern is, for all that there's a very large amount of change, enough to be quite excited about, there isn't as much changing as the opportunity that we have external to the firm recommends we make. We are developing a method and we are gaining in improvement, reducing cost and increasing value, we're teaching people how to do more, and we're growing. But I believe that the opportunity could absorb growth at a much higher rate.

[Later]

Robert: In time, surely. And more than one computer going at one time . . . let me particularize this for a minute—and I won't do it particularly well. You have said that you would like to go through all our software and document it. You haven't had the opportunity to do that because you've been working on other things, but you would like to have the opportunity to do more statistical analysis, and realistically, all you've had an opportunity to do so far is to have a couple of meetings with a consultant that would be helpful. That you would like to have more free time for your personal life and that you find yourself having to make trade-offs between competing programs. Those all say that at present you are already a constraint on the growth and competence of this firm. Without having any new programs yet.

[Later]

Norton: We've done that this year, but not nearly to the degree that we'll do it next year.

Robert: And I hear you say that, and I want to believe it, and I don't. The reason I don't is that, with very few exceptions, I have not been advised by a manager to change my behavior. I have not heard in the meetings that we have had together recommendations of a frequent and recurring character from managers. There are only about half a dozen specific suggestions, and they—really, I think the only ones I can think of are the two that you've come up with, Marge. And I look for a lot more initiative from the managers.

Note again that Robert requests that managers confront their superiors when the superiors are not fulfilling their responsibilities. We are now witnessing at the manager level the same request that was made of the vice-presidents in the previous session.

John: Let me say it a little bit differently. I have heard, over the last 12 months, lots of assertions by the managers about things they would like to do [gives examples]. If you look back on it, they are really not happening. I think that's partially what you're responding to. That we're all fully booked, and that's why they are not happening, and I think Robert's concern at this moment—and I guess mine—would be that if those things don't ever happen, are not allowed to happen, we're not going to be able to grow up, and we're going to be increasingly concerned with the internal stuff. Maybe what we do need to do is make some places to downscale, but the trade-off has to be that we get things done instead of continuing to talk about them and do statistical analysis and do that write-up of the programs, that kind of thing. A common theme that I hear going around is "Yeah, we're going to do that," and I don't see a lot of those things coming through. I see the firm continuing to be a little bit sloppy, especially on consulting letters with a lot of mistakes that are embarrassing to us, but we continue to cover up that that's not excellence—

Robert: Would you own that there has also been, at the same time you're saying that, lots of change?

John: Absolutely. Absolutely. And we may grow a lot and get a lot more people. But I would wonder how we break past the stuff in here.

Carol: The fatigue factor is up because for two years that I've been here, almost every day it's pulled another way, whether it's developing another universe or go out and do a million interviews. When I tried to figure out what was going on, I figured out that the reason that my energy was low was that I just got pulled ten too many ways and got too tired.

Vince: And I'm saying it happens and we don't even know it happens. That's where my dander goes up. Robert says there's no change—

Don: He didn't say there was not change—

John: Let me play back what I think you're saying. I think you're saying last year we all agreed on a plan and agreed we wouldn't change that. Then Bill goes out and sells a bunch more clients in Program B, expands the number of interviews, and really doesn't come to the managers and say, "Is that OK?" He kind of does it and then leaves it up to you.

Vince: Well, it isn't only Bill. It was done in the planning meeting [gives example]. The response is "Can you do it?" Of course, you can do it.

Carol: And our background—part of my breeding is "Can do, yessir, yessir!" And what we did in two years is accommodate because, gee, that was more sales or "that's what our clients need." And we didn't have the numbers to say the ramifications of that would be 1, 2, 3. We didn't know the numbers then, and our nature was to say yes, you want it—*my* breeding was to say that.

Vince: Not only that, but when I attempt to say no, I can't do it, it sounds negative.

Robert: Do you have plans to extricate yourself? We're here to support them.

Vince: I haven't really had a chance.

Robert: Well, we'll let you go through the plan. I—left-hand side for just a second—I heard both of you saying something to the effect of "We are not able to—not being allowed to—assert our views, either because we don't have information we consider valid or because you really make assertions about what those constraints are and to honor those assertions." If I'm wrong on that, I need to be—

Carol: You heard it wrong. It's not you. It's me. Me, as a manager. I didn't have the information, and my breeding is not to be assertive and say no.

Note again how confrontation of distancing leads the parties to examine their responsibility for not taking initiatives. Recall that Jack was even unaware of his passivity. Carol, in contrast, is more aware of it and realizes the difficulty involved.

Robert: Are you prepared to change that and to ask us specific ways in which you can help each other?

Carol: I . . . am intellectually prepared to do it. I don't know if I can do it, and if I can't, then I have to go somewhere else.

Robert: Are you prepared to ask us to help in practical and useful ways?

Carol: Yes. Yes.

Robert: Would you see it as a sign of strength if you asked for help? [Pause. Laughter. Robert jokingly leads Carol on to say yes.] *I* would see it as a sign of strength.

John: Let me talk specifically about that because I was in specifically the same situation two years ago. I used to think, "Never ask for help, it's a sign of weakness." At first when I started doing that, it was really uncomfortable. I really didn't think I was going to like it, and I didn't think it was going to be productive and didn't think that the people nearby would be as supportive as has been alleged. Trust. My experience was that as I tried that more and more often, I couldn't get over the difficulty that I was having. It was a very productive and very helpful effort. It was valid and it really did

John is referring to the sessions described in Chapter Twelve. Note how the learning two years ago is remembered by John and used to help Carol.

John relives the difficulties he had in asking for help and the positive response he received from others. He realized that, at the outset, he did not trust people who said they would help him.

help quite a lot. And so I would
be now in a position where I
think that would be easier to ask.
But it is the support around, so
when Robert asserts, and the rest
of us assert, that we would be
willing to help, the natural tendency would be not to trust that.
But what you find is that if you
do trust it, and try it, you'll get a
choppy transition period, but
you'll find it useful after that. It
allows you to move to a different
level of working relationship.

[Later]

Robert: Let me be careful as to what I intend to say. There is a real
compact, and I've said this to you as individuals and as a group, between this firm and the managers. You have a real stake in this firm.
You've proven that by the work that you've done. You're entitled to
a special significance in consideration. The nature of the work that
we do is so turbulent and fraught with difficulty of catching on to it,
each of us has gone through some sort of dreadful Valley of the Shadow of Death is what comes to my mind, which you're [Carol] right
in the middle of and coming up through the side, maybe up through
the foothills and out over the side.

   Everybody goes through it. . . . Some special kind of qualitative tolerance of the difficulty of doing the work, a special appreciation of the fact that enormous amounts of late-night and tension-
filled exhausted special effort that have been done by every individual person, is a part of it. I value that greatly. I have a very strong
personal commitment to this firm's future, that it's crucial that that
special consideration be part of being what a manager is.

   It is not without some real limits, and while I continue to
assert that we'll get through it, I think I owe it to you to say that if
an individual becomes a constraint on the first strategy, I know me
and my ambitions enough to know that I would not be comfortable
being tolerant for long. While there's progress being made, yes. While
you still have hope, yes. But when you come to the time where you
say no, this isn't going to work, I think the changes ought to be
made. It doesn't have to be that somebody gets cashiered. It could be
a structural change in the organization that allows that person to do

the things that [he or she is] good at and provides the firm with opportunities to do other things as well . . . it's up and out for the principals and the vice-presidents.

For the managers, I think, frankly, it's up and over, because [we have so much work] that there's plenty of work to be done by people who are really good at doing one kind of work and don't happen to have interest, ambition, skills, or whatever, to do a different kind of work. I don't know if we'll be able to accommodate the up-or-over kind of approach. I would hope we can.

⮑ 16

Dealing with
Ineffective
Managerial
Performance

The three episodes in this chapter focus on two problems. The first concerns Carol, a manager who has worked very hard and produced acceptably in the past. As the number of persons in her department and the complexity of the tasks increased, it became evident to Robert, Bill, John, and later Don that she might not have the ability to reconceptualize her job so that it would be more manageable (for example, redefining tasks, hiring more people, redefining relationships).

Robert, who was her partner contact, or sponsor, reported to the other officers over a year's time that he found Carol could not deal with the new complexity effectively. It appeared that she expected to manage her present group in the same way that she had done when it was significantly smaller.

Robert was especially concerned because whenever he met

with Carol, the conversation seemed to move through the phases of Carol's (1) admitting some things were behind but not others, (2) blaming other people, and (3) blaming the pressure in the firm. Robert would then offer to provide whatever financial and administrative support Carol needed to overcome the barriers, but she could not come up with a viable solution to her problems. He would then design possible solutions, which, for the most part, she would accept and execute competently.

Robert knew that, with the continued growth of the firm, Carol's job area would expand, and he had serious doubts that she would be able to manage it. If he was correct, given Carol's strong sense of responsibility and loyalty, performance would eventually become a psychological problem for her. Moreover, her below-par performance would become a problem for the other managers. Robert wanted to avoid establishing a norm of reward for below-par performance. The partners had long ago established a clear policy that vice-presidents and managers, like partners, had to produce at high quality levels or leave.

A second problem is one already identified—the differences in the way the partners each implemented the firm's policies on excellence and individual recognition and growth. Robert, for example, believed in advocating forthrightly his evaluation of Carol and encouraging her disconfirmation of it. If she could not disconfirm it and could not alter her performance with whatever resources and internal conditions she requested, Robert saw that as evidence of her ineffectiveness. He was willing to redesign her job, willing to reassign her, willing to provide whatever consulting or educational help she needed, but he was not willing to continue the present situation.

All the partners agreed that it was the policy of the firm to give managers the freedom and the responsibility to design and manage their jobs and that once the designs were approved, the managers should get the financial and other resources needed. No manager had ever been denied such resources.

Although the partners believed that Carol was not denied financial and material resources, they disagreed about their own culpability in unilaterally creating deadlines, altering commitments, and so on. They were committed to reducing these demands for all managers and felt that they had not done this adequately. In other words, Carol and other managers could justifiably blame some of their low performance on the unilateral actions of their superiors. The partners also disagreed on how candid they should be with Carol. They all agreed that she was loyal but that her performance was inadequate. Robert said that if they did not agree with his strategy of confronting Carol, then he would prefer that one of them become her sponsor, because Robert would have to withhold his views of her in order to carry out the wishes of the other partners to go easy. Therefore, Don became her sponsor.

Although the partners have continually espoused that their firm should reward excellence and should create a culture of "all for one and one for all," the actuality is quite different. As we have seen in previous cases, each partner has a different criterion for "excellence." The partners also vary in the degree to which they are willing to advocate their views and encourage confrontation of them. The variance in confrontation becomes especially high when the partners are dealing with difficult issues, such as Carol's performance.

Because these differences are not yet resolved, whenever a discussion such as the one about Carol is held, it is interwoven with the unresolved issues of the partners' different views on excellence and on candor. As we shall see, whenever Robert makes an assertion about Carol's level of performance, at least two of the partners differ with him. But the way they differ makes it hard to test the attributions, and this frustrates both sides. When Robert asks for a test with Carol herself of the attributions they are making about Carol's performance, the partners voice their fear that a well-intentioned, constructively oriented confrontation of the issue would upset Carol. Moreover, argues Don, the managers could interpret such action and consequences to mean the partners are not genuinely concerned about Carol. These arguments are not only attributions that compound the problem, but they are attributions that, if publicly tested, could lead to a cure that makes the illness worse. Let us turn to a brief description of each session.

Session 1

The partners are faced with discussing Carol's performance because they must decide her new compensation and whether she receives any bonus. Robert advocates (with illustrations) that Carol's performance is not up to the firm's standards now, though it was adequate when the firm (and her job) was significantly smaller, and that she has not shown the capacity to reconceptualize her job in such a way that she could hire additional help and remain in control. Robert also presents examples of how he has evaluated Carol, asking her to respond and especially to disconfirm. He is able to illustrate to the partial satisfaction of Don, Bill, and John that her responses are further evidence of her difficulties.

Underlying Robert's concern is the long-range problem that could be created if they do not act decisively to move ineffective managers. The partners are also concerned about Carol and her impact on the firm. Don and Bill clearly differ with Robert concerning Carol's performance. They agree that it is problematic, but they also believe it is better than Robert suggests. Second, Don and Bill are concerned about Carol's mental health. If she "cracked up" on the job, it would have a significantly negative effect on the entire firm.

Robert suggests that Carol not be given any raise. The other partners believe she deserves a cost-of-living raise. Robert is anxious about the message that will be communicated to Carol if she gets a raise. He is concerned that Don (her mentor) and the partners are not leveling with her. Every time Robert takes the position that the partners ought to level with Carol and encourage her to respond, he is told (especially by Bill and Don):

> "Carol is so emotionally upset that she will not hear us" (Don).
> "She looks terrible" (Bill).
> "I'm really scared that she is overloaded" (Don).
> "I'm very nervous for her state of mind. I really think that she could flip out" (Bill).
> "We must give her [a cost-of-living increase] or else it'll finish her off" (Don).

When Robert asks for relatively directly observable data to illustrate these attributions, he is told that it would be inappropriate to go after further data because that in itself would be upsetting. When Robert suggests that he has data, Don tells him, "It is ridiculous to speculate because none of us really knows what the hell is going on." Robert appears frustrated but agrees to the cost-of-living increase. Don agrees to tell Carol that she has to hire a first-class manager to help her. Robert believes that she should be involved in selecting the new manager, but Bill and Don believe that Carol does not wish to be involved. The meeting ends with Don repeating the message that he will deliver to Carol when he notifies her of the salary increase.

There are several points to highlight in this session. First, Robert appears to advocate his position and to encourage, or at least to listen to, disconfirmation. The partners, especially Don and Bill, do not agree and say so. However, Don and Bill are not able, nor do they take the initiative, to illustrate and test their attributions about Carol. When Robert asks for data, they either respond with more attributions or assert that the very act of obtaining data could be counterproductive. Don, it should be noted, is the newest partner and has had little exposure to the theory-of-action perspective. At best, he espouses aspects of Model II, but as we have seen and will continue to see, his predominant strategy under difficult conditions is unilateral face saving. Bill, the partner who has been uncomfortable with interpersonal confrontation but who is beginning to change, is not yet ready to be candid with an employee who he believes is emotionally distraught. It is not clear where John stands on this issue. Most of his participation in these sessions is as a group facilitator. When he does speak on this issue, he appears to agree with Robert that Carol's performance is poor and with Bill and Don that now is not the time to discuss the issue openly. One could argue that if Don's and Bill's descriptions are correct, they have responded to Carol's tensions by becoming unilaterally responsible for protecting her, which to them means not requiring that she discuss the issue. As we shall see, their decision was not shared by Carol or the other managers.

Session 2

Two months later, the partners discuss, among other things, the agenda for the partners/managers' meeting in the afternoon. During these two months, Carol has continued to perform her job, and Robert's views have not changed. Don, Bill, and John are now more convinced that Carol is not able to meet the present performance standards, never mind the additional demands of the future.

Robert then asks that there be a discussion with the managers about how Carol's job could be redesigned so she can stay and that a new manager be hired to take whatever part of her job she will choose to divest herself of. Robert believes that Carol herself should be offered the opportunity to redesign her job. He also believes that the other managers should be involved because the change would affect their jobs.

Don disagrees. He reports that Carol was upset when she learned (two months ago) that she would receive only a cost-of-living raise. He reports that Carol is working very hard and she continues to be under considerable stress; yet neither she nor Don has yet taken the initiative to redesign her job. Robert states that it is time to "face reality" because now Don, Bill, and John are coming to agreement. He does not believe that this emerging consensus should be kept from Carol. At a minimum, she should have the opportunity to question it.

Don then reveals that he has acted unilaterally in the matter. He has promised Carol and Ruth (personnel director) that the redesign of Carol's job will not be discussed during the meeting with the managers.

Robert is surprised and notes that Don has committed the other partners without consulting them. Don replies that he had to make that judgment on the spot.

Robert wants to go ahead and discuss the issues with the managers because he believes that (1) Carol can do it, (2) her colleagues are ready to do so, and (3) a forthright, concerned discussion should lead to a decision that will help Carol and the firm.

Bill is worried. On seeing Carol immediately after Don had talked to her early in the morning, he thought, "I wouldn't be surprised if she quit." Bill is not able to offer any data. Such a sudden unilateral action on Carol's part would jeopardize the firm because her essential post would be vacant, since an additional manager has not been hired yet.

Don adds more unillustrated attributions. "I am not only concerned about Carol, but I am concerned about the spillover effect on the . . . organization." He continues, "I can't give you data, but my nose tells me to be careful. I do think Carol will leave. But she has a high sense of responsibility [and would not leave the firm] in the lurch."

Robert points out that if Carol decides to leave, it will be on her own decision, because "I thought that we were committed to working with her." The partners now agree with Don's serious doubts that Carol can extricate herself from the bind she herself has created.

Robert pleads for a chance to obtain data from Carol. Don becomes adamant. "All I can say is no. It's the best judgment that I can bring to the process."

Bill supports Don. He agrees that everything Robert is saying is accurate but asserts that "her system is so overloaded that there is no way that she will hear any of that except the last paragraph (which she will hear as 'I'm fired')."

The meeting continues with Robert asking for an open discussion while Bill warns, "You could push her over the wall," and Don reiterates, "We can harm the fabric of the firm." Robert points out that an agreement had been made with all the managers to discuss such issues. Don states, "If you do it, that will undercut me, because I said no."

Robert: Could you not change your mind?

Don: No, because I think it would be wrong.

Don is willing to discuss the new job only without Carol present, after the managers' meeting. Robert asks what it is about Carol's state of mind that "it makes sense for us to say that we should not discuss it during the meeting but to discuss it unilaterally after the meeting. Will not Carol find out?" Don reiterates, "I do not believe that Carol can take it. The managers know it, and they do not want to discuss it." Robert appears to agree.

Session 3

A few minutes later, in the meeting of partners and managers, the managers announce that they have unanimously decided that Carol's job should be discussed openly and candidly. All the partners agree. Don, Bill, and John reported later that they were surprised. Don also reported feeling embarrassed and betrayed.

Don: [I remember that] I thought that I had a lot of evidence that an open discussion with Carol would do harm to the fabric of the firm. That really bothered me. And I told Robert I didn't want to be a part of the process [of talking openly about the Carol issue].

Then they [managers, including Carol] reversed the whole thing on me. I was so disgusted. I just sat there sort of stunned. I should have explored it more.

The managers describe in detail several important doubts about the redesign of Carol's job. Robert raises the question whether anyone else sees an inconsistency in the discussion. On the one hand, the managers describe the new person as one who would advance to equal status with Carol. On the other hand, they describe the same person as a "back-up," a "second," with lower salary.

Carol responds that eventually the firm may need someone as senior as she, but not now. Robert asks if it isn't true that Carol has reached her limit, that she feels "I just can't do it," "It won't work" —a feeling, he continues, that others have had in their own jobs. Carol admits this. Robert continues to suggest that if Carol feels overwhelmed, it is all right to say so. "We *really* are committed to find means by which you can be, as an individual, a success within your sphere of importance." Carol says, "I'm not avoiding working. I have been here long enough to know you work really hard in this firm." Robert and others agree that they see her working hard. It is because she is working so hard that they want to redesign the job. Robert says, "I really don't agree with simply 'Let's do the rational thing.' I'd like to do the humane thing—the thing that all of us will be pleased with when we look back on it."

Later Robert states an attribution that he wishes to test about what he believes is in the managers' left-hand column. They see Carol as a terrific human being, working very hard, and they do not want her performance to deteriorate to a point at which she will be terminated. So "let's shore her up with another person until she gets back on top of the job." Several managers say yes, that is how they feel. Robert says that he does not see how shoring Carol up will relieve the tension and strain Carol is experiencing.

Carol: I'd like to try to explain my feelings. I feel the job is difficult. I work very hard. I also believe I have learned . . . and whatever happens, I know that I will walk away from it a much better person.

The thing is, I do want my life back. I'm tired of waking up at two o'clock in the morning figuring out whether so-and-so was done correctly.

Bill then asks Carol whether she would feel diminished if her present job were split into two parts with a coequal new manager. Carol replies yes. Robert asks in what way, and before Carol can answer, John intervenes.

John: I'd like to test out something with you, Carol, if I might. Is, on the left-hand side of your column, the fear that we are advocating hiring a coequal [because you think] our left-hand side is that we intend to push you out?

Ruth (personnel manager): Yes. Say it, Carol.

John: Is that your perception?

Carol: Yes.

John: OK. Because that is important if that is your perception, because it is really wrong.

This leads Carol to inquire about the partners' view of her present performance. The response is, in effect, that she is working hard but her performance is not adequate, that they want her to get help. The discussion continues with Robert, Bill, and John supporting the idea of a new manager and redesign of the job in ways that lead to a realistic job for Carol.

Carol: I can't make that split. [Still, if you think so], damn it! [Starts crying] You need a good manager! And maybe I'm not a good manager. Maybe I'm good at personnel. [She hiccups from crying and everyone laughs.] I want to succeed. I want it very badly.

John: I know.

Robert: Are you willing to succeed where you are strong, which is what I care about. . . .

Carol: I know you do.

The session ends with Carol describing her dilemma. On the one hand, she wants her life back (that is, less pressure). On the other hand, she does not want to fail. John and Robert empathize and suggest that the way to "get her life back" and to succeed is to redesign her job to fit her strength or to use whatever resources the firm can offer to find a job outside the firm. The partners are clear. They want her to stay on the same conditions that she seeks—namely, that she be in control of her life and that she succeed.

This session ends with change in the pattern of Don's and Bill's taking responsibility for Carol. It is clear that although she was under a great deal of emotional stress, the attributions made about her represented Don's and Bill's interpretations, none of which was ever tested. One may suggest that she began to "get her life back" the moment she made it clear that she wanted it back.

17

Facilitating
Understanding
and Reducing
Distancing

You may recall that, throughout several of the episodes with the partners, Robert expressed increasing dissatisfaction with the low commitment the partners showed toward the internal management of the firm. He felt that most of the problems were delegated to him even though all the partners had formal responsibilities in the management of the firm. Robert had not expressed dissatisfaction during the early years because he felt the partners were swamped with building a client practice. Now that they had achieved that goal with distinction, and new vice-presidents were being added, Robert wanted the partners to take more initiative in administrative matters. Whenever Robert discussed his dissatisfactions, he was met with agreement and a promise by the partners that they would do more. But the promises, in Robert's view, were never fulfilled. Robert decided to confront the situation.

The meeting began with Don saying that he agreed with Robert's analysis that he was doing a disproportionate share of the work. He worried about this because (1) the burden on Robert was inhumane, (2) the other partners' dependency on Robert was bad for the firm in the long run, and therefore, (3) it was time to reallocate responsibilities. Don also added that he wanted specific commitments on changes because "We'll say we're going to do it, but because most of us are busy chasing the rabbit—that is, the client—we don't do it." He concluded, "It is not going to be easy to fill in some of the responsibilities that Robert is presently filling, because most of us are not good at administration."

Robert said that he had been willing to be exploited because he knew that it was not long-term. "The time is now," he added; yet if necessary, he could wait a while longer. Don responded that a delay would be harmful.

Robert reiterated his desire for the firm to "shoot for the moon." He said that he could interpret some of Don's remarks to mean that the firm should slow its rate of growth. "I am afraid," he continued, "if we slow down, we will fail. I am willing to make major efforts to keep up our pace. I'm less willing, I find, to do so when I find that my efforts are not matched by those of others."

One of the most perplexing problems faced by the partners of a very successful, fast-growing organization is that they soon outgrow the relationships that characterized the early years. As the firm grows and adds more personnel, there is pressure for more structure, more rules, and more bureaucratization. As we saw in Part Two, officers of such firms acknowledge the importance of internal management, but they distance themselves from it. The same was beginning to occur in this firm. Robert had periodically expressed the opinion that Bill, Don, and (recently, less so) John were not fulfilling their responsibilities related to a growing firm and especially to the people in it.

Another equally perplexing problem is that in many cases the distancing is partly caused by the fact that the entrepreneur who created the business dominates. Dominance during the early years is usually accepted because the entrepreneur is making vital decisions and everyone is working hard, putting in long hours to build the firm. However, if the dominance by the entrepreneur continues as the firm grows and stabilizes, the other partners may withdraw from having any but the most required relationship with the dominator and instead extend involvement with clients.

As the firm develops, and the partners must deal with internal

management matters, they often reluctantly vote for still more bureaucracy. They want to continue their distancing stance because
they attribute to the entrepreneur that he will probably never change.

This chapter describes several key episodes in the all-day meeting when this issue was discussed. In the next chapter, I will analyze
those episodes.

Don is repeating his desire not to let Robert continue his present work pace because "I think it is dangerous for you, for the partners, and for the firm. We've developed a dependency [on you]
which has become a conscious or tacit conspiracy to keep you working. It is time to change this." Bill, Don, and, slightly less so, John
believe that Robert may want to be in control because, as Don states
it, "Robert likes the pain."

Robert says that he wishes the partnership would take on
more responsibility for defining first-rate client work and providing
alert, tough monitoring of performance. Robert asks Bill to give his
views on whether the firm should speedily "shoot for the moon."
Bill replies, "Of course," and then adds, "I would like to discuss that
because I have a different perception and would like to test it out."

Bill: I really feel that you have a significant lack of confidence in my
commitment to our firm which gets me angry. And maybe I then
block off listening to you. So I'm going to need help [in this meet-
ing] to articulate my views. For example, I go into a partners' meeting and express an idea, and boom!

Don: What do you mean, you get "the boom!"?

Bill: Well, this may be wrong, but I believe that Robert really wants
to have the good ideas. [But he discounts the ideas of others.] That
has driven me away from contributing new ideas.

Note that Don, who has rarely taken the initiative during past meetings, is the first to talk; that Bill, who in the past has acknowledged
that he disliked dealing with interpersonal conflict, is telling Robert
that he resents Robert's mistrust of his loyalty and that he does not
believe that Robert values his ideas. He suggests that Robert puts
down his ideas only to surface them later as his own.

Robert, who might once have flushed with anger and withheld
immediate response, now answers by checking his understanding of
what Bill is saying: "The feeling that you have is, if you have an

idea, I would say that since I didn't invent it, it can't be very good."
Bill replies yes, "but I am not sure." Bill puts Robert and the partners on notice that although Robert may be tired of doing most of
the administrative work, Bill is tired of having his commitment and
loyalty questioned by Robert.

Bill surfaces for the first time that he doubts that Robert
wants the other partners to contribute new ideas.

Robert then gives several illustrations of situations in which
Bill took the initiative to produce certain memos but never completed them on time and, in Robert's view, did not even do a good
job. Bill replies that this evaluation of poor performance rankles him,
but what upsets him more is his own reaction: "I don't say, 'Robert,
what do you mean by a good job?' I don't confront you." He adds
that he now realizes this may be primarily his responsibility, since
Robert does invite people to disagree.

Robert continues with several examples to illustrate his fear
that Bill will not do a good job. "You appear not to realize how
much time these memos would take. I then see you swamped with
client work, and I wonder how you can do a good job. It will all be
done at the last minute," and this places Robert in a bind. If he confronts Bill about a memo, he may be accused of overcontrolling. If
he says nothing, he is likely not to receive a superior product.

Bill admits that he does put client work ahead of internal management responsibilities. As he gives his explanation, he comments
that he himself finds his explanation confused and inadequate. Robert immediately responds by giving a recent example of some first-
class work by Bill.

This interaction illustrates that whenever Robert senses Bill
may be hurt and upset, he quickly finds a legitimate way to say
something positive to Bill and to provide support. But as Bill points
out, he does not seek or need such support. If he appears confused or
in trouble, then he should learn to deal with it. Otherwise the "support" that he is getting only reinforces the unequal relationship that
he abhors. Again, it is important to recall that Bill was not only disagreeing with Robert, he was simultaneously examining his own responsibility for the problem.

Instead of supporting this self-examination, Robert gives additional examples of Bill's broken promises. It is as if Robert felt that
the breach was broken, and he must get in as many of his views as

possible before Bill closes it. Robert seems to be concerned that Bill may withdraw, a strategy that Bill has used in the past. However, Bill does not withdraw in this meeting. Indeed, he identifies the withdrawal strategy in order to make it less likely that he—or others—will let himself use it.

The interventionist interrupts Robert to ask his reasons for giving Bill more negative examples when Bill is trying to explore his responsibility in the negative aspects of their relationship. "I did not intend to evaluate him negatively but to illustrate examples of poor communication," answers Robert.

Bill, who was thinking about one of Robert's examples (that of Bill's missing a deadline), then said, "I saw the date and never told him I could not meet it. I think the problem is that I've allowed him [to place me] in a response mode [in which] I don't even think of saying [what is on my mind]. I can see the position Robert is in. He never hears from me, so the only thing he knows is that I did not meet the deadline." This adds several new organizational and interpersonal dimensions to Bill's diagnosis.

> *Organizational:* Apportionment of role and structure in the Executive Office.
>
> *Interpersonal:* The attribution by Bill, Don, and John that Robert wants to be in control and enjoys the pain.
>
> The attribution by Robert that Bill can be brittle; that the brittleness is illustrated when Bill talks in a confused manner; and the attribution that it is Robert's responsibility to support Bill.
>
> Bill's admission that he does not confront Robert when he believes Robert is in error.
>
> Bill's realization that such action makes it unlikely Robert will know what he is thinking and allows him to conclude that Bill is not as committed to the firm as he espouses.

The interventionist's reaction to Bill's comments is that he is not only being candid with Robert but constructively confronting himself. The interventionist then asks: If Bill sees Robert as confrontable, if Bill is working to reduce his automatic "saluting" of Robert, then what is the source of Bill's anger toward Robert? Part of it may come from pent-up feelings. Another source may be the issue of competence alluded to in previous meetings.

Interventionist: To what extent is your problem with Robert one of deadlines, and to what extent is it that you believe that he may believe that you cannot produce the quality you and he desire?

Bill: No, I believe that I can do it. I have a strong feeling for high quality.

Int.: I buy that. But how about the other possibility that you cannot produce the high quality that you value?

Bill: No, I do not think so.

Int.: So your withdrawal, as you see it, is that you do not want to confront Robert.

Bill: Yes, but more so in the past.

Bill explores another possibility, which the interventionist expressed in the form of a rule: If I do not confront Robert, then I can expect the same treatment from him. Bill had laughed at this and said he doubted it.

Bill: What I am more concerned about is my ability to avoid confrontation when I see it. I'm recognizing more and more that that's the worst thing to do because you build up all the left-hand-column stuff. I'm not imputing anything to others. I'm imputing it to my own behavior. I can build a case that I can't lose.

Int.: You can't lose?

Bill: Well, if Robert does [in my opinion, something unfair], and I don't confront him and later he confronts me, then I can say Robert is being unfair. After all, I didn't confront him. I don't have to change, and that's not good.

The interventionist then points out that what Bill has just described is close to the rule "If I'm nice to Robert, then he should be nice to me," and that is not confronting Robert. Bill may also reduce the probability that anyone will confront him on his errors. If, for example, he confronts Robert on what he means by "high-quality performance," Bill may have to confront his own views on the same subject, "which are not all that clear," adds Bill.

Robert gives an example to illustrate that Bill used "imaginative devices to gain control and maintain control, and not make his work subject to the inspection of others." Such inspection is a policy of the partnership. Bill agrees that he prefers to get evaluations of his work from the other partners, but he wants to be free to take or leave the advice. That assumes the communication process on these issues should be one-way. "I don't see how we will learn from each other!" exclaims Robert, who then makes a short speech including several examples of times when he could have taught Bill things. He does not mention the possibility of learning from Bill—thereby illustrating a one-way communication process.

Robert: . . . If we'd sat down together, you would have seen why I was doing [such-and-such], and you would have changed your [views to conform to mine].

And I would have been able to show you exactly why you would make them better, and that we would have learned more, and the report would have been better.

Instead, where we wind up is, I give you feedback, you take the easy ones, and we never talk about the tough ones . . . [under these conditions], you can't improve because you don't go through a learning experience.

It appears to the interventionist that Robert is telling Bill that Bill has a lot to learn and should seek his aid. The interventionist waits for Bill to confront Robert, but he does not. A few minutes later, the interventionist questions this.

Int.: Did you hear Robert tell you that if you and he had a two-way discussion, you would see how wrong you were?

Bill: Yes, that's what I get all the time. I heard him say to me, "Look, every single change I [Robert] made, you would have learned from it, and I could have proven that [my] changes are correct."

Robert: [In disbelief] That's what you heard?

Int.: I would confirm Bill's reaction.

Robert: What you heard was that all my changes were good changes that you should have taken, and you'd have learned something from me!? [Bill and interventionist both answer yes.]

Robert: Then I have said something badly, because what I want to be saying was very different from that.

I am really upset that you all see it so clearly in a way that is so different from what I meant.

I want to be free to advocate my views but also to learn.

Int.: I believe that is your intent. And there are many times that I have observed you behaving that way. But not a few minutes ago.

By the way, I think Bill also wants to learn and be confrontable, [but as he has stated], he does not behave that way all the time.

The interventionist thinks this may be an excellent example of how Robert expresses pent-up feelings about Bill and is not aware of the unilateralness of his statements. Bill then says that the incident has helped him to see more clearly what he feels Robert is communicating: (1) This is a bad piece of work. (2) If you would spend the time with me, I could prove to you why it is bad. (3) If you do everything I say, it will be quality work.

Bill: And that sends me into orbit because I say if my work is so bad, then what am I doing here for so many years?

The other side is, I say, "OK, that's Robert. He is always going to say it is terrible."

Int.: And when Robert hears or senses the latter, he feels unfairly judged, and the situation is polarized. He may then respond in a way that makes it easier for you to withdraw.

Bill: Yes.

Int.: So if you become more confronting of Robert, you, too, may behave in ways that you object to Robert using [such as polarizing or doubting whether a person will change].

Bill: Yes, and I think that his and my relationship has become more difficult.

Don: Why? How?

Bill: Because I believe that I am confronting him more in the partners' meetings.

Robert: I wish you would do more of it, not less.

We now have an example in which Robert does behave in ways that make Bill angry. But we also see that Robert is unaware that he is communicating these negative messages. For the first time, Bill sees more clearly the degree to which Robert is unaware. For the first time, he has reason to question his attributions about Robert, attributions based on yet another attribution, that Robert knew he was communicating the putdown messages and hence mistrusted Bill and was angry with him.

In exploring this example, Bill is able to express more of his tacit reasoning about Robert. In doing so, he learns that he, too, polarizes and distorts Robert's intentions. Hence, he mistrusts Robert. Thus, the mistrust he feels from Robert is not a one-way affair.

Bill then notes that, as long as he does not confront Robert, he will never learn the extent to which Robert is right or the true extent of his own abilities. Nor will he overcome his withdrawal response.

Bill then adds that his reactions have important consequences for the new vice-presidents. They come to believe that the approval that really counts is Robert's because they cannot depend on Bill to be as tough or because they come to believe he has low performance standards. "If we're not careful, we will create a situation where no vice-president will trust me. Moreover, if they go to Robert, that places him in the position of doing more work, which is what we are telling him not to do."

A second organizational consequence is that the new vice-presidents have learned to give their reports to Robert early so that if they receive a tough evaluation, as they expect, they will have adequate time to rework the reports. This annoys Robert because he reads reports that he considers of poor quality, and he begins to believe that the vice-presidents may not be as competent as he thought. "And that is dangerous for all of us," says Don. "We cannot sustain what's going on now. We're dependent on Robert."

Then Don adds, "I think Robert has brought this on himself. He is not an unwilling partner [in it]." The interventionist remembers that Don had said that he thought Robert "enjoyed the pain." "Yes," responds Don, "which is dangerous, and it scares me."

Bill: Yes, Robert said that in order to build a firm he doesn't mind being screwed. I wonder if he doesn't have some left-side resentment about being screwed for the sake of the firm.

Robert: I'm willing to work what I see is disproportionately hard to accomplish the firm's objectives because [if you people do your part], the extra work is self-liquidating.

Int.: If I understand you, you do not see them working to help re-

reduce the disproportionate share of the work they say that you do, but if they could show you a compelling argument that you're wrong, you would listen.

Robert: I think there is evidence that I want to learn. I value tough critiques [gives examples in which he has encouraged the partners to confront him].

Int.: What is it, then, that Robert does that suggests to you [Bill and Don] that he enjoys the pain?

Bill replies that Robert is usually in control of the major decisions (Bill illustrates) and that Robert does not want others to be in control. He adds that he does not discuss this with Robert, to "save a lot of agony." The interventionist asks what evidence Bill has to illustrate his attribution that Robert seeks unilateral control.

Bill: I didn't say he wants unilateral control.

Int.: I thought all of you said it here in your cases. Have you and Don, for example, not asked in this meeting, "Does [Robert] *really* want to make this an equal partnership, or does he want to be in control?

Bill and Don: Yes.

Bill: OK. I see I am making attributions and giving no data. OK. [Asks himself]: What [are] the data?

[Later]

Bill: We all agree Robert is overworked. But I don't think anybody says to him, "You are not going to take on such-and-such a responsibility."

Robert: [You, Bill, used the phrase *wrest away from me*.] That phrase disturbs me because it suggests that I'm holding onto a whole bunch of responsibilities that I refuse to let go of.

Bill and John: Yes.

Robert: I think that the evidence is that, during the past several years, I have been pleading for you fellows to do the things you promised to do [illustrates]. If these are not done because you are swamped, how could you take on more work?

Bill: Nor have we confronted you when you have not met your commitments.

Robert: Which ones?!!

Bill: Now, don't get angry.

Int.: If Robert chooses to get angry, let him, and let's deal with that. Perhaps one reason why you may not level with him is your fear if he gets angry.

Robert: I'm just not going to let him keep on. [I'd like some data.]

Int.: May I ask you to let him go on so that he tells you what is in his mind? Then let us examine it.

Bill repeats his attribution that no one confronts Robert when he does not "perform." The interventionist states that this may be true, but he fails to see how that illustrates that Robert wants and likes pain and unilateral control.

Bill: I didn't say that.

Don: Well, I did [and I think you did].

Bill: Well, maybe, yes. I say that we place him in the position of not having confidence that we can do these things.

Int.: And up to this moment, you all make an attribution that he likes the pain, which may help you to continue placing him in that position.

Bill: I recognize that. All I am saying is that we are not as strong advocates of Robert fulfilling his commitments as he is of us fulfilling ours. I think that is wrong on our part.

Int.: Something funny is going on. On the one hand, you say that your error is not to confront him on the commitments he misses or on those he takes. On the other hand, you attribute to him that he likes the pain and wants the overwork.

Bill: No, I do not say he likes the pain and wants to overwork.

Robert: But did you not say the agony of wresting these responsibilities away from me is too great?

Bill: Don says that [Robert] likes it. I say I don't think so.

Int.: OK, but is not Robert caught? One partner says he likes pain; the other says he does not like it, but you can't take the responsibilities away from him.

[Silence]

Bill: . . . [I'm confused.] We say that we all work hard. I say that I work as hard as Robert or anyone else. Yet when he asks, we say we can't do it because our volume is too high, and he always says, "I can do it."

[Silence]

Int.: He may be brighter?

Bill: No, I don't think so.

Don: Or more efficient.

Bill: More efficient, but not brighter.

Int.: By "brighter," I mean that he may be better analytically and have a clearer concept of the firm [illustrates from examples Bill and Don gave that Robert does have a clearer concept].

To review, we see Bill realizing that he may behave in ways that cause Robert to have a mistrust of him that he does not believe is valid. He has stated: "I do not confront Robert; hence, I do not tell him when I think he is wrong; and hence, he comes to believe that I have no doubts about him and that his attribution about me [less loyal to the firm on internal administrative matters] is true." What would happen if Bill confronted Robert? We had a partial answer because Bill was confronting Robert. Robert's reactions were (1) to test his understanding of the attribution that Bill was making (that Robert did not acknowledge others' ideas) and to illustrate that this was not so; (2) to get angry at the attribution that he was not fulfilling some commitments and to ask immediately for illustrations, a request that the interventionist blocked so Bill and Don could give their views. But when free to do so, they were unable to produce illustrations of their views; all they could do was describe their feelings.

The inability of Don and Bill to give relatively directly observable data suggests that they do not have any, that the attributions they made are automatic responses to cues for which Robert may not be responsible. When questioned, Bill explores his reasoning openly and concludes with a statement that suggests Robert is not *the* problem.

To return to the meeting: The interventionist breaks the silence by mentioning a reason that was discarded earlier, Robert's time pressure. Bill responds, "Yes, sometimes I hear Robert say that if he had more time, he could produce better reports." Bill continues with a lengthy description of how Robert has worked hard to integrate new partners and help them build up a clientele. He ends by questioning how Robert can possibly continue this type of commitment. The interventionist states that the illustrations show that Robert does take on more responsibility than the others but that they do not illustrate the attribution that Robert loves pain and over-control. The discussion continues, and eventually it is concluded that Robert must be in a double bind. If he keeps doing all the adminis-trative work, then he will feel misused or unfairly used. If he does not do it, he will feel he has let the firm down, because these tasks must be done, especially if the firm is to be first-rate.

Robert agrees with the double-bind interpretation. However, he also believes that it would be hard for him to turn over the re-sponsibilities they are discussing without evidence that they will be done, and done well. He then adds that he wants to create an envi-ronment where the partners make equal contributions, with himself in a central role on such activities as hiring new officers.

Don: OK, I found this helpful. Now the problem is, how can we de-sign a situation where the burden is appropriately shared?
Bill: What burden?
Don: The burden of leadership. [That is what a partnership is all about.]

Don continues, saying that the focus on growth and volume has re-duced Bill's and his attention to quality and innovation—that under those conditions, Robert, who has always maintained the firm should produce the highest-quality service, feels that he must become the quality control. "This has [understandably] led Robert to delegate less and to control functions to a degree that is not sustainable." John says that he now sees more clearly that the responsibility lies in the actions of all the partners, not simply Robert.

Robert reiterates that he prefers a collegial partnership in which each partner has his fair share of the important functions (for example, hiring new professionals and managers, new development). He draws a diagram (Figure 6) of four partners, all equally powerful in, and responsible for, the firm and equally accessible to one an-other. He repeats the metaphor of "all for one and one for all."

Robert then describes what actually goes on. Because he is re-sponsible for most of the important internal functions, he contacts each of the other partners separately in order to get tasks accom-plished. They not only tend to miss deadlines, but they also impose

Figure 6. Ideal Interaction Among the Partners

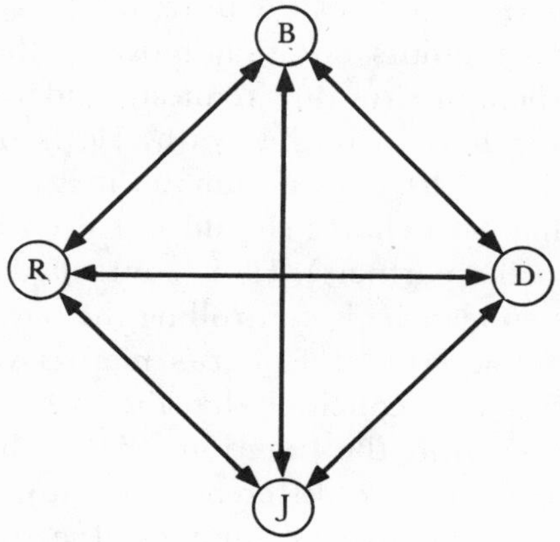

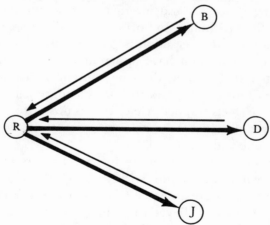

pressures on the staff below to meet their own needs. Robert contacts them to find out when they are going to fulfill their commitments or to clear up internal staff problems. The diagram of actual interaction looks like Figure 7.

Figure 7. Actual Interaction Among the Partners

Robert is initiating much more action than the other three partners are initiating toward him or toward one another. If the diagram were shifted to put Robert's circle at the top, the map would show a pyramidal structure. Robert says that is not what he prefers.

But if the others prefer that arrangement, then he wants the formal structure and policies to reflect the pyramidal reality. To compound the problem, Robert points out that most of the actions between him and the partners are routine requests and routine monitoring, which he does not like to bother with. He is overseeing a lot of single-loop activities. If he does dominate, it is in regard to precisely those activities that he believes should not even have to exist (that is, checking up on the partners). He is controlled by the partners in such a way that it appears he is controlling the partners.

The partners agree that Robert's map is valid. Don remarks that he is not prepared to conclude that the three of them are unwilling or unable to perform the functions that Robert wants to shed. The diagram arrows are then differentiated into "chicken shit" and "important" arrows. The greatest number of arrows, from Robert to the partners, are "chicken shit" arrows, representing routine monitoring tasks, which Robert resents. Bill asks, "Why don't we simply reduce the chicken-shit arrows? Once we do that, then let us see how we take on more responsibility for the important arrows. We have," Bill continues, "unwittingly created a situation which is no good for any of us or the firm."

Robert's diagram makes further connections between the partners' reasoning processes and interactions and the structure of the Executive Office. Although the office is structured as one of equals, the actual pattern of interaction is more akin to a pyramidal structure. Bill, Don, and John have apparently focused on this aspect. Robert points out, however, that the content of his initiation of action is related mostly to issues that they and he agree are "chicken shit." Hence, he feels trapped. He exercises power to deal with issues that he believes should not be his responsibility if the partnership is to be "all for one and one for all."

Herein may be one source of anger for Robert. He believes that he has created a firm and, with the help of the partners, a compensation scheme to create equality of partners and to reward high performance. He also believes that the partners value the collegial model that he calls "the Three Musketeers." Yet he finds himself in a situation in which the partners make attributions about his motives that they do not test, they deal with him in ways that create and maintain a dependency relationship, and then they assert that the dependency is bad while acting in ways that strengthen it in the important areas (such as recruiting). To compound the problem, they force him to take initiative on "chicken shit" issues, a condition that they had all promised themselves never to create in their firm.

Don then states that he is not sure they can fulfill the important responsibilities better than Robert.

Bill: And the reason for that is . . . ?

Don: I don't know. [When I reflect on my actions], I do not think I do these jobs as well as I would like. [Maybe it's because I'm swamped, but I'm not sure.]

The partners continue giving further examples of organizational consequences. Bill gives an example in which, in a previous meeting, he had agreed with John on the impact of a projected management information system on the firm's employees. Robert then cites data showing that Bill never said he agreed with John. "The reason I press this," says Robert, "is that I believe that you have a great desire to be in agreement, and that is somehow associated with your need not to confront and to say openly when you do not agree."

The interventionist sees this as an opportunity to remind Robert and the others of the difference between "needs" and automatic reactions.

Int.: As Bill has stated, his reactions are to agree. If they are automatic, it is probably tacit, and therefore he is unaware.

I suggest that he invite you, John, and Don to confront him when he appears to be nodding automatically.

Instead of seeing him as having a need, I would see him as having a learned automatic reaction. The way to help Bill is, whenever any of you see him agreeing in this automatic manner, ask him about the meaning of the agreement.

Bill: Yes. I know when I do it; I see it as a trivial point . . . I'll agree in order to keep going where I want to go. Sometimes I also mean I'll agree in order to return later to discuss it, but I never say that.

Int.: So it could be a form of staying in control of yourself and others. If the other person thinks there is agreement, then he may go on to something else, which gives you the time to develop your response or not to give one.

Robert: I'd like to underline that because [some staff people] have told me that they no longer trust you when you say yes.

Bill: Yes, I've heard about that, Robert.

Robert: And perhaps even some of your clients.

Bill: Yes, that's something I recognized six to eight months ago. I now realize that people catch me on this easing-in method. I then try to back and fill, which must tell them that there must be something wrong. I've got to be more straightforward.

Then Robert asks Bill to illustrate his attribution that Robert becomes upset when Bill is late in finishing a commitment. Bill responds only that he has that feeling, that he recognizes that he is making an attribution and not illustrating it.

The interventionist agrees that Bill has a right to express his feelings, but Robert has an equal obligation to himself not to act on Bill's feelings and attributions until Bill can illustrate them. Bill agrees and says that it is important for the partners to meet their commitments. Bill says that it will not be easy, but he is trying to learn how to meet his commitments and to question Robert's performance when it appears necessary.

Robert: Let me give you some very clear quick examples.

Bill: That's frustrating. I'm getting angry now . . . because I'm struggling with my own incompetence, trying to understand this. I don't need more data to tell me that I've screwed it up in the past. I recognize that. I recognize that the burden is on me. . . .

Bill is feeling angry, expressing it, and simultaneously telling Robert why he is not being helpful. The interventionist asks Bill, "What would you wish Robert to do?"

Bill: Be open to allow me to prove that. I'm fearful that his distrust will not allow him to do that.

Int.: And whose responsibility is it to let him know if he is open or not?

Bill: I don't know. I guess I do. It is mine. . . . If I don't feel he's open, I should confront that. . . : And do so when it is happening rather than waiting.

Robert agrees but says that he wants more feedback. "I need the data that you believe illustrate your feelings about me. I want you to express your views, but I don't want to have to accept them as valid without evidence." Bill and the interventionist agree, and the interventionist sums up what he thinks Bill is trying to say:

Int.: I believe my attributions about Robert are correct.

But I realize that I do not have the data.

So now I am putting everyone on notice that when I see some of these actions occurring, I will say so.

Bill: Yes, that's what I'm trying to say.

Don returns to his original theme that some decisions should be made on routine issues. "I realize that these are small and symptomatic, but they build up into a fairly big bill." Don suggests, for example, that the firm hire an editor in order to standardize a particular report style. Robert agrees that an editor would speed up the writing. But "the real problem is that the principals are not completing the writing tasks that they defined for themselves." Robert says that the same problem would exist if an administrator were hired, a conclusion with which Don disagrees. He points out that certain programs did not achieve the quality to which the firm aspired because no one paid adequate attention to such routine matters as printing errors and "crummy" table arrangements. Moreover, an effective administrator, states Don, would provide the partners with a precious gift—namely, time.

Robert believes that if the managers can become a cohesive team, they can deal with the administrative problems as a group in the same way that the partners function as an Executive Office group. Bill wonders whether one first-rate senior manager might not be better than five managers. Robert voices his fear that if they hire a high-priced general manager, he or she will then want more managers to manage.

The interventionist interrupts the substantive discussion to reflect on the way Don and Bill have been stating the case for hire of an editor and a general manager. They suggest, raise the possibility, inquire into, and so on. But they do not appear to have developed a case that is compelling, even to themselves. If true, this would invite Robert to confront their ideas while reinforcing his fear that they do not think their positions through adequately. Don responds that some of the board members had suggested the possibility of appointing a high-level manager. Bill adds that, with a general manager, the partners would have more time for long-range planning.

Robert repeats that he doubts the partners would find the time to do the long-range planning. This comment leads Bill to return to his feeling that Robert does not trust their commitment to the firm. "You believe the firm must come first, above all other things," says Bill. Robert disagrees: "I've never asked you to put the firm above all things." Bill answers, "But that is what I hear." Robert asks how he can communicate to Bill without being misunderstood. He repeats that he believes Bill's performance on administrative matters has not been good, while Bill believes it is good. Bill agrees that Robert's evaluation is more accurate than his own but believes that Robert should separate Bill's performance from his commitment. Bill may feel "I may be dumb and not so competent. But one thing I'm not is a guy who does not take our firm seriously."

Bill: Yes, I think [the interventionist] has hit on something. I think what really frosts me is—I think you hit on it, which I wasn't really aware of—was the implication that because I missed a date, I'm not working hard or I'm not loyal and committed.

Robert: That is not what I intend to say, nor is it on the left-hand side of my column. [What worries me is that you believe that you are really close to managing yourself and I see you really far from it.]

Bill answers that he does not feel as effective as he wants to, that he is working on improvement, and that Robert is too biased to see the changes he is making. He concludes that it may be best to stop the discussion and to continue it again after he and Robert are able to collect fresher, more recent examples. Robert agrees that he has made his point and that the important thing is the future. But neither Robert nor Bill closes the discussion by glossing over their differences. Robert says that he hears Bill's assertions that adequate progress is being made but that he cannot accept the data as adequate evidence. However, he will look to the future. Bill responds that he is not sure that Robert will see the evidence but that it is important he first collect it and then discuss it with Robert. Bill adds, "I feel that [Robert considers me] guilty until proven innocent [given, in his view, my performance history]. "I'd like to emphasize," adds Robert, "I hope to be open and encouraging of what you intend to be doing [and if you do not think I am, please tell me]."

Robert also emphasizes that his major concerns are related to the commitments made, but not kept, by the partners regarding internal administration and development of the firm. Bill points out that Robert has done most of the work in such key areas as recruiting, conceptualizing the firm, and long-range planning. Which of these activities would he be willing to delegate to the other partners? Robert says that the first step is to reduce all the necessity for him to monitor and police the partner commitments.

Bill: I understand that. Let's assume that's done. Now, look at the seven or eight key activities on the board. Which ones do you want to do and which ones do you not?

Robert: I should answer your question, but I have difficulty because [I'm not sure, if I gave up something, that I would feel secure it would be done by one of you].

Bill: OK, now we're right back in the box [where we're assumed to be guilty].

Int.: Robert, would you be willing to identify the activities that you are willing to delegate and let us see if the other partners can do them?

Robert: Yes, for example, the write-ups for the directors' meeting. But I do not want to be in the position where you make the commitments and then you set it up in such a way that we do not meet them, or if we do, I have to do them.

Bill: OK, let me go out on a limb now, OK? How about recruiting?

Robert: I hear implicit in the question—and maybe I'm oversensitive to this—that [you believe] that I am your typical founder/entrepreneur who cannot give up and delegate anything that is important. It is my view that a lot of important things have been delegated [illustrates].

I also believe that I understand the firm better and can articulate it well out on the circuit.

On recruiting, I do not think that Bill, Don, and John would be as effective at presenting the firm and creating the excitement that I sense we need to have in recruiting. Also, I think I should spend more time on recruiting partners than VPs.

The meeting ends with Robert inferring that his fellow partners see him as the typical entrepreneur who does not wish to let go. The inference is valid. What difference would it have made if Don and Bill had stated this attribution at the outset? Perhaps Robert would have better understood some of the assertions they were making about his motives and the reason that they seek such remedies as a general manager.

Moreover, if such a discussion had occurred, it might have made it easier to identify several puzzles. Note that Don and Bill's recommendations would create a formal pyramidal structure within the Executive Office. Yet during the discussion, they all agreed that the Executive Office interactions were primarily pyramidal and that they should be more collegial. If they held a theory of management that suggested a collegial relationship was best for the partners, why would this theory not hold for the senior managers? A general manager in a formal pyramidal structure would create a layer of authority between the partners and the managers and officers. This would probably accelerate distancing on such important issues as innovation and risktaking. Finally, if the reason for a general manager is that they believe Robert is unchangeable and the partners are swamped, wouldn't the general manager sense this and see it as his or her duty to minimize pressures on the partners?

The second day of the meeting began with the partners reviewing where they stood. Don is anxious that Robert not continue doing all the extra tasks, agreeing with Robert that he is not in a position to help him out, that, though dissatisfied, he cannot come up with a solution. Robert feels that he has communicated his conviction that he does not want to play policeman with the partners or do the routine tasks that they have not completed on time. Robert also learns that, at times, he may not be hearing Bill correctly.

Bill says that he has given yesterday's discussion much thought and is now clearer about his feelings. Some sentences that illustrate this are the following:

> "The [interventionist's] comments really helped clarify it. I hear Robert saying that I'm not committed. I will fight that because I work harder, as hard as he does. I'm breaking my hump for the firm. I'm as committed as anyone."
>
> "Commitment and ability may be two different things."
>
> "I bridle [when Robert implies I'm not committed], and I block at hearing other things."

"If Robert could say—and maybe he is and I'm not hearing it—'Look, I understand you guys are committed, but I'm tired of [playing policeman and doing the routine things],' then I could focus on that."

"[Robert is correct, and] I'm trying to break the habit [of running from one last-minute crisis to another]."

"I know that we three partners have taken the pledge—more than once—[to change our habits]. I don't think we've changed our actions. I wonder if we really mean to change them. I mean, I wonder if we really believe that firm work is important [as opposed to client work]."

Bill: One final problem . . . I heard Robert and the [interventionist] say that he is ready to give up authority and that the real problem is us [although we did point out that Robert may be a coconspirator]. I'm not sure I buy that we are the major cause, but then I ask myself why don't we confront Robert. I think of yesterday's episode.

Robert: What was that?

Bill: You [Don] said that we needed a manager. Robert said that he did not agree. You said, "I think that we do," and it dropped. And that happens a lot. But dropping it is a joint responsibility, and why do we do that?

Robert should throw that back to you, Don, and say, "If you think we need a manager, make the case, let's explore it."

So Robert says no to one of our ideas; we let it go by and think, "Oh, that son-of-a-bitch is not open to ideas." [But is that fair?] Maybe we're not willing to spend the hours it takes to develop the idea.

Don: Not willing. . . .

Bill: Yes, [I don't like admitting it]. *Willing,* I think, Don.

Don: I think we're willing. But if we do that, we're going to sacrifice client work.

Bill: But Robert is able to do both. Moreover, he says [because of us] he has to sacrifice a lot of his precious time to keep us on the ball.

The interventionist points out a feature of the discussion that illustrates Bill's last point. Don expresses serious concern about the way the firm is managed. Bill is concerned about Robert's unfair attribution that he is not committed to the firm (which was important) and about why the other partners do not take the initiative more often. The feature to which the interventionist is referring is that here are two more examples in which the two partners have identified the problem but say nothing about how to overcome their part of it.

Don: But in order to overcome many of these problems, you have to allocate energy and brains. [We need more help.]

Int.: Yes . . . but what is it that you recommend, and what is the reasoning behind it?

Don: All right. I hadn't said anything about that yet.

Robert interrupts, saying that before they get to this issue, he wants to respond to Bill's views about commitment. He believes that all the partners are about equally committed to performing client work. He does not believe they are equally committed to the task of building a manageable, innovative firm. He adds, "As I see it, I have more creative skill than you guys. [I consciously decided not to hire more imaginative and creative people because many of them eventually harm an organization.]"

Bill points out a dilemma. It is true that Robert fills in the breach whenever there is a gap. But Robert's very willingness to fill in the gap may lead Bill to let Robert do so, and then Bill feels "an enormous amount of guilt."

The interventionist is surprised that the partners do not pick up on Robert's statement that he hired them because he judged them to be less creative than he. The interventionist asks the partners how they feel about Robert's view that he is more creative than they in conceptualizing the firm's mission and more imaginative in building new programs. Bill replies, "At the level of firm work, I say yes." Don adds, "I have no problem with thinking that Robert is more creative than I am. I don't take it as an insult." Robert says, however, that he feels that they are glad they have this crazy, innovative person, but they do not appreciate him. "Every time you turn around, he [speaking of himself] keeps saying, 'You guys ought to appreciate me. I'm different.' He keeps sending on signals to tell [you] that he is different. Eventually you distance yourself from him, and he feels 'Life is not good.' "

Bill replied that he had no problem utilizing Robert's creative talents, but he doesn't want to utilize them for everything. There are times that the incremental help he might receive from Robert is not that valuable. But he feels he is going to get that help whether he wants it or not, and it is that pressure that Bill feels is counterproductive. He and Don agree that they want Robert to focus on precisely what he is good at (conceptualizing) and to delegate more routine issues to others (for example, hire an editor, hire new managers). Robert says that he would be delighted to work on the conceptual issues. But he feels that the editorial and managerial problems are temporary and solvable if the partners meet their administrative commitments.

Don doubts that the issues are temporary. Robert's scenario of how these problems will be solved (VPs will soon be up to speed, the staff will be upgraded and will be self-sufficient) is, Don feels, optimistic. Bill says maybe what the firm needs is an administrative manager. Don agrees. They doubt that Robert can continue to do first-class client work and also be a first-rate administrator, even if the partners meet all their commitments. Don says, "[To repeat], I have no problem with Robert's role in the firm work. I think that it is extremely well done. Where we clearly have a problem is the visible and emotional support we have shown Robert in that work. I don't think that can be changed until [we add some more people and develop a clearer reporting structure at the levels below us]." The interventionist says that he hears Bill's and Don's concern clearly, but what he has not heard is any ideas about what they would do to solve the problem.

Robert: [You guys just questioned my effectiveness as administrative manager], and my feeling is one of "You bastards, that's not fair. You haven't asked what I'm doing. You're making attributions about me and never testing them out." . . . So you'll still be saying, "I don't have any evidence for this, but I sure know how I feel about it. I feel that Robert doesn't do the job; he takes on more than he can perform and then is not confrontable," and you're stuck.

And that is a really negative experience for me, to have the impression that that may be taking place.

Bill: Yes, I think it is taking place. [We are dissatisfied on issues and not confronting you.]

[Later]

Bill: And what really [provokes me] is that I don't confront Robert. . . . Why do we do that? Are we such weak characters that we can't confront across the board?

Or is it something that Robert does that closes off confrontation? I don't know. But I do know that something is wrong.

Int.: My hunch is that five years ago Robert was less confrontable. He is now more confrontable, but you appear to have remained more dependent [and maybe the new mismatch is upsetting both of you].

Bill: I see myself enormously more confronting than I was five years ago.

Int.: You're right. But I guess what we've done is upped the ante as to what has to be discussed.

Bill: Yes.

Robert: What I hear is that you are more confronting of me as a person but not more confronting of the issues.

Bill: That may be true.

[Robert gives more illustrations.]

Bill: OK, let me get to the left-hand side of the column while it's fresh. I was feeling that you were going to beat my example to death, so I quickly agreed.

Robert: And this is what we did yesterday.

Bill: And then I say, who needs it?

Don: I understand that.

Robert: Let me add my left-hand column. Bill says, "I'm going to make a point with an example. Then I'm going to say, 'Robert, you can't attack my example.' That'll leave you [Robert] stuck. I'll get to say what I want to say. As soon as [the example] starts to weaken, I'm going to say, 'It doesn't make any difference whether the evidence is there or not, my assertion is valid.' "

Bill: [Here we go again.] I say, "Here is something that I'm concerned about." Now I've got to defend the one example to death. I'm not up to that. What I'm raising is an issue and not advocating it.

Int.: To the extent that you do not advocate your position, you may be remaining in the dependent position that I mentioned before.

If you pick an example that illustrates a point, which, if correct, challenges the core of what Robert believes is true, then I can understand how he would wish to challenge it.

Bill: But can't I raise an issue without having complete documentation?

Int.: Yes, but what I heard was an assertion about Robert and not an invitation for inquiry.

Bill: I guess what I see is us backing off from Robert. It is better, but it is still too high.

Int.: It may be still high. How do you react to the confrontation that you people had with Robert on the management information system?

Bill: Yes, that is a good example where we confronted and he listened. [But] something happens in our meetings so that we do not discuss our differences. We get submissive and back off. Robert interprets that as us not understanding, and we place Robert in a position that alienates him from us, which causes him personal problems and us, too.

Int.: That is a nice analysis. Is not the next question "What are you partners going to do about this?"?

The partners are not clear what they will do. Bill and Don wonder whether they should create a traditional presidential role. When asked what difference that would make, Bill responds that it would be easier to take orders under those conditions. The interventionist points out that this would formalize the dependent relationship between them and Robert, a relationship to which Bill objects. The Three Musketeers concept will work only if the partners do not withdraw when Robert confronts their reasoning processes and if they initiate a higher proportion of the actions related to the internal management and development of the firm.

Don wonders whether that alternative is realistic. The interventionist then points out a dilemma. On the one hand, the partners believe that Robert is too much in control (and that he may actually seek that control). When we examine the actions Robert initiates, actions that lead the partners to feel that he is too much in control, an estimated 90 percent are actions related to details and monitoring unkept (or half-kept) promises. On the other hand, the partners offer no alternative solution except creation of a traditional presidential role, which would formalize Robert's unilateral actions and their dependency, a condition they object to. Moreover, they are not confident that they can meet internal issue commitments so that the police role and other unilateral actions of Robert (which he does not like) are eliminated.

Bill acknowledges the dilemma. He returns to the idea that Robert hired them because he believed they were not as creative as he.

Bill: If he believes that he can add to the creative discussion, then will he not be involving himself in all the important decisions? We're back full circle.

Int.: The idea of the Executive Office is that all the partners are to have a voice in all the major decisions. So he will be driven to participate, as you are also. However, in order for this concept to work, the partners must be able to confront each other if anyone's contributions are not helpful.

Bill: But that is where we have the problem. Will we confront?

Bill acknowledges that the Three Musketeers concept will work if the partners are more active. The interventionist agrees, adding that if they are tougher on Robert, it will enable him to be tougher on them. The concept of the Executive Office requires that each partner use his unique skills as fully as possible.

Bill: And I see if we take more initiative and show our skills, then Robert will value our contributions.

Int.: Yes, as I see it, the three partners appear to be dragging their feet on becoming equals.

Bill: But will this concept work on the next lower level?

Int.: It can, but only if it works on your level. If we have the present situation, then I believe the next level below will feel confused and bewildered.

Don, who has doubts about the practicability of the concept in this firm, is correct, but in my opinion only because the collegial concept is not being implemented correctly. We now have a tacit pyramidal structure with Robert on top and the partners disgruntled because he has too much power. He, on the other hand, believes that most of his unilateral actions come in routine areas and police-type actions, which he hates.

Bill then identifies a dilemma—namely, that Don believes the Three Musketeers concept won't work. The interventionist believes that this is quite possible because it is a self-fulfilling prophecy on the part of the partners. The partners agree. Bill suggests that the partners could try to make the concept work at the manager level, and if it is not successful, they can design a more traditional mode.

Robert, turning to Don, says that he understands Don has doubts about the collegial structure they have been trying to create at the partner and manager levels. He asks Don to present his doubts and the reasoning behind them. "I'm beginning to develop some anxiety that you have not told us everything that you can now tell us. I would *not* like us to make a decision without having *all* your views. I do not want the idea of a collegial or matrix organization to be undiscussable."

Bill suggests that the partners, as a group, should first define *collegial*. Robert responds that before they do that, he would like to hear Don's and Bill's concerns and that they should take whatever time they require to build their case. Bill replies that the next step should be a group discussion about the collegial concept so that they will be clear about what they are criticizing.

The interventionist infers that another discussion is in the making in which Robert and Bill will not hear each other correctly. He believes that part of the problem is that Bill has been asserting Robert does not really want a collegial relationship, but he is unable to illustrate his attribution even to his own satisfaction. This upsets Robert, who then seeks data. However, what Robert does not see, in the interventionist's view, is that Bill is becoming aware of his errors.

Robert: I don't buy that at all.

Bill: I really buy that.

Robert: What is it that you really buy?

Bill: Well, for example, when I say that we do not feel free to confront you, you take it as an accusation against you. "Not confrontable?! Damn it, how can you say that? I'm openly confrontable!"

But I'm not necessarily making an attack on you. I may be wholly responsible. I don't know.

Int.: Or if it is an attack on you, then through discussion he could become aware of it. [To put it another way], Bill said something an hour ago that was understandably seen by you as an attack. Now, after an hour's discussion, he begins to have doubts about the validity of his attack. Do you see that?

Robert: I do not see that as what we have just gone through. Bill never said, "A while ago I asserted that administrative issues are not confrontable. I no longer agree with that view." So he hasn't taken that back. I said, "All right, I'm prepared to discuss it. I invite you to develop whatever basis you wish." Then I hear Bill saying, "Oh, we must do that as a group."

Bill: What I'm saying is:

The three partners do not confront Robert.

Robert *is* wholly open and confrontable and would be confronted [let us say] by everybody except, as Don would say, these three partners that he selected.

Or there may be something that Robert says or does that may give cues that he is not confrontable.

I admit I get that feeling [that you are not confrontable]. I also admit I can't document it. . . . Or could Robert have chosen individuals who [at some level] he knew would not confront him?

Robert is bewildered. He finally says that he doubts any discussion is going to change Bill's and Don's views. The interventionist points out that Bill and Don have similar feelings about his changing.

Bill: Look, I think you [Robert] feel that I am throwing rocks at you. I'm not.

Robert: Yes. I feel you are.

Int.: It is not only you. Aren't all of you throwing rocks? [Illustrates.]

Robert agrees and is bewildered. Yesterday the partners pleaded with him that when they have an idea, he should not "grab ahold of it and shake it." Today Bill presents an idea, and Robert responds by saying, "Fine, take all the time you need to develop it. I'm trying to model what you asked for yesterday." Bill then answers that he doesn't want to develop the idea—the partner group should do that. "I'm stuck!" exclaims Robert.

The interventionist agrees that Bill may appear inconsistent to Robert. The inconsistency can be understood if Robert sees Bill as changing his mind. Bill made accusations about Robert acting unilaterally, and so on. However, as a result of their group conversation, he begins to see that he, Don, and John are responsible for creating the situation that they condemn. Consequently, Bill now asks the partners to join in the discussion of his new idea so that it will evolve from the Executive Office as a group.

Robert, however, is still smarting from the accusation that he espouses a collegial partnership but does not act to reinforce it. He was told, for example, that he was not giving others an opportunity to explore their views. Hence, when Bill and Don respectively raise some views with which he disagrees, he invites them to develop those views and present them to the group. But Bill and Don interpret this as "OK, you guys, build your cases individually and then we'll have a go at them." They want first to have a group discussion. Robert asks whether the discussion would not be more effective if they advocated their respective views and then encouraged inquiry into them. Moreover, if they want to work in any kind of subgroup, that is acceptable.

Bill does not respond to Robert's question. He says that what is troubling him is that Robert is communicating that Bill and Don feel he has "screwed up" as a president who wants collegial relationships. "You [Robert] are communicating that 'I think I am confrontable; hence, your statement is not fair. I'm going to prove it [by asking you to develop your plans in any way that you wish].'" Bill says that he wants to look forward. "I'm putting me and all of us on notice that I'm going to be looking for this problem. I'd like to be able to say, "Look, here's a problem, let's look for some data."

The interventionist says that he is concerned about Bill's comment because it still places him in the position of raising a question (inquiry) but not advocating his views. Bill may be designing a situation that continues the dependent, passive relationship he creates with Robert. Bill responds that this means he must not bring up an idea until he can advocate it. "OK, that makes me nervous about my idea being confronted, and I may not bring a point up until I can prove it beyond a shadow of a doubt. That is not being open."

The interventionist suggests that Bill introduce his views and state ahead of time the degree of confidence he has in his conclusions, noting the gaps that would have to be closed, and so on. Otherwise, although Bill complains about not having the opportunity to state his ideas, he would only be asking a question. Under these conditions, Robert would feel free to confront the nascent idea, and that is the very condition that Bill is trying to avoid. Robert would indeed be in a bind.

Don adds that another reason they may not take the initiative is that they do not have the time to think through an issue, and if there is agreement, they could not follow up. The partners might say to him, for example, "Don, if you have a point and we agree, do it; don't just complain." If he did not follow through, he would feel guilty. If he said that he could not follow through, he would feel irresponsible. "Better to forget about it, particularly since we have a workhorse [Robert], and wait until he takes some action. Thus," Don concludes, "there are other reasons than our personalities that administrative commitments are not met. We cannot build a company the way we are going."

Robert says that he can develop the managers into an effective team so that they can handle many of the items that Don is understandably worried about. Bill and Don don't agree that this is possible.

The interventionist asks whether they are willing to experiment. They could develop a list of issues that the manager group should be able to solve, and give them to Robert. If the manager group does not solve them, they have good data for requesting changes in that group. "What prevents you from trying this out?"

Don: It is extraordinary, isn't it? [Laughs]
Bill: Yes.

Robert smiles, adding that he is willing to be the workhorse for another year or so as long as the partners are jointly designing and implementing ways to reduce the counterproductive features that have been identified. He repeats his request for confrontation any time he appears to be inhibiting them from taking initiative or undermining the collegial atmosphere.

The partners then examine ways to reduce Robert's workload in the administrative area. As Don and Robert are exploring what can be reduced, Bill suddenly becomes quite upset. He feels that Robert is not sincerely trying to reduce his commitments.

Bill: I hear the same message. "Eliminate the routine activities and give me a commitment to meet your promises, and nothing has to change."
Robert: [Interrupting] Hold it, Don! Bill says, "Damn!" Drops his pad down, and says we're not making any progress.

Bill: No, no! We're doing fine!

Robert: Look, Bill, I'm trying very hard to inquire into what you said were unconfrontable issues. In my view, you are making it difficult. I believe that you are making it harder to do what you espouse. I don't understand why you don't join us in inquiring.

Bill: OK. Keep going. I'm willing to learn. I'm willing to learn.

Don: [Turns to their list] In my view, none of these functions are being performed at the level to which we aspire.

Robert: I agree.

Don: The only way I know how to do better is to increase the attention that is paid to them. I just can't believe that we can expect you to do that. You are overworked, and that is a risk for the firm.

[Robert and Don explore why the firm has not been able to hire a new personnel manager.]

Don: OK, to take the hard line, I would hold you [Robert] responsible for failing in eight months to get a new manager.

Robert: I partially agree. [Explains]

Don: I remember saying that I think it is a mistake to expect the present manager to recruit her replacement.

Robert: We did find three who turned us down.

Bill: But I thought that we agreed no longer to be satisfied with nice tries.

Bill points out that, in effect, the tables are being turned. Now it is Robert who has not met the time commitment, and he is giving excuses in the same way they give excuses to him when they do not meet their commitments.

Int.: I hear Bill saying that he is tired of being in a group where there are valid reasons for lousy results. "So I am seeking to reduce this by asking that we hire an office manager."

Bill: Yes. You are making excuses, just as we made excuses. It is time that we hire someone to be office manager.

Robert: I hear you as critical of things that do not work out and as not balancing it with statements about the things that have worked out.

Bill: Well, I'm trying to help all of us change.

Robert: But the example that you use is, in effect, tails you win, heads you weren't involved.

Int.: That's the situation Bill wishes to change.

Robert: I find that exciting.

Don: You've been in a position that you lose both ways. We've put you, and you've put yourself, in that position.

We're not going to solve the problems by balancing the minuses with pluses.

Robert: I'm not asking for that.

Don: That is what I heard you say a moment ago.

Robert: The way to solve this problem is not look backwards but look forwards to prevent this from happening again.

Don: That is what we are trying to do.

Bill: Yes.

Int.: They are right with you on that.

The discussion continues with Bill and Don repeating that they understand there are valid reasons for the delay in hiring an office manager, but they want to raise the performance level of all the partners in administrative issues. In effect, Don and Bill are now trying to get Robert to raise his own performance level in an area for which he has responsibility.

18

Analyzing Reasoning in Problem Solving

The partners agree that the firm should "shoot for the moon," which means, above all, that they will be known as the firm with premier products and services. They also agree that, because of heavy pressures from extreme growth, employees are at times making errors that threaten the quality of client services. Therefore, one immediate goal is to strengthen the performance of managers and employees. Don and Bill (and, to some extent, John) believe the firm should hire a general administrative manager to whom the managers responsible for production, financial, and personnel functions will report. This should free the officers to get on with expanding and strengthening client services and should simultaneously reduce the grueling work pace of the partners.

Robert agrees with the idea of strengthening internal managerial activities and reducing the work pace of the partners, but for him, "shooting for the moon" also includes creating a firm that is administratively unique. He hopes to minimize the predisposition of most organizations to solve problems by hiring more managers, which not only layers people but also compounds unilateral control. Robert prefers to err in the direction of giving managers and employees as much autonomy and responsibility as possible to keep them challenged and involved. He hopes, for example, to institute the collegial concept at the manager level. Instead of having a general administrative officer, the managers would execute those responsibilities as a group. The managers would then be more in charge of their own and the firm's destiny, would create a better-quality work life among themselves, and ideally would seek ways to do the same for their subordinates.

It is not clear to what extent Bill and John are committed to these goals. They appear to be more committed than Don, but like Don, they believe that these aspirations will take too long to implement and will extract too great a toll from the partners. Robert believes the risk is worth taking, and he would accept another year or two of heavy work load to achieve these goals. He also believes that if Bill and John organized their client work more effectively, and if they were more committed to the administrative health of the firm, they could take on more responsibility than they have. Robert does not believe that Don can shoulder his share of the administrative responsibilities now because he is swamped with several new client programs. Bill and John support this view unhesitatingly, and so does Don, though reluctantly. He wants to do his share of the administrative load.

There is agreement among the partners that Bill, Don, and John have, in varying degrees, not fulfilled commitments they made regarding routine administrative issues or commitments to share their client reports with one another. An especially thorny issue is the quality of the firm's report writing. Robert believes that it is mixed, that he knows how to do reports better than the other three partners and should be given a chance to edit all reports. Although Bill, Don, and John agree that Robert is a fine writer, they doubt that his way is the one best way or that client service can be enhanced only by Robert's editing. They believe that a professional writer should be hired to deal with all editorial issues.

The partners also agree that they should concentrate on the most prestigious and largest clients. Robert seeks this not just for sales survival or prestige but, more important, because he believes the best way for the partners to be challenged, and to challenge the dominant assumptions of their firm continually, is to reflect on their practice with the chief executives of their clients. Robert has the view that the firm can best survive by reflecting on its practices; the best reflection comes from self-examination of activities, and that holds for routine report writing as well as for client interaction.

All the partners agree that to date Robert has shown the greatest skill in reflecting on practice, conceptualizing dominant business ideas, and producing innovations for the firm. But they do not necessarily agree that this will always be so. They believe, to varying degrees, that once they are out from under the tremendous pressures of fast growth, they will be able to increase their own contributions along these dimensions. This is, in their minds, another reason they should get on with hiring new administrative personnel.

A position taken by the three partners appears to contain some internal inconsistencies—for instance, their espoused committal to the concept of "one for all and all for one" when the reality is quite different.

Bill, Don, and John believe that Robert's work load is inhumane and that they should carry some of his important administrative responsibilities, such as recruiting and producing innovations. If they do not, they believe, there is a danger of being dependent on Robert, thereby converting the collegial structure into a traditional pyramidal structure.

Robert agrees with this diagnosis and asserts that he is ready to turn over major responsibilities to them. But he hesitates to do so for two reasons. One, as they agree, they are too swamped to meet even routine administrative commitments, much less the more important ones (such as training the vice-presidents). Second, as they also agree, to date he has shown the best performance in conceptualizing and selling the firm to potential partners; hence, what sense does it make for him to withdraw? Moreover, if it is "one for all and all for one," what sense does it make to rigidly define duties? Why not remain fluid and organic, with every partner a resource to every other one?

The interventionist does not see that Bill, Don, and John respond to these inconsistencies. They interpret Robert's raising them as evidence that he does not wish to relinquish control. Let us examine in more depth the problem-solving processes related to these issues.

Nested Levels of Problem-Solving Processes

Bill's, Don's, and John's diagnosis may be formulated as in Figure 8 (admittedly, somewhat simplified).

Figure 8. Bill's, Don's, and John's Diagnosis

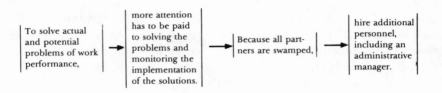

Robert agrees that the problems deserve more attention and that everyone is busy. But he is worried about the potential unintended consequences of hiring more people. For example, general managers typically seek to strengthen their role by hiring new subordinates and by defining top-down tighter control systems. A new layer of management will be created that distances the partners from the managers who have direct access to employees. These and similar consequences could lead the firm to become more bureaucratized. This would not only lead to greater rigidity but would reduce the opportunities for challenging work and the space for free movement. To add insult to injury, it would cost, over a ten-year period, several million dollars. Why is the concept of peer collegiality acceptable at the officer level and not at the manager level?

Robert suspects that some of the employee complaints of feeling pressured and confused, with resultant error, are caused by partner actions. For example, there is evidence that the partners have acted unilaterally and violated schedule commitments, that they have misunderstood the managers' plights, and that the managers have hesitated to complain.

Before new personnel are added and bureaucracy is created, why not strive to correct the partners' contribution to the problems and simulaneously strengthen the manager group? After these are accomplished, then determine whether additional personnel and bureaucracy are needed.

Robert's diagnosis may be formulated as in Figure 9.

Figure 9. Robert's Diagnosis

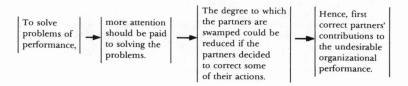

| To solve problems of performance, | → | more attention should be paid to solving the problems. | → | The degree to which the partners are swamped could be reduced if the partners decided to correct some of their actions. | → | Hence, first correct partners' contributions to the undesirable organizational performance. |

Formulating the two diagnoses helps us see a second-order problem—the difference in view of what is the cause of the first-order problem (that is, inadequate firm performance).

In Robert's view, a good deal of the problem is correctable without adding further top-level personnel and bureaucracy. The second-order problem, therefore, is the recalcitrance of Bill, Don, and John to alter their actions and to help train the managers.

Bill's, Don's, and John's view of the second-order problem is that Robert does not want to add new top personnel and bureaucracy because he wants to remain in control; he is an entrepreneur who does not want to give up power. Don and John (and, somewhat less so, Bill) explain Robert's recalcitrance by attributing to him that he seeks, and may enjoy, the pain of being overworked.

Don believes (as, to a lesser degree, do Bill and John) that all these attributions represent core characteristics of Robert's personality: They are not likely to change. Hence, it follows, hire a new general manager and create more bureaucracy.

Figure 10 diagrams the partners' second-order view of the problem.

Implicit criticism of Robert is embedded in this diagnosis. The diagnosis implies that the issues, in addition to being unchangeable, are undiscussable and uncorrectable.

Robert does not believe the attribution that he seeks to maintain control and enjoys the distress of overwork. He also rejects the idea that he is not changeable. He cites as evidence the fact that he is begging to be rid of the "chicken shit" unilateral interaction on routine issues. He also cites as justification for his involvement in the

Figure 10. Bill's, Don's, and John's Second-Order Diagnosis

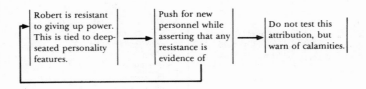

more profound issues (such as conceptualizing the firm and recruiting officers) that the three partners have a poor record in meeting their commitments, and anyway, they agree that he is better at such activities.

Figure 11 shows Robert's second-order view of the problem.

Figure 11. Robert's Second-Order Diagnosis

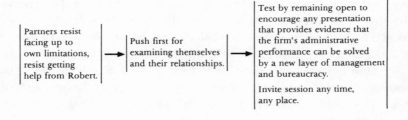

Robert's diagnosis implies that Bill, Don, and John are resisting because they are not genuinely committed to a collegial firm, with minimum bureaucracy, where each partner contributes according to his strength. The partners may also resist because they are trying to reduce his dominance by stripping him of responsibilities in areas where they agree that he has very fine skills.

To the interventionist, the partners do not respond to Robert's attributions as he does to theirs. Don deals with the issues by saying, in effect, "The time has passed for discussion. The lower-level employees require strong leadership and clearly defined roles." Bill partly agrees with Don but also believes the partnership would be better off if he and others were not so quick to salute Robert. He seeks a partnership in which ideas are explored and decisions are arrived at by consensus. Robert is agreeable to that but asks them to take more initiative.

Let us now add a third-order problem. Robert's view that the partners resist examining themselves is related to a third level of attributions that he makes about the partners. He sees Don as a product of several decades in a large bureaucracy who automatically seeks traditional answers to difficult problems. Don acknowledges that this may be partly true.

Robert also sees Don as panicking more than the situation calls for. For example, Don insisted that it would be a disaster for the partners to talk about Carol with the managers (see Chapter Sixteen). Yet when the meeting began, the managers themselves brought up the issue.

Robert also sees Don as feeling out others before he gives his opinion and as being too quick to gloss over interpersonal difficulties. (Yet Robert acknowledges that Don is becoming more proactive, and Robert twice reinforced this by saying how much he valued it.) Thus, whatever controversial contributions Don may make about the substantive issues of bureaucracy and new personnel, Robert (and, less so, Bill and John) will doubt their validity.

These attributions represent features of personality. Don, in his discussion of Robert, has said that personality features are unchangeable. Although Robert may not believe this, he does believe that it is unproductive to force Don to talk about these attributions, because Don has ruled them out in previous discussions.

Turning to Bill, Robert believes that he is unable to manage his work schedule and pressures; that his level of aspiration for high-quality service is not adequate; and that he is unable to present ideas compellingly. Moreover, Robert believes that Bill is unaware of these characteristics (except the first) and that the unawareness is probably a defense that Robert had better deal with carefully, as he does not wish to upset Bill. Robert sees Bill as predisposed to interpret any remarks that he makes on these issues as questioning his loyalty and commitment to the firm. He believes he has said repeatedly that he does not question Bill's loyalty. He also believes he has invited Bill to illustrate his attributions. Bill either has been unable to do so even to his own satisfaction or has merely said he will point out examples in the future.

Furthermore, Bill admits that he backs down too quickly when confronted by Robert because (1) this is his usual way of moving the conversation on, (2) he realizes he does not have a well-thought-out argument, and (3) he expects Robert to "beat his examples to death." Yet Bill simultaneously admits that Robert is confrontable on issues like these if he can present data and make his attributions subject to test. As Bill and Robert realize, the latter is probably not going to happen, because Bill's predisposition is to back off and simultaneously to blame Robert.

To summarize: There are problems of organizational structure and of the hiring of a general manager for the office and an editor for reports. Bill, Don, and John believe the time has come to introduce more bureaucracy and to hire for these two key jobs. Robert prefers first to correct actions of the partners and managers that cause organizational errors and to strengthen the partner and manager groups. Once this is accomplished, then they can decide what additional bureaucratization and personnel are needed.

We have a situation similar to Case B in Chapter One, in which there is a standoff between two sets of partners. As in the previous case, each side holds pessimistic attributions about the other's motives and influenceability. In Chapter One, these attributions are, typically, neither discussed nor tested. However, in this case the attributions are made public and subject to test. Robert, Bill, and John are open to having their positions tested (Don is ambivalent because sometimes he would rather bureaucratize and get on with it). Robert is more able to illustrate his attributions and receive confirmations from the partners than they are. The session ends with Bill and Don promising to keep more of their administrative commitments; Bill and John will take on new administrative commitments. All three seek evidence that Robert is unable to let go and may enjoy his stress. Finally, Bill ends with a renewed commitment not to agree so easily with Robert and to surface his doubts more clearly.

Thus, we see that the fears expressed in most organizations regarding a discussion of typically undiscussable issues are not necessarily realistic. The partners leave the session even more committed to obtaining data to test their views. They leave, in other words, as a more learning group than they were when the meeting began.

One facet of the relationship between Bill and Robert appears to be triggered by defenses irrelevant to the present situation. Bill, for example, is predisposed to be angry at Robert because Robert believes that Bill is not as loyal and as committed to the firm as he himself is. Robert denies that he feels this about Bill in respect to client work, but he confirms it in respect to administrative work. As a result, Bill is predisposed to be angry at Robert, to mishear him, and to act in ways to dethrone him.

Robert also has some defensive feelings toward Bill, because he does not hear him, nor does he reward Bill for his continuous struggle to understand better his predisposition to blame Robert and to see him as unchangeable. At least half a dozen times in this meeting, Bill was angry at himself for not confronting Robert or for attributing to Robert motives for which he had little evidence. Instead of empathizing and supporting this self-inquiry, Robert responded either by adding further examples of Bill's "faults" or by telling Bill how much better off he would be if he took Robert's advice. These reactions upset Bill even more, and he expressed this. At the same time, he remained aware that a large part of his distress was his own fault.

Therefore, in addition to the three levels of attributions already described, there is a fourth-order problem—that Robert and Bill sometimes interact in a manner that automatically triggers each other's defenses. We must find a way to identify the cues that set off these automatic reactions, which Robert and Bill realize are counterproductive to progress.

Reasoning During Interpersonal Encounters

My analysis suggests the following relations among interpersonal relationships, effective problem solving, and organizational effectiveness. The partners made attributions about one another in order to make rational sense of one another's actions. Thus, Don explains Robert's willingness to work at an inhumane pace and his apparent commitment to such activities as recruiting and conceptualizing the main business ideas of the firm by attributing to him certain personality features: (1) he hates to let go—he is an entrepreneur who needs to be in control—and (2) he enjoys the pain of overwork.

Both these attributes imply that Robert is not in control of his actions, and hence what he espouses cannot be trusted. Thus, Robert espouses "one for all and all for one," but his personality is such that he seeks to be on top. He espouses that all work schedules should be reduced; yet he works very hard. Moreover, the attributions, if valid, imply that Robert cannot change these personality features. Hence, Don tells Robert these attributions, never expecting that he will be able to change them. That is one reason that Don is recommending the addition of new personnel and the development of additional bureaucratic structures. Moreover, if these personality features are unchangeable, an implication is that Robert's reasoning processes are influenced by factors over which he has little control. That is, Robert's reasoning processes are distorted in ways that Robert is unaware of, and so his conclusions should be respected (Model I politeness) and simultaneously discounted and disbelieved. (In most organizations, Don would think all this covertly and act as if he were not thinking it.)

Under these conditions, it is difficult to see why Don would ever accept Robert's reasoning as a basis for modifying his own. What sense does it make for Don to alter his reasoning by listening to reasoning he considers distorted? To genuinely listen to such reasoning would be irrational.

In a Model I world, people normally reason as Don is now reasoning, keeping this reasoning undiscussable, so that it is also untestable. Since it is untestable, the errors embedded in it are unlikely to be identified. Because all the players usually believe the errors exist on the other side, and because that, too, is undiscussable, it is not surprising that self-fulfilling prophecies, self-sealing processes, and escalating errors result.

This case illustrates some of the consequences of such interactions. First, if such interactions take place millions of times in everyday life, people can come to believe that it is human nature not to deal with these problems candidly. It is also understandable that people make rational sense of this belief by holding another one—that to discuss these matters would be dangerous and would open a Pandora's box. Finally, it is understandable that people become alarmed and bewildered by the suggestion that we make the undiscussable more discussable. Such an act, these persons maintain, ranges from being inept and uncivilized to being stupid and punishing. And if these attributions become norms of a culture, then discussing these issues will be dangerous or even immature or insane.

The second consequence of this type of interaction is that it initiates action that ignores these issues and hides the concealment. In this case, for example, actions that are rational according to the partners' theories-in-use would include hiring a general manager, hiring an editor, and defining roles and responsibilities more clearly. This would add, over a decade, millions of dollars in costs (the salary of a senior manager alone, plus benefits, was estimated conservatively at $100,000 a year). It would also add another layer between the partners and the managers and thereby increase the probability of distancing. Finally, it would increase the proportion of the managerial machinery that unilaterally controls the performance of others, as well as the evaluation of that performance. This could lead people to become defensive in order to ensure survival and could result in the sort of organizational games that prevent learning—or, worse yet, base learning on distorted data.[1]

In making this analysis, I have not proved that the new appointments are unnecessary or that additional bureaucracy would not be beneficial. My point is that if the players use reasoning processes that necessarily lead to escalating errors, self-fulfilling prophecies, and self-sealing processes, these processes ought to be corrected before additional people are hired, before bureaucracy is put in place, and most important, before belief that people cannot double-loop learn is reinforced. The decisions about structure and personnel will then be informed and more freely made (Model II governing variables).

This case illustrates that double-loop issues can be discussed, that such discussions do not lead to chaos, that people are not irreparably damaged by such discussions, and so on. Indeed, the case also illustrates that the partners as a team became more of a learning system after the meeting than they were before it.

The case does not show that such discussions are sweetness and light, that conflict is suppressed (criticisms from those who advocated structural changes were frequent), or that the new world means nobody gets upset. Robert, Don, and Bill did become upset at differ-

---

[1]Chris Argyris and Donald Schön, *Organizational Learning* (Reading, Mass.: Addison-Wesley, 1978).

ent times during the session, but (with the possibility of one episode) it was, as one put it, "no big deal." To put it more technically,
the discomposure was discussable and manageable in such a way that
the participants learned new ideas and took new actions.

An issue that is still not effectively managed by the group relates to areas in which the partners are not in adequate control of
their own actions. Recall that Robert told Bill, in effect, "If you
would take my advice, then you would be better off." Recall also
that Robert was stunned that this was what others heard. He added
that he wanted to understand that better because that was not the
message he intended. Recall also that he asked for, and received,
quite a bit of feedback. Robert did not find all the feedback convinc-
ing, but he did embark on a program to learn more about this apparent blindness.

Bill learned that his automatic reaction to certain comments of
Robert's is anger. Once he becomes angry, still other automatic reactions are triggered. Bill privately discounts Robert ("There he goes
again, being punishing") and almost simultaneously ignores the comment by continuing his own line of reasoning. But the price of ignoring Robert is submission to him, and the price of that is dependence
on him. When Bill goes into his private acts of discounting and ignoring, no one knows what his thoughts and feelings are. Robert, unaware of the negative messages, may feel that he is getting through.
Later, because Bill does not fulfill what Robert had assumed was an
agreement, Robert may feel that this is yet another example of Bill's
failure to control work pressures and meet his commitments. He may
also feel Bill has betrayed and misused him.

Whenever Robert expresses those feelings, Bill becomes upset
because he interprets them to mean Robert believes he is not loyal
and not committed. We now have a circular process that produces
the dynamics illustrated in the previous chapter. The assumption is
that Robert and Bill, with the help of the interventionist, John, and,
less so, Don, can be helped in the same way that they helped John
(Chapter Ten).

Some important implications for learning are embedded in this
analysis. The ultimate objective, for example, of courses in leadership
and organizational learning should not stop at examining what people do to one another. It is important to get at the actual behavior,
but that is not adequate. It is necessary for human beings to explore

the reasoning processes that lead them to design and produce their behavior. This implication should also hold for emotions and feelings. It is important to acknowledge relevant feelings, but it is even more necessary to explore the reasoning processes that lead to those feelings.

Part Four

Linking Theory and Practice

19

Improving Individual and Organizational Development

Conditions for Double-Loop Learning

We have identified some of the important conditions for double-loop learning in organizations, be they large or small, private or public, voluntary or nonvoluntary. Briefly stated, the conditions are that individuals, acting as agents for the organization, must produce Model II action strategies and at the same time introduce and maintain O-II learning systems in their organization. In theory, the way for an interventionist to help clients (whether individuals, groups, or organizations) achieve these conditions is to use Model II action strategies. Thus, the skills needed to get from here to there and the end results that we are trying to achieve are similar.

What makes it difficult to specify how we get from here to there, and when, is that we cannot predict how individuals and the organization are going to react to Model II action strategies. As we have seen, both are likely to be threatened because their governing variables, their way of life, and the actions that to date have led to success (as well as to problems) are all placed in question. Further, if the intervention activity is designed to give organizations and their agents genuine choice about moving into Model II, even they cannot specify ahead of time the degree and nature of their defensive reaction. Indeed, to require or encourage such early specification may rob clients of some very important learning, including the iterative nature of progress and awareness of their inability to accurately predict their own reactions. Moreover, the very unpredictability of responses can be used by the interventionist to design powerful learning experiences for the clients. Instead of seeing client responses as resistance to be overcome, the actions are seen as grist for the learning mill.

Another important reason that clients should be responsible for their own pace is that it allows them to make informed judgments about continuing double-loop activities. It is conceivable, for example, that organizational development activities may be classified as successful even though the clients have made an informed decision to slow them down or even to halt them.

Although every client situation has its unique qualities, there are similarities among individuals and organizations that enable an interventionist to make valid plans regarding diagnosis and implementation. In this research, we have identified five features that every double-loop learning activity (whether of one person or in some larger social system) will contain: (1) the extent of client commitment, (2) the probable level and scope of threat, (3) the role of reasoning, disconnectedness, and distancing, (4) the role of organizational and societal factors, and (5) the advisability of generating and maintaining choice about entry into and exit from the learning activity, as well as the pace of progress.

Briefly, the implications of our findings are as follows:

Finding	*Implication about*
People value Model II theory-in-use and O-II learning systems but doubt their own or others' ability to produce them and the organization's ability to accept them.	*Commitment:* The underlying attitude of most people to individual and organizational double-loop learning will be ambivalence. Those who are "completely for it" may have as much difficulty as those who are completely against it.

Finding	*Implication about*
People are unaware that they cannot produce Model II simply by wanting to do so and intellectually understanding it. They are also unaware of the program that makes them unaware.	*Level of threat:* Double-loop learning activities will lead people to question the basis of their sense of competence and confidence, as well as their capacity to create the kind of justice that they value.
People use reasoning processes that decrease their ability to detect and correct double-loop errors; most are disconnected from their reasoning processes; they remain sane because they deal with this root problem by distancing themselves from the consequences (all of us tend to do this).	*Key role of reasoning, disconnectedness, and distancing:* People will come to learn that suppression or unawareness of one's feelings is important but not as basic an issue as disconnectedness from one's reasoning processes and the flaws in those reasoning processes. People will also learn that the distancing they use to make their everyday life manageable leads to a social pollution that, in the long run, may make them feel they are prisoners, leading an impossible life.
Organizations contain learning systems that reinforce the organizational entropy in any given situation.	*Key targets:* Organizational activities that focus on altering individual theories-in-use must also focus on altering learning systems, which include such features as the politics, the win/lose dynamics of coalition, the norms against risk taking, the hiding of error, and the hiding that error is being hidden. Alteration of organizations so that they can double-loop learn will be genuine (and not bypass or be limited) if individ-

Finding	*Implication about*
	uals learn to produce actions in congruence with Model II theories-in-use. Such learning will lead to Model O-II learning systems in organizations.
Model I theories-in-use are probably one of the most powerful consequences of the socialization process. They are at the core of the society and culture in which we are embedded.	All organizational development programs necessarily impinge on the larger social and cultural milieu in which individuals and organizations are embedded. Strictly speaking, there is no organizational development (of the kind that we are referring to) without societal and cultural changes.

Different people learn at different paces, and the pace may vary for the same person under different conditions.
 	
    This implies that the pace at which organizational factors will change will also vary.
	Pace of learning: Although the processes used and the objectives can be defined relatively clearly, the pace of achievement cannot be accurately determined ahead of time. A slow pace is not necessarily a sign of resistance, nor is a fast pace necessarily a sign of genuine acceptance. Nor is a fast pace followed by a slow pace necessarily a sign of difficulty; it may be a sign that the person is upping the ante.
	
	    Organizational development activities should continually and publicly test for the genuineness of learning and its ability to spread and not to wash out.

Practitioners interested in helping clients learn to double-loop learn are likely to be faced with certain conditions. Their clients' commitment to learning is probably going to be, at best, ambivalent.

The clients are probably unaware of the threat to their competence, confidence, and sense of justice. They are probably also unaware that the primary teaching target is their reasoning processes, the processes that they would consider least in need of examination. Nor are they aware of their disconnectedness and distancing, nor of the programs in their heads that keep them unaware. Clients are not likely to realize that double-loop learning, if it is to be genuine and not a bypass of basic problems, requires changes in the organizational learning system that, when combined with changes in individual theories-in-use, will question important features of the socializing processes and the norms of the culture.

In creating conditions for double-loop learning in a social system, the interventionist is likely to be faced with clients who believe they have the competence to be in control of their everyday lives and responsibilities. The interventionist must help clients experience the paradox of counterproductive control in such a way that it cannot be ignored. They must be helped to realize that the very competences that keep them in control prevent double-loop learning. Next, clients must be helped to learn an additional set of skills in the learning of which they will experience still another paradox—that to succeed they will have to create for themselves conditions of failure and a sense of not being in control. Being able to reflect on failure and lack of control is, paradoxically, the first step toward being in control.

In order to produce these conditions, interventionists and clients have certain responsibilities.

1. Interventionists not only should have a relatively clear idea of the threats involved in double-loop learning but should be masters of models, processes, and skills required to overcome the threats and build new competences. Unfortunately, too little is known about these models. What is helpful, however, is that the models, processes, and skills the interventionist uses to get the clients from here to there are the same ones that the clients require to become effective in double-loop learning and to help others do the same.

2. Clients must be free to stop their learning whenever they wish. The only obligation they should have is to test publicly with one another and with the interventionist the attributions they are making that lead them to exit. The point of this obligation is to help clients test the validity of and the consequences of their actions, not

to try to keep them in a context that they wish to terminate. They could even reject this obligation if they so chose, but that choice should be made public. Public discussion of their decision not to test their attributions would require that they think through the meanings they are communicating to the lower levels of their organization. This, in turn, would provide the lower levels with information about the genuineness of the top people's commitment to double-loop learning.

3. Clients must be willing to reflect on their actions and policies. Without reflection, there can be little learning because, as we have seen, people must examine their actions to get at their theories-in-use, and they cannot examine their actions until after they act. However, reflection is not easy because most of us reflect not so much to learn as to alter our actions in order to win and not lose, in order to remain in unilateral control, and in order to protect ourselves from feeling vulnerable.

4. Clients must be willing to experiment with new systems designs. Almost anything about the way organizations are managed will be questioned because organizations themselves are basically structures and processes to accomplish intended consequences. Most organizations are presently designed and managed in ways that are consistent with, and reinforce, Models I and O-I. Double-loop learning will require that clients reexamine such basic managerial technology as organizational structures, management information systems, financial and budget processes, quality control activities at all levels, and reward and morale systems.

The material in Chapters Thirteen through Eighteen shows that commitment to Models II and O-II does not mean that those in authority become soft or that the solution to problems is to give subordinates more power. Power equalization may be useful; it may be counterproductive. As to the former, we have seen in those chapters that many activities that are associated with excellence are emphasized much more *and* more openly. Robert strove hard to have such difficult issues as money, power over decisions, career paths, ownership, ineffective performance, and loyalty to the firm discussed among the partners, officers, and managers. In this sense, the firm was providing power equalization. But along with it went responsibility equalization. If the managers were to be in control of their jobs, then they would also have to be responsible for such difficult decisions as reassigning or firing themselves. If the officers were to require that the partners fulfill their commitments to train them, the officers would have to be responsible for not distancing themselves when the partners were not providing the training. They were as responsible for identifying and correcting the training oversight as the partners. As Parker noted, this was a new concept to him, for he had learned not only to act diplomatically with his superiors but to use any gaps they might have created to gain some space of free movement on his job.

Finally, clients will find themselves applying their learning to all aspects of their lives. Robert, Bill, and John, for example, held several sessions with their wives with the purpose of enhancing the quality of their home life. All have reported that the learning experiences have helped. Interestingly, with one exception, the wives acted in ways that stopped the partner/spouse sessions. It is not completely clear what led them to do so. It does appear that the wives wanted more attention from their husbands and more opportunity to influence them, but as they realized that these goals were achievable, they also realized the achievement would increase their responsibility for changing aspects of themselves that they had not expected to be in question.

Given clients who are willing to commit themselves to the conditions just described (where commitment includes freedom to stop, coupled with an obligation to test that decision), and given competent interventionists who can produce the required learning processes, it is possible to design double-loop learning conditions in any system.

Steps in an Organizational Development Program

Simply put, the interventionist has to design learning conditions that allow clients to learn how to *discover* problems, *invent* solutions, *produce* the solutions, and *evaluate* the effectiveness of the production. *Initially*, the problems to be discovered are related to the clients' theories-in-use and effective double-loop learning. Our prediction is that there are many problems, that they are not trivial, and that they should not be ignored or bypassed. We also predict that it is not possible to discover the problems of individual theories-in-use without discovering how the context in which people are embedded reinforces the theories-in-use. Our way of understanding the context is through the concept of the learning system. If clients and interventionist focus on the learning system, they will have focused on most of the relevant systemic factors that are facilitating or inhibiting double-loop learning.

The first step in the process of double-loop learning is to provide credible data for clients about their theories-in-use and learning systems. How can this be accomplished? Clients can be asked to assess the degree to which they may be unrealizingly contributing to the organizational problems that they wish to overcome.

The method used to collect the data should make it possible for clients (1) to commit themselves publicly to what they believe to be important problems, (2) to provide their espoused theory of how they would correct the problem if they were free to do so, (3) to illustrate (in the form of a conversational scenario) how they would implement what they espouse, and (4) to provide insight into what they believe they must unilaterally censor in order to be successful. The case described by Gerry (Chapter Six) is an example.

A case similar to the X and Y case may be used as a first step. The limitation of the X and Y case is that it does not give the clients insight into what they believe to be crucial problems in their own organization, although this limitation is often overcome once clients connect the learning with their organizational context. In one organization, the problems of budgets and management information systems were surfaced once people began to inquire into what would inhibit them from seeking to learn, and to use, Model II in their organization.

The context in which the results are discussed is important. For a client group of 25 to 30 people, at least a one-day session, without interruptions, is advisable. The interventionist can begin the session by providing a collage of the kinds of problems identified by the participants, communicating the patterns he or she has identified in the way the group dealt with the problem. It is possible to use a case written by one of the participants. The interventionist could ask the group to evaluate how effectively the case writer dealt with the problem. The group members become, in effect, consultants to the case writer. Whether the case writer is identified should be determined in advance between the participants and the interventionist. (I usually recommend that participants indicate their preference when they mail me their cases. The sooner people strive to be open, the better; however, candor that is forced can easily be counterproductive.)

I usually select a case whose substantive issue is important and, if possible, one that deals with the problem in an easing-in manner. The logic for preferring the easing-in approach is as follows. Recall that the group members are asked to evaluate the effectiveness of the case writer's actions. Their evaluations are written on an easel until everyone publicly agrees that his or her view is included. Next, I examine the implicit causal theory in their cases. Usually it is similar to the one they used in their X and Y cases. I then develop the finding that they use in their problem diagnoses the same causal theories that they discourage others from using. Usually participants state that they would not say aloud what they are thinking; that is, they would "ease in." I then either ask them to roleplay the easing in and get their reactions to it or point out that they have just made a critical diagnosis of an easing-in case.

The result is that participants recognize important inconsistencies in their diagnoses, in their actions, and more fundamentally, in their reasoning processes. As indicated in Chapter Eight, their reactions range from surprise to bewilderment, frustration, incompetence, anger, resignation, and fear. An individual can experience many of these feelings at different times, and a group can experience all of them at the same time.

The rest of the day is spent dealing with Type A or Type B defenses; helping participants see that dealing with their sense of failure is an important early step toward success; helping them explore the organizational and contextual factors that reinforce features counterproductive to double-loop learning; and helping them experiment and practice with new actions and design and implement new organizational environments.

At the end of the day, participants should have generated an understanding of their programmed incompetence in double-loop learning; an understanding that superiors and subordinates (young or old, powerful or not, male or female) are equally responsible for problems; and an understanding that the organization's learning system reinforces incompetence and counterproductive behavior. With such knowledge, participants can begin to discuss whether, when, and how they can correct the situation.

The second step is to generate sessions where participants can practice unfreezing from Model I and learn to produce Model II. There are two possibilities. The first is to use the normal meetings of the organization where the use of Model II actions would be important. Examples are the sessions in which officers evaluate the performance of managers or the case team evaluates its own performance; the regularly scheduled officer and officer/manager meetings in which important policy and administrative issues are discussed; ad hoc sessions that might be generated by individuals.

The second possibility is the session created by the clients and the interventionist specifically to practice producing Model II actions. For example, in one organization six officers each produced cases (in the X and Y format) of difficult problems they had with subordinates or with each other. The cases became the focal point for discussion of (1) the effectiveness with which the case writer dealt with the problem, (2) the effectiveness with which the group members counseled the case writer, and (3) the implications of their discussions for those organizational features that would require changing if Model II governing values were to be emphasized and an O-II learning system were to be instituted. Examples of the latter category included reexamination of the salary system, of the reward system for administrative duties, of time and opportunity for product and service innovations, and of the ongoing substantive and market education required by officers and managers.

Selection of the type of session—whether specifically created or a normal organization meeting—was usually left up to the participants. The interventionist was notified of the client's preference in order to coordinate schedules and do any necessary planning. The amount of planning varied with the type of meeting proposed and the participants' competence. For example, during the early phases, the interventionist met with two officers who were to evaluate the performance of a manager. One officer was the office administrator who normally conducted the evaluation process, and the other officer was selected by the manager. The officers used their preliminary sessions to clarify what they intended to say to the manager and to design their approach as much as possible in congruence with Model II (providing directly observable data, encouraging inquiry and confrontation of their views, publicly testing their attributions and evaluations). They also explored ways they could express differences so that the manager would see he was not necessarily dealing with offi-cers who were "against" him. They also designed ways to encourage the interventionist to help them examine errors they might make during the meeting. Finally, during the early stages, the two officers and the interventionist spent a half to a full hour reviewing each meeting with the manager. Whenever it seemed helpful, they would replay sections of the tape, or the interventionist would have a par-ticularly difficult or well-handled episode transcribed for review. Often officers and managers listened to the tapes of performance evaluations at their leisure, meeting with the interventionist if they felt it would be helpful. As the officers involved became increasingly competent, the amount of review time required before and after each evaluation was shortened significantly, barring the rare difficult case.

Almost no planning was required for the sessions in which case team performance was being evaluated. Some case teams met for one session without the interventionist (usually for two or three hours). Other teams met for one session, asking the interventionist to cri-tique their interaction. In Case E (Chapter Six), the group met a sec-ond time to discuss the interventionist's analysis. The officer also met separately with the interventionist to review further the implica-tions of the analysis. In Case F (Chapter Seven), the officer and man-ager each met separately with the interventionist.

The interventionist's role in the administrative meetings was to intervene whenever he felt he could facilitate the problem-solving and decision-making processes. Occasionally he would summarize progress to date, illustrating with signs of progress as well as signs that further work had to be done. The preceding chapters in Part Three include several examples of his role (a more detailed publica-tion is in progress).

As noted earlier, my preferred intervention strategy is to begin at the top level. I worked with the officers (in one organization) and the partners (in the other) until they were ready to manage the pro-cess of helping their immediate subordinates to become more profi-cient in Model II. In the larger firm, this was done almost immediate-ly because some officers selected sessions in which their immediate subordinates had to be involved.

In the smaller firm, I worked first with the partners. When they showed evidence that they could use Model II actions with one another and with their subordinates, a session was held for the managers, with myself as the educational leader. The partners and managers would meet with and without me. Whenever I could not be present, the sessions were tape-recorded so that I would provide feedback. As the firm has grown larger and added more officers and managers, a second interventionist has been introduced to work with the partner/officer/manager interface while I continue to work with the partners and board of directors.

The pattern of development and growth is therefore relatively straightforward. It is composed of learning opportunities to help those on top first. As those on top prove by their actions that they are able to use Model II whenever it is appropriate and can help create an O-II learning system, learning activities are introduced to the next level below. As those on each level become competent, they, in turn (with the help of a professional whenever necessary), work with the next level below.

In the smaller firm, all the partners were committed to learning Model II and to creating an O-II learning system before the next level was approached. This was not so in the larger firm. A few of the officers felt that Model II could be dangerous if people really "opened up." Some believed that Model II was not particularly necessary, that if everyone were technically superlative, human problems would rarely occur. These issues were dealt with openly. How can Model II be dangerous if it encourages free and informed choice as well as confrontation about its use or misuse? If some officers were fearful about what might happen if people "opened up," it would be related to the fear that openness might mean discussion of the undiscussable. In some cases, as we have seen, expressing what was in the left-hand column did destroy inquiry. People did have to learn that many of their private thoughts were counterproductive. They had to ask themselves why, in certain cases, they framed the issues in such counterproductive ways. In other cases, the material on the left-hand side could very well be brought out in the open and tested for its validity. People soon learned that Model II was not to be feared.

What was to be feared legitimately was that people would become "open" in order to control others or win others over (that is, using Model II strategies in the service of Model I governing variables). But that fear could be discussed, and people could decide to confront such actions. Another fear that a few persons expressed was related to the potential destructive dynamics of the group. Could there be a contagion about criticism that might escalate beyond the members' control? Again, if these fears are discussed, and action is taken to deal with them, there is little to fear. We have many examples in which the members were able to manage the conditions that could bring on fear, and hence the fear was greatly reduced.

At the same time, it became easier for certain officers in the larger firm to state publicly that they had doubts about Model II and to do so without suggesting that others should not learn it. To date, all those who had doubts have had them reduced by observing the changes in others (who they were sure were uninfluenceable) and the changes in the internal environment of the firm. Incidentally, recall the case in Chapter One in which officers described as liberals and conservatives were working on a career development policy. It is interesting to note that the conservatives have made more progress than those who described themselves as liberals.

How much time do these learning activities consume? At the outset, they do consume a little more time. For example, evaluation sessions that usually took about one hour now required two. But this was temporary. As people became more competent, the time required was reduced. More important, the number of meetings held to correct "misunderstandings" of previous meetings was reduced, as was the number of private one-to-one meetings to deal with "difficult" people.

Moreover, important consequences occurred throughout the organization that had never occurred before. For example, the evaluation of managers was now reconceptualized as follows: There is no such activity as "manager evaluation." Whenever a manager is evaluated, the officers, too, are being evaluated, and the culture of the firm—especially its norms and values about justice—is being greatly influenced. (In a forthcoming publication, we hope to show how the sense of injustice and its uninfluenceability held by the consultants and managers was reversed over a two-year period.) Moreover, bureaucratic controls, such as career development committees, were dismantled because more officers were carrying out their career development responsibilities without need of bureaucratic checkup. More officers were dealing with difficult evaluations more effectively. Finally, the office administrator initiated meetings where any professional or staff member could raise questions about the firm's policies and practices, as well as the norms of justice. Rather than opening up new controversies, quite the reverse happened. Because the office administrator was able to create a genuine climate for discussion, more people found that the organization was influenceable and realized that it was being as just as it knew how. Perhaps even more important, subordinates learned that they were better at complaining than they were at recommending workable solutions. Soon they asked for fewer such meetings because they had little new to add.

Although I believe that the data obtained (and to be obtained) will show that many counterproductive consequences that emanated from poor evaluation practices were significantly reduced, and the overall sense of justice increased, the point is that all members have gained a sense that the internal organization is more influenceable. Along with this sense of influenceability, there has been a reduction in grievances as lower levels have learned that often the top had not corrected some policy simply because it did not know how to deal with the variance in views. When the subordinates took on the challenge, they were no more successful.

It now takes less time to deal with difficult issues, and every successful resolution spreads outward to influence many parts of the firm. When more time is needed, it is because the members are upping the ante of what is discussable. In the large firm, for example, some younger officers believed that there were older officers who were not pulling their weight and thus were overly compensated. When this was first raised publicly in the officer group, some of the older senior officers (obviously hard-working and leaders in their field) became indignant. They believed that the younger officers had a debt to the older officers that could never be repaid. This issue was discussed but to date has been only partially resolved. In the smaller and younger firm, we have seen that this issue is discussable by the partners, officers, and managers. Indeed, Robert, Bill, John, and Don are continually monitoring their actions. Their current problem is how to help one another reduce the overload in such a way that the younger officers do not feel they are being given the less productive accounts.

Finally, the real issue about time is how much is genuinely accomplished during the time spent. For example, the issue of whether Robert was a domineering entrepreneur had been building up in the organization for several years. As our data show, it was discussed from time to time. It came to a head when all concerned felt that they had enough data to illustrate their point and when Bill and John (and, less so, Don, because he was the newest partner) believed that they could constructively confront Robert and deal with any angry feelings. At the time of this writing, it appears the problem is re-solved. Robert is doing as he and the other partners wish. The situa-tion is being managed by all the partners because the issue is dis-cussable and all actors are influenceable. Moreover, the new officers and managers see, in actual sessions, that such issues can be discussed. Hence, they soon learn that issues "I would never have thought of discussing in my previous job" are now discussable. But as Parker found out, when issues are discussable and partners are influenceable, it is less likely that the officers can distance themselves from the double-loop issues of the firm.

Indeed, as we have seen, this is one of the most pervasive re-sults of the organizational activities described in this book. Distanc-ing and disconnectedness exist at the highest levels. They can have a deleterious effect on the entire organization and can lead to bureau-cratization and a reinforcement of the distancing and disconnected-ness.

Distancing and disconnectedness can be reduced, and in doing so, the organization becomes increasingly influenceable and in greater control of its internal system and hence of its destiny. Inter-estingly, issues such as job satisfaction and morale become less im-portant. What become more important are opportunities for self-responsibility and excellence in performance, these embedded in a culture where learning and justice are dominant.

Two major features of organizational development have been emphasized in this book. The first is double-loop learning, and the second is to tackle head on the individual, organizational, and cul-tural factors that inhibit it. The latter activity is very important be-cause it appears that much of the present practice in organizational development focuses on translating double-loop issues into single-loop issues, bypassing the underlying causal factors that inhibit effec-tive solution.[1]

Often the pressure to perform bypass organizational develop-

---

[1] Chris Argyris and Donald Schön, *Organizational Learning* (Reading, Mass.: Addison-Wesley, 1978).

ment (OD) interventions and deal with single-loop issues comes from top people who, on the one hand, expect to see relatively quick changes in human behavior and, on the other hand, expect no changes that will touch underlying causes such as their theories-in-use and their reluctance to discuss the undiscussable. OD professionals are understandably sensitive to these conflicting expectations, and often they try to deal with them in an incremental approach. The logic of this approach is that if there is enough success with single-loop learning programs, then one can risk designing some genuine double-loop learning programs, especially at the top. I am not aware of any published instances during the last two decades in which this logic has worked as intended. Indeed, it appears that the greater the apparent success with interventions that bypass issues we have focused on in this book, the greater the insistence by the top to continue on the same course. Why tamper with success, especially if line management's evaluation of the seminars and other learning experiences is laudatory? Moreover, as has been stated before, probably 75 percent of all organizational problems are single-loop, and hence there is a genuine need for such activity.

But this philosophy has several unintended consequences. First, when OD programs are geared to single-loop issues, the organization may not see that many organizational factors are slowly but surely polluting the system, increasing the likelihood that single-loop solutions will someday be found inadequate.[2]

Second, to the extent that the OD programs remain within the Models I and O-I of the organization, they can become fads and teaching skills that may be viewed as "gimmicks." A gimmick, you will recall, is any skilled action that is congruent with Model II behavioral strategies (such as advocacy combined with inquiry) but is used to satisfy Model I governing variables (for example, be in control; win, do not lose). A fad is an organizational program that espouses double-loop changes but remains within single-loop limits, the participants acting as if this were not the case. Fads most often exist to satisfy the concerns and defenses of the top. Once they run their course, they can be easily dumped, usually in such a way as to place the responsibility on those below, including the OD specialists.

[2] Argyris and Schön, 1978.

Finally, the more OD professionals design their programs to remain within the boundaries of single-loop issues, the more they will become what are affectionately known in the organizational world as "techies." They are viewed as highly skilled professionals tinkering with technical issues and therefore are not very informative or helpful to top people who are trying to understand the bigger picture. This has happened to industrial psychologists, operations researchers, and marketing researchers and is now happening to strategic planners. The irony is that originally they did focus at the highest levels. As each area succeeded and developed cadres of professionals, they defended their empires by producing what they promised in ways that kept line management from rejecting or interfering with them. One of the most frequent ways of defending themselves was to remain within single-loop domains, where it was more likely that their technology would apply and simultaneously less likely that they would deal with problems of major concern to the people at the top.

20

Developing
Action Science

Essential Features of Action Science

This has been a story about a research program designed to understand and alter the reasoning and learning process of individuals and organizations. Such stories are always reconstructed, because it is impossible to describe everything that is happening or has gone on. We could easily produce millions of pages of manuscript if we transcribed all our tape recordings, and these tapes represent only a small fraction of all the encounters which we observed and in which we were involved.

If descriptions are necessarily selective, then it is important to be clear on how we decide what data to select, on how we construct and organize them, and that we are not kidding ourselves and others about their validity. We have available two basic resources to answer these questions: theory and method. A theory is a set of interrelated constructs that purport to explain the phenomena we are studying and are so designed that they can be publicly tested to be either confirmed or disconfirmed. Research methods are the rules of the game in order to ascertain that we are not deluding ourselves or others.

Elsewhere[1] I have tried to show that many of the established views about theories and research methods contain inner contradictions and hence can be counterproductive for double-loop learning. The perspective that guides our research may be called action science. Some of its basic tenets can be summarized as follows:

1. The ultimate purpose of action science is to produce valid generalizations about how individuals and social systems, whether groups, intergroups, or organizations, can (through their agents) design *and* implement their intentions in everyday life. The generalizations should lead the users to understand reality and to construct and take action within it.

We have seen, beginning with the X and Y case, that people use different theories when they try to discover and understand double-loop issues than when they act to deal with them. Propositions such as those related to easing in, undiscussability of the undiscussable, distancing, and nonresponsibility would probably never have become as prominent as they did if we had not made the distinctions between espoused theory and theory-in-use and between single- and double-loop learning.

2. A complete description of reality requires not only a description of the universe as it is but a description of its potential for significantly reformulating itself (its potential being part of what it is). But as we have seen, people tend to be highly conservative about, and even unaware of, the potential for double-loop changes. Most people whom we studied doubted that double-loop changes were possible in individuals and organizations. This is understandable because, being programmed with a Model I theory-in-use, the only alternatives they could create would be single-loop ones. Model II, as an espoused theory, is not particularly rare. The big problem and challenge is to translate the espoused theories into theories-in-use.

Action scientists hold normative views about alternative ways of living. These views are, however, continually subject to empirical test. But in order to test them empirically, we must be able to produce them, even in a world that is not hospitable to such ideas. Hence, action scientists not only describe the world as it is and

---

[1] Chris Argyris, *Inner Contradictions of Rigorous Research* (New York: Academic Press, 1980).

as it might be, but they must also specify how to get from here to there.

3. All actions that have intended consequences are based on reasoning. The reasoning that people use to discover problems and invent solutions to problems is often, as we have seen, very different from the reasoning used to produce the invented solutions. For example, the consultants dealing with the X-Y case acted contrary to the advice they gave others and to their own intentions.

A second feature about reasoning for use is that it is remarkably resistant to change, whereas reasoning for understanding is more easily altered. For example, within one hour most participants agreed that they did not deal with Y as they intended or as they advised Y to deal with X. However, many could not alter their reasoning-in-use after hours of trying. We found it easy to change espoused theories (attitudes, beliefs, and values), compared with changing the values and the reasoning processes embedded in action.

The third feature of reasoning for use is that it is based on a theory-in-use. The theory-in-use is the master program in people's heads by which they determine what actions will tend to lead to what consequences. The theory-in-use is a master guide about causality and design in human relations.

If we know the theory-in-use, we can predict the type of meanings that people will produce when dealing with double-loop issues. For example, we can predict that people programmed with a Model I theory-in-use will tend to produce unillustrated attributions and evaluations and will neither test them nor encourage others to do so (even though they may espouse otherwise). Note that the prediction does not concern the behavior (the first rung of inference) or the culturally accepted meanings (second rung). The variance there is great. The prediction is for rungs 3 and above on the ladder of inference.

One of the basic assumptions of our perspective is that predictions should be aimed at rungs 3 and above. There are several reasons. First, these rungs contain causal explanations and probable consequences. For example, we can predict that it is unlikely the recipient of an unillustrated attribution will understand and be able to test it. This will create or reinforce a sense of being misunderstood and probably feelings of defensiveness.

Second, generalizations about rungs 1 and 2 would require an understanding of so much variance that it would not be possible to store and retrieve so much information in everyday life. Focusing on generalizations about rungs 1 and 2 would be comparable to developing generalizations about how different leaves fall to the ground.

As I have said, action science should be usable in a given situation. How do we square that requirement with the idea that prediction should be limited to rungs 3 and above? The answer is that if we can help people be aware of, and in control of, the master programs in their heads, then they will be able to manage effectively their personal responsibility, the meanings that they create, and the effectiveness of their actions. The key to making the world manageable is to conceptualize it. The key to effectiveness lies in the conceptualization being useful for effectively producing the meanings and consequences that the user intends. The user's exact words may vary; the meanings may not.

If people understand and are in control of their reasoning processes, then they will also understand the causal theories they use to design and implement their actions. A fundamental task of action science, therefore, is to specify these reasoning processes.

4. People's ability (1) to design and implement their actions or (2) to understand the actions of others is dependent first on being able to see accurately the relatively directly observable data (rung 1 on the ladder of inference) and to infer correctly the cultural meanings embedded in these data (rung 2). Second, in order to do this under real-time conditions, people must have theories-in-use that they use to organize what they see and to infer causal patterns. These causal patterns become the basis for the design and implementation of new action. Action science, therefore, focuses on how people come to understand rungs 1 and 2 in order to act. Such understanding is found in rungs 3 and above on the ladder of inference.

The reason that action scientists try to produce generalizations about rung 3 and above is that that is what people also do. The variance on rungs 1 and 2 is usually so great that people cannot manage it under real-time conditions. Indeed, they would become immobilized if everyday life had to be dealt with at rungs 1 and 2. Their theory-in-use (which, you will remember, is as much a societal phenomenon as it is an individual one) is the key to making their lives manageable. Understanding people's theories-in-use, therefore, must also be a key focus of action science.

5. The theories that action scientists produce to understand

action, as well as to design and implement it, should be directly usable by individuals and organizations. Otherwise they will compound already complex problems by creating theories that human beings cannot use. The theories-in-use of the interventionist in all the examples in this book would be those of the clients as they learned to use Model II competently. The theories-in-use that the interventionist applies to help a client should be usable by the client to help and to educate others in double-loop learning. Basic theory in action science —theory about everyday life—should be the same as the theory people use in everyday life.

Often social scientists, using the normal science rules for research, react to these views by saying, "Oh, I see, you do not seek a theory that generalizes beyond the specific case." I hope this book illustrates that this response is based on a misunderstanding. The propositions about Models I and II, for example, are applicable to a very wide domain. Moreover, as we shall see below, they tend to be much tougher in the sense that they permit very few exceptions without being falsified.

Normal science and action science researchers aspire to produce knowledge that is ultimately generalizable and simultaneously usable in concrete situations. The difference is that the former tend to separate it into generalizable knowledge for basic research and applicable knowledge for developmental or applied research. They even have different theories and rules of evidence for applicable knowledge, and they usually believe that the generalizable knowledge must precede. Action scientists, in contrast, do not separate generalizable knowledge from knowledge that can be used in a specific situation. Propositions about the consequence of advocating in such a way as to unilaterally control others in order to win and not lose are applicable in almost any situation in which people are acting in this way. The propositions about easing in would hold for a person in the X and Y seminar, for people in budget meetings, for people dealing with difficult clients, and so on. The theory and research technologies for basic and applied research are the same in action science. Therefore, basic and applied research are designed into every study from the beginning.

6. Basic research in action science, as in normal science, requires methodology to make certain that social scientists are not deluding themselves or others and hence that (1) their propositions are

testable and falsifiable, which requires (2) propositions containing causal statements and (3) accomplishing this as elegantly as possible (that is, with the minimum number of concepts and axioms).[2] Action science differs from normal science in its commitment to produce knowledge under conditions in which (1) the knowledge being produced is designed to be usable by those producing the knowledge (subjects and action scientists) and (2) precision is in the service of producing accurately, in the noncontrived world, the consequences embedded in the propositions.

The two conditions imply some very important consequences. First, the knowledge produced should be stated in a form in which people can use it in everyday life, where they seldom have great control over the environment or other people. In other words, the propositions should not require that users have the unusually high unilateral control over others that researchers have when they conduct experiments. The conditions of unilateral control, though rarely mentioned in most normal science generalizations, are a part of them. For example, reinforcement learning theories produce generalizations such as "Given such-and-such a reinforcement schedule, the following degree of learning is expected." What is rarely added is that the generalization holds only if the relationship between reinforcer and reinforcee is similar to the relationship between experimenter and subject.[3]

Second, the knowledge should be stated precisely enough so that the user can produce the consequences embedded in the propositions without inhibiting the outcome. If generating the precision embedded in a proposition requires conditions that will be counterproductive to implementing the consequences embedded in the proposition, then the precision is itself counterproductive. For example, if the proposition specifies a curvilinear relation between X and Y, then trying to find the precise location of X and Y in a given situation may require more time than is available. Elsewhere[4] I have tried to show that this means that the highest degree of accuracy necessary in everyday life will probably be obtained by the use of heuristics, or rules that are not very precise. The trick is to combine opti-

---

[2] Argyris, 1980.
[3] Argyris, 1980.
[4] Argyris, 1980.

mal sloppiness with accuracy (that is, achieving the intended consequences).

Focus of This Book

1. Double-loop learning for individuals and social systems (such as groups and organizations) must necessarily be studied together. As we have seen, individual theories-in-use are based on the social system and culture in which individuals are embedded. However, double-loop changes in O-I learning systems cannot be achieved without first changing individual theories-in-use. In short, although individuals and social systems are identifiable as separate entities, double-loop learning cannot occur without both of them being taken into account.

2. It is necessary to understand the unawareness that is programmed into human beings, for which they have a program in their heads to keep them unaware. To be unaware of something is to be ignorant of its existence. To be unaware that we are unaware is to have a tacit program that maintains the initial unawareness. We are not simply ignorant of something; we are ignorant of the theory-in-use that keeps us unaware.

The hypothesis that I propose for explaining the massive unawareness is that it is due to the fact that our actions are learned through socialization and therefore are highly skilled. The essential feature of highly skilled actions is that they can be performed without giving attention to the mental programs required to produce them. The programs are tacit—hence our unawareness.

3. We must understand those human actions produced under a high degree of involvement if we are to provide propositions about human actions that are central to everyday life.

The more research deals with the entire cycle of discovery/invention/production/evaluation and generalization under everyday-life conditions, the greater will be the involvement of the actors, and the higher the probability that the systems studied will be central, rather than peripheral, to the society and culture in which they are embedded.

The more research deals with action that produces successes and failures, the more it deals with the inner contradictions in people's theories-in-use and in the sociopolitical environment in which people are embedded. Therefore, it will produce knowledge that will be able to take risks with individual and system stability. That is, if individuals take action based on knowledge that questions underlying inconsistencies that are currently sanctioned (sanctioned because they appear to maintain the social structure and our sanity), the risk to the complicated, fine-tuned individual and system balance will seem great. The greater this risk, the greater also the risk that such individuals will be seen as deviants.

4. The first step in any such research is to activate and surface the inner contradictions embedded in everyday actions. But the essential feature of inner contradictions is that they are hidden by layers of taken-for-granted action. These layers of action, and any defenses that surround them, must be unpeeled. But to unpeel them requires that people become aware of the defenses (individual and societal) that they use to keep these actions from surfacing into their awareness. People are not about to collude in such unpeeling unless they believe that it is necessary, that it can be done without uncorrectable and uncontrollable strain to themselves and to their world, that knowledge and skills exist which can be used to correct the identified errors, and that these skills can be learned.

Thus, the fourth characteristic of the domain of action science is the production of knowledge about the universe as it is and about ways of changing its inner contradictions so that we learn the knowledge and skills that can alter the inner contradictions. This requirement suggests that people who produce the data should be viewed as clients rather than subjects. Clients engage the professional expertise of another in order to be helped. Subjects are under the control of professionals so that the latter can obtain the knowledge they seek. The traditional subject relationship may not be an appropriate one to study inner contradictions, because it is based on a Model I relationship, which supports and reinforces the learned unawareness and defenses of a Model I world.[5]

The studies described throughout this book were guided in their design and execution by the rules of action science and the imperatives of double-loop problems.

[5] Argyris, 1980.

Nature of the Data Collected

The objective of action science is to predict to rungs 3 and above on the ladder of inference in such a way that meaningful predictions can also be made at levels 1 and 2. The key to understanding is to infer the reasoning processes embedded in the actions. In effect, we observe what people say and do; we infer the culturally accepted meanings; and then we reconstruct the reasoning that must have been used to produce what we observed.

Not surprisingly, the predominant data collected were observations of situations between clients and action scientists. The situations ranged from those designed and implemented mainly by the action scientist (the X and Y seminars) to those designed and implemented mainly by the clients and influenced by the action scientist (the case team sessions, the evaluation sessions, and the confrontations among the partners) to those in which design and implementation was completely the responsibility of the clients (the sessions on Carol).

The primary mode of collecting the observations was tape recordings. The secondary mode was observations made by a second researcher present in some of the meetings. Tape recordings were listened to and transcribed. The amount of material transcribed varied. During the early stages of the research, almost every tape was transcribed. As patterns developed, it became easier to differentiate between single- and double-loop issues, and then only tapes with primarily double-loop data were transcribed.

Over a thousand 90-minute cassette tapes were collected in the research reported in this book. Each tape yields about 75 pages of transcription. Transcribing every tape would mean producing 75,000 pages of data. And we taped only a small fraction of what actually occurred in the organization. This implies that a relatively complete documentation is probably not possible and that even an incomplete description would mean a monumental expense in typing, filing, reading, categorizing, and so on. The financial resources were simply not available.

But even if they had been, I am not convinced that complete descriptions are what is needed. If we had described everything that we had observed, we would have thousands of pages of transcript. Not only would we have become immobilized, but so would the actors if they had to pay attention to such descriptions. Human beings have ways of making such complexity manageable, and action scientists must discover and use those ways in their research.

Organizing the Data

I began this research believing that the best way to organize the data was to define units that could be used to categorize the information and to count the categories. This would provide the basis for the study of patterns as well as the ability to quantify the pattern.

The first question that arose concerned the size of the unit. During a previous research program, I developed procedures to analyze transcriptions into units that could be produced with a respectable interobserver reliability score.[6] To obtain these scores, units were developed that were easily observable and teachable to observers. To obtain the desired precision, the units used cut the stream of action into very small micro-units. As a result, the meanings experienced by the clients were often lost. When I fed back simple quantitative data that illustrated the frequency with which individuals produced the different categories, the clients found the scores interesting primarily as an exercise in discovery. The quantitative scores did not help them invent or produce new actions. One reason was that the categories represented, as theoretical categories always do, the meanings embedded in the theory itself. Such meanings are on the third rung of the inference ladder or higher. To use the categories, the clients had to connect them with the second and first rungs of the ladder. Although in many cases this was possible, the amount of time required to do it constantly would rarely be available. Moreover, the researcher cannot present all the directly observable data (rung 1) and the culturally accepted meanings for each data point. The meeting of the partners (Chapter Seventeen) alone would have required nearly 900 pages, and again, even if we presented it, how would anyone be able to make sense of it without a theory?

A second reason that the categories in the earlier research were not helpful was that they contained little insight into how the indi-

---

[6]Chris Argyris, *Organization and Innovation* (Homewood, Ill: Irwin-Dorsey, 1965).

vidual could be more effective. Nor could such propositions be created by combining many of the categories, because they were propositions related to discovery and understanding, not invention and implementation. Like many of my colleagues, I considered the propositions related to discovery to be basic research. The propositions related to invention and production were considered applied research, to come later. But as we have seen throughout this book, the basic cycle of human action is discovery/invention/production/evaluation, and paying attention to all these processes may lead to different generalizations than when attention is paid only to the discovery phase.

A third reason that the quantitative scores inhibited learning is illustrated by the consequences that occurred frequently when, let us say, A had a score of 80 and B one of 40. Immediately the clients saw A as twice as good (or bad, depending on the category) as B. The quantitative patterns triggered automatic Model I responses of competition. When the clients examined how the scores were arrived at, they realized the arbitrariness of the numbers. For example, one sentence could produce a unit of unilateral advocacy, as could two paragraphs. We might have produced an even more microscopic scoring procedure, giving the two paragraphs a higher quantitative score than the one sentence, as in many of the sophisticated scoring procedures used by social scientists today. But when we tried these procedures, we found that the more the categories, and the higher the scores, the quicker the results passed human information-processing limits for invention and production. The clients, in other words, may have found the pattern interesting as an exercise in discovery, but the very complexity inhibited making inventions and then producing them. One reason research subjects may cooperate is that they believe we need the data for our satisfaction, not necessarily for their learning.

It is important to emphasize that the clients were, as we have seen, extremely bright and highly motivated to learn. The problem was that the quantitative patterns contained a degree of precision and complexity that made it difficult for them to use them under real-time conditions. The constraints, in other words, are related to human information-processing capacities, not to intelligence.

This does not mean the limits cannot be pushed back. Information theorists have shown, for example, how books can become external memories to help the actor retrieve knowledge. But what kinds of external memories are helpful? Using a handbook on leadership could actually cripple a leader. Imagine a leader faced with an intergroup problem, knowing that there are propositions about dealing with such problems in chapter 5 of a leading handbook. Does the leader stop the stream of activity while he rereads chapter 5? Does the leader go through an assortment of cards that summarizes these data? Won't the very act of referring to data upset the other participants? If they, too, had equal access to the handbook, would they not seek equal time?

If this ad hoc research did not immobilize human action, the nature of most of the propositions in the handbook would. The propositions would probably be incomplete for the complexity being dealt with. More important, they would be packaged in the form of a proposition stating a quantitative relationship among several variables. But this proposition (let us say that it asserts a curvilinear relationship between a and b, and for the sake of argument, let us assert that a and b are the only relevant variables) is so information-rich that the practitioner would have to perform some very complex information gathering to find at what point on the curve a and b were for his or her particular situation.

The first way out of this dilemma, I believe, is to respect the limits of human information processing and to study how human beings learn complicated schemes. This would enable us to develop action maps of the reasoning processes that people use when they act on double-loop issues. For example, the map of the reasoning processes that Parker used to deal with a superior whom he did not wish to upset represented an easing-in strategy. An easing-in strategy, as we have seen, is used in many situations in which people fear the defensiveness of others. An action map of the easing-in process could, therefore, be highly generalizable across many situations and interactions.

One of the major unanswered questions is the makeup of these action maps. At the moment, we are relatively clear about some of the features of maps that describe how people reason and act in order to get from here to there. Thus, we can specify the reasoning processes and the behavioral strategies by which the clients in Chapters Two and Three, and the participants in the case team meetings, produced self-fulfilling prophecies—self-sealing processes that led to escalating error. We can also begin to specify how distancing and disconnectedness make it highly likely that people will be unaware of what is in their action maps. However, we are terribly inadequate in specifying the action maps that can correct all these unintended consequences.

Nothing in what has been said implies that quantitative maps are necessarily ineffective. Much more research is needed to determine the quantitative maps that clients can use. For example, Marasigan-Sotto[7] has developed a scoring procedure based on Models I and II that conforms to the normal science requirements. Under the direction of Professor De Cock at Katholieke Universiteit, Leuven, she has used the scheme to study the degree of Model I action strategies used by any given actor. They are now beginning to inquire into how the resulting quantitative map can be used in reeducation. My strategy is to postpone the development of such maps until much more is known about what is required to help people produce Model II actions and O-II learning systems under zero to moderate stress and how, given our limited information-processing skills and the pressures of real time, we go about learning, storing, retrieving, and using such information.

Finally, there is the problem that most generalizations currently produced in research have little to do with double-loop learning. In a series of reviews of research in social psychology, organizational psychology and sociology, political science, and behavioral theories of organizations, theorizing and empirical research were found to be limited mainly to single-loop issues. The major reason for these limitations was not that social scientists were uninterested in double-loop issues. The limitations were due to the research methods and the type of theories presently accepted in most of social science. Such theories are usually limited to descriptive theories of the universe, which means that double-loop options are rarely found. Current research methods require a precision that may produce knowledge that actually reinforces distancing and disconnectedness.[8]

A second way out of this dilemma is to use other human beings as external memories and helpers in achieving what we intend. Other people can serve as on-the-spot resources in reducing gaps be-

---

[7] Betty Marasigan-Sotto, "Construction of a Scoring Method for Analyzing Argyris's Theories-in-Use" (thesis, Katholieke Universiteit, Leuven, 1980).
[8] Chris Argyris, *Inner Contradictions of Rigorous Research* (New York: Academic Press, 1980).

tween knowledge and action and can monitor our action with a view to increasing its effectiveness. But in order for others to serve as facilitators, we must create the conditions under which they will minimally distort the information they give us. Using Model II theories-in-use and O-II learning systems are two critical requirements to help us achieve these conditions.

In order to create O-II learning systems, not only theories-in-use must be altered but also the traditional pyramidal structure, financial systems for planning and budgeting systems for control, reward and pay systems, and so on. All of us are incomplete resources to ourselves, but we can create conditions to reduce that incompleteness through the cooperation of others and the redesign of the context in which we work.

Validity of the Data and Analysis

The first question about data is: How do we know that what they suggest occurred actually did occur? Or how do we know that what is reported to have happened is what actually happened?

Let us begin with the written cases, such as the X and Y case. It is not difficult to produce the actual cases so that one can read the scenarios that participants wrote. Thus, it is possible to provide the actual scenarios for their inspection and study.

A more difficult question to answer is: How do we know that the scenarios the participants wrote represent what they actually did or would say? For example, how do we know that Gerry's scenario is an accurate representation of what was said with T? Gerry and T may have spoken different words.

We do not know with certainty that the scenario is a valid reproduction of the words actually used (that is, the first rung on the inference ladder). But neither do we need to know. The important question, for our purposes, is to establish the validity of the meanings Gerry produced (rungs 2 and 3 on the ladder). Did he produce meanings that could be scored as untested attributions or evaluations? If so, then he was acting in accordance with Model I. Because it is not possible to produce Model II meanings without Model II theory-in-use, we should not find any Model II actions in the entire scenario. We should not find, for example, any illustrated attributions and evaluations where the intent is public testing with the others involved. Gerry withheld important information (in the left-hand column). This is further evidence of Model I (self-censorship to unilaterally protect self and others). Again, we should not find any instances in which Gerry made public to T the material he censored. If predictions such as these are not disconfirmed, then we believe that our inference that Gerry used a Model I theory-in-use is valid.

But could someone fake a more Model II scenario? Probably not, except by copying a Model II scenario written by someone else. But if a participant did produce such a fake scenario, it would soon be discovered by the way he reacted to the analysis of his case by others or the way he tried to help others learn. The reasons are as follows. Recall that people programmed with Model I theory-in-use are using a highly skilled theory-in-use. Recall also that the same theory-in-use necessarily leads them to become distant from their personal responsibility for creating self-fulfilling prophecies, self-sealing processes, and escalating error. Remember that these factors combine to create a state of disconnectedness from the actors' own reasoning processes. Hence, the reasoning processes will go on automatically, even if the actors do not want this to happen. (For example, Gerry deeply believed in Model II.) Because all this is true, it is possible for the interventionist in the X and Y seminars to predict that the participants will not be able to produce Model II actions and meanings even though they wish to do so.

Turning to the tape recordings, the same reasoning holds. People who have only a Model I theory-in-use should not be able to produce Model II meanings in dealing with any double-loop problem that requires confronting the actors' respective theories-in-use. It may be possible for people to solve an organizational double-loop problem if (1) none of the participants holds differing views and (2) the logic required to solve the problem is explicit, easily understood, and easily producible. For example, suppose A and B agree that the organization should change its objective from marketing to manufacture and service. If the technology is known, if the participants agree, if the resources are available, and if their present skills do not inhibit them from learning the required new skills, a change in organizational objectives can occur without learning Model II. But if there were any major disagreements about the goals or the way to reach them, then the participants would be facing a situation similar to the one described in Chapter One—namely, two competing factions making private attributions about each other, each trying to assure the other side that it has nothing to fear. The prediction would be that we would never observe a meeting in that organization where the participants, by design, are dealing with threatening double-loop problems in a Model II manner.

Not all the transcriptions available have been included, because of space limitations and the redundancy of the findings. Someday, when appropriate theories are known and effective ways to categorize the data are available, it will be possible to code the data and present summary pictures of the findings. The only additional stumbling blocks would be training people to analyze and code the data and finding the financial backing to develop such resources.

Again, I recommend moving slowly toward such expensive studies until we know better the value of such knowledge for science and for practice. It is by no means self-evident how much more knowledge is needed in order to be helpful and valid to the practitioner. Nor, as pointed out earlier, is it self-evident how detailed action maps should be if they are to describe our understanding in valid and generalizable propositions.

Perhaps there are different action maps for different basic or generic problems. This book, for example, concentrates on excerpts from transcriptions of ongoing situations in the organizations (1) when changes toward Model II are being attempted and (2) when people are dealing with double-loop substantive issues. The reason is to document the extent to which these problems are dealt with in a Model II manner; the extent to which O-II learning systems are created; the actors' awareness when discrepancies exist between Model I and Model II actions; and their actions and reactions toward these discrepancies. Even though the sessions are tape recorded, it is still possible to miss an important episode. The best guarantee against such a gap is to rely on the actors present to tell the interventionist. To increase the probability that the clients will do so, it is necessary for such action to be in their interest. It is at this point that research and learning are intimately related. If the subjects are truly clients and are committed to learning Model II and to creating O-II learning systems (and if the interventionist is committed to helping them do so), they are more likely to call his or her attention to sessions that contain important episodes related to their learning progress. We have been asked, for example, to meet with several clients who wanted to reflect on a meeting in which they acted consistently with Model II. In doing so, they spent quite a bit of time trying to re-create the situation (and all this was tape recorded). Listening to the tape, a researcher would consider it a dream opportunity. Here are clients (because they do not see themselves as subjects) striving to make sure their re-creation is as valid as possible, for otherwise they will not learn.

The analysis of the case team's performance used earlier in the book was done because the officer and subordinates believed that they could learn something if they re-created the situation and reflected on it. We were called in to observe and to facilitate the discussion. This example also illustrates another important feature in support of assessing the validity of the recollection. An analysis of the conversation and meanings produced in recollecting what happened contained features that were congruent with those of the original situation. In other words, if people can act consistently only with their theory-in-use, then when they try to reflect on their Model I behavior, the reflection and re-creation will also contain Model I features.

The most important way to assess the adequacy of the sample and the validity of the inferences made is to publicly test inferences as people act. Again, when the goal is to help people learn Model II, testing the validity of the data is the necessary first step for learning. Clients are not interested in spending precious time and experiencing frustration and pain over invalid data.

Examples of Predictions Made

At least three types of predictions are relevant to an action science study of the movement from Model I toward Model II by individuals and organizations. First are the predictions about how people programmed with Model I deal with such situations as the X and Y case or manage case teams or deal with ineffective performance. The predictions can range from the meanings that will be produced to the probable self-censoring (left-hand column) to the impact on others and on double-loop learning. Second are predictions that can be made about the processes involved in moving from Models I and O-I to Models II and O-II. Third are predictions made once people have learned Model II sufficiently so that they can use it under little to

moderate stress. I have presented examples of all these types of predictions.

Predictions Related to the X-Y Case

Four kinds of data were collected at the outset in the X and Y
case: the diagnoses made by the participants, their advice concerning
how Y could have behaved more effectively, the conversations they
designed to show how they would communicate with Y, and the information that they would not communicate during the conversation.

Simple quantitative analyses were fed back to the participants
in the form of a collage depicting the range of meanings found in the
written diagnoses. Participants were asked to read the feedback carefully, noting whether their important meanings (in their eyes) were
included in the collage. This was the first public test of the inferences
made by the interventionist.

Next, the causal theory inferred by the writer to be embedded
in these analyses was made public in order to test its validity. The
discussion continued until a representation was generated that the
participants believed was a valid representation of their views. In all
situations to date, consensus has been possible, though in a few cases
only after lengthy public discussion. In other words, agreement is not
guaranteed.

Next, further confrontation of the causal theory was encouraged. The interventionist pointed out that if participants communicated to Y the information in their diagnostic frame, they would be
using the causal theory that they were advising Y not to use with X.
You may recall that this led many participants to seek new ways to
disconfirm the diagnosis. The interventionist tried to respond to all
confrontations for two reasons. First, they represented additional opportunities to test the validity of the inferences he had made. The clients were, in effect, generating arguments that could falsify his inferences. Second, the very content of the discussion could be used to
confirm or disconfirm the analyses. The taped dialogue should produce evidence consistent with the inferences made by the interventionist.

For example, this prediction was made and stated openly to
the participants:

You will act toward one another and toward me consistently with the way you acted toward Y, as illustrated in the conversation that you wrote.

You will therefore be using the same kind of reasoning processes in evaluating one another and me as you used in evaluating Y.

This meant that the participants would make unillustrated attributions and evaluations; that they would withhold specifiable information; that they would act in ways that created self-fulfilling prophecies, self-sealing processes, and therefore escalating error; and that they would create consequences that they advised others not to create. Moreover, they would be largely unaware that they were acting in these predictable ways. And once they were told the predictions, and even after they witnessed others behaving in ways that were consistent with these predictions, they would still behave in such ways, even when they consciously intended not to do so.

These are hardy predictions, not only because they can be both operationalized and disconfirmed but because making them public does not alter the probability that the predictions will not be falsified or disconfirmed. They are hardy predictions because the interventionist is asserting that the participants will behave in these ways in this and in *any* other setting where the performance evaluation requires communication of difficult and threatening information.

None of these types of predictions has been disconfirmed in the 27 X-Y-case sessions held so far. We have even had participants who get together outside the classroom, with all the time they need, to roleplay how they would deal with Y. So far, no one has ever asserted that he or she behaved in accordance with Model II (in most cases, they had tape-recorded the roleplaying so that an independent assessment could be made). We also have had many people collect data about how they tried to behave according to Model II in settings outside the seminar. None has reported being able to do so.

Finally, our seminars have been designed in various ways so as to permit testing of these predictions under different conditions. One seminar consisted of two sessions (about ten hours each) nearly six months apart. In neither session were the participants able to behave according to Model II.[9] Three seminars contained three sessions of about ten hours each, four months apart, with the same results. Four seminars of seven sessions (about two hours each) one week apart produced similar results. Four seminars of seven sessions (about two hours each) one day apart produced the same results. Finally, six one-and-a-half-day seminars produced the same result. In previous research,[10] we have presented observations and tape recordings of Model I meetings in many settings and in several cultures. In none of these tapes could we find examples of Model II actions or Model O-II learning systems.

It is this experience that leads us to suggest that Model I theories-in-use and O-I learning systems are probably the most powerful and frequent and that they exist "in" all individuals and systems (at least in industrialized societies). We assume, therefore, that Model I is probably taught through early socialization and continually reinforced by the socialization processes used in most social systems.

However, as we have also seen, underlying these persistent processes is a powerful capacity to unfreeze. Human beings are able to learn Model II and (perhaps more easily) to produce O-II learning systems. To move toward Model II, people do need help from someone who is already competent in producing Models II and O-II, although it may be possible for people committed to constructive self-reflection to learn Model II by themselves. Donald Schön and I required three years of hard work and long hours to formulate Models I and II. Both of us are still learning to produce it. I myself am so involved in trying to make the experience of learning Model II more

---

[9]Jack Heller, *Increasing Faculty and Administrative Effectiveness* (San Francisco: Jossey-Bass, 1982).

[10]Chris Argyris, *Understanding Organizational Behavior* (Homewood, Ill.: Dorsey Press, 1960); Chris Argyris, *Organization and Innovation* (Homewood, Ill.: Irwin-Dorsey, 1965); Chris Argyris, *Management and Organizational Development* (New York: McGraw-Hill, 1971), Chris Argyris, *Behind the Front Page: Organizational Self-Renewal in a Metropolitan Newspaper* (San Francisco: Jossey-Bass, 1974); Chris Argyris, "Theories of Action That Inhibit Individual Learning," *American Psychology*, 31(9) (September 1976): 638-654; Chris Argyris, *Increasing Leadership Effectiveness* (New York: Wiley-Interscience, 1976), Chris Argyris and Donald Schön, *Theory in Practice: Increasing Professional Effectiveness* (San Francisco: Jossey-Bass, 1974); Chris Argyris and Donald Schön, *Organizational Learning* (Reading, Mass.: Addison-Wesley, 1978).

effective and efficient that I have not concerned myself until recent-ly with observing how long it would take people to learn it by them-selves. I have chosen to spend my energies to create, through research, instruments that people can use for self-instruction and to study the effectiveness of those instruments. It may be, as Henderson[11] sug-gests, that double-loop changes can evolve naturally, but such evolu-tion is extremely slow, even on an individual scale. Our goal is to gen-erate knowledge about such change so that it can occur as rapidly as possible when we choose to produce it.

Predictions Related to Moving Toward Model II
Outside the Learning Environment

Predictions related to moving toward and using Model II (and hence establishing a Model O-II system) are predictions about rare events. All the examples I have presented are illustrations of experi-ments that occurred "naturally" because an O-II learning system was being created. They were all experiments that would not have been permitted in the O-I learning system.

A prophecy is an espoused guarantee that a specified some-thing will happen. A prediction is a hypothesis that a specified something will occur under specified conditions and will not occur under other specified conditions. Thus, it is possible to predict that people embedded in an O-II learning system will tend to deal with difficult, embarrassing, double-loop problems, *or* if they do not, they will be aware that they are not doing so, and they will be confront-able about the matter.

Action scientists do not guarantee that a particular event will occur, because if Model II conditions exist, people are free to choose their actions. Thus, the existence of Models II and O-II means that the actors now have two degrees of freedom. They can choose Model I or Model II, or some hybrid. But whatever the choice, to the ex-tent that they use Model II theories-in-use and are embedded in an O-II learning system, the actors' decisions will be discussable and confrontable.

---

[11] Bruce Henderson, *Henderson on Corporate Strategy* (Cambridge, Mass.: Abt Books, 1979).

The method we have used to test whether unnatural or rare occurrences were produced was (1) to observe the stream of behavior, (2) to note any potentially embarrassing double-loop issues that arose, and (3) to observe how the participants dealt with them. If the issues were not dealt with in a Model II manner, we would predict that the participants (1) were aware and could explain their actions or that they (2) were unaware but were confrontable and willing to learn and (3) tried to produce plans for dealing with such occurrences in the future. Data to the contrary would disconfirm our hypotheses. We observed the above results under two conditions, when the interventionist was present and when absent. During the early phases, his presence was required to a greater extent. However, as people continued to learn, they also tended to up the ante of what was discussable. Thus, the Robert group were able to produce Model II actions for certain difficult problems (such as Carol's case) without aid; yet they requested such aid when it came to confronting the other difficult issues described in Chapters Fourteen through Eighteen.

Careful reading of the transcripts uncovers examples in which Model I and Model II actions were used but the overall results were consistent with Model II. It appears, therefore, that not all the actions must be Model II in any given session in order for double-loop learning to be achieved. One reason may be that when people behave in a Model I fashion toward each other (for example, when feeling hurt or angry), they appear to identify it as they are doing it and to recognize that it is not the competent action they want to produce. Another reason is that when someone behaves in a Model I manner that can have counterproductive results, the others present can identify the negative impact and ask whether the actor was aware, whether such consequences were intended, or both.

A third reason for successful double-loop learning even with Model I actions is that people discount some Model I actions. They do so because they recognize how difficult it is to produce Model II actions or that the Model I actor had good intentions. This discounting occurs in both the Model I and Model II worlds. The difference between the two is that, in the Model II world, the discounting should be discussable, and there should not be an assumption that it will go on forever because the actor is unable to discuss it.

Some examples of rare events that occurred without the interventionist present are these:

1. Discussing the possibility that John may have taken a client away from Robert.
2. Discussing jointly with managers the criteria by which they would be promoted, demoted, or asked to leave. Discussing ways in which the persons involved and their peers could jointly arrive at such decisions.
3. Consultants discussing with managers and officers their view that they had been unfairly penalized in terms of earnings.
4. Consultants now being told when they are heading for dismissal and, moreover, being given all the data available and encouraged to design with the officer any tests that could be used to disconfirm the officer's evaluation.

The following are examples of rare events that occurred with the interventionist present:

1. Discussing John's integration into the firm, his feeling of betrayal, Robert's anger that John felt betrayed. (Two years later, you will recall, not only did John feel a part of the group, he also said that being in the firm had led to unexpected learning experiences.)
2. A more open evaluation of managers, in which more directly observable data were used; in which the behavior of any participant during the session could be discussed; and in which officers, as well as the managers, were having aspects of their behavior evaluated.
3. Discussion about the future of Bill's, Don's, John's, and Robert's roles in the partnership and the present frustrations that each partner had with the others.
4. Manager and officer discussing candidly how difficult it was to work with each other, the objective being not only to air differences but to devise new approaches to correct the situation.
5. Self-exploration of inadequate performance by a first-rate case team.
6. Discussing issues related to distancing by officers from their responsibility for dealing with internal administrative issues and the career development of younger professionals.

Action Science and Quasi-Experimental Designs

Action science, as described in this book, is similar to, yet different from, the quasi-experimental design described by Campbell and Stanley.[12] Much of what we do can be described as experimental in the sense that the action scientist is producing an experimental treatment. The experimental treatment consists of designs (1) to help people become aware of their theory-in-use and the learning systems that they create, as well as any programs in their heads to keep them unaware of both, and (2) to help people move toward Model II and O-II learning systems. The designs represent long, complex processes, the different parts of which are placed into action as a response to the client's reactions.

The action scientist, to use the normal science terminology, is very much a part of the experimental treatment. It is therefore important that we make the actions of the interventionist, and the theory-in-use behind them, clear, explicit, continually observable, and continually subject to empirical test. The shorter and more efficient the interventions, the more likely that they will be reproducible and also the more likely that we will be able to teach others how to become effective interventionists.

The action scientist, unlike the normal science experimental researcher, has little or no control over the environment. But it is not necessary to have such control. The predictions are stated to hold true no matter what occurs in the environment, and to date the environment is Model I/O-I. Models II and O-II conditions will not occur under Model I and O-I conditions, because the latter are self-reinforcing and self-sealing. If they ever do occur, it will be a powerful disconfirmation of the theory.

All these hypotheses are subject to test in every learning environment, every organizational condition that we study. For example, in the X and Y seminars, there is no guarantee that the clients will confirm their Model I theory-in-use. Indeed, as we have seen, many rejected the idea initially. But the very way they rejected it helped to produce more data that disconfirmed their stand and produced

[12] Donald T. Campbell and Julian C. Stanley, *Experimental and Quasi-Experimental Designs for Research* (Chicago: Rand McNally, 1963).

further learning, which, in turn, strengthened the experimental manipulation. When the case team members reflected on the causes of their failure, there was no guarantee that distancing and disconnectedness would be seen as critical variables. When this was found to be the case, many of the members rejected the idea. They were encouraged by the action scientist to design any test or inquiry they wished, but in every case they concluded that the results were in favor of the hypothesis they had rejected.

When clients began to redesign their cases, there was no guarantee that they would succeed in producing Model II. As we have seen, it takes many experimental attempts to produce Model II actions. But every attempt, if effectively dealt with initially by the interventionist and later by the clients, should produce further learning, and all of it should be consistent with the theory.

In a traditional experiment, researchers intend that their experimental treatment take effect fully. Those who do not respond as predicted represent instances of failure. If enough respond in ways that were not predicted, the experiment is considered a failure. The same rules were not operative in this research. We worked hard to make the experimental treatment as powerful as possible but always made it explicit and confrontable. Actions that disconfirmed its effectiveness indicated that participants were exercising their free and informed choice. This made it possible for the action scientist to examine the choice and, hence, continue the experiment. If the clients were to continue to question and reject the experimental treatment, the conclusion was that they chose to do so. Hence, in our research the experimental treatment cannot work unless the clients choose to make it work. Sometimes their choice may be tacit; nevertheless, it can be shown that they were personally causally responsible for the success of the experiment.

Because of these differences, it is difficult to imagine the usefulness of a control group. The purpose of a control group is to ensure that the results are due to the experimental set-up and not to some other variable. But how does one create a control group in an X-Y seminar or a seminar to learn new Model II skills? Does one select a comparable group and place its members in a learning situation that differs from the experimental set-up in order to see whether they learn Model II? Wouldn't they have to know Model II in order to produce it in some other way? If they learned Model II and were placed in a situation that violated its concepts, and if the interventionist acted as if this were not the case (because the fact that they were the control group must be kept secret), thus making all these conditions undiscussable, wouldn't they be an inadequate control group?

Participants may act as their own control group. The theory predicts (and as we have seen, our data do not yet disconfirm the predictions) that people will produce Model I meanings even when they understand, value, and intend to produce Model II actions. People are socialized with skills to produce Model I and, through programs they are unaware of, programmed to be unaware that this is the case. How could they ever produce something that requires reasoning processes and theories-in-use that they do not have? The very distancing and disconnectedness that make Models I and O-I viable also make it unlikely that anyone will produce Models II and O-II, even if he or she wishes to do so.

Under these conditions, it is hard to see how history (that is, events occurring between different measurements) or the passage of time (maturation) could influence our results. Nor is testing a problem because, as we have seen, clients and interventionist create any test that they wish, and yet the clients continue to produce Model I. Similarly, we have changed instrumentation by varying observers and scores, and the results were the same. Selection is not a problem because almost everyone is hypothesized to be Model I, and so far the empirical data support the hypothesis overwhelmingly.

This does not mean that we do not seek conditions that are different. We continue to seek clients of different cultures, different age groups, different sexes and races, different organizations, different political systems. The theory, as it presently exists, states that if people complete cases (such as X and Y) and are scored to be Model I, then all the predictions follow, no matter what other conditions hold.

Role of the Action Scientist

It is important to emphasize that the action scientist is critically important in producing change. The action scientist, in the language of normal science, is an important part of the experimental manipulation. As suggested, it is doubtful (given our present learning technology) that people will learn Model II by themselves. The clients, as well as the facilitator, are researchers of their actions. They are as concerned, if not more so, about the validity of the data and the inferences they are making as normal science researchers are about theirs. The action scientist may be more concerned because his or her credibility is on the line in every decision made. Clients could act in ways that could harm themselves or their system. Action scientists could act in such a way that they failed as professionals. Action scientists are not neutral participants—if we are correct, they are essential to change.

There is a question of whether the capacity for double-loop learning continues when the action scientist is no longer present, and if so, how long. Our answer to date is that, in all situations in which the clients have chosen to go beyond the Type A defensiveness that they experienced at the outset, they were able to learn in such a way that they produced double-loop learning with and without outside aid. In the case of longest record (the case of Robert, Bill, John, and Don), the time span is nearly ten years.

This does not mean that these clients always produce double-loop learning whenever they wish to do so. Many of their attempts contain hybrids of Models I and II theory-in-use. For reasons not yet clear, hybrids produce more pure O-II learning systems than we initially expected.

Nor does it mean that the action scientist is never needed. For example, the session in which Robert, Bill, John, and Don discussed issues of distancing and commitment raised the level of threat in the issues discussed, and the interventionist was helpful. Other examples were presented, however, in which the partners dealt with one another and with the managers on threatening issues in a manner that enhanced double-loop learning, a type of learning that we believe is rare in the present world.

Index